STUDIES IN CH'AN AND HUA-YEN

KURODA INSTITUTE

STUDIES IN EAST ASIAN BUDDHISM

STUDIES
IN CH'AN AND
HUA-YEN

Edited by
Robert M. Gimello
Peter N. Gregory

UNIVERSITY OF HAWAII PRESS
Honolulu

Published by University of Hawaii Press in association with the Kuroda Institute for the Study of Buddhism and Human Values

The Kuroda Institute for the Study of Buddhism and Human Values is a non-profit, educational corporation, founded in 1976. One of its primary objectives is to promote scholarship on Buddhism in its historical, philosophical, and cultural ramifications. The Institute thus attempts to serve the scholarly community by providing a forum in which scholars can gather at conferences and colloquia. To date, the Institute has sponsored five conferences in the area of Buddhist Studies. The present volume is the outgrowth of the first such conference, held at the Institute in May, 1980. Volumes resulting from other and future conferences, as well as individual studies, are also planned for publication in the present series.

Library of Congress Cataloging in Publication Data
Main entry under title:

Studies in Ch'an and Hua-yen.

(Studies in East Asian Buddhism ; no. 1)
1. Zen Buddhism—Addresses, essays, lectures.
2. Hua-yen Buddhism—Addresses, essays, lectures.
I. Gimello, Robert M., 1942-   . II. Gregory,
Peter N., 1945-   . III. Series.
BQ9266.S78 1983   294.3'927   83-18188
ISBN 0-8248-0835-5 (pbk.)

CONTENTS

FOREWORD

It gives me great pleasure to introduce the
Kuroda Institute's Series on East Asian Buddhism with
the publication of this, its first volume. In doing
so, I would also like to say a few words about the
activities and goals of the Institute, within which
this series, published in cooperation with the University of Hawaii Press, figures in an important way.

The Kuroda Institute for the Study of Buddhism
and Human Values is a non-profit, educational corporation, founded in 1976. One of its primary objectives
is to promote scholarship on Buddhism in its historical, philosophical, and cultural ramifications. The
Institute thus attempts to serve the scholarly community by providing a forum in which scholars can
gather at conferences and colloquia. To date, the
Institute has sponsored five conferences in the area
of Buddhist Studies. The present volume is the outgrowth of the first such conference, held at the
Institute in May, 1980. Volumes resulting from other
and future conferences, as well as individual studies,
are also planned for publication in the present
series.

The series represents the Institute's commitment to make available to the scholarly community some
of the increasing body of advanced work currently
being done in the area of East Asian Buddhism.
Despite its growth in recent years, there has as yet
been no vehicle in the English speaking world designed
to meet the scholarly needs of this expanding field of
research. It is our deep hope that the Institute's

series will fulfill this need. The series is not tied to any sectarian position or methodological approach. Indeed, it is our intention that the works to be published within it represent a wide spectrum of scholarly methods, ranging from the philological, historical, philosophical, and cultural to the comparative. It is our sincere hope that they be of interest not only to buddhologists, but also to scholars working in broader fields, such as Asian Studies and the Study of Religion. While the series will focus on East Asia, it will by no means be confined to publishing works dealing exclusively with East Asian Buddhism. For instance, the Institute is currently organizing a conference on Buddhist Hermeneutics, a topic of especial interest precisely because it cuts across the geographical boundaries that all too frequently prevent Buddhist scholars from sharing their work with one another. Although the initial volumes in the series will present the fruits of the Institute's on-going series of conferences in Buddhist Studies, the series is also intended to publish other worthwhile scholarly ventures in the general field of East Asian Buddhism. Indeed, the Institute welcomes the submission of such works for consideration.

In closing, I would like to take this opportunity to express our thanks to Stuart Kiang at the University of Hawaii Press for his understanding and cooperation, as well as to Robert Gimello, Luis Gómez, Peter Gregory, and William LaFleur, who will serve as the general editors for the series.

Armando D. Grant
Director

PREFACE

In the nearly four decades that have passed
since the end of World War II, the study of East Asian
Buddhism has made rapid, manifold, and significant
advances in the West. One general effect of its
remarkable progress, apart from the enormous increment
it has produced in the sheer quantity of knowledge,
has been to draw the study of Buddhist thought and
history away from the obscure periphery of scholarship
on China, Japan, and Korea into the very center of
those fields of academic focus. Students of East
Asian history and culture, therefore, are no longer so
inclined as they once were to follow traditional
prejudices--e.g., the residual biases of Confucianism
or of the European Enlightenment--in regarding
Buddhism as an entirely arcane subject beyond the pale
of, say, sober Sinology or main-stream Japanology.
Rather, it is now widely recognized that Buddhism is a
subject worthy of study not only in its own right, as
a subtle and sophisticated system of religious belief
and practice, but also because of the variety of very
consequential roles it has played in the formation of
East Asian society and civilization. Conversely,
Buddhist Studies itself has begun to outgrow that part
of its previous isolation which was self imposed.
Buddhist scholars, that is to say, are now less
inclined than they once were to abstract their subject
from its various, complex, and ever-changing cultural
contexts. They are as much interested in exploring
the web of its relationships with other components of
East Asian civilization as they are in tracing the

intricacies of its philology and the internal patterns of its thought.

The factors contributing to this change in the nature and place of East Asian Buddhist Studies are too numerous to list in their entirety, and it is likely that not all of them are yet fully understood. No doubt influential are the new definitions of Religious and Intellectual History that have been entertained throughout the academy. New designs of advanced graduate training in the relevant disciplines and areas have surely also had their effects. However, two rather more specific factors deserve special notice, particularly in view of their relevance to the work here at hand. The first of these that needs to be appreciated is the extent to which western scholars of Chinese, Japanese, and Korean Buddhism have put themselves wisely in debt to Japanese scholarship. The Japanese have led the field of East Asian Buddhist Studies for several generations, and in recent decades they have succeeded in adding to the breadth and depth of their traditional learning in the subject a measure of critical sophistication in Philology and History that has set the standard which all others in the field must match. No serious work on East Asian Buddhism is now being done in Europe or America that has not been deliberately informed by the Japanese model. The other particular factor to be noted is the importance of the discovery and exploitation of previously unknown or very little known primary sources of information. Foremost among these, of course, are the manuscripts and xylographs of the now well known Tun-huang trove. Of a significance for the study of East Asian Buddhism comparable to the significance of the Dead Sea Scrolls for the

early history of Judaism and Christianity, these texts
have had especially revolutionary effects upon our
knowledge of the origins and early phases of Ch'an
(Zen). Again, it has been Japanese scholars who have
taken the lead in editing, analyzing, and interpreting
the hundreds of these texts in Chinese and Tibetan
that bear on the early history of Ch'an, but now
French scholars are also making very important contributions, and for some years yet to come the study of
early Ch'an will continue to be one of the most
exciting frontiers of advancement in East Asian
Buddhist Studies wherever conducted. Also to be
considered are the many other primary sources, apart
from the Tun-huang materials, that have come to light
in the past forty years or so and are now attracting
scholarly attention. One thinks particularly of texts
discovered in Korean monastic libraries or in hitherto
little explored Japanese collections. These too have
helped stimulate the growth and redefinition of East
Asian Buddhist Studies that is currently underway.

It is the belief of the editors of the present
volume that the essays which comprise it exemplify the
trends sketched above. They either broach new topics
or address older topics from new theoretical and methodological perspectives, and they are based in large
measure on primary literature--much of it from the
Tun-huang collection--which has been only recently
discovered or which has previously eluded extended
investigation. Moreover, all five of the essays are
written by scholars who owe much to their Japanese
teachers and who try to emulate those teachers in
philological and historiographical rigor.

Ch'an and Hua-yen (Kegon) Buddhism have been
chosen as the dual focus of this group of studies

essentially for three reasons: First, because they are major traditions of East Asian Buddhist thought and practice which were roughly contemporary with each other in their origins and which influenced each other in important ways during the early centuries of their development.   Second, because they both loom large as examples of the East Asian transformation of Buddhism, i.e., of the remarkable process by which that originally Indian tradition took on the shape and substance first of a Chinese, and later of a Korean and a Japanese, religion; as such they serve as valuable case studies in one of world history's most fascinating examples of religious change. Third, because they happen to be the subjects of some of the best work now being done, here and abroad, in the field of Buddhist Studies and so can serve well to index the changes underway in that field.

The articles by Broughton, Gómez and McRae deal with early Ch'an and are based on texts in Chinese and Tibetan that were found among the Tun-huang manuscripts.   All three shed substantively new light on the rise of what was to become one of the most crucial East Asian developments of Buddhism.   The articles by Gregory and Gimello treat somewhat of Ch'an but mostly of Hua-yen--the latter especially in its "classical" phase during the eighth and ninth centuries, although they give some attention also to its later influences in other traditions of East Asian Buddhism. The Hua-yen articles are based primarily on materials which have long been available in standard editions of the Chinese Buddhist canon but which have been studied hardly at all in the West and only in the most preliminary way even in Japan.   It is hoped that they will show, among other things, that the Hua-yen tradition is something more than its conventional reputation as a purely theoretical and rather cerebral form of Buddhism might lead one to believe.

Four of the five articles are much revised and expanded versions of papers delivered in 1980 at a Conference on East Asian Buddhism held in Los Angeles under the sponsorship of the Kuroda Institute for the Study of Buddhism and Human Values. The fifth, that by Luis Gómez, was especially solicited for the volume well after the conference. All of the articles were designed to comprise a collection that would serve not to introduce, survey, or sum up a field of study but to communicate new and ongoing advanced research. This will be the purpose also of the series, Studies in East Asian Buddhism, which this volume inaugurates.

We cannot conclude these remarks without an expression of our gratitude to the Kuroda Institute for its support and patience, and especially to its former Director, Dr. Michael Soulé. Thanks are also due to Barbara Cook, who performed so well the tedious task of preparing the typed copy of this volume, and to Mr. Sheng-kuang Lee, who inscribed its Chinese characters. We are indebted to others as well, too numerous to mention, but, of course, none of those whose help we have received is responsible for any of the volume's flaws.

Robert M. Gimello
Peter N. Gregory
1983

EARLY CH'AN SCHOOLS IN TIBET
by
Jeffrey Broughton

I. Introduction

The thousands of manuscripts from the hidden cave library of Tun-huang 敦煌 range over an enormous span of Chinese history, from the time of the great translator Kumārajīva to the time of the compilation of the Ch'an history Ching-te ch'uan-teng lu 景德傳燈錄 , that is, from about A.D. 400 to 1000. The Chinese Ch'an manuscripts within the Tun-huang corpus date from about 750 to 1000;[1] the Tibetan Ch'an manuscripts date to the period of the Tibetan occupation of Tun-huang, from the 780's to 848. It is clear that during the Tibetan occupation period there was intense Chinese-Tibetan cultural intercourse; in fact, many Tun-huang Chinese, having forgotten characters, knew only the Tibetan script. Interest in Chinese Buddhism and Ch'an in particular on the part of the Tibetans acted as a magnet. Fortunately, from the point of view of early Ch'an studies, the Tibetan "window" on Ch'an opened up at about the end of the early Ch'an period, and the shutters were drawn before the reworking of the tradition carried out in Hangchow and Nanking during the Late T'ang and Five Dynasties. In short, the Tibetans saw a fairly representative survey of the Ch'an literature in circulation during the eighth century--the records or histories, the dialogues, the treatises, and the "Ch'an sutras." Scholars, of course, have been working on the Chinese Ch'an manuscripts for decades, and if one could

synthesize all the piecemeal work they have done, a
new picture of early Ch'an could be assembled.[2] The
Tibetan Ch'an manuscripts, which only very recently
have come to receive the attention they deserve,[3]
provide several potential avenues of research: the
recovery of lost Ch'an sayings, perhaps even lost
works; the reconstruction of lost or corrupt portions
of known Chinese works; help in interpreting difficult
passages in Chinese works, and so on.

In the realm of Tibetology, research into
Tibetan Ch'an has begun to undermine the traditional
view of early Tibetan Buddhism. Western-language
treatments of Tibetan religion, which show the pervasive influence of the traditional view, minimize the
role of the Chinese party, the all-at-once gate (ston
mun = tun-men 頓門), slighting it as a heresy
defeated at the so-called debate of the Council of
Tibet in the late eighth century and suppressed soon
thereafter. Now it is thought possible that even the
debate itself is an invention of the later Tibetan
Buddhist historians.[4] Tibetan Ch'an documents have
enabled us to see that historians after the time of
Atīśa, the eleventh century, more or less expunged the
role of Chinese Ch'an from the record and in the
process naturally overemphasized the role of Indian
masters in the introduction of Buddhism and culture to
their country. Perhaps Ch'an was even the dominant
strain of Buddhism in eighth-century Tibet. In any
case, though the circumstances are as yet quite
unclear, during the ninth century Ch'an teachings went
underground and lingered on, in disguised form, within
the Rdzogs-chen tradition, that ancient tradition of
the imperial era which is thought of as most distant

from the core of Buddhism by the new traditions
established from the late tenth century onward.

Since those Chinese Ch'an schools which formed
the <u>ston</u> <u>mun</u> (all-at-once gate) of Tibet are among
those schools which are imperfectly known from Chinese
sources, there is the possibility of learning more
about them from a comparative study of Tibetan and
Chinese materials. The schools in question are the
Reverend Kim or Ching-chung lineage, the Wu-chu or
Pao-t'ang lineage, and the post-Shen-hsiu Northern
lineage, the last of which we might call the late
Northern. This is not to suggest that the names and
texts of other schools of Ch'an are not to be found
among the Tibetan-language texts of Ch'an: fragments
of Shen-hui's 神會 sayings, for instance, have already
been identified.[5] But the above three schools would
be central in any tentative reconstruction of the history of Chinese Ch'an in Tibet. The principal sources
for the study of the <u>ston</u> <u>mun</u> are: miscellaneous
Ch'an materials in Tibetan found in the cave library
of Tun-huang early in this century, in particular
Pelliot Tibetan 116;[6] Ch'an materials in Tibetan preserved in central Tibet among the Rdzogs-chen, the
most important of which, as of now, are the <u>Lamp</u> <u>of</u>
<u>the</u> <u>Ch'an</u> or <u>Dhyāna</u> <u>Eye</u> (Bsam-gtan-mig-sgron)[7] and the
<u>Five</u> <u>Classes</u> <u>of</u> <u>Orders</u> (Bka-than-sde-lṅa);[8] and
Chinese materials, both Tun-huang texts and Kuei-feng
Tsung-mi's 圭峰宗密 (780-841) writings on the Ch'an
schools.[9]

II. History of Ch'an Transmissions to Tibet

It is useful to view the history of Tibetan
Ch'an against the background of T'ang and Tibetan history. The T'ang histories[10] note the abilities of the
Tibetans (Bod), and it is apparent that China was losing ground in its Tibetan wars. From the late 750's
the Bod held much of the T'ang province of Kuan-
chung 關中 (Shensi 陝西) west and north of the capital Ch'ang-an 長安 and the mountainous areas of Chien-
nan 劍南 (Szechwan 四川). Within a few years the
capital itself was lost to Bod troops and the Chinese
reduced to partisan activity under the renowned general Kuo Tzu-i 郭子儀. There were intermittent
periods of relative peace when Chinese and Tibetan
envoys met, made sworn covenants, and erected boundary
markers. In the 780's Sha-chou 沙州 (Tun-huang) fell
under Tibetan occupation.[11] It is no mere coincidence
that the routes by which Ch'an went to Tibet fit in
with this geography. Ch'an reached central Tibet from
two areas: Szechwan and the Central Asian holy city
Tun-huang.

Imperial and aristocratic patronage played an
important part in the introduction of Ch'an to Tibet.
Two Tibetan clan names are connected with the transmission of the three Ch'an lineages mentioned above,
the Sba in central Tibet, one of the powerful families
producing ministers for the Tibetan state from the
early sixth century, and the 'Bro, located on the
fringes of the Tibetan empire southeast of Tun-
huang.[12] To a degree they remind us of some of the
great clans (uji) surrounding the imperial family in

early Japan. The Sba were instrumental in Ch'an transmissions from Szechwan and the 'Bro was a patron of the Chinese Ch'an master Mo-ho-yen 摩訶衍 (Tibetan Ma-ha-yan with variations), whose name appears in so many Tibetan texts.

So far our sole Tibetan historical sources for the introduction of Ch'an comes from the hand of a member of the Sba family. The Statements of the Sba Family (Sba-bźed)[13] is really a chronicle dealing with the famous Bsam-yas Monastery, two members of the Sba family having been successive abbots of that monastery, which played a role in Tibetan Buddhism analogous to Tōdai-ji 東大寺 in Japan.[14] From the Statements of the Sba Family we learn of two pilgrimages to China on the part of Tibetans, both of which were to be of enormous significance in the transmission of Buddhism to their country.

Japanese scholarship on the Statements of the Sba Family allows us to reconstruct the following two sequences of events.[15] The first of two pilgrims sent to China was the son of a Chinese commissioner (shih 使)[16] to the court of Emperor Mes-ag-tshoms[17] (r. 704-755). When the commissioner was about to return to China, Mes-ag-tshoms prevailed upon him to leave behind his son, referred to as "the Chinese boy, the dancer,"[18] to join the entourage of Mes-ag-tshoms' son, who was eventually to become the Emperor Khri-sroṅ-lde-bstan. This Chinese boy, known to us as Sba Saṅ-śi,[19] spoke and read Chinese, and, presumably with these talents in mind, in 751 Mes-ag-tshoms sent Saṅ-śi, at the head of four young Tibetans, off to T'ang in search of the Dharma, a small group of trial candidates for ordination. It is very likely that their route from the Bsam-yas region to the Szechwan plain passed through the kingdom of Nan-chao 南詔 (Yunnan 雲南), a route taken on occasion by raiding Tibetan armies.[20] The Statements of the Sba Family explicitly states that the group received the teaching of the most famous Ch'an master of the time in I-chou 益州 (Ch'eng-tu 成都), Reverend Kim (using his Korean name rather than Chin ho-shang 金和上),[21] also known as Wu-hsiang 無相 , a Korean aristocrat from Silla who had come to the court of Hsüan-tsung 玄宗, and in time had made his way to Szechwan. Saṅ-śi's meeting with Reverend Kim must have been around the time Reverend Kim had two audiences with the fleeing emperor, who had entered Szechwan in 755 in the wake of the An Lu-shan 安祿山 Rebellion. Reverend Kim, it seems, had connections to the imperial house.

Reverend Kim gave Saṅ-śi three Chinese texts, and the Tibetan party remained in China for several months after that. When, after eight years abroad, Saṅ-śi and his party return, the balance of forces at the Tibetan imperial court has shifted drastically. Saṅ-śi's patron Mes-ag-tshoms is dead; his son Khri-sroṅ-lde-bstan is not yet thirteen, the age at which he would inherit the throne; power resides with one faction of great ministers, and a suppression of Buddhism, under the banner of Bon, is underway. With no patron to sponsor the propagation of the Chinese-style teaching, Saṅ-śi prudently decided to hide away "the Chinese Dharma."[22] It was then 759 and the texts remained hidden for the next two years, only the first of several burials of Chinese teachings in Bod. With the lifting of the suppression in 761, Saṅ-śi "removed them from [their hiding place in] Mchims-phu and distributed the sayings of Reverend Kim [Kim ha-saṅ gi luṅ ba]."[23] Working with two Chinese, presumably

masters in the Reverend Kim tradition, Saṅ-śi translated these sayings into Tibetan.[24] It is possible
that Saṅ-śi had been recognized as a teaching master
in the Reverend Kim lineage. In time he became abbot
of Bsam-yas Monastery[25] and surely taught a Chinese-
style teaching within its precincts.

There is another member of the Sba who played a
key part in bringing Chinese Ch'an to Tibet, and that
is Gsal-snaṅ, the author of the family compendium
Statements of the Sba Family.[26] Gsal-snaṅ was a minister of the Emperor Khri-sroṅ-lde-bstan; in time he
left home and took the name Ye-śes-dbaṅ-po. His trip
to T'ang in search of the Dharma occurred sometime in
the later years of the 760's, his earliest departure
date being 763; it is quite possible that he was in
China for most of the late 760's, the years immediately following the An Lu-shan Rebellion. The Statements of the Sba Family tells us that the Chinese
emperor himself summoned Reverend Kim in order to
instruct Gsal-snaṅ in Buddhism,[27] but from the Chinese
Tun-huang text Record of the Dharma Treasure Down
Through the Generations (Li-tai fa-pao chi 歷代法
寶記) it is known that Reverend Kim died on the
evening of June 15, 762,[28] before Gsal-snaṅ had even
left Tibet. Again the imperial connection is prominent. It is most likely that here the Statements of
the Sba Family is trying to enhance the author's reputation by connecting him to Reverend Kim and Hsüan-
tsung. Japanese scholarship has suggested, with good
evidence, that it was not Reverend Kim that Gsal-snaṅ
encountered in Szechwan, but another Ch'an master in
I-chou 益州 , Pao-t'ang Wu-chu 保唐無住 .[29] Wu-chu
was a northerner and martial arts adept. His disciples at Pao-t'ang 保唐 Monastery in I-chou went to

lengths to emphasize that their master was Reverend Kim's successor; in fact, they composed the Ch'an history Record of the Dharma Treasure Down Through the Generations with this objective in mind. The actual connection between Reverend Kim and Wu-chu was much more tangential than this record would have us believe and becomes clear only upon an examination of independent Chinese materials. Judging from what is already known from the Tibetan literature on Ch'an, both Tun-huang texts and texts preserved among the Rdzogs-chen in central Tibet, where Wu-chu's sayings appear quite frequently, one is inclined to accept the hypothetical Wu-chu/Gsal-snaṅ meeting, even though the Statements of the Sba Family nowhere mentions Wu-chu's name. In any case, it is reasonably certain that there was a transmission of Pao-t'ang (Wu-chu) Ch'an around the late 760's. Reverend Kim Ch'an and Pao-t'ang Ch'an were the first Ch'an schools to reach central Tibet.

The next Ch'an transmission came a decade or more later from the Tibetan outpost of Tun-huang in the North, which did not fall into Tibetan hands until the 780's. This third known transmission involved one strain of the post-Shen-hsiu or late Northern school. The Chinese Tun-huang text Settling the Correct Principle of Suddenly Awakening to the Great Vehicle (Tun-wu ta-ch'eng cheng-li chüeh 頓悟大乘正理決) tells us that the Northern Ch'an master Mo-ho-yen, a student of two of Shen-hsiu's 神秀 successors,[30] came to central Tibet from Tibetan-occupied Tun-huang in either 781 or 787[31] at the invitation of the Tibetan emperor. Mo-ho-yen returned to Sha-chou (Tun-huang) in the next decade and continued to teach there. There has been some confusion over the identification of this

Mo-ho-yen. Kuei-feng Tsung-mi lists a Mo-ho-yen as a student of the Southern Ho-tse Shen-hui school.[32] Mo-ho-yen's teaching in Tibet as the famed proponent of the all-at-once gate can be summarized as "gazing-at-mind" (k'an-hsin 看心 = sems la bltas) and "no-examining" (pu-kuan 不觀 = myi rtog pa) or "no-thought no-examining" (pu-ssu pu-kuan 不思不觀 = myi bsam myi rtog).[33] "Gazing-at-mind" is an original Northern (or East Mountain Dharma Gate) teaching. As will become clear, Pao-t'ang and Northern Ch'an dovetail in the Tibetan sources. Mo-ho-yen's teaching seems typical of late Northern Ch'an. It should be noted that Mo-ho-yen arrived on the central Tibetan scene somewhat late in comparison to the Ch'an transmissions from Szechwan.

III. Materials for the Study of Tibetan Ch'an

To summarize the previous section, the tentative chronology runs as follows. In the late 750's the Ch'an of Reverend Kim arrived through Sba San-śi, but immediately upon arrival had to go underground for several years because political conditions did not permit its propagation. We have sayings in the Tibetan materials attributed to Kim-hu, Kim-hun, and other similar names,[34] but it is questionable whether these are transliterations of Reverend Kim's name. By the 770's the Ch'an of Pao-t'ang Wu-chu had arrived, most likely through Sba Gsal-snan. Judging from its imprint in Tibetan Tun-huang texts and in central Tibetan texts, its influence was substantial. Parallels to its history, Record of the Dharma Treasure Down Through the Generations, are found at many points in the Tibetan literature;[35] its twenty-

eight patriarchs theory shows up repeatedly; apocryphal "Ch'an sutras"[36] associated with Pao-t'ang (and
Northern) Ch'an circulated in Tibet; and, its form of
the name of the first patriarch of Ch'an in China,
P'u-ti-ta-mo-to-lo 菩提達摩多羅 (= Bodhidharmatrāta), rather than the Bodhidharma form used in other
Ch'an schools, is the name by which the first patriarch is usually known in the Tibetan literature. A
sayings record of the first patriarch, corresponding
to the Chinese Tun-huang text Treatise on The Two
Entrances and Four Praxes (Erh-ju ssu-hsing lun 二入四
行論), was known in Tibet under such titles as
the Great Chinese Instructions on Ch'an (Bsam-
gtan-rgya-luṅ-chen-po) of Bodhidharmatrāta.[37] Lastly,
by the 780's late Northern Ch'an, in the person of Mo-
ho-yen, arrived in central Tibet. The corpus of
Northern Ch'an in Tibetan includes: a version of the
Northern history Record of the Masters and Disciples
of the Lanka School (Leng-chia shih-tzu chi);[38] sayings of Mo-ho-yen's teacher Hsiang-mo Tsang,[39] a
student of Shen-hsiu; a Tibetan translation of an
important Northern dialogue;[40] and a number of Tibetan
works[41] specifically dealing with Mo-ho-yen's teaching, of which Stein Tibetan 468[42] is representative.
The Tibetan materials thus include potential sources
for any study of late Northern.

III.A.   Tibetan Tun-huang Texts and Rdzogs-chen Texts

Let us briefly focus on four key Tibetan works:
Pelliot Tibetan 116; Pelliot Tibetan 996; the Lamp of
the Ch'an or Dhyāna Eye; and the Five Classes of
Orders. Other Tibetan Tun-huang texts have been
researched and there is the possibility of finding

still others which will yield valuable information.
Also, much probably lies hidden in the Rdzogs-chen
literature.[43]   Pelliot Tibetan 116, the Lamp of the
Ch'an or Dhyāna Eye, and the Five Classes of Orders
contain the sayings of numerous Ch'an masters. The
following is a condensation of those sections of
Pelliot Tibetan 116 (VI.b-VIII) which record such
sayings:

    And in the Treatise on the Essence of
Causation by Master Nāgārjuna who teaches the
great vehicle: "In this there is nothing
which can be made manifest; there is no
[provisional] attribution at all.   In reality
gaze [lta] at the real. When one sees [mthoṅ]
the real, it is liberation."   Thus it
appears.[44]

    And Bo-de-dar-ma-ta-la,[45] the first of
seven generations,[46] said: "As to entering
principle [don la 'jug pa = li-ju], one awakens to the purport by means of the teaching;
the ordinary person and the True-nature [yaṅ
dag pa'i ṅo bo ñid = chen-hsing] are one without difference, and so, because covered by
false, adventitious dust, one does not realize
that the True-nature is manifest. If one puts
aside the false and reverts to the real, puts
aside discrimination and abides in light, then
there is neither self nor other. The vulgar
and the sage are equal, are one; if, without
moving, one abides firmly, then, beyond that,
one will not follow after the written teaching. This is the peace of reality, without
discrimination, quiescent, without action, and

this is entering into principle." Thus it appears.[47]

And in the teaching of Ch'an master Bu-cu [Wu-chu]:[48] "No-mind [myi sems pa = wu-i] is morality; no-thought [myi dran pa = wu-nien] is concentration; and non-production of the illusion mind is insight." Thus it appears.[49]

And in the teaching of Ch'an master [Hsiang-mo Tsang]: "Having nothing at all to be mindful of is Buddha-mindfulness." Thus it appears. "If you always [practice] Buddha-mindfulness and objects do not arise, then directly it is markless, level, and object-less. If you enter this place, the mind of mindfulness becomes quieted. There is no further need to confirm [that it is the Buddha]; if you gaze at this itself ['di ñid la bltas] and are level, then it is the real Dharma-body of the Thus-come-one." Thus it appears.[50]

And in the teaching of Ch'an master A-rdan-hver: "The mind as it is, level, is the real path of yoga." Thus it appears.[51]

And in the teaching of Ch'an master 'Gva-lun [Wo-lun]: "When thoughts follow after mind as it moves and one perceives objects, it is not necessary to draw them in; it is not necessary to check them." Thus it appears.[52]

And in the teaching of Master Ma-ha-yan [Mo-ho-yen]: "The Dharma-nature not being in thoughts, we set up no-thought no-examining [myi bsam myi rtog = pu-ssu pu-kuan]." Thus it appears.[53]

After a saying of A-rya-de-ba and a short work by
Master Ma-ha-yan, the Book Which Explains the Six
Perfections and Ten Assemblages in No-Examining, the
text continues:

Quoted from the Ch'an record of Master Bu-
cu [Wu-chu]: "As to the fact that morality,
concentration, and insight are no-thought [myi
sems ba = wu-nien], morality is non-
discrimination, concentration [lacuna] and
non-production of the illusion mind is
insight. These are the dhāranī gate."54

Quoted from the Ch'an record of Ch'an
master Kim-hun (= ?Reverend Kim): "When the
mind is level, all dharmas are level. If you
know the True-nature, there are no dharmas
that are not Buddha-dharmas. When you awaken
to principle, the mind of attachment does not
arise. At the time that one is not possessed
of the reality sphere in the mind, there is no
understanding. If you ask why this is so, it
is because the thusness of the perfection of
insight, by being level from the outset, is
objectless."55

This Kim-hun saying is followed by sayings of
Ch'an master Dzaṅ,56 Ch'an master De'u-lim,57 Ch'an
master Lu, Master Kim-hu (= ?Reverend Kim), Ch'an
master Pab-śvan, Ch'an master Par, Ch'an master Dzva,
Ch'an master Tshvan, Ch'an master Vaṅ, Ch'an master
Dzvaṅ-za, and the Chinese layman Keṅ-śi. The text
continues:

Quoted from the Ch'an record of Ch'an master Śin-ho [Ho-tse Shen-hui]:[58] "Always understand the real mark of no-thought [dran ba myed pa = wu-nien]. If you ask what this is, as to the fact that the mind-nature [sems kyi raṅ bźin = hsin-hsing] from the outset has the nature of non-abiding, there is nothing to obtain and the mind is pure, and so, in concentration there are no objects...."[59]

This Śin-ho saying continues, followed by sayings of Reverend 'Byi-lig, another of Master Maha-yan, and one of Ch'an master De'u. The text continues:

Quoted from the Ch'an record of Master Bu-cu [Wu-chu]:[60] "By the mind of reality the maṇḍala is made. Having lit the incense of complete liberation with the fire of markless-ness, and having done the unobstructed con-fession/repentance, practicing the morality of no-thought [bsam pa myed pa = wu-nien] and the concentration in which there is nothing to obtain, taking non-duality as wisdom, do not ornament the maṇḍala with worldly conditions." [Bu-cu] also taught: "Because all sentient-beings are, from the outset, completely pure, and, from the outset, perfect, there is neither increase nor decrease. Because of following after thought, the mind is defiled by the three realms, receiving various aggre-gate bodies. If, depending upon a good teacher, one sees the self-nature, then one becomes a Buddha [raṅ bźin mthoṅ na saṅs

rgyasu 'grub bo = <u>chih</u> <u>pen-</u> <u>hsing</u> <u>chi</u> <u>ch'eng</u>
<u>fo-tao</u>]. If one attaches to marks, it is
saṃsāra. Because sentient-beings have
thoughts, we name it and speak of no-thought
[<u>bsam</u> <u>ba</u> <u>myed</u> <u>pa</u> = <u>wu-nien</u>]. If [sentient-
beings] had no thoughts, no-thought would not
even be delineated. [Extinguishing][61] the
mind of the three realms, dwelling in neither
the place where the self expires nor in marks,
it is not that there is no effort. As to
divorcing from illusion, it is complete liberation. If there is mind, it is like waves on
water. If there is no-mind [<u>sems</u> <u>myed</u> = <u>wu-
hsin</u>], it is like the heretics. To follow
after arising is the defilement of sentient-
beings. To depend upon quiescence is movement
in nirvāṇa. Do not follow after arising nor
depend upon quiescence; do not enter concentration; have no arising; do not enter ch'an;
have no practice. The mind has neither
obtaining nor losing; there are neither
reflections nor forms; one dwells in neither
nature nor marks."[62]

The mixed Pao-t'ang/Northern cast of Pelliot
Tibetan 116 stands out: the form of the first
patriarch's name is clearly a Tibetan transliteration
of Chinese P'u-t'i-ta-mo-to-lo, the Pao-t'ang form of
that name; several lengthy Bu-cu (Wu-chu) sayings
dealing with his three phrases and "no practice"; the
sayings of the Northern master Mo-ho-yen with his "no-
thought no-examining" teaching; and the saying of Mo-
ho-yen's teacher Hsiang-mo Tsang, which is found in
the Northern history <u>Leng-chia</u> <u>shih-tzu</u> <u>chi</u>. Much the

same mix occurs in central Tibetan writings such as
the Lamp of the Ch'an or Dhyana Eye and the Five
Classes of Orders, indicating that much the same Ch'an
literature circulated in Tibetan-occupied Tun-huang on
the outskirts of the Tibetan empire and in the heart-
land of central Tibet.[63] It is unclear whether the
first set of names, Nāgārjuna/Bo-de-dar-ma-ta-la/Wu-
chu/Hsiang-mo Tsang/A-rdan-hver/Wo-lun/Mo-ho-yen/A-
rya-de-ba, is meant to be taken as a lineage or not.
Even if not, perhaps there is some significance to the
order, which in general fits with the chronology of
Ch'an transmissions to Tibet.

The circumstances behind this mixing of Pao-
t'ang and Northern Ch'an motifs are puzzling. In the
Five Classes of Orders Ma-ha-yan is presented as the
seventh emanation of Dha-rmo-ttā-ra-la (= Ta-mo-to-
lo),[64] that is, Ma-ha-yan is presented in a Pao-t'ang
context. As a solution Japanese scholarship[65] has
suggested that the Northern master Mo-ho-yen, finding
upon arrival in central Tibet that Pao-t'ang was
already established there (with patronage), took over
some Pao-t'ang teachings, and, in particular, that Mo-
ho-yen found the legendary biography of P'u-t'i-ta-mo-
to-lo of the Pao-t'ang school useful. In any case,
the association of Pao-t'ang and Northern is a close
one. Evidence suggests that, even though the name of
the Northern master Ma-ha-yan is the most prominent
one in the Tibetan Ch'an literature, Pao-t'ang Ch'an
was an important strain of Ch'an in early Tibet.

Pelliot Tibetan 996[66] describes a Ch'an lineage
that flourished in Central Asia and Tibet, a lineage
which traces its succession through an Indian, two
Chinese, and a Tibetan, the last being active in the
early ninth century. A-rtan-hver, the Indian founder,

shows up in Pelliot Tibetan 116, the Lamp of the Ch'an
or Dhyāna Eye, and the Five Classes of Orders.[67] He
is said to have migrated from India to the city-state
of Kūcha on the northern route of the Silk Road, where
he collected three-hundred disciples and declared the
"gate of all-at-once entering into the meaning of the
great vehicle." His successor was a Chinese known as
Reverend Be'u-siṅ active in Tun-huang and Kan-chou.
Be'u-siṅ's successor was another Chinese, known by the
Tibetan name Man, who travelled to China, and,
finally, Man's successor was the Tibetan Tshig-tsa-
nam-ka.[68] The mention of Kūcha is intriguing--we
know nothing of Kūchan Buddhism during the eighth and
ninth centuries. Ch'an literature shows up not only
in Tibet, but elsewhere in Inner Asia as well. Among
the Uighur Turkish manuscripts and block prints
brought back from Turfan, one has been found which
contains passages parallel to the Northern Ch'an text
Treatise on Examining Mind (Kuan-hsin lun); another
has been identified as four sheets of a Uighur Turkish
translation of an unknown Chinese commentary on the
Perfect Enlightenment Sutra (Yüan-chüeh ching), a
sutra associated with Ch'an.[69] The Uighur literature
found at Turfan at the beginning of this century and
carried away to distant libraries and museums may
contain other Ch'an-related materials.

III.B. Chinese Tun-huang Texts and Kuei-feng
        Tsung-mi's Writings

        Two of the three Ch'an schools important in the
formation of the ston mun of Tibet, the Ching-chung
(Reverend Kim) and the Pao-t'ang, were all but forgotten in China by the Sung, even by the late T'ang.

What were the Szechwan Ch'an schools like during their heyday in the eighth century? To answer this we must begin with the Tun-huang text, Record of the Dharma Treasure Down Through the Generations, a Ch'an history which emerged from the Pao-t'ang school, and to the writings of Kuei-feng Tsung-mi, who claimed to be in the Ho-tse Shen-hui lineage. Tsung-mi was writing some time after the flourishing of the Szechwan schools, in the 820's and 30's; nevertheless, his descriptions and critiques of these schools are useful. He was a native of Szechwan, born and raised not far from I-chou. Judging from his Ch'an writings, which might be described as scholarly and syncretic, he was quite familiar with Pao-t'ang and Ching-chung. It is necessary, though, to keep in mind that Tsung-mi's directions in both Ch'an and the canonical teachings may have been determined to some extent by his critical stance toward aspects of Pao-t'ang Ch'an.[70] Also, in his General Preface to the Collection of Explanations of the Ch'an Source (Ch'an-yüan chu-ch'üan chi tu-hsü 禪源諸詮集都序 , hereafter abbreviated as Ch'an Preface) he certainly ranked Pao-t'ang low in the critical classification of the Ch'an schools, as a sort of Yogācāra or Consciousness-only Ch'an like the Northern, as opposed to the Mādhyamika or Voidness Ch'an of Oxhead and the Dharma-nature or Tathāgata-garbha Ch'an of Shen-hui and Hung-chou.[71] Tsung-mi spent the last years of his life amassing a collection of the Ch'an literature in circulation, but all that has come down to us is his introduction to its contents, the Ch'an Preface, wherein he states that he has faithfully recorded the teachings of each school, even those of which he is critical:

The former wise ones and the later eminent ones each have their strong points. The ancient noble ones and the present-day worthies each have their benefits. This is the reason I have collected the goodness of all the houses and recorded their lineages. There are some which make me uneasy, but even these have not been changed.[72]

His detailed notes in the Subcommentary on the Perfect Enlightenment Sutra (Yüan-chüeh ching ta-shu ch'ao 圓覺經大疏鈔) on both the Reverend Kim school, which he calls the Ching-chung 淨眾 school or the school of Chih-hsien in the South, and the Pao-t'ang school mesh well with the Record of the Dharma Treasure Down Through the Generations and the Tibetan materials.

The Record of the Dharma Treasure Down Through the Generations pictures Reverend Kim and Wu-chu as two successive patriarchs of one Szechwan lineage, but it is from the hands of Wu-chu's followers, and is in effect the recorded sayings of Wu-chu with Bodhi-dharmatrāta to Reverend Kim tacked on as a pedigree. The following is a condensation of the core of the Record of the Dharma Treasure Down Through the Generations,[73] the very lengthy Wu-chu section:

(18) The Ho-shang [Wu-chu] was a man of Mei-hsien 郿縣, Feng-hsiang 鳳翔 [west of Ch'ang-an]. His family name was Li and Dharma name Wu-chu....In strength he surpassed others. He was a martial arts expert....He unexpectedly met the white-robed layman Ch'en Ch'u-chang 陳楚章, whose origins are

unknown. People of the time called him a
magical apparition body of Vimalakīrti. He
spoke the all-at-once teaching. On the very
day the Ho-shang met him, they intimately
coincided and knew each other, and [Ch'en]
silently transmitted the mind-dharma....For
three to five years [Li] engaged in the white-
robed [layman] practice. During the T'ien-pao
天寶 years [742-756] he unexpectedly heard of
Reverend Ming 明 of Tao-tz'u Shan 到次山 in
Fan-yang 范陽 [northern Hopei], Reverend
Shen-hui of the eastern capital [Lo-yang], and
Reverend Tzu-tsai 自在 of the superior prefecture of T'ai-yüan 太源 [Shansi], all disciples
of the sixth patriarch [Hui-neng] who spoke
the Dharma of the all-at-once teaching. At
that time the Ho-shang had not yet left home.
He subsequently went to T'ai-yüan and paid
obeisance to Reverend Tzu-tsai.

After giving a short discourse by Tzu-tsai the text
continues:

[Li] said goodbye to his previous path...and
subsequently cut his hair and took the robe.
Having received the full precepts in 749, he
said goodbye to the old Ho-shang [Tzu-tsai]
and went to the Ch'ing-liang 清涼 Monastery on
Wu-t'ai Shan, where he spent a summer. He
heard lectures on the deportment of Reverend
Ming of Tao-tz'u Shan and the idea behind
Reverend Shen-hui's sayings. Since he already
understood their meanings, he did not visit
them and pay obeisance (亦不往禮).[74] In

the fullness of the summer of 750 he came out
of the mountains and went to the western capital [Ch'ang-an]. He went back and forth
between the An-kuo 安國 Monastery and the
Ch'ung-sheng 崇聖 Monastery. In 751 he went
from the western capital to Ling-chou 靈州 in
the North [Ninghsia 寧夏] and dwelled on Ho-
lan Shan 賀蘭山 [north of Ling-chou] for two
years. Unexpectedly there was a merchant
Ts'ao K'uei 曹瓌 who made obeisance and asked:
"Has the Ho-shang ever gone to Chien-nan
[Szechwan] and met Reverend Kim?" He
answered: "I do not know him." K'uei said:
"The Ho-shang's countenance is just like that
of Reverend Kim...." The Ho-shang asked Ts'ao
K'uei: "Householder, since you have come from
Chien-nan, what sort of Dharma does that Ho-
shang speak?" Ts'ao K'uei answered: "He
speaks of no-remembering, no-thought, and no-
forgetting."

Ts'ao K'uei relates his experience with
Reverend Kim's ordination ceremony and the text
continues:

Wu-chu subsequently left Ho-lan Shan and went
to Ling-chou for traveling papers in order to
go to Chien-nan and pay obeisance to Reverend
Kim....The Ho-shang gradually went south and
arrived at Feng-hsiang [west of Ch'ang-an]....
In February/early March of 759 he arrived at
the Ching-chung Monastery[75] in the superior
prefecture of Ch'eng-tu. When he first
arrived he met Master An-ch'ien 安乾 who led

him in to see Reverend Kim. When Reverend Kim
saw [Wu-chu] he was extraordinarily pleased.
Reverend Kim ordered An-ch'ien to serve as
host and An situated him in a courtyard
beneath the belltower. It was precisely the
day for receiving conditions [receiving the
precepts]. That night, following the multitude, he received conditions. It only lasted
for three days and three nights. Each day
Reverend Kim, in the midst of the great
assembly, said: "Why don't you go enter the
mountains? Of what benefit is it to stay for
a long time?" Those disciples who personally
served Reverend Kim on the left and right were
alarmed: "Reverend Kim has never talked like
this before. Why does he suddenly come out
with these words?" Reverend Wu-chu silently
entered the mountains....Master Tao-i, who was
dwelling with him, practiced chanting, obeisance, and mindfulness. The Ho-shang [Wu-chu]
intently cut off thoughts and entered the
realm of self-realization (一向絕思斷慮入
自證境界). Tao-i, together with other
young masters in the community, said to the
Ho-shang: "I and the others wish to request a
twenty-four hour obeisance and confession. We
would like the Ho-shang's permission." The
Ho-shang said to Tao-i and the others: "Here
food will be cut off. Each of you has
advanced into the deep mountains....No-thought
is viewing the Buddha. Having thoughts is
samsāra. If you desire to be able to do obeisance and mindfulness, then go out from the
mountains....If you desire to be able to dwell

together in the mountains here, intently [practice] no-thought (一向無念)." Master Tao-i's view did not accord with this idea and so he said goodbye to the Ho-shang and emerged from T'ien-ts'ang Shan 天蒼山 [i.e., Po-yai Shan 白崖山 , north of I-chou 益州]. He came to Ching-chung 淨眾 Monastery in I-chou [Ch'eng-tu 成都]. He first saw the elder K'ung 空 and said to him: "In the mountains Ch'an master Wu-chu does not allow obeisance, confession, mindfulness, and chanting, but merely sits in voidness and quietude (只空 閑坐)." When Ho-k'ung 何空 and the others heard this they were startled [and said]: "How can this be the Buddha-dharma?" They led Master Tao-i 道逸 to see Reverend Kim. Before Tao-i had finished bowing Ho-k'ung and the others reported to Reverend Kim: "Ch'an master Wu-chu of T'ien-ts'ang Shan merely sits in voidness and quietude. He is unwilling to practice obeisance and mindfulness (不肯 禮念) and does not teach those who dwell with him to practice obeisance and mindful-ness. How could such a thing be the Buddha-dharma?" Reverend Kim scolded Ho-k'ung, Tao-i, and the others: "You should retreat! When I was in the stage of study, I did not eat but merely sat in voidness and quietide. Even in going to the bathroom I made no effort. You don't know. In the days when I was on T'ien-ku Shan 天谷山 [northwest of I-chou] I also did not practice obeisance and mindfulness ...." The Ho-shang [Wu-chu] said to Hsüan 璿: "Layman, the patriarch Dharma's one branch of

the Buddha-dharma has flowed to Chien-nan and
Reverend Kim is it. If you do not receive the
precepts, then you return from the precious
mountain empty-handed." Having heard, Hsüan
clasped his hands and rose. The disciple then
went to the superior prefecture to receive
conditions [i.e., ordination]. The Ho-shang
[Wu-chu] said: "Here is one-half catty of
bud-tea. If you go, take this bud-tea as [a
seal of] faith, give it to Reverend Kim,
transmit my words, and bow your head to
Reverend Kim. If Reverend Kim asks about me,
say that Wu-chu does not yet intend to emerge
from the mountains." Hsüan then said goodbye
to the Ho-shang, took the present of bud-tea,
and left. On May 11, 762 he arrived at the
Ching-chung Monastery in the superior prefecture of Ch'eng-tu....Tung Hsüan 董璿 met
Master P'u-t'i 菩提 who led him in to see
Reverend Kim. [Tung Hsüan] related the matter
of Wu-chu's gift of bud-tea and transmitted
the bow. Reverend Kim heard his words, saw
the bud-tea, and was unusually pleased. He
said to Tung Hsüan: "Since the Ch'an master
Wu-chu had [a seal of] faith to send, why
didn't he come himself?" Tung Hsüan answered:
"Ch'an master Wu-chu, on the day that I came,
said: 'I do not yet intend to come out from
the mountains.'" Reverend Kim asked Tung
Hsüan: "Who are you?" Tung Hsüan lied to
Reverend Kim in his answer: "I am a disciple
who personally serves Ch'an master Wu-chu."
Reverend Kim said to Tung Hsüan: "On the day
you return to Po-yai Shan I have [a seal of]

faith for you to take. You must come see me."
On the fifteenth day he saw Reverend Kim and
Hsüan said: "I am about to return to Po-yai
Shan and take the Reverend's present." At
that time [Reverend Kim] dispatched the disciples who personally served him on the left
and right: "All of you go outside the hall."
He then summoned Tung Hsüan into the hall.
The Ho-shang subsequently took the robe, rare
among men, and showed it to Hsüan: "This is
the robe that Empress Tze-t'ien 則天 gave to
Reverend [Chih-]hsien 智詵 ; Reverend Hsien
gave it to Reverend T'ang 唐 [Ch'u-chi 處寂],
and Reverend T'ang gave it to me. I transmit
it to Ch'an master Wu-chu...." "You take this
robe and secretly send it to Ch'an master Wu-
chu and transmit my words: 'It is important.
Make effort! Make effort! It is not yet time
to come out from the mountains. Wait three to
five years, until there is an important person
to welcome you, then come out.'"[76] Then he
dispatched Tung Hsüan saying: "Go in a hurry.
Do not teach anyone." After seeing Tung Hsüan
off, Reverend Kim said to himself: "Even
though this thing goes late, it will in the
end return." As Reverend Kim was saying these
words, there was no one around him. But the
disciples outside the hall heard Reverend
Kim's voice and all at once entered the hall,
asking Reverend Kim: "What were you saying to
yourself?" [Reverend Kim responded:] "I was
just talking." Reverend Kim's manner was
agitated; they noticed and asked: "Ho-shang,
where is the robe of faith which has been

transmitted to you? To whom has the Ho-
shang's Buddha-dharma been handed over?"
Reverend Kim said: "My Dharma has gone to Wu-
chu. The robe is hanging on the tip of the
tree. No one else can take it." Reverend Kim
said to the others: "This is not your realm.
Each of you go to his own place...." On June
15, 762, he ordered his disciples: "Bring me
a new clean robe. I will now bathe." By the
evening, sitting sternly, he expired.

(19) Deputy Commander-in-chief, Vice-
President of the Imperial Chancellery, Minister Tu 杜 [Hung-chien 鴻漸],[77] when he first
arrived in the superior prefecture of Ch'eng-
tu [in late March or early April of 766],
heard of the inconceivable things about
Reverend Kim [and said]: "Since the Ho-shang
has expired, there must be disciples to pass
it down." Subsequently, he went to the Ching-
chung Monastery and the Ning-kuo 寧國
Monastery on Heng Shan 衡山 [in Hunan] and saw
the traces of when Reverend Kim was alive.
The minister asked the young masters: "There
must be a disciple to continue the succession.
Is there a monk who has obtained the robe and
the bowl?" The young masters answered: "No
one has succeeded. While the Ho-shang was
alive there were two robes, one at the Ning-
kuo Monastery on Heng Shan and one remaining
at the Ching-chung Monastery to receive offerings." The Minister did not believe this. He
also asked some Vinaya Masters: "I have heard
from a distance that Reverend Kim was a great
teacher and that he received the robe and bowl

transmitted down from master to master until now. Reverend Kim having expired, where is the disciple who succeeded him?" A Vinaya Master answered the Minister: "Reverend Kim was a foreigner and did not possess the Buddha-dharma. When he was alive he did not discourse on the Dharma much, being unable to speak correctly.[78] When he was alive he was sufficient in making offerings and giving, but [Ho-]k'ung is the only disciple blessed with virtue. But even he does not comprehend the Buddha-dharma." The Minister, with his far-reaching vision, knew that this was a lie. So he returned home and asked his attendants, K'ung-mu officials Ma Liang 馬良 and K'ang-jan 康然 : "Do you know whether in Chien-nan there is a famous monk, a great worthy, of high practice?" Ma Liang answered: "Within the courtyard I usually hear the generals talking, and they say: 'West of the Ts'an-yai Pass 蠶崖關 on Po-yai Shan there is Ch'an master Wu-chu. He has obtained Reverend Kim's robe and bowl and is his successor. This Ch'an master's virtuous karma is deep but he has not come out of the mountains.'"

(20) On October 31, 766, special commissioner Mu-jung Ting 慕容鼎 , district officials, and Buddhist and Taoist monks went to Po-yai Shan and invited the Ho-shang [to come down]....They bowed their heads and said: "We wish the Ho-shang would not put aside compassion for the sake of living beings of the three Shu [Szechwan] and would serve as a great bridge."

After Wu-chu has come down from the mountains he is
visited by Minister Tu:

> The Minister entered the courtyard and saw
> that the Ho-shang's countenance was immobile,
> sternly pacific. The Minister bowed, came
> down the stairs, bowed, clasped his hands, and
> asked them to rise. The various secretaries
> and officials had never seen such a thing.
> They saw that the Ho-shang did not welcome him
> and did not rise. They looked at each other
> and asked: "Why doesn't he get up to welcome
> [the Minister]?"...When the Minister first
> sat down, he asked: "How did the Ho-shang
> come to arrive here?" The Ho-shang said:
> "From afar I came to commit myself to Reverend
> Kim...." The Minister asked: "Reverend Kim
> spoke of no-remembering, no-thought, and no-
> forgetting, did he not?" The Ho-shang
> answered: "Yes." The Minister also asked:
> "Are these three phrases one or three?" The
> Ho-shang answered: "They are one, not three.
> No remembering is morality; no-thought is con-
> centration; and no-falseness is insight." He
> also said: "The non-arising of thoughts is
> the gate of morality; the non-arising of
> thoughts is the gate of concentration; the
> non-arising of thoughts is the gate of
> insight. No-thought is morality, concentra-
> tion, and insight together." The Minister
> also asked: "This one wang character, is it
> 'woman' beneath the wang [as in 'falseness']
> or 'mind' beneath the wang [as in 'forget']?"

The Ho-shang answered: "'Woman' beneath the wang."

(25) [To a master Ching-tsang from Ch'ang-an who is versed in a Vimalakīrti commentary and has practiced sitting-ch'an the Ho-shang says:] "No-remembering is the Way. No-examining [pu-kuan 不觀] is Ch'an.[79] Do not take and do not put aside; when objects come, do not condition them. If you read commentaries, then it is thought movement."

(27) [To a Master Chung-hsin who is versed in the Odes and History he says:] "At all times self-existent. Do not pursue; do not turn. Do not float; do not sink. Do not flow; do not coagulate. Not moving, not vibrating. Not coming, not going. All lively walking and sitting is Ch'an" (活鱍々行坐 總是禪).

(33) One day when the Ho-shang was drinking tea, thirty military secretaries and officials bowed and sat down, asking: "Does the Ho-shang like tea a lot?" The Ho-shang said: "Yes." He then recited Verses on Tea ....The secretaries thereupon asked: "Why does the Ho-shang not teach others to read the sutras, perform Buddha-mindfulness, and do obeisance? We disciples do not understand." The Ho-shang said: "Self-realization, the ultimate nirvāṇa, I teach people about these. I do not use the implicit teaching of the Thus-come-one...." The master's springs and autumns were sixty and one.[80]

Notable points include the following: Wu-chu's (Li Liao-fa's) association with laymen, in particular his first master Vimalakīrti Ch'en Ch'u-chang and his successor Deputy Commander-in-chief Vice-President of the Imperial Chancellery Tu Hung-chien; Wu-chu's association with military men, the generals and secretaries of the Szechwan armies, a master-disciple relationship which brings to mind those of Japan; an opposition between the disciples who personally served Reverend Kim and Wu-chu, the only one who really understood Reverend Kim's suggestion to enter the mountains; Wu-chu's avoidance of ordinary Buddhist practices; and the critical response that Wu-chu's teaching evoked from some of his own followers and some of the followers of Reverend Kim at Ching-chung Monastery. The Record of the Dharma Treasure Down Through the Generations' account sounds a bit contrived in places (Reverend Kim's defense of Wu-chu's not practicing; Reverend Kim's transmission of the robe to Wu-chu through an intermediary; the prediction of Minister Tu's arrival, and so on). It would seem that the unknown Pao-t'ang compiler(s) of the Record of the Dharma Treasure Down Through the Generations were connected to the official/military milieu.

It is clear from Tsung-mi that, although Wu-chu recognized Reverend Kim as his master (認‧金和上 為師), the Reverend Kim house and the Wu-chu or Pao-t'ang house were in fact two distinct lineages. The Record of the Dharma Treasure Down Through the Generations does mention that Wu-chu received the precepts at one of Reverend Kim's public assemblies. In his Chart of the Master-Disciple Succession of the Ch'an Gate Which Transmits the Mind-Ground in China (Chung-hua ch'uan hsin-ti ch'an-men shih-tzu ch'eng-

hsi t'u 中華傳心地禪門師資承襲圖 , hereafter
abbreviated as Ch'an Chart) Tsung-mi gives Reverend
Kim's successor not as Wu-chu, but as I-chou
Shih 益州石 (Ching-chung Shen-hui), tracing Ching-
chung from Hung-jen to Tzu-chou Chih-hsien to Tzu-chou
Ch'u-chi to I-chou Kim to I-chou Shih, and from the
Record of the Northern Mountain (Pei-shan lu 北山錄)
of Shen-ch'ing 神清 (d. 806-820), who was in the
Ching-chung line, we know that Ching-chung and Pao-
t'ang were not just separate lineages, but antagonis-
tic ones.[81]   All of this, of course, fits with the
split in the Record of the Dharma Treasure Down
Through the Generations between Reverend Kim's students at the Ching-chung Monastery and Wu-chu.   This
is Tsung-mi's description in the Subcommentary on the
Perfect Enlightenment Sutra of the Ching-chung house:

> Those who say "use mind in the manner of the
> three phrases which correspond to morality,
> concentration, and insight" are the second
> house. At its origin it is collaterally
> descended from the fifth patriarch through one
> named Chih-hsien.   He was one of the ten main
> disciples [of the fifth patriarch].   He was
> originally a man of Tzu-chou 資州 [southeast
> of Ch'eng-tu], and he eventually returned to
> Te-ch'un 德純 Monastery in his native prefec-
> ture and converted [beings].   His disciple
> Ch'u-chi 處寂 , whose family name was T'ang,
> received the succession.   T'ang produced four
> sons, the first of which was Reverend Kim of
> Ching-chung Monastery in the superior prefec-
> ture Ch'eng-tu, Dharma name Wu-hsiang 無相 .
> He greatly spread this teaching. (As to Kim's

disciples, Chao 召 [= I-chou Shih = Ching-chung Shen-hui], who is presently at that monastery [i.e., Ching-chung], Ma of Ch'ang-sung Shan 長松山, Chi 李 [= ?Li] 李 of Sui-chou 逐州, and Chi 李 [= ?Li] 李 of T'ung-ch'üan 通泉 county have all succeeded him.) The three phrases are no-remembering, no thought, and no-forgetting. The idea is: Do not recall past objects; do not anticipate future glories; and always be joined to this insight, never dark-ening, never erring; we call this no-forgetting. Sometimes [the Ching-chung says]: Do not remember external objects; do not think on internal mind; dried up without support. (No-forgetting as above.) Morality, concen-tration, and insight correspond respectively to the three phrases. Even though [the Ching-chung's] expedients in opening up the purport and discoursing are numerous, that which their purport is tending toward lies in these three phrases. Their transmission ceremonies (傳 授儀式) are like the expedient of receiving the full precepts on an official mandala [ordination platform] at the present time in this country. I mean that, in the first and second months, they first pick a date and post notices, collecting monks and nuns and laymen and laywomen. The arranging of the broad bodhi-seat, obeisance, and confession some-times takes three to five weeks. Only after this do they transmit the Dharma. All of this is carried on at night. The idea is to cut off externals and reject confusion. The Dharma having been transmitted, immediately

beneath the words [of the master] they stop
thoughts and practice sitting-ch'an. Even
when people arrive from a great distance, even
nuns and laymen, before they have stayed long
at all, they have to do a week or two of
sitting-ch'an. Afterwards, following later
conditions, they disperse. It is very much
like the Dharma of mounting the platform of
the [Nan-shan] Vinaya School [based in the
mountains of that name just south of Ch'ang-an
and using the Dharmaguptaka version of the
Vinaya]. It is necessary to have a group.
Because of the tablet of the official statement [i.e., because Ching-chung grants
official licenses], it is called "opening
conditions." Sometimes once in a year, sometimes once in two or three years, it is
irregular in its opening.[82]

Ching-chung was a sort of Ch'an ordination
lineage which held periodic night-time transmission
ceremonies, enormous public gatherings. It utilized a
form of Buddha-mindfulness (mentioned in the Reverend
Kim section of the Record of the Dharma Treasure Down
Through the Generations) and emphasized sitting-ch'an.
Szechwan was a center of nien-fo 念佛 (Buddha-
mindfulness) Ch'an, for, in addition to Ching-chung,
there were the lineages of Ch'eng-yüan 承遠 and Kuo-
lang Hsüan-shih 果閬宣什 .[83] In chart form:

34

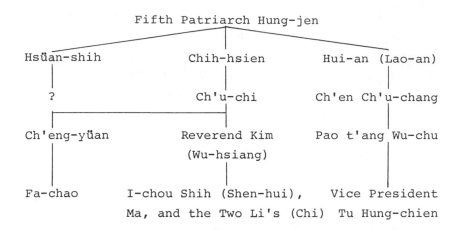

Ch'eng-yüan (712-802) was a native of Han-chou 漢州 in Chien-nan and once served Ch'u-chi, who is likely to have practiced some form of Buddha-mindfulness (nien-fo), since two of his students did. Ch'eng-yüan later studied under the Pure Land teacher Tz'u-min 慈愍; Ch'eng-yüan's disciple Fa-chao authored the Praises on the Pure Land Dharma-body (Ching-t'u fa-shen tsan 淨土法身讚), which shows the extent of the nien-fo/Ch'an fusion in some quarters.[84] The following selected verses from the Praises on the Pure Land Dharma-body, a Tun-huang manuscript, teach that the pearl of the mind is intrinsically pure but dust on it must be eliminated; that the practitioner sees the Pure Land during sitting-ch'an; that Buddha-mindfulness is identical to the no-thought of Ch'an; that the Pure Land is in the mind and is not dependent upon contemplative imagery; and that reliance upon the written teaching leads into the realm of discrimination:

    The pearl of the mind is always intrinsically
        pure;

The rays of spirit pervade the ten directions;
Know that the mind has no place to abide in;
Upon liberation you will obtain purity and
    coolness....
The mirror of wisdom has no darkness;
The pearl of knowledge is always functioning
    brightly;
Dust and toil must be cut off;
And the treasury will be welcomed
    spontaneously....
People at present specialize in the nien-fo;
Mindfulness-practitioners enter into deep
    ch'an;
The first night they sit with upright mind
The Western Land is before their eyes.
If one practices mindfulness [nien 念], he
    knows no-thought [wu-nien 無念];
No-thought is thusness;
If one understands the intention herein,
It is called the pearl of the Dharma-nature.
The Pure Land is in the mind;
The stupid seek it on the outside;
Within the mind there is the precious mirror;
It does not know to stop throughout one's
    lifetime....
The pearl of the mind is always of penetrating
    splendor;
The self-nature from the outset is perfectly
    bright;
Awaken to principle and know where the real is
    tending toward;
If you practice nien-fo, then no-arising....
The Buddha-marks are void and markless;
Thusness is quiescent and wordless;

Chatting about the written teaching,
From this comes the Ch'an of false
thoughts....[85]

Tsung-mi refers to Kuo-lang Hsüan-shih's Ch'an
as the Ch'an of the Nan-shan Nien-fo Gate[86] (the Nan-
shan in Szechwan) lists him as a disciple of the fifth
patriarch in the Ch'an Chart,[87] but claims to lack
accurate knowledge of the transmission. Subcommentary
on the Perfect Enlightenment Sutra classifies Hsüan-
shih's school under the rubric "preserves the Buddha
by transmitting the incense" (傳香而存佛):

"Transmitting the incense" refers to the fact
that, when they first collect the multitude
and perform such ceremonies as obeisance and
confession, it is like the Reverend Kim
school.[88] When they are about to hand over
the Dharma, they take transmission of the
incense as the faith between master and disciple. The Ho-shang hands it over; the
disciple hands it back to the Ho-shang; and
the Ho-shang hands it back to the disciple,
like this three times. It is the same for
each person [attending the ceremony].
"Preserving the Buddha" means that, just when
handing over the Dharma, they first speak of
the Tao-principle of the Dharma-gate and the
significance of practice, and only afterwards
order the one-character [i-tzu 一字] nien-fo.
In the beginning they stretch the sound of the
one character 引聲由念] , and afterwards
gradually lower the sound to a finer sound,

until no sound at all. They send the Buddha
to thoughts, but thoughts are still coarse.
They also send [the Buddha] to mind, from
moment to moment preserving [such] thoughts,
[and so] there is always Buddha within the
mind, until they arrive at no-thoughts [wu-
hsiang], at which they have obtained the
Way.89

Hsüan-shih's one-character or one-sound nien-
fo90 which leads to no-thoughts (wu-hsiang 無想.) is
clearly similar both to the nien-fo/no-thought (wu-
nien) of Fa-chao 法照 and to the nien-fo of Reverend
Kim in the Record of the Dharma Treasure Down Through
the Generations:

Reverend Kim, in the first and twelfth months
of every year, for the sake of thousands of
monks, nuns, and lay people, held a ceremony
of receiving conditions. In the ornamented
bodhi-seat he sat in the high seat and dis-
coursed upon the Dharma. He first taught
stretching the sound of the nien-fo [yin-sheng
nien-fo] to the point of exhausting one
breath's thoughts. When the sound had died
down and thoughts had been stopped, he said:
"No-remembering, no-thought, and no-
forgetting. No-remembering is morality. No-
thought is concentration. No-forgetting is
insight. These three phrases are the dhāraṇī
gate."91

Ching-chung practiced nien-fo and sitting-
ch'an; followed a rigorous variety of disciplinary

formalism; had state recognition as an ordination center; and propagated Ch'an at enormous mass gatherings. This is the Ch'an Saṅ-śi and his Tibetan party encountered in I-chou and transmitted to Tibet.

Concerning the Pao-t'ang house, Tsung-mi observes in Subcommentary on the Perfect Enlightenment Sutra:

> "Adhering to neither the teachings nor the practice and extinguishing perception" (教行 不拘而滅識) is the third house. It is also descended collaterally from the fifth patriarch, by way of Reverend Lao-an. At sixty years of age he left home and received the precepts. Crossing over sixty summers later, he was one-hundred and twenty. That is why he was called "Old An." An was his given name. He was respected as a master by the Empress Tzu-t'ien. His power in the Tao was deep, and his will was singular. All the famous worthies compared unfavorably with him. He had four students who were all high in the Tao and famous. Among them was a lay disciple called Ch'en Ch'u-chang (the other three were T'eng T'eng, Tzu-tsai, and P'o-Tsao to), at that time known as Ch'en Ch'i-ko. There was a monk by the name of Wu-chu who met Ch'en's instruction and obtained awakening. He was also singular in his will. Later Wu-chu traveled into Shu [Szechwan] and encountered Reverend Kim's opening of Ch'an [k'ai-ch'an] and also attended his assembly. [Wu-chu] merely asked questions and, seeing that it was

not a matter of changing his previous
awakening, he wished to transmit it to those
who had not yet heard it. Fearing that it
would not be proper to have received the
succession from a layman [i.e., Vimalakīrti
Ch'en Ch'u-chang], he subsequently recognized
Reverend Kim as his master. Even though the
idea of his Dharma of instruction is just
about the same [as that of Reverend Kim], his
transmission ceremonies are completely different.[92] What I mean by different is that [Wu-
chu Ch'an] carries out none of the marks of
the Śākya gate [shih-men shih-hsiang i-ch'ieh
pu-hsing]. Having cut their hair and put on
robes, they do not receive the precepts. When
it comes to obeisance and confession, turning
[the rolls of the texts] and reading, making
drawings and paintings of the Buddha, and
copying sutras, they revile all of these
things as false thoughts. In the halls where
they dwell they do not set up Buddha arti-
facts. Therefore, I say they "adhere to
neither the teachings nor the practice." As
to their "extinguishing perception," this is
the Tao which they practice. The idea is
that, taking all samsaric wheel-turning as the
arising-of-mind, and since the arising-of-mind
is falseness, they do not discuss good and
evil. Since non-arising [of mind] is the
real, they are not like those who engage in
the practice of marks. They take discrimination as the enemy and non-discrimination as
the real Tao. They also transmit the spoken
teaching of the three phrases of Reverend Kim,

but they change the character for "forget" to
the one for "false," saying that various
students have made a mistake in the words of
the former master entrusted to them.[93] The
idea is that, since no-remembering and no-
thought are the real and remembering-thoughts
is the false, then remembering-thoughts is not
allowed. Therefore, they say no-falseness
[rather than no-forgetting]. Moreover, their
intention in reviling all of the teaching
marks lies in extinguishing perception and
becoming the completely real. Therefore,
where they dwell they do not discuss food and
clothing, but trust that men will send offerings. If they are sent, then they have warm
clothing and enough to eat. If they are not
sent, then they let hunger and cold take their
course. They also do not seek to teach
[beings] and do not beg food. If someone
enters their halls, they do not discuss
whether he is highborn or a thief; in no case
do they welcome him, nor do they even get up.
In singing hymns or praises and making offerings, in reprimanding abuses, in everything,
each lets the other take his course. Indeed,
because their purport speaks of non-
discrimination, their practice gate has
neither "is not" nor "is." They merely value
no-mind as the ultimate. Therefore, I call it
"extinguishing perception."[94]

Whereas the Record of the Dharma Treasure Down
Through the Generations goes to great lengths to trace
Wu-chu through Reverend Kim, Tsung-mi portrays Wu-chu

as a lay disciple of Vimalakīrti Ch'en (Ch'en
Ch'u-chang) who did not change his views upon coming
to one of Reverend Kim's assemblies, but merely
obtained authentification as a teaching master. The
two schools differed drastically: Ching-chung
stressed obeisance, confession, mindfulness, and so
on; Pao-t'ang did not receive the precepts, did not
perform obeisance and confession, did not chant and
copy texts, used no incense and Buddha images, went on
no begging rounds, but merely "sat in voidness and
quietude." The official patrons of Pao-t'ang ("Protect the T'ang"), among whom there seem to have been
many civilian officials and military men such as Tu
Hung-chien and his subordinates, enabled it to flourish from the late 760's. Perhaps the students of Wu-
chu at Pao-t'ang Monastery came to overshadow Reverend
Kim's successors at the Ching-chung because of their
patronage.

IV. Conclusion

Most Western-language treatments of Tibetan
Buddhism, when dealing with the first diffusion of
Buddhism into Tibet during its imperial period, follow
the Kamalaśīla view, which becomes the orthodox post-
Atīśa view, and describe the Chinese party as teaching
the following: Due to the power of karma which arises
from mental discrimination, sentient-beings revolve in
saṃsāra; if they think of nothing at all (na kiṃcic
cintayanti = ci yaṅ mi sems) and do nothing at all
(nāpi kiṃcit karma kurvanti = ci yaṅ mi byed pa), they
will escape from saṃsāra.[95] Almost automatically the
word "Taoist" is applied to this position. Such
descriptions of the ston mun are found not only in

sources hostile to the Chinese-style teaching. For instance, the Rdzogs-chen Five Classes of Orders makes it clear that the ston mun was not overly engaged in "works":

As the last successor of Bo-dhi-dha-rmo-tta-ra, the principle of Ma-hā-yā-na ho-shang: By completely perfecting the all-at-once entrance, one arrives at the many meanings and principles of the sutras. That desired principle exists in [Tibetan] script and in the Great Chinese Instructions of Dhar-mo-ttā-ra [the Treatise on the Two Entrances and Four Praxes]. It is in the lineage of the pure origin of the instruction of doing nothing at all [ci yan byar med]. The Indian master Kāma-śī-la [Kamalaśīla] did not completely perfect the sutras whose meaning requires to be drawn out [neyārtha]. He cut through doubts concerning the learning of stages [rim pa] and so on. He established miniature clay images [of Buddhas and other figures which are placed in large numbers on the ledges of stupas] and did muttering prayers; he erected bridges to voidness and cleansed the footpaths [to the bar do or intermediate state]; he built many stupas and set up many academies. He established a great community of ordained monks. He did readings aloud of the great Indian sutras; he did the explanations and hearings of the great Dharma circles; he made friendships with those in grief; he impartially cured sick persons; to great giving to a high degree, to whatever becomes

43

great, he applied himself. Ma-hā ho-shang
[Mo-ho-yen] practiced the twelve expedients of
the practice. In the secret mantras of the
great vehicle he received many stages of
powers; he served at many maṇḍalas of realization; he did tastings of medicines, multitudes
of offerings, and overcomings of fire; he
applied himself to founding schools of cultivation and so on. He did not honor the community of ordained monks and objects to which
offerings are made. He rejected any method or
system [tshul 'chos chos lugs] and gazed
[blta] apart. These are the twelve expedients
of the practice of the secret mantras.[96]

The Indian pandit is presented as the activist mis-
sionary, the Chinese Ch'an master as the esoteric
yogin. The former built stupas, academies, and
medical clinics; the latter practiced sitting-ch'an
and gazing-at-mind. The tantric patina is camouflage
applied at a later date when the Chinese teaching had
become "heretical."

The historical circumstances surrounding the
Council of Tibet are far from clarified. Each side
probably received its information about the other
through hearsay, and even hearsay had to pass through
a formidable language barrier. Under such conditions
it is unlikely that the Indian pandits would have had
much patience for the ston mun's "gazing-at-mind," a
Ch'an-style meditation with antecedents in the East
Mountain Dharma Gate and the earliest Northern Ch'an
teachings, and "no-examining." For them "no-
examining" only came after effortful examining or
analysis. What they would have made of Pao-t'ang

Ch'an's "no-practice" is even more problematical, assuming that traces of Pao-t'ang remained by the time tension was accelerating. In a Chinese context Mo-ho-yen's Northern teaching of "gazing-at-mind"/"no-examining" and the Pao-t'ang emphasis on "all lively walking and sitting is Ch'an" can be distinguished. However, since both led to a neglect of many ordinary Buddhist practices, particularly to a neglect of the intricate structure of Yogācāra meditation as expounded by Kamalaśīla, in Tibet all strains of Chinese Ch'an must have appeared to opponents such as Kamalaśīla as the same heretical Chinese teaching of no-effort.

What became of the Chinese-style ston mun? Certainly, Ch'an was not banished from Bod simply by the wave of a hand, even an imperial hand. There are indications that the eventual Rdzogs-chen response to Ch'an lore was some sort of p'an-chiao or classification of the teachings, to use a Chinese term. Such a development is suggested by several texts. Vimala-mitra, a very important figure in early Tibetan Buddhism, translated many tantras and visited China.[97] He compiled a Sanskrit treatise which was translated into Tibetan under the title Meaning of the All-At-Once Entrance No-Examining Cultivation (Cig-car-'jug-pa-rnam-par-mi-rtog-pa'i-bsgom-don).[98] This work, which is based on Kamalaśīla's Steps of Cultivation (Bhāvanā-krama) and the Ch'an portion of Pelliot Tibetan 116 or similar materials, absorbs the calming/discerning of the former from a ston mun position.[99] Stein Tibetan 709[100] breaks down into a progression. The earlier sections,[101] which rely on the Sutra Which Explains the Hidden Meaning (Samdhi-nirmocana Sūtra) and the Steps of Cultivation, discuss

such topics as: four errors in dhyāna;[102] the triad
of hearing/pondering/practicing; the cause and fruit
of calming/discerning; obstacles in calming/discern-
ing; and antidotes. It is said that if novice yogists
(las daṅ po pa'i rñal 'byor pa) do not practice
calming/discerning, they will not be able to obtain
the unexcelled fruit.[103] The final sections[104] are
Ch'an-oriented. They include: the sayings of an
unidentified Ch'an master 'Gal-na-ya; a citation of
Bodhidharmatrāta's Book of Ch'an (Bsam-gtan-gi-yi-
ge); and the division of Ch'an into three levels, with
Tathāgata Ch'an (de bźin gśegs pa'i bsam gtan)[105] as
the highest. It is said that Mahayogists (rñal 'byor
chen po pa) must specialize in practicing the teaching
of Tathāgata Ch'an.[106] And, finally, the Lamp of the
Ch'an or Dhyāna Eye[107] expounds, in ascending order,
the purports (gźuṅ) of the step-by-step gate (tsen man
rim gyis 'jug pa), the all-at-once gate (ston mun cig
car 'jug pa), the Mahāyoga (rñal 'byor chen po), and
the Rdzogs-chen (rdzogs pa chen po). This even sounds
something like Tsung-mi's arrangement of the Ch'an
schools into three tenets (tsung). The teachings of
the lower rungs are expedients for those of lesser
abilities.

NOTES

1. Ueyama Daishun, "Tonkō ni okeru Zen no shosō," Ryūkoku Daigaku ronshū, 421 (October, 1982), pp. 90-116.

2. A preliminary descriptive catalogue of the Chinese-language Ch'an materials is: Tanaka Ryōshō, "Tonkō Zenshū shiryō bunrui mokuroku shokō," Komazawa Daigaku Bukkyō gakubu kenkyū kiyō, No. 27 (March 1969), pp. 1-17; No. 29 (March 1971), pp. 1-18; No. 32 (March 1974), pp. 30-49; and No. 34 (March 1976), pp. 12-14. See also Yanagida Seizan's "Zenseki kaidai" in Nishitani Keiji and Yanagida Seizan, Zenke goroku II, Sekai koten bungaku zenshū, 36B (Tokyo: Chikuma shobō, 1974), pp. 445-514, and Yanagida's brief list in Yanagida Seizan, Shoki Zenshū shisho no kenkyū (Kyoto: Hōzōkan, 1967), pp. 51-53. For an overview see Tanaka Ryōshō and Shinohara Hisao, eds., Tonkō butten to Zen, Kōza Tonkō, 8 (Tokyo: Daitō shuppan-sha, 1980).

3. Tibetan Ch'an studies began in 1939 with publication of a Ch'an-related Tibetan Tun-huang text: Marcelle Lalou, "Document tibétain sur l'expansion du Dhyana chinois," Journal Asiatique, CXXXI (October-December 1939), pp. 505-522. In the early 1950's Paul Demiéville published a study of the Council of Tibet: Le Concile de Lhasa, Bibliothèque de l'Institut des hautes études chinoises, Vol. VII (Paris: Impr. nationale de France, 1952). Six years later Giuseppe Tucci published a study of the Ch'an portion of a Rdzogs-chen "discovered treasure," this being the first indication that Ch'an-related materials had survived in central Tibet: Giuseppe Tucci, Minor Buddhist Texts, Part II, Serie Orientale Roma, IX, 2 (Roma: Instituto Italiano Per Il Medio Ed Estremo Oriente, 1958). Japanese scholarship began with the publication in the late 1960's and early 70's of Ueyama Daishun's articles on a Tibetan translation of the early Ch'an history Leng-chia shih-tzu chi and on the Tibetan Tun-huang manuscript Pelliot Tibetan 116, which contains the sayings of many Ch'an masters. During the 70's Ueyama, Obata Hironobu, Yamaguchi Zuihō, Kimura Ryutōku, Okimoto Katsumi, Imaeda

Yoshiro, and Harada Satoru published a series of
detailed articles on Tibetan Ch'an texts and related
matters. An excellent descriptive summary of the
Japanese scholarship down to 1977 is: D. Ueyama, "The
Study of Tibetan Ch'an Manuscripts Recovered from Tun-
huang, A review of the field and its prospects," tr.
K. W. Eastman and Kyoko Tokuno, to be published in
Early Ch'an in China and Tibet, edited by Lewis
Lancaster and Whalen Lai (Berkeley: Lancaster-
Miller, forthcoming). In 1980 Tanaka and Shinohara,
eds., Tonkō butten to Zen, appeared. As the first
survey of the Tun-huang manuscripts and Ch'an, it
devotes a lengthy section (pp. 377-466) to Chinese
Ch'an and Tibetan Buddhism. Pelliot Tibetan numbers
refer to the 2216 Tibetan manuscripts collected at
Tun-huang by Paul Pelliot and catalogued in Marcelle
Lalou, Inventaire des manuscrits tibétains de Touen-
houang conservés à la Bibliothèque Nationale (Paris:
Bibliothèque Nationale, 1939, 1950, and 1961), Vols.
I-III; Stein Tibetan numbers refer to the 765 Tibetan
manuscripts collected at Tun-huang by Aurel Stein and
catalogued in Louis de la Vallée Poussin, Catalogue of
the Tibetan manuscripts from Tun-huang in the India
Office Library (Oxford: Oxford University Press,
1962). A preliminary descriptive catalogue of the
Tun-huang Tibetan-language Ch'an materials is: Kimura
Ryūtoku, "Tonkō Chibettogo Zen bunken mokuroku shokō,"
Tokyo Daigaku bungakubu Bunka kōryū kenkyū shisetsu
kenkyū kiyō, 4 (1980), pp. 93-129. This catalogue
lists thirty-two manuscripts related to Ch'an:
Pelliot Tibetan 21, 102, 116, 117, 118, 121, 623, 635,
699, 811, 812, 813, 817, 818, 821, 822, 823, 827, 829,
835, 996, and 2105; Stein Tibetan 468, 667, 689, 703,
704, 705, 706, 707, 709, and 710. It also contains a
list of seventy-one publications, mainly articles,
useful in the study of Tibetan Ch'an.

4. Yoshiro Imaeda, "Documents tibétains de
Touen-houang concernant le concile du Tibet," Journal
Asiatique, CCLXIII (1975), p. 146. See also Ueyama,
"The Study of Tibetan Ch'an Manuscripts," pp. 20, 35,
and 36.

5. Fragmentary Shen-hui sayings have been found
in three Tibetan Tun-huang manuscripts, Pelliot
Tibetan 116, Pelliot Tibetan 813 and Stein Tibetan
709. See Okimoto Katsumi, "bSam yas no shuron (1)--
Pelliot 116 ni tsuite," Nihon Chibetto gakkai kaihō,
XXI (March 1975), p. 7; Kimura Ryūtoku, "Tonkō
shutsudo Chibettobun shahon Stein 709," Nihon Chibetto
gakkai kaihō, XXII (March 1976), p. 11; Obata

48

Hironobu, "Kodai Chibetto ni okeru tonmonha (Zenshū) no nagare," Bukkyōshi gaku kenkyū, XVIII, 2 (March 1976), p. 75; and Obata Hironobu, "Pelliot tib. n. 116 bunken ni mieru shozenji no kenkyū," Zen bunka kenkyūjo kiyō, VIII (August 1976), pp. 7-8 and 28-30.

6. Pelliot Tibetan 116 is a compilation of a number of texts. It is included in Ariane Macdonald and Yoshiro Imaeda, eds., Choix de Documents tibétains conservés a la Bibliothèque Nationale, Tome Ier. (Paris: Bibliothèque Nationale, 1978). Ueyama Daishun, "Tonkō shutsudo Chibettobun Zen shiryō no kenkyū--P. tib. 116 to sono mondai ten," Bukkyō bunka kenkyūjo kiyō, 13 (June 1974), pp. 1-11, describes this manuscript and gives a detailed outline of its contents. The following is a brief description of each section according to Ueyama's numbering system: I. Tibetan translation of Sanskrit Arya-bhadra-pranidhāna-rāja; II. Tibetan translation of Sanskrit Vajracchedikā Sūtra; III. a summary of the various features of the great and small vehicles, a genre found in other Tibetan Tun-huang manuscripts; IV. a very short exposition of the three "views," "equanimity by existents," "equanimity by entrance," and equanimity by practice"; V. This is a handbook for "Mahāyogists" (rñal 'byor chen po pa rnams), to be used to "counter the disputations of those who, from without beginning, have been attached to the manifestations of real things and words, to avert their views and serve as a summary reminder of necessary points." This work is cast in the form of objections and answers. The answers are mostly quotations from sutras, including a number of Chinese compositions translated into Tibetan. Many of these sutras were favored by the Pao-t'ang and Northern schools of early Ch'an. To suggest the flavor of this important section here are the tenth through fourteenth objections: "Another persons says: 'Not to do effortful offerings and so on is wrong.' An explanation thereof: In the Ratnakūta Sūtra: 'If there is no thought of the Buddha and no thought of the community, it is known as a true offering.' Thus it appears and so, yogists' not doing effortful offerings and so on is not wrong. Another person says: 'Not performing the speaking of bad deeds and confession/repentance is wrong.' An explanation thereof: From the Phyogs-su-rgyas-pa'i-mdo [i.e., the Chinese composition Fang-kuang ching]: 'Whoever wishes to perform confession/repentance sits straight and really gazes. He really gazes at the real. If he really sees, he will be completely free [of the sins]. That is known as the most excellent

repentance.' Thus it appears and so, it is evident
that the unmoving cultivation is the most excellent of
repentances. Another person says: 'For people who
are cultivating the path not to rely on the characteristics of antidotes is wrong.' An explanation
thereof: From the Ākāśa-garbha Sūtra: 'In thoroughly
calmed dharmas antidotes are not necessary.' Thus it
appears and so, it is evident that, if the mind does
not examine marks, it is not necessary to attend to
antidotes. Another person says: 'As to producing the
thought of enlightenment, if at first the thought is
produced from the gate of analysis, later no-examining
[myi rtog pa] is accomplished.' An explanation
thereof: From the Gstug-tor-chen-po'i-mdo [i.e., the
Chinese composition Ta fo-ting ching]: 'If at first
one produces the thought which has neither arising nor
extinguishing, at the end he will obtain the fruit
which has neither arising nor extinguishing. If at
first he produces the thought which has arising and
extinguishing, at the end he will not obtain the fruit
which has neither arising nor extinguishing.' Thus it
appears....It is evident that practice from the gate
of analysis becomes focussing-of-the-attention solely
on marks, and it is always useless for examining the
realm which has neither arising nor extinguishing."
(fols. verso 18.2-22.2); VI.(a). This section contains twenty-three questions on no-examining (myi rtog
pa = pu-kuan); the answers quote many of the same
sutras as the previous section and one treatise, the
Rta-skad-byan-chuḥ-sems-dpa'i-mdo (Aśvaghosa-bodhi-
sattva Sūtra = the Chinese composition Ta-ch'eng ch'i-
hsin lun/fol. verso. 33.3-34.1). Here are the first
three questions: "'In no-examining what does producing the thought of enlightenment consist of?' From
the Vajracchedikā Sūtra: 'Completely abstaining from
all thoughts is producing the thought of unexcelled
enlightenment.' Thus it appears. 'In no-examining
what does cultivating the perfection of insight consist of?' From the Prajñā-pāramitā Sūtra: 'The mind
not moving to any dharma--that is known as the most
excellent yoga of the perfection of insight. Thus
spoke the Lord.' 'In no-examining how is the great
vehicle manifested?' From the Rdo-rje-tin-ne-'dzin-
kyi-mdo [i.e., the Chinese composition Chin-kang san-
mei ching]: 'If there are no thoughts, origination is
not produced, and reality as it is does not move.
That is the great vehicle.' Thus it appears." (fols.
verso 23.2-24.4); VI.(b). This section begins with the
line: "This gate of all-at-once entrance does not
contradict the instructions of those many sutras above
and is also in agreement with the learned [Ch'an]

masters below." (fol. verso 40.3-4) It then gives
sayings for Na-ga-rdzu-na, Bo-de-dar-ma-ta-la, Wu-chu,
Hsiang-mo Tsang, A-rdan-hver, Wo-lun, Ma-ha-yan, and
A-rya-de-ba. This list has the look of a partriarchal
succession for Tibetan consumption. The final line
is: "[Here] ends the book [which serves as] a support
for remembering the necessary meanings for Mahayogists
who are of the purport of the one nature wherein there
are no objects." (fol. verso 47.2-3); VII. a short
work entitled Book Which Explains the Six Perfections
and Ten Assemblages in No-Examining [myi rtog pa], by
Master Ma-ha-yan; VIII. the sayings of eighteen
Chinese Ch'an masters and laymen, including Wu-chu,
Shen-hui, and Ma-ha-yan; IX. This section is a Tibetan
translation of the Tun-wu chen-tsung chin-kang pan-jo
hsiu-hsing ta pi-an fa-men yao-chüeh, a Northern Ch'an
dialogue which shows a tendency to fuse characteristic
Northern teachings with Shen-hui teachings. The position of the text is: if one exerts effort to finely
gaze (bltas = k'an), in time the gazing ripens into
seeings (mthon = chien); this position shows an affinity to the teaching of Mo-ho-yen. The Tibetan rendering is perhaps 30% longer than the text which can be
assembled from the Chinese Tun-huang manuscripts
(Stein Chinese 2799, Pelliot Chinese 3922, and Stein
Chinese 5533); X. a short work dealing with the "five
fears of errors"; and XI. four lines of verse entitled Book Which Teaches of the Dharma-dhātu Nature.
Obata, "Pelliot tib. n. 116 bunken," pp. 4-12, provides a transliterated text and Japanese translation
of VI.(b), VII, and VIII. Ueyama Daishun, "Chibettoyaku Tongo shinshū yōketsu no kenkyū," Zen bunka
kenkyūjo kiyō, VIII (August 1976), pp. 33-103, provides a transliterated text of IX, a Japanese translation, and editions of the Chinese texts. See also
Kimura Ryūtoku, "Tonkō shutsudo Chibettobun shahon
Pelliot 116 kenkyū (sono ichi)," Indogaku Bukkyōgaku
kenkyū, XXIII, 2 (March 1975), pp. 281-284; Okimoto
Katsumi, "bSam yas no shuron (1)," pp. 5-8; and
Kimura, "Tonkō Chibettogo Zen bunken mokuroku shoko,"
pp. 97-104. Okimoto (p. 6) says that a part of the
text between fol. 40 and fol. 41 has been lost and
hence Ueyama's VI.(a) and VI.(b) should be VI and VII,
the manuscript thus containing twelve separate texts
instead of eleven.

  7. The Bsam-gtan-mig-sgron is an early ninth-
century Rdzogs-chen text by Gnubs-chen Saṅs-rgyas-ye
šes (b. 772). Rdzogs-chen (Great Perfection) is a
section of the Rñiṅ-ma doctrine. Section 5, which
deals with the all-at-once gate (ston mun cig car

'jug pa), contains the sayings of many Ch'an masters. A copy of this text was found in India in the mid-1970's. See Gnubs-chen Saṅs-rgyas-ye-śes, Rñal 'byor mig gi bsam gtan or Bsam gtan mig sgron, Smanrtsis shesrig spendzod, Volume 74 (Leh, Ladakh: S. W. Tashigangpa, 1974). See Okimoto Katsumi, "bSam yas no shūron (2)--Tonkō Chibettobun ni okeru shozenji," Nihon Chibetto gakkai kaihō, XXII (March 1976), pp. 7-8, for a chart of all the Ch'an masters in the Bsam-gtan-mig-sgron, Bka-thaṅ-sde-lṅa, and Pelliot Tibetan 116. The overlap is striking.

8. The Rdzogs-chen text Bka-thaṅ-sde-lṅa, a compendium of royal and aristocratic lore, contains a section, the "Blon-po-bka'i-thaṅ-yig" ("Reports of the Ministers"), which records Ch'an sayings. The Ancient School follower O-rgyan-gliṅ-pa (1323-1379), one of the numerous discoverers of hidden literary treasures, discovered the Five Classes of Orders (of the Indian master Padamasambhava to the demons, kings, queens, ministers, and clergy) together with a biography of Padmasambhava. See Hellmut Hoffmann, Tibet. A Handbook (Bloomington: Research Center for the Language Sciences, Indiana University, undated), pp. 24 and 160. Tucci, Minor, pp. 68-81, provides a transliterated text and English translation of the Ch'an sayings of the fourth section, the "Reports of the Ministers."

9. Among the Chinese Tun-huang texts the following are relevant. The (tentatively titled) Erh-ju ssu-hsing lun is generally considered an authentic record of Bodhidharma's teaching. For text and Japanese translation see Yanagida Seizan, Daruma no goroku, Zen no goroku, 1 (Tokyo: Chikuma shobō, 1969). It is quoted in Tibetan documents as the Rgya-luṅ (Chinese Instructions), the Rgya-luṅ-chen-po (Great Chinese Instructions), or the Bsam-gtan-rgya-luṅ-chen-po (Great Chinese Instructions on Ch'an) and attributed to Bodhidharmatrāta. For instance, see Gnubs chen Saṅs-rgyas-ye-śes, Rñal 'byor mig gi bsam gtan, fols. 130.2-4 and 179.1-4. See Obata, "Pelliot tib. n. 116 bunken," pp. 12-16; Obata Hironobu, "Chibetto den Bodaidarumatara Zenji kō," Indogaku Bukkyōgaku kenkyū, XXIV, 1 (December 1975), pp. 229-232; and Okimoto Katsumi, "Chibettoyaku Ninyū shigyō ron ni tsuite," Indogaku Bukkyōgaku kenkyū, XXIV, 2 (March 1976), pp. 39-46. The Ldan-kar-ma Catalogue, compiled in 812, records a Bsam-gtan-gyi-yi-ge rgya las bsgyur ba ("Book of Ch'an, translated from China"). See Yoshimura Shūki, Denkaruma mokuroku no

kenkyū (Kyoto: Ryūkoku Daigaku Tōhō seiten kenkyūkai, 1950), No. 614. There is some possibility that the Tibetan titles are closer to the original title than Erh-ju ssu-hsing lun. The Leng-chia shih-tzu chi (T no. 2837) is a Northern history. For text and Japanese translation see Yanagida Seizan, Shoki no Zenshi I, Zen no goroku, 2 (Tokyo: Chikuma shobō, 1971). Stein Tibetan 710 is a Tibetan translation of a version of the Leng-chia shih-tzu chi which ends in the midst of the account of Tao-hsin. See Ueyama Daishun, "Chibettoyaku Ryōga shiji ki ni tsuite," Bukkyōgaku kenkyū, XXV-XXVI (May 1968), pp. 191-209, and Ueyama Daishun, "Chibettoyaku kara mita Ryōga shiji ki seiritsu no mondai ten," Indogaku Bukkyōgaku kenkyū, XXI, 2 (March 1973), pp. 597-602. Okimoto Katsumi, "Ryōga shiji ki no kenkyū," Hanazono Daigaku kenkyū kiyō, 9 (March 1978), pp. 59-87, provides a transliterated text of Stein Tibetan 710, a Japanese translation, and the Chinese text. The Li-tai fa-pao chi (T no. 2075) shows many parallels in the Tibetan texts. For text and Japanese translation see Yanagida Seizan, Shoki no Zenshi II, Zen no goroku, 3 (Tokyo: Chikuma shobō, 1976). This volume contains an essay by Obata, "Rekidai hōbō ki to kodai Chibetto no Bukkyō." For a more detailed treatment see Obata Hironobu, "Chibetto no Zenshū to Rekidai hōbō ki," Zen bunka kenkyūjo kiyō, VI (June 1974), pp. 139-176. The Tun-wu ta-ch'eng cheng-li chüeh (Pelliot Chinese 4646) deals with the Ch'an master Ma-ha-yan of the Council of Tibet. For a reproduction of the manuscript and a French translation see Paul Demiéville, Le Concile de Lhasa. We have no Chinese texts attributed to Ma-ha-yan/Mo-ho-yen, but numerous Tibetan texts. Stein Tibetan 468 is representative. See Ueyama Daishun, "Tonkō shutsudo Chibettobun Mahaen Zenji ibun," Indogaku Bukkyōgaku kenkyū, XIX, 2 (March 1971), pp. 124-126; Okimoto Katsumi, "bSam-yas no shūron (3)--nishu no Mahaen ibun," Nihon Chibetto gakkai kaihō, XXIII (March 1977), pp. 5-8; and, G. W. Houston, "The System of Ha Sang Mahāyāna," Central Asiatic Journal, Vol. 21, 2 (1977), pp. 106-110. The Tun-wu chen-tsung chin-kang pan-jo hsiu-hsing ta pi-an fa-men yao-chüeh (Pelliot Chinese 2799 and others) is an expository work of late Northern provenance, a series of questions and answers between a layman and a Northern master (actually, the same person). A Tibetan translation of it is found in Pelliot Tibetan 116 (IX). Ueyama, "Chibettoyaku Tongo shinshū yōketsu no kenkyū," pp. 33-103, provides a transliterated text of the Tibetan, a Japanese translation, and the Chinese texts. For all of the above, see Tanaka and

Shinohara, eds., Tonkō butten to Zen, pp. 414-425.
Three works by Kuei-feng Tsung-mī (780-841), the
Ch'an-yüan chu-ch'üan chi tu-hsü (T no. 2015), the
Chung-hua ch'uan hsin-ti ch'an-men shih-tzu ch'eng-hsi
t'u (ZZ 2, 15, 5, pp. 433b-438b), and one section of
the Yüan-chüeh ching ta-shu ch'ao (ZZ 1, 14, 3, pp.
277b-280a), include treatments of the schools of
eighth-century Chinese Ch'an. For texts and Japanese
translations see Kamata Shigeo, Zengen shosenshū tojo,
Zen no goroku, 9 (Tokyo: Chikuma shobō, 1971).

10. Chiu T'ang-shu, 196, and Hsin T'ang-shu,
216. See S. W. Bushell, "The Early History of Tibet.
From Chinese Sources," Journal of the Royal Asiatic
Society of Great Britain and Ireland, 12 (1880), pp.
435-541. Tibet is referred to as T'u-fan.

11. The Tibetan occupation is dated 781-848 by
Fujieda Akira and 787-848 by Demiéville. See Fujieda
Akira, "Toban shihaiki no Tonkō," Tōhō gakuhō, XXXI
(March 1961), pp. 199-292.

12. For references on these two families see
Hugh E. Richardson, "The Dharma that Came down from
Heaven: a Tun-huang Fragment," in Buddhist Thought
and Asian Civilization, ed. Leslie S. Kawamura and
Keith Scott (Emeryville, Calif.: Dharma Publishing,
1977), pp. 224 and 226. The 'Bro family is mentioned
in the Tun-wu ta-ch'eng cheng-li chüeh (Demiéville, Le
Concile, fol. 127a.4 and pp. 25-30). They were originally of Źań-źuń stock, a people who were absorbed
into the Tibetan empire at an early date.

13. For a text of the Sba-bźed see R. A. Stein,
Une chronique ancienne de bSam-yas: sBa-bźed, Publi-
cations de l'Institut des Hautes Etudes Chinoises,
Textes et Documents, I (Paris: Centre National de la
Recherche Scientifique, 1961). Stein's text is the
Sba-bźed "with a supplement." See Hoffman, Tibet, p.
26.

14. These two famous monasteries are close in
time. As with Tōdai-ji, Bsam-yas had kokubunji or
provincial reflections. Within the Bsam-yas complex
there was a "Hall of Unmoving Ch'an" (mi g'yo bsam
gtan glin = ?pu-tung ch'an yüan). See Tucci, Minor,
p. 113.

15. Obata, "Chibetto no Zenshū," pp. 142-152,
brings the Chinese perspective to bear on the Sba-
bźed, focusing on coordinating the trips of Śań-śi and

Gsal-snaṅ with the figures of Szechwan Ch'an. See
also Yamaguchi Zuihō, "Chibetto Bukkyō to Shiragi no
Kin ōsho," Shiragi Bukkyō kenkyū (June 1973), pp. 3-
36.

16. This commissioner's name occurs in the Sba-
bźed as 'Ba'-de'u, the Chinese original of which is
unclear. See Yamaguchi, "Chibetto Bukkyō to Shiragi,"
pp. 5 and 26 (n. 13).

17. Regal name Khri-lde-gtsug-brtan.

18. Stein, Sba-bźed, p. 5.2.

19. Yamaguchi, "Chibetto Bukkyō to Shiragi," p.
26 (n. 9), says that San-śi is not a transliteration
of Chinese ch'an-shih ("Ch'an master"), but an abbreviation of San-śi-ta.

20. Obata, "Rekidai hōbō ki to kodai Chibetto no
Bukkyō," in Yanagida, Shoki no Zenshi II, p. 328.

21. Eg-cu'i Ñi-ma ha-san of the Sba-bźed = I-
chou Chin ho-shang (Stein, sBa-bźed, p. 6.14 et
passim).

22. Stein, sBa-bźed, p. 9.14. The hiding place
was Mchims-phu in the mountains outside Ra-sa (later
Lhasa).

23. Stein, sBa-bźed, p. 10.6-7.

24. Stein, sBa-bźed, p. 10.13-15. The two
Chinese were Rgya (China) Mes-mgo and Rgya A-nan-ta.
There is a saying in the Bka-thaṅ-sde-lṅa attributed
to a Ch'an master Sbab Śan-śin: "Ch'an master Sbab
Śan-śin said: 'The all-at-once knowledge without dis-
crimination is like the lion, the king of the animals,
who looks down, in the four positions unafraid.'" See
Tucci, Minor, p. 73.16-19.

25. It seems that San-śi = sBa dPal-dbyaṅs the
abbot of Bsam-yas = dPal-dbyaṅs the author of the
Mahāyoga text Pelliot Tibetan 837. See Ueyama
Daishun, "Peyan cho no mahāyoga bunken--P. tib. 837 ni
tsuite," Bukkyō bunka kenkyūjo kiyō, 16 (June 1977),
pp. 9-11. Here we have a striking example of the link
between Ch'an and Mahāyoga, in the person of an abbot
of early Tibet's most important monastery.

26. Stein, sBa-bźed, p. v.

27. Stein, sBa-bźed, pp. 19.16-20.1.

28. T 51, pp. 185a and 187c. Yanagida, Shoki no Zenshi II, pp. 143 and 172.

29. Obata, "Chibetto no Zenshū," p. 153, discusses the high probability that Gsal-snaṅ actually met Wu-chu rather than Reverend Kim. He concludes that the author of the Sba-bźed, due to conditions at the Tibetan imperial court, converted Wu-chu into Reverend Kim. This seems quite likely. It is difficult, however, to say just what those conditions were. Perhaps Reverend Kim's reputation at the court was substantial and to be called upon.

30. The Tun-wu ta-ch'eng cheng-li chüeh (Demiéville, Le Concile, fols. 156b.6-157a.1) says that Mo-ho-yen had heard the Dharma fifty to sixty years earlier from Hsiang-mo Tsang, Hui-fu, and I-fu. For all three, see Ui Hakuju, Zenshū shi kenkyū (Tokyo: Iwanami shoten, 1939), pp. 287-289, 290, and 276-279. Hsiang-mo Tsang probably studied under Shen-hsiu at Yü-ch'üan Monastery in Ching-chou (Hupeh) during the last quarter of the seventh century. He subsequently entered T'ai Shan (Shantung), where he collected many disciples and lived to a very advanced age. Hui-fu and I-fu are listed by the Northern history Leng-chia shih-tzu chi as two of the four heirs of Shen-hsiu: "Ch'an master P'u-chi of Sung-kao Shan [Sung Shan] in Lo-chou [outside the eastern capital Lo-yang], Ch'an master Ching-hsien of Sung Shan, Ch'an master I-fu of Lan Shan in Ch'ang-an, and Ch'an master Hui-fu of Yü Shan in Lan-t'ien [southeast of Ch'ang-an] are all students of the same master, Dharma-brothers with the flight formation of wild geese, and they have all succeeded Ta-t'ung ho-shang [Shen-hsiu]." T85, p. 1290c. Yanagida, Shoki no Zenshi I, p. 320. Little is known of Hui-fu (Hsiao-fu or Little Fu), but he was important in metropolitan Northern Ch'an; I-fu (Ta-fu or Big Fu) continued Shen-hsiu's imperial connection and died in 736. Mo-ho-yen, then, must have studied Northern Ch'an in Shantung and Ch'ang-an during the first half of the eighth century. He subsequently migrated to Tun-huang and was resident there when Tibetan troops captured it in the 780's. His fame was sufficient to elicit from the Tibetan emperor an invitation to come to central Tibet.

31. Demiéville, Le Concile, fols. 154a.6-154b.1:
"Your subject, Śramaṇa Mo-ho-yen, says that, in Sha-
chou [Tun-huang] on the day of its submission [to
Tibet], receiving the order of universal kindness [of
the Tibetan emperor], I went seeking afar in order to
open up and illustrate the Ch'an gate and eventually
arrived in Lo-so." Mo-ho-yen's arrival date thus
depends upon whether one dates Sha-chou's surrender as
781 (Fujieda) or 787 (Demiéville). During this period
the center of Tibet was Yar-kluṅ or Brag-mar (the
Bsam-yas region). The Tibetan imperial entourage
still moved from place to place according to the
seasons. Chinese Lo-so transliterates Tibetan Ra-sa
(= Ra-ba'i-sa), "the walled ground." Ra-sa was only
one of the summer residences of the emperor; the Bsam-
yas area was the winter residence. Mo-ho-yen did not
meet the emperor in Ra-sa, but probably in the Bsam-
yas area. Tucci, Minor, pp. 32-34.

32. Tsung-mi, in his Chung-hua ch'uan hsin-ti
ch'an-men shih-tzu ch'eng-hsi t'u (ZZ 2, 15, 5, p.
435a; Kamata, Zengen, p. 290), lists a Mo-ho-yen among
the eighteen students of Ho-tse Shen-hui. However, he
says nothing else about this Mo-ho-yen in his Ch'an
writings, and we can only assume that this Mo-ho-yen
of the Ho-tse school is unrelated to the one of
Tibetan Ch'an. Jao Tsung-i, "Shen-hui men-hsia Mo-
ho-yen chih ju-tsang," Symposium on Chinese Studies
Commemorating the Golden Jubilee of the University of
Hong Kong 1911-61, Vol. I (1964), pp. 173-181, argues
that the Mo-ho-yen of Tsung-mi's chart is indeed the
one famous in Tibet, and in the process Jao identifies
the Hsiang-chou Fa-i of Tsung-mi's list of Shen-hui's
students with the Ta-mo-ti (= Dharmamati) who worked
in tandem with Mo-ho-yen to "open the Ch'an teaching."
Demiéville, Le Concile, fol. 154b.4.

33. See the Tun-wu ta-ch'eng cheng-li chüeh
(Demiéville, Le Concile, fol. 135a.2-4); Pelliot
Tibetan 116 (fol. verso 48.1 et passim); and Stein
Tibetan 468 (fols. 1b.3-2a.2). On Mo-ho-yen see
Harada Satoru, "Mahaen Zenji kō," Bukkyōgaku, 8
(1979), pp. 109-133; Harada Satoru, "Mahaen Zenji to
tonmon," Indogaku Bukkyōgaku kenkyū, XXVIII, 1 (1979),
pp. 428-432; and Tanaka and Shinohara, eds., Tonkō
butten to Zen, pp. 379-407 and 422-425.

34. Obata, "Pelliot. tib. n. 116 bunken," pp.
23-24. Kim-hun and Kim-hu appear in Pelliot Tibetan
116; Kyin-hu in the Bsam-gtan-mig-sgron; Kin-hun in
the Bsam-gtan-mig-sgron; and Ke-hun in the Bka-thaṅ-

sde-lña. For more on such variants see Yamaguchi, "Chibetto Bukkyō to Shiragi," p. 28 (n. 28).

35. Obata, "Kodai Chibetto ni okeru tonmonha," pp. 75-76.

36. A number of Chinese sutras, that is, Chinese compositions, circulated during the eighth century and were used by the Pao-t'ang and the late Northern of Mo-ho-yen. In fact, both seem to have relied solely on sutras, not on treatises and commentaries. The opening passage of the Li-tai fa-pao chi lists twenty-five sutras as support, but no treatises or commentaries (T 51, p. 179a; Yanagida, Shoki no Zenshi II, p. 39). Four of the twenty-five are Chinese compositions: Ta fo-ting ching (T no. 945); Chin-kang san-mei ching (T no. 273); Fa-chü ching (T no. 2901); and Ch'an-men ching (Stein Chinese 5532). The Tun-wu ta-ch'eng cheng-li chüeh states: "I, Mo-ho-yen, for all of my life have practiced only great vehicle Ch'an--I am not a Dharma-master. If you wish to hear of dharma-marks, then listen at the side of the Brahman Dharma-masters. What Mo-ho-yen says does not rely upon the commentaries or treatises. I depend upon the texts of the great vehicle sutras to instruct. Mo-ho-yen's cultivation relies upon the Mahā-prajñā, Lañkā, Viśeṣa-cinti, Ghana-vyūha, Vajra, Vimalakīrti, Ta fo-ting, Hua-yen, Nirvāna, Ratna-kūta, Pu-chao san-mei, and other sutras, which are faithfully received and practiced." (Demiéville, Le Concile, fol. 156b.3-6) The Tun-huang text Chu-ching yao-ch'ao (T no. 2819), an anthology of sutra quotations which was used by Ch'an people, shows a great deal of overlap with both the Li-tai fa-pao chi list and the Tun-wu ta-ch'eng cheng-li chüeh list. It quotes the same four apocryphal sutras as the former. Concerning the Handbook for Mahāyogists and Questions on No-examining contained in Pelliot Tibetan 116 (V and VI.a), several observations can be made. (See n. 6.) With the exception of the Ta-ch'eng ch'i-hsin lun, only sutras are quoted, and this pool of sutras shows a great deal of overlap with those listed in the Li- tai fa-pao chi and the Tun-wu ta-ch'eng cheng-li chüeh, and those quoted in the Chu-ching yao-ch'ao. Four apocryphals appears: Ta fo-ting ching, Fang-kuang ching (T no. 2871), Chin-kang san-mei ching, and the Fa-wang ching (T no. 2883). Perhaps those disputatious ones putting forth the objections in the handbook, the "ones who, from without beginning, have been attached to the manifestations of real things and words" (thog med pa nas dños po dañ sgra la mñon bar

58

źen pa rnams), are related to the followers of the
Brahman Dharma-masters who "wish to hear of dharma-
marks" (yü t'ing fa-hsiang). However, Kimura, "Tonkō
shutsudo Chibettobun shahon Pelliot 116 kenkyū (sono
ichi)," p. 281, argues that the handbook material is
not directly related to Mo-ho-yen and the questions
and answers of the Tun-wu ta-ch'eng cheng-li chüeh.
See Obata Hironobu, "Chibetto no Zenshū to zōyaku
gigyō ni tsuite," Indogaku Bukkyōgaku kenkyū, XXIII, 2
(March 1975), pp. 170-171; Okimoto Katsumi, "Zenshū
shi ni okeru gigyō--Hō-ō-kyō ni tsuite," Zen bunka
kenkyūjo kiyō, 10 (July 1978), pp. 27-61; and Tanaka
and Shinohara, eds., Tonkō butten to Zen, pp. 351-
376.

37. See n. 9. However, in Stein Tibetan 710 he
is referred to as Bodhidharma (Bod-de-dar-ma) or
Dharma (Dar-ma). See Okimoto, "Ryōga shiji ki no
kenkyū," p. 66.

38. See n. 9.

39. See Obata, "Pelliot tib. n. 116 bunken," pp.
16-18. Hsiang-mo Tsang has sayings in Pelliot Tibetan
116, the Bsam-gtan-mig-sgron, and the Bka-than-sde-
lṅa.

40. See n. 9. The Tun-wu chen-tsung chin-kang
pan-jo hsiu-hsing ta pi-an fa-men yao-chüeh (or chen-
chüeh) speaks of "gazing at the place of wu" (k'an wu
so-ch'u = myed pa'i gnas la bltas). See Ueyama,
"Chibettoyaku Tongo shinshū yōketsu no kenkyū," pp.
96-97.72-74 et passim.

41. See n. 9.

42. For an English translation (but with
Sanskrit equivalents rather than Chinese) see Houston,
"The System of Ha Sang Mahāyāna," pp. 108-110; for a
Japanese translation see Okimoto, "bSam yas no shūron
(3)," p. 6.

43. Ueyama, "The Study of Tibetan Ch'an Manuscripts," p. 22.

44. Parallels the Yin-yüan hsin lun sung yin-
yüan hsin lun shih by Nāgārjuna, T 32, p. 490b.

45. The Pao-t'ang school used this form of the
first patriarch's name. See Philip Yampolsky, The
Platform Sutra of the Sixth Patriarch (New York:

Columbia University Press, 1967), pp. 8-9, for a table
of the twenty-eight Indian patriarchs according to the
various Ch'an histories. See Paul Demiéville,
"Appendice sur 'Damoduoluo' (Dharmatrā/ta/)," Mémoires
archéologiques, XIII, fasc. I (1978), pp. 43-49.

46. "Seven generations" (bdun rgyud) crops up
elsewhere in the Tibetan Ch'an literature. Ma-ha-yan,
for instance, is said in the Bka-thaṅ-sde-lṅa to be
the seventh emanation from Dha-rmo-ttā-ra-la (Tucci,
Minor, p. 68.1-3).

47. Parallels the Erh-ju ssu-hsing lun.
Yanagida, Daruma no goroku, pp. 31-32. However, for
the key line ning-chu pi-kuan ("in a coagulated manner
abides in wall-contemplation"), the Tibetan reads rtog
pa spaṅs te lham mer gnas ("puts aside discrimination
and abides in light or brightness"). This may be an
interpretative translation; if that is the case, it
could shed some light on Bodhidharma's famed "wall-
contemplation." Stein Tibetan 710, a Tibetan translation of a version of the Northern history Leng-chia
shih-tzu chi, shows a more literal rendering of the
Chinese: gtsaṅ mar 'dug ste rtsig ṅos la bltas pa
("remains in purity and gazes at the wall-surface";
fol. 28b.3-4). See Okimoto, "Ryōga shiji ki no
kenkyū," p. 68.4-5. The Bsam-gtan-mig-sgron, in quoting the Rgya-luṅ-chen-po, gives rtogs pa spaṅs te lham
mer gnas (Gnubs chen Saṅs-rgyas-ye-śes, Rñal 'byor mig
gi bsam gtan, fol. 130.2-3); it gives exactly the same
rendering somewhat earlier in a quotation from "the
teaching of the Great Master Bodhidharmtrāta" (fol.
57.6). The Bka-thaṅ-sde-lṅa also gives lham mer gnas
in a saying of the "Great Master Bodhidharmatrāta"
(Tucci, Minor, p. 70.28). The bltas ("gazing") in
Stein Tibetan 710 brings to mind Mo-ho-yen's characteristic teaching, but we are left with the problem of
what "abiding in light" or "abiding in brightness"
might mean. Perhaps this comes from a form of the
Erh-ju ssu-hsing lun which circulated in the Pao-t'ang
school. Obata, "Pelliot tib. n. 116 bunken," pp. 12-
30, discusses each of the following Ch'an masters of
Pelliot Tibetan 116 and provides transliterated versions of related Tibetan materials (Bsam-gtan-mig-
sgron, Bka-thaṅ-sde-lṅa, and the Tibetan Tun-huang
manuscripts).

48. Tibetan transliterations vary a great deal:
Wu-chu = Bu-cuṅ, Bu-cu, Bhu-cu, 'Jug-du, and so on.

49. Parallels Li-tai fa-pao chi, T 51, p. 189a. Yanagida, Shoki no Zenshi II, p. 200. These are the so-called "three phrases" (san chü-yü). Tsung-mi noted that Reverend Kim's teaching centered around a form of the three phrases, but that Wu-chu's followers, the Pao-t'ang lineage, changed the last of the three from "no-forgetting" (mo-wang) to "no-falseness" (mo-wang).

50. Parallels Leng-chia shih-tzu chi, T 85, p. 1287a. Yanagida, Shoki no Zenshi I, p. 192. The Leng-chia shih-tzu chi, however, does not attribute these words to Hsiang-mo Tsang: "The Ta-p'in ching [25,000 Prajñapāramitā Sūtra] says: 'Having nothing to be mindful of is called Buddha-mindfulness' [wu so-nien che shih ming nien-fo; T 8, p. 385c]. [If you ask] what is it that is called 'having nothing to be mindful of,' the mind which is mindful of the Buddha is called 'having nothing to be mindful of.' Apart from mind there is no separate Buddha; apart from Buddha there is no separate mind. Being mindful of the Buddha is precisely being mindful of the mind; seeking mind is precisely seeking the Buddha. Why is this so? Consciousness is formless; the Buddha is characteristicless. If you understand this principle of the Tao, then it is pacification of the mind. If you always remember Buddha-mindfulness and objects do not arise, then in quiescence it is markless, level, non-dual. If you enter this position, the mind which remembers the Buddha disappears, and there is no further need to verify [that it is the Buddha]. Then gaze at this level mind [k'an tz'u teng-hsin]--it is precisely the body of the real Dharma-nature of the Thus-come-one." I would like to thank Bernard Faure for this identification.

51. This is the India master whose lineage is traced in Pelliot Tibetan 996. His name in variant transliterations also appears in the Bsam-gtan-mig-sgron and the Bka-thaṅ-sde-lṅa.

52. Parallels the opening lines of the Wo-lun ch'an-shih k'an-hsin fa (Stein Chinese 1494 and others). See Suzuki Daisetsu, Suzuki Daisetsu Zenshū, Vol. II (Tokyo: Iwanami shoten, 1968), p. 452, and Wu Ch'i-yü, "Wo-lun ch'an-shih i-yü Tun-huang T'u-fan wen (Pelliot 116) i-pen k'ao-shih," Tun-huang hsüeh, 4 (1979), p. 44. In the light of the Chinese the myi of myi dmyigs na has been deleted. Very little is known of Wo-lun. However, discussion of gazing in the Wo-lun ch'an-shih k'an-hsin fa suggests an affinity to

the teaching of Mo-ho-yen and the Tun-wu chen-tsung chin-kang pan-jo hsiu-hsing ta pi-an fa-men yao-chüeh: "[The mind] is intrinsically, always quiescent, neither arising nor extinguishing, markless and inactive. Because of no-awakening, we falsely speak of movement; in reality it is unmoving. Therefore, the practitioner, as to the thoughts which follow mind-movement, merely faces the interior of mind, abides connected to the one-mind, and internally and externally ripens gazing [shu-k'an], until there is neither the finest mark of movement nor non-movement. This is called the great samadhi. As to this sort of great samadhi, all common men and sages themselves possess it. Because of the false thoughts of sentient-beings, they incorrectly speak of movement. By incorrectly speaking of movement one becomes a common man. Because this mind-nature is intrinsically unmoving, therefore, for those who can train in it, movement produces quiescence and we call them sages. It is like the inside of a mine. Even though there is real gold, if you do not put forth effort, in the end you will not obtain it. The one who makes effort gets the gold. The mind is also like this. Even though one knows that from the outset it is constantly quiescent, one must avail oneself of examination-illumination [kuan-chao]. If one does not examine-illuminate, then he will be together with false movement." Suzuki, Suzuki Daisetsu Zenshū, Vol. II, pp. 452.6-453.2, and Wu Ch'i-yü, "Wo-lun ch'an-shih,' p. 45.7-12. "Gazing," of course, is closely associated with Mo-ho-yen. The "ripening of gazing" is discussed at several points in the Tun-wu chen-tsung yao-chüeh: "You should investigate-examine and make your gazing ripen, and then it is the purity of the original nature" (ju tang ti-kuan k'an-shu chi-shih pen-hsing ch'ing-ching = khyod kyis rtag par ltos te byaṅ na gdod mthoṅ ṅo//khyod kyi ṅo bo ṅid gtsaṅ gdaṅ ba yin no; Ueyama, "Chibettoyaku Tongo shinshū yōketsu," p. 98.82); "You merely ripen gazing and minutely gaze and from time to time you will see brightness in the room" (ju tan shu-k'an hsi-k'an huo chien wu-chung ming = khyod kyis ci nas kyaṅ byaṅ bar bltas//ẑib du bltas na//bar bar ni khyim gyi nan na snaṅ ba mthoṅ; p. 99.85). In addition to the above manuscript there is also the Wo-lun ch'an-shih chi (Stein Chinese 5657 and others). Also, see Obata, "Pelliot tib. n. 116 bunken," pp. 19-21.

53. See Obata, "Pelliot tib. n. 116 bunken," pp. 21-23.

54.   Parallels Li-tai fa-pao chi, T 51,   p. 189a.
Yanagida, Shoki no Zenshi II, p. 200.

55.   No parallel in Chinese materials has yet
been discovered.

56.   Ch'an masters Dzań, Lu, Pab-śvan, Par, Dzva,
Tshvan, Van, Dzvań-za, the Chinese layman Keń-śi, and
Ch'an masters 'Byi-lig and De'u remain unidentified.
Luo Charngpei, T'ang wu-tai hsi-pei fang-yin, Series
A, No. 12 (Shanghai: Kuo-li chung-yang yen-chiu yüan
li-shih yü-yen yen-chiu so, 1933), is very useful in
attempting to reconstruct the Chinese originals of
Tibetan transliterations.

57.   Probably Niao-k'o Tao-lin (781-824).   See
Okimoto, "bSam yas no shūron (1)," p. 7.

58.   See Okimoto, "bSam yas no shūron (1)," p. 7.

59.   This saying shows parallels with a Chinese
Tun-huang text, the Nan-yang ho-shang tun-chiao chieh-
t'o ch'an-men chih liao-hsing t'an-yü (Pelliot Chinese
2045 and others).   See Hu Shih, Shen-hui ho-shang i-
chi (Taipei: Hu Shih chi-nien kuan, 1968), pp. 235-
236.

60.   The following Bu-cu sayings parallel Li-tai
fa-pao chi, T 51, pp. 185c-186a. Yanagida, Shoki no
Zenshi II, pp. 163-164.

61.   Supplied from Li-tai fa-pao chi, T 51, p.
186a.9.

62.   Pelliot Tibetan 116, fols. verso 41.1-67.4.
For a transliteration and Japanese translation of all
these sayings see Obata, "Pelliot tib. n. 116 bunken,"
pp. 4-12.

63.   Ueyama, "The Study of Tibetan Ch'an Manuscripts," pp. 20-21. For instance, the Bsam-gtan-mig-
sgron has the same sayings for Bo-dhe-da-rmo-
ta-ra, 'Dug-ba (Wu-chu), Bdud-'dul-sñiń-po (Hsiang-mo
Tsang), A-dha-na-her, 'Ga-'lun (Wo-lun), and Ma-ha-
yan, as well as ten of the eighteen Ch'an masters
mentioned in section VIII.   The Bka-thań-sde-lńa has
the sayings for Bo-dhi-dha-rmo-tta-ra, 'Jug-du, Bdud-
'dul-sñiń-po, A-dhan-her, and Ma-hā-yā-na, as well as
six of the eighteen sayings of VIII.   For a chart of
all these masters, see Okimoto, "bSam yas no shūron
(2)," pp. 7-8.

64.   Tucci, <u>Minor</u>, p. 68.2-3.

65.   Obata, "Chibetto no Zenshū," p. 166, and Obata, "Kodai Chibetto ni okeru tonmonha," p. 78.

66.   Lalou, "Document tibétain sur l'expansion du Dhyāna chinois," pp. 505-522.

67.   For the relevant passages see Obata, "Pelliot tib. n. 116 bunken," pp. 18-19.

68.   It has been suggested that this Man is identical to the Ch'an master Ma-ha-yan of the Council of Tibet, Man's departure for China being Ma-ha-yan's return Tun-huang after the council, but there is nothing to substantiate this. See Okimoto, "bSam yas no shūron (2)," p. 5.

69.   Kudara Kōgi, "Unidentified Mahāyāna Text in Uighur," MS, describes the former. Its reconstructed Chinese title, <u>Kuan shen-hsin lun</u> (<u>Treatise on Examining Body and Mind</u>), is curiously close to the Northern <u>Kuan-hsin lun</u>. It is a translation from Chinese executed by a Uighur translator active in the tenth century. The fragments of the <u>Yuan-chüeh ching</u> commentary were discovered in Stockholm (personal communication). It does not seem to be one of Tsung-mi's commentaries.

70.   The question of Tsung-mi's motives is an important one. Yanagida Seizan has suggested that both Tsung-mi and Ma-tsu Tao-i established their positions in opposition to Pao-t'ang. See "The <u>Li-tai fa-pao chi</u> and the Ch'an Doctrine of Sudden Awakening," pp. 10, 26-27, 31, and 41-43, to be published in a volume in the Berkeley Buddhist Studies Series. This English version is based on Yanagida Seizan, "Mujū to Shūmitsu: Tongo shisō no keisei o megutte," <u>Hanazono Daigaku kenkyū kiyō</u>, 7 (March 1976), pp. 1-36; the latter is itself a revision of Yanagida's introduction to <u>Shoki no Zenshi II</u>. Tsung-mi's attitudes toward Ching-chung, Pao-t'ang, Northern, and Hung-chou deserve further attention. We must make distinctions among the following: Tsung-mi's descriptions of the Ch'an schools and attempts to trace their lineages; his critiques of the teachings of the Ch'an schools and his <u>p'an-chiao</u> (or <u>p'an-ch'an</u>) evaluations; and his lineage claims for himself, that he is in the fifth generation of the Ho-tse Shen-hui line. Tsung-mi's description of the situation in the halls of the Pao-t'ang school, their lack of ritual, study,

imagery, and so on, is corroborated by criticism of
Pao-t'ang in the Pei-shan lu of Hui-i Shen-ch'ing, who
was in the Ching-chung line (T 52, p. 612c).   On the
other hand, his p'an-chiao evaluations and critiques
are less reliable.   He ranks Ching-chung, Pao-t'ang,
and Northern in the lowest rung of his schema as
Yogācāra Ch'an, but Wu-chu Ch'an clearly comes out of
the wu-nien of Shen-hui and has little to do with
Yogācāra.   Tsung-mi's evaluation of Northern is part
of the complex of distortions passed down with the Ho-
tse tradition.   Perhaps Tsung-mi saw his own teachings, the positivistic or expressive Knowing of Shen-
hui and the Tathāgata-garbha teachings, as upāya or
skill-in-means to counteract the excesses in both Pao-
t'ang and Hung-chou; his p'an-ch'an in that case would
be part of such an upāya.   In the early (Szechwan)
phase of his career Tsung-mi had almost Neo-Confucian
misgivings about Pao-t'ang's antinomian interpretation
of Shen-hui's wu-nien; in the later (Ch'ang-an) phase
of his career he had the same sort of misgivings about
Hung-chou's antinomian interpretation of the
Tathāgata-garbha teachings.   In short, Tsung-mi was a
Neo-Confucian before the advent of Neo-Confucianism.
Finally, we come to Tsung-mi's lineage claims.   As in
the case of so many Ch'an figures of this period, such
as Wu-chu and Ma-tsu, we probably cannot take these at
face value.   Hu Shih argued that Tsung-mi was in the
fifth generation of the Reverend Kim line, not in the
fifth generation of the Ho-tse Shen-hui line.   According to Hu Shih, Tsung-mi obscured his descent from
Ching-chung Shen-hui (whom he always refers to as I-
chou Shih rather than "Shen-hui") and, by sleight of
hand, converted Ching-chung Shen-hui into Ho-tse Shen-
hui.   See Hu Shih, "Pa P'ei Hsiu te T'ang ku Kuei-fcng
ting-hui ch'an-shih ch'uan-fa pei," Chung-yang yen-
chiu yüan li-shih yü-yen yen-chiu so chi-k'an, 34
(1962), pp. 3-8; or Yanagida Seizan, ed., Koteki
Zengaku-an (Kyoto: Chūbun shuppansha, 1975), pp. 397-
402.   We must remember that the pull to connect with
Hui-neng was very powerful--Ma-tsu also began in the
Ching-chung line and only later made the Hui-neng
connection.   However, I find it difficult to imagine
that no one at the time would have challenged such a
fabrication.   One thing stands out: Szechwan Ch'an
was pivotal in the world of eighth-century Ch'an.

    71. The Ch'an-yüan chu-ch'üan chi tu-hsü lists
ten lineages: Kiangsi (Hung-chou); Ho-tse (Shen-hui);
Shen-hsiu in the North (Northern); Chih-hsien in the
South (Ching-chung); Oxhead; Shih-t'ou (of which

Tsung-mi knew virtually nothing); Pao-t'ang; Hsüan-shih (Nan-shan Nien-fo Gate Ch'an); Ch'ou-Na (actually two lineages descended from Buddhabhadra and Gunabhadra); and T'ien-t'ai. T 48, p. 400c. Kamata, Zengen, p. 48. Tsung-mi divides these lineages into three tenets (tsung or siddhānta), corresponding respectively to Yogācāra, Mādhyamika, and Tathāgata-garbha teachings and texts.

72. T 48, p. 412c. Kamata, Zengen, p. 251. The Korean Sŏn (Ch'an) master Pojo Chinul (1158-1210), who made a lengthy study of Tsung-mi's Ch'an writings, in his Fa-chi pieh-hsing lu chieh-yao ping ju-ssu chi (a reworking of the Chung-hua ch'uan hsin-ti ch'an-men shih-tzu ch'eng-hsi t'u with commentary) speaks of the unbiased nature of Master Mi: "Master Mi's intention is not yet clear to some. Does he mean to slander or praise the purports of the two lineages [Hung-chou and Oxhead]? However, he merely destroys later students' grasping of the words and makes them perfectly awaken to the Knowing-seeing of the Thus-come-one and has neither a mind of slander nor a mind of praise toward the two lineages." See Yanagida Seizan, ed., Kōrai hon, Zengaku sōsho, 2 (Kyoto: Chūbun shuppansha, 1974), p. 153. Chinul, of course, is not writing from a historical perspective. Nevertheless, he may have accurately perceived the underlying tone of Tsung-mi's Ch'an writings.

73. The numbers in parentheses refer to the section numbers in Yanagida, Shoki no Zenshi II.

74. This is revealing of the relationship between Wu-chu's teaching and that of Ho-tse Shen-hui. Wu-chu's wu-nien teaching did not come from direct study under Shen-hui, but from lectures on Shen-hui sayings.

75. Only a few years earlier San-śi and his Tibetan party had attended one of the mass assemblies at the Ching-chung.

76. Reverend Kim was known for predictions; he also makes one to the Tibetan party of San-śi. The important person who will welcome Wu-chu in the future is Minister Tu Hung-chien (709-769). See following note.

77. Biography Chiu T'ang-shu, 108, and Hsin T'ang-shu, 128. Tu came to Szechwan to suppress an insurrection; he was in charge of all Chinese armies

in Szechwan and at times himself negotiated with the
Tibetans. His patronage was instrumental in bringing
Wu-chu to the forefront of the Buddhist world of
Ch'eng-tu.

78. Presumably, as a Korean, his command of
spoken Chinese was poor.

79. "No-examining" (pu-kuan = myi rtog pa) is
prominent in Ma-ha-yan's teaching in Tibet. It also
appears in Shen-hui's writings. See Hu Shih, Shen-hui
ho-shang i-chi, p. 236. The locus classicus is the
Vimalakīrti: "No-examining is enlightenment" (T 14,
p. 542b).

80. T 51, pp. 186a-196b. Yanagida, Shoki no
Zenshi II, pp. 168-317.

81. Ch'an Chart, ZZ 2, 15, 5, p. 435a; Kamata,
Zengen, p. 289. For biographical information on
Ching-chung Shen-hui (720-794), see the Sung kao-seng
chuan, T 50, p. 764a; Shen-hui's surname was Shih.
The Pei-shan lu reference is T 52, p. 612c. For bio-
graphical information on Hui-i Shen-ch'ing, see the
Sung kao-seng chuan, T 50, p. 740c.

82. ZZ 1, 14, 3, pp. 278a-278b. Kamata, Zengen,
p. 305.

83. For Ch'eng-yüan see Ui Hakuju, Zenshū shi
kenkyū, I, pp. 175-177, and for Hsüan-shih, pp. 179-
192.

84. See Ueyama Daishun, "Tonkō shutsudo Jōdo
hosshin san ni tsuite," Shinshū kenkyū, 21 (1976), pp.
62-71. Ueyama points out (p. 65) that during this
period the tendency to versify doctrine for chanting
shows up not only in the Pure Land tradition but in
Ch'an as well. In Pelliot Chinese 2690 we find the
Praises on the Pure Land Dharma-body accompanied by
two sets of Ch'an verses, the Ch'an-men shih-erh shih
and the Nan-tsung tsan, and in Pelliot Chinese 2963 we
find it accompanied by the Nan-tsung tsan. This
suggests that Ch'an people used these scrolls.

85. Verses 3, 7, 9, 10, 11, 15, and 17 in
Ueyama's edition.

86. In Yüan-chüeh ching ta-shu ch'ao, ZZ 1, 14,
3, p. 279b.

87. ZZ 2, 15, 5, p. 435a. Kamata, Zengen, p. 289.

88. Thus, great assemblies with lay people present ("the multitude") were characteristic of both the Hsüan-shih and Reverend Kim schools. Both also seem to have been oriented to disciplinary formalism.

89. ZZ 1, 14, 3, p. 279b. This is obviously speaking of an oral recitation or nembutsu.

90. Presumably fo.

91. T 51, p. 185a. Yanagida, Shoki no Zenshi II, p. 143.

92. In Tsung-mi's terms, the ideas (i) of the Wu-chu and Reverend Kim houses are the same (the idea of the Yogācāra texts), but their praxes (hsing) are radically different.

93. Perhaps those around Shen-hui of Ching-chung Monastery (that is, I-chou Shih) were transmitting the "no-forgetting" form of the three phrases. Clearly, Pao-t'ang held that Ching-chung was distorting the teaching of Reverend Kim.

94. ZZ 1, 14, 3, p. 278b. Kamata, Zengen, p. 306.

95. This evaluation appears in Kamalaśīla's third Bhāvanā-krama (Demiéville, Le Concile, p. 348). See Ueyama Daishun, "Chibetto shūron ni okeru Zen to Kamalaśīla no sōten," Nihon Bukkyō gakkai nempō, 40 (1975), pp. 56-57.

96. Tucci, Minor, p. 69.1-22.

97. Tucci, Minor, pp. 115-121. Vimalamitra was an Indian who visited Tibet and then China. Tucci connects him to Vairocana and Myan-tin-ne-'dzin. The former also traveled to China.

98. Peking No. 5306.

99. Harada Satoru, "bSam yas no shūron igo ni okeru tonmonha no ronsho," Nihon Chibetto gakkai kaihō, XXII (March 1976), pp. 9-10.

100. Kimura, "Tonkō shutsudo Chibettobun shahon Stein 709," pp. 11-13, gives an outline of its contents.

101. Sections II-VII in Kimura's numbering.

102. Fols. 14b.5-15a.4. The text gives Tibetan transliterations and translations of Shen-hui's famous aphorisms criticizing Northern Ch'an. However, it simply labels them four errors of understanding and mentions nothing of the Northern/Southern context. They run as follows: rgya skad du/śab śim 'do'i je 'u//bod skad du sems bsdu śiṅ naṅ du rtog pa//rgya skad du/khi sim pa'u hve'i//bod skad du sems ldaṅ śiṅ skye ba'o//rgya skad du/'giṅ śim śa byi deṅ//bod skad du/sems lhan ne 'dug ciṅ rtse gcig du 'jug pa//rgya skad du/the'u sim khan tseṅ//bod skad du/sems gnas śiṅ dben ba la dmyigs pa//. In Shen-hui's writings these four phrases ("coagulate mind and enter samadhi; abide in mind and gaze at purity; raise mind and externally illuminate; collect mind and internally realize"/ning-hsin ju-ting chu-hsin k'an-ching ch'i-hsin wai-chao she-hsin nei-cheng) are said to be the teaching of the Northern masters P'u-chi and Hsiang-mo Tsang. The order in the Tibetan version is different. See Hu Shih, Shen-hui ho-shang i-chi, pp. 133-134, 175-176, 239-240, and 287-288. The original target of these criticisms was no longer relevant in Tibet.

103. Fol. 40b.3-5.

104. Sections VIII-IX in Kimura's numbering.

105. The term Tathāgata Ch'an (ju-lai ch'an) seems to have begun with Shen-hui and to have been inherited by Pao-t'ang. The Li-tai fa-pao chi states: "Reverend Shen-hui of the Ho-tse Monastery in the eastern capital each month made a platform and dis-coursed on the Dharma for people. He destroyed purity Ch'an and erected Tathāgata Ch'an." T 51, p. 185c. Yanagida, Shoki no Zenshi II, p. 154.

106. Fol. 43a.2-43b.5.

107. Gnubs chen Saṅs-rgyas-ye-śes, Rñal 'byor mig gi bsam gtan, Contents.

THE DIRECT AND THE GRADUAL APPROACHES OF ZEN MASTER MAHAYANA[1]: FRAGMENTS OF THE TEACHINGS OF MO-HO-YEN

by

Luis O. Gómez

This essay has the modest goal of introducing the reader to a small group of manuscript materials belonging to the formative stage of Ch'an Buddhism. These documents are the putative work, or contain the teachings, of an eighth-century Ch'an Master who assumes one of the most radical positions on the side of sudden enlightenment in the sudden vs. gradual enlightenment controversy. Yet these texts are also a good example of how early Ch'an did not exclude (1) rigorous meditational practice, (2) the possibility of a gradual approach, and (3) conceptual schemata to explain the relationship between (1) and (2) and the ineffable, indivisible state of enlightenment. The teachings in question are those of the Chinese Master Mahāyāna (Chinese: Ho-shang Mo-ho-yen 和尚摩訶衍) which are preserved in Chinese or Tibetan translation in several manuscripts from Tun-huang. These texts-- seen as Ch'an teachings, and not simply as curious manuscripts from Tun-huang--can offer some insight into the internal dialectics of Zen.

Master Mo-ho-yen is known to us not only through these fragments. The Tibetan chronicles tell us that he was a Teacher of Meditation at the Tibetan court for a short period towards the end of the eighth century A.D. At that time he participated in a controversy that tradition presents to us as a "Council" held under the aegis of the King of Tibet. The first account of this debate to be known in the West was

that of the seventeenth-century Tibetan chronicler Sum
pa mkhan po, but Obermiller's translation of Bu-ston's
Chos-'byun introduced more detailed information on
what Tibetan tradition claims to have been the actual
proceedings of a "Council." It was Obermiller himself
who suggested that the source for Bu-ston's exposition
of the issues of the controversy was Kamalaśila's
Third Bhāvanākrama, the manuscript of which he had
brought back to Leningrad from Tibet.[2]

The complexity of the issues, doctrinal and
historical, did not become apparent until, under the
title of Le concile de Lhasa, Paul Demiéville published and translated a Chinese manuscript from Tun-
huang (Pelliot 4646), the Tun-wu ta-sheng cheng-li
chüeh 頓悟大乘正理決 , which purports to be the
actual "dossier" or minutes of the debates.[3] It is of
some interest and perhaps significant that of all the
issues discussed in this work the only two that are
unquestionably explicit points of conflict with the
Bhāvanākramas are the two chosen by Bu-ston from the
polemic section of the Third Bhāvanākrama as a summary
of the conflict.[4]

Bu-ston's exposition of these two points is
very concise, and is worth reproducing here--as they
recur in another form in the fragments that occupy us.
According to this account from the fourteenth century,
the Ho-shang's first thesis was:[5]

As long as one carries out good or evil acts,
(kuśala-akuśala) one is not free from transmigration as [these acts] lead to heaven or hell
[respectively]. It is like clouds which cover
the empty sky irrespective of their being
white or black.

The second thesis explains the Ho-shang's alternative
to the path of action:[6]

> Whoever does not think of anything, whoever
> does not reflect, will be totally free from
> transmigration. Not thinking, not pondering,
> non-examination, non-apprehension of an object
> --this is the immediate access [to libera-
> tion], it is the same as the Tenth Stage
> (bhūmi) [of the Bodhisattva].

Spokesmen for gradual enlightenment were the
masters Kamalaśīla, Śrīghoṣa, and Jñānendra, who took
issue with both theses. For them there could be no
direct access to liberation. To leap into no thought
is to sink into quietistic indifference and insensi-
tivity. Although the highest experience is a state of
non-discrimination or non-conceptualization (rnam-par
mi rtog pa: avikalpa), it is the result of very
specific causes. These causes have to be cultivated
gradually. They can be discerned or defined ration-
ally, and have distinct moral and practical implications.

* * *

These were points at issue not only at the
Tibetan Court in Lhasa and not simply as a result of
the theoretical insight of a handful of hermits. The
question of the non-discursive character of the
Buddhist religious experience was a burning issue in
the cultural milieu in which early Ch'an Buddhism--and
consequently, early Tibetan Buddhism--developed. The
same questions--of stages and degrees, of sudden and
gradual--were of great concern in China at that time,

as can be seen in what remains of the monumental work
of Tsung-mi. Through recent research into other
Tibetan and Chinese materials it has now become
obvious that the controversy raged well beyond the
confines of what is today political Tibet. It is too
early to pinpoint the exact chronological or geo-
graphic focus of the controversy, as it seems that
various sets of questions similar to, but independent
of, those collected in the Cheng-li chüeh circulated
in the Tun-huang area as well as in the Tibetan heart-
land. There are, for instance, the famous Twenty-two
Questions on the Mahāyāna by T'an-k'uang, studied by
Ueyama and more recently by Pachow.[7] There is also
Pelliot 116, which contains what could be described as
a manual for debate, as was suggested by Okimoto.
Several pericopes found in the latter text seem to
have been used in the composition of a work attributed
to Vimalamitra, Cig car 'jug pa.[8] The Tun-huang manuscripts have yielded other interesting fragments and
pericopes which also point to an extended controversy
that cannot be adequately described even by
Demiéville's revised terminology, "les conciles du
Tibet."[9]

Among the texts discovered in Tun-huang, and
again researched mostly by Japanese scholars, there
are several fragments of the teachings of the Ho-shang
Mo-ho-yen preserved in Tibetan translation. The content of four of these fragments was summarized systematically by Ueyama Daishun in a short article published in 1971.[10] He worked with four manuscripts:
Pelliot 116, verso ff. 171b[1]-173b[2]; Pelliot 117, verso
ff. 5.1-7.5; Pelliot 812, complete, one folio; and
Pelliot 813, ff. 8a1-8b2. Number 813 contains the
first two parts of 117, while number 116 only contains

the third topic covered in 117, and one line from its beginning (see chart III below). Ueyama also identifies 812 with the beginning of 117, but the correspondences are only approximate. I rather take Pelliot 812 as a summary, but this is getting ahead of my own argument.

Ueyama also mentions a fragment from the Stein Collection, number 468, which is likewise attributed to the Ho-shang Mo-ho-yen, but he does not discuss its contents in detail. This text seems to me most probably another fragment from the same work which yielded the other fragments discussed by Ueyama. It bears the same title as the fragment in Pelliot 117, Mkhan-po Ma-ha-ya-na-gi Bsam-gtan cig-car 'jug-pa'i sgo.[11] It is unfortunately fragmentary, but it seems to overlap with the other fragments at its very end, suggesting that Stein 468 is the beginning of the work that continues with Pelliot 117.

If this is the case, we may be on our way to reconstructing a sizable portion of a work of Mo-ho-yen--or at least of a collection of his "sayings" or yü-lu 語錄. Thematically, the reconstructed work can be analyzed as follows: (1) a description of perfect samādhi or the dhyāna without examination or conceptions--this is the sudden approach (cig car 'jug), the path to liberation (grol thar pa'i lam sgo); (2) a description of the five meditational stages or processes (thabs, standing for Chinese fang-pien 方便), through which one may pass if one fails to reach the non-conceptual state by the direct method;[12] and (3) an explanation of how the ten perfections can be achieved by the single practice of non-discrimination.

The importance of Stein 468 was pointed out by Mark Tatz in an article in the Tibet Journal, but his observations unfortunately were based exclusively on la Vallée Poussin's extract in the India Office Catalogue.[13] Tatz' observations show that even a cursory glance at the catalogue entry confirms the relevance of Stein 468 to the Tibetan debates of the eighth century, a point proven more rigorously by Okimoto.[14] Its importance should become more evident as we summarize the contents of the whole fragment (only two folia, recto and verso, are translated).

The root cause for human suffering (saṁsāra), says the Ho-shang Mo-ho-yen, is the mental construction of false distinction (vikalpa-citta; rnam par rtog pa'i sems).[15] This type of thought is moved by the force of beginningless habits. Its movements affect our perception of the world and our actions in it. In this sense everyone--from Buddhas to the denizens of hell--is magically generated (sprul ciṅ) from vikalpa. Consequently, if the mind did not move, dharmas would not obtain.

Therefore, in order to put an end to the discriminating mind, and thereby stop saṁsāra, one should sit in a lonely spot in the lotus posture, keeping the back straight. Once one has entered dhyāna, as he then looks into his own mind, he does not conceive of any living being whatsoever. If he finds himself driven to consider and ponder with his discursive faculties, he should become aware of it (tshor 覺). In the agitated mind itself he does not discriminate (myi brtag) agitation or non-agitation, being or non-being (yod-pa daṅ-myed-pa), good or bad, blemishing afflictions or purification; he does not discriminate a single dharma. When one becomes aware of the mind's

movements in this fashion, then no self-nature (raṅ
bźin myed) is discovered in it.

After a detailed discussion of the nature of
this knowledge, the text explains that one cannot
obtain even that perception of the moving mind which
is the awareness sought by the meditator. It is the
boundless thought that does not think. One becomes
free from attachment even to no-thought.

With this the fragment concludes. Okimoto
Katsumi, in his "Bsam-yas no shūron (III)--nishū no
Makaen ibun,"[16] claims that the two folios of Stein
468 are in fact the beginning of another fragment from
Tun-huang--Stein 709 (which begins with folio 4). The
two manuscripts seem indeed to be written by the same
hand and are quite close in size and format. This
hypothesis is suggestive, for, as pointed out above,
the title of Pelliot 117 is the same as that of Stein
468. Therefore, if Okimoto's presumption is correct,
we must have an even larger portion of this particular
work of Mo-ho-yen. Since Pelliot 116 also overlaps
with Pelliot 117 and Pelliot 813, the fragments must
fall together somehow to form at least part of the
original text of Mo-ho-yen's Bsam-gtan cig-car 'jug-
pa'i sgo (* 禪頓入門   ).

Unfortunately, Stein 709, though extensive and
marred by only a few lacunae, is still a pastiche of
pericopes and not a full text, as shown by Kimura
Ryūtoku.[17] This difficulty notwithstanding, the fragments could be assumed to link together; probably by
admitting Stein 486 as part of the introduction to the
treatise of the Ho-shang, followed by Stein 709, and
completed by the fragments studied by Ueyama. In this
way Stein 468 would serve as a bridge between the main
issues discussed in the Cheng-li chüeh and the

Bhavanakramas and the discussion on the five upayas
and the ten perfections. Stein 468, as we have seen,
begins by taking up the same controverted point as the
"third new question" of the Cheng-li chüeh, namely,
whether the transmigration of living beings is due to
vikalpa irrespective of the nature of their actions.[18]
After answering in the affirmative the fragment
attempts to justify its theory and method of meditation on the basis of this doctrine. The connection
suggested is very similar to that found in the Cheng-
li chüeh, that is, since all conceptions lead to
transmigration they are all equally pernicious and
therefore should be abandoned. The path is consequently understood to consist exclusively in the
elimination of vikalpa. Of course, very much like the
Cheng-li chüeh, Stein 468 falls into a circle that it
fails to explain and that would take us by surprise if
we were not familiar with it in other writings: the
abandonment of vikalpa is not brought about by active
suppression of vikalpa, but rather by acknowledging
its presence. This is what the Ch'an Master Mo-ho-yen
calls at the same time "looking into one's own mind"
(sems la bltas 看 心) and "the unthinkable" (bsam
gyis myi khyab pa), or "not thinking" (myi sems).

* * *

The positions of Stein 709 and Pelliot 812
within the puzzle deserve a more careful scrutiny.
Pelliot 812 is clearly another work, or simply a
summary of Mo-ho-yen's works. We shall return to this
text; for the time being let us turn our attention to
Stein 709 which would appear to be more problematic.
Though Okimoto's suggestion of a link with Stein 468
is attractive, and on the face of it quite plausible,
what he presents as arguments are insufficient to

prove his thesis.[19]   There would seem to be important differences in style, content, and intended audience between Stein 468 and Stein 709, as well as between the latter, on the one hand, and Pelliot 116, 117, 812, and 813, on the other. The first of these (Stein 468) presents constructive or systematic arguments, describing the direct (or "sudden") approach to enlightenment. Pelliot 117, 812, and 813 describe the indirect or mediate ("gradual") approach, intended for those who cannot enter directly into no-mind or no-thought.   The two approaches clearly balance each other perfectly and form a logical unity that could easily be interpreted as one continuous text.   Stein 709, on the other hand, does not provide a smooth transition between these two sets.   It is primarily a polemic text, sometimes almost in the style of the Cheng-li chüeh, and clearly alludes to many of the issues in the Bhavanakramas.

Finally, one must point out the fact that most Tibetan manuscripts from Tun-huang are pastiches or agglutinations of pericopes or mere fragments, and Stein 709 evidently is no exception to this.[20]   Even assuming that Stein 468 was originally the beginning (folia 1-2) of a manuscript that continued with Stein 709 (f. 4, lacuna, ff. 7-23, lacuna, f. 25, lacuna, ff. 27-45, lacuna) nothing would guarantee that the work or fragment of a work beginning on f. 1 of Stein 468 did not end on folio 3.

There is no doubt that folio 4, and at least part of folia 7-11 of Stein 709 represent fragments from the teachings of Mo-ho-yen. But Okimoto has pro-posed that the pericopes in Stein 709 formed one single work, which originally began with f. 1 of Stein 468.   In light of the preceding discussion, his position would not be as strong if it were not for an additional piece of evidence which he has mustered in his paper.[21]   The Bsam-gtan mig sgron, a Tibetan com- pilation attributed to the Nin-ma-pa eighth-century Master, Gnubs-chen Sans-rgyas-ye-ses, contains several fragments attributed to Mo-ho-yen.[22]   One of these is identified as belonging to the "Ma-ha-yan-gyi Bsgom lun."[23] Following this is another fragment introduced with the expression "de nid las," which generally is synonymous with our ibid. Now, the first passage is taken verbatim from the same text as Stein 468 (ff. 28b1-29a3), the second corresponds to Stein 709 (f. 4a2).   The Bsam-gtan mig sgron thus completes the web of evidence that suggests that Stein 468, Stein 709, and Pelliot 116, 117, 812, and 813 contain different portions of what was originally a single text, the Bsam-gtan cig- car 'jug-pa'i sgo.

There There would thus seem to be three slots (A, B, C) for the fragments from Pelliot 116, 117, 812, and 813.   Upon closer analysis, however, it appears that

Now that (1) Stein 468 and 709 are linked by the above reasoning, (2) the connection between Stein 468 and Pelliot 117 is confirmed by a similarity in title, and (3) the connection between Pelliot 117 and Pelliot 116, 813 and part of 812 is established by contents, one may further relate Stein 709 to all of the above by the following exercise in hypothetical reconstruction.   If one places Stein 468 as the open- ing passage of Mo-ho-yen's Bsam-gtan sgo, the next step would have to be the placing of the fragments from Pelliot 116, 117, and 813 relative to Stein 468 and 709. Now, the latter can form the frame of refer- ence for the location of the other fragments as represented in Chart I on the following page.

There would thus seem to be three slots (A, B, C) for the fragments from Pelliot 116, 117, 812, and 813.   Upon closer analysis, however, it appears that

Chart I

Structure of a Presumed Manuscript Stein 468/709

Extant Fragments	folia	Topic
Stein 468	1-2	Introduction: the way of immediate access.
Lacuna A	*3	?
Stein 709	4	Polemics: response to objections
Lacuna B	*5-6	?
Stein 709	7	The perfections are all included in the one practice of immediate access.
Stein 709	8a-8b	The highest perfection, wisdom.
Stein 709	8b-9a	Immediate access to the meditation of a Tathagata.
Stein 709	9a-11a	The Madhyamika position and non-conceptual meditation.
Lacuna C	?	?

these fragments do not form a unit. The first part of
Pelliot 117--identified by title as part of The Gate--
corresponds to Pelliot 813 and to the second part of
Pelliot 812 (see Appendix I).

The second part of Pelliot 117, however, is
clearly marked by what appears to be the title of
another work: Mkhan-po Ma-ha-yan-gyi Bsam-brtan myi-
rtog-pa'i nang-du / pha-rol-tu phyin-pa drug dang /
bcu yang 'dus-par bshad-do //. The first lines in
Pelliot 116 (f. 171b1) confirm this: Mkhan-po Ma-ha-
yan-gis // Bsam-brtan myi-rtog-pa'i nang-du pha-rol-tu
phyind-pa drug dang / bcu 'dus-pa bshad-pa'i mdo //.[24]
This means that Pelliot 116, verso 171.1-173.2, and
Pelliot 117, verso 6.4-7.6, probably belong to or
constitute another work of Mo-ho-yen, another "record"
of his sayings.

The first part of Pelliot 812 (recto 6.2-8.2)
belongs to still another work--as will be explained
below.

We are therefore seeking to locate within the
matrix of the fragments of The Gate, as represented in
Chart I, only a short passage from Pelliot 813 (f.
8a2), the second part of Pelliot 812 (recto 8.3-lo.1),
the first part of Pelliot 117 (verso 5.1-7.6), and
possibly an additional two lines from the Bsam-bgtan
mig sgron (see the chart in Appendix I, nos. III-
IV). This amounts to approximately 185 syllables.
Now, each folio (recto and verso) in Stein 468 and 709
has approximately 220 syllables. Therefore, any of
the available slots in Chart I could be the location
of this passage in the original text of The Gate, so
that any arguments for its placement would have to be
contextual.

There is, unfortunately, no decisive argument favoring any one of these three positions. I would like to suggest, nevertheless, that the most intelligent guess on the basis of what is available to us is to assume that the passage in question best fits as the missing portion identified above as lacuna A. The first fragment of the passage can be understood to continue the thoughts expressed at the end of Stein 468, while the main body of the passage--dealing as it does with the five fang-pien 方便 (or "upayas")-- would seem to be the most likely object for the qualifications expressed in f. 4a of Stein 709. The composite picture of the extant portions of The Gate and its thematic structure could be represented then in an outline such as the one suggested in Chart II, on the following page.

This hypothetical reconstruction gives us something approaching the fabric of an integral text. I have attempted to translate this hypothetical text in an appendix to the present paper (Appendix II). The translation is as provisional as the reconstruction, for there are still many obscure passages--mostly in the characteristic syntax of Tun-huang Tibetan translations of Chinese texts. Still, I believe this exercise to be a necessary step in trying to understand the teachings of Mo-ho-yen as a system, and not simply in terms of its opposition to the gradualists.

To this end I have included other fragments in Appendix II. Pelliot 812 begins with the words "Mkhan-po / Ma-ha-yan // Bsam-gtan-gyi snin-po /," a clause that Demiéville interprets as a title, which he renders into Chinese as Ch'an-yao 禪要 or "Essentials of Meditation."[26] It is not clear, however, whether this fragment should be considered part

Chart II

Hypothetical Original Structure of "The Gate"[25]

Extant Fragments	Actual Folio Number	Hypothetical Folio Number in Reconstructed Work	Topic
Stein 468	1-2	*1-2	I. Introduction: The way of immediate access
Pelliot 812	8a3-4	*3a	II. Transition
Pelliot 813	8a2		
Pelliot 812	8a5-10al		III. The possibility of means
Pelliot 813	8a2-b2	*3a-b	
Pelliot 117	5bl-6b4		
Bsmi	165.4-5	*3b	IV. Transition
Stein 709	4a	*4a	V.1. Still, no means is the ultimate doctrine of Mahayana
Stein 709	4a-b	*4a-b	V.2-3. It is not like the teaching of tirthikas and sravakas
Lacuna B2	X	*6b (part)	[*transition]
Stein 709	7	*7	The perfections are all included in immediate access
Stein 709	8a-8b	*8a-8b	The highest perfection-- prajna

Chart II, page 2

Stein 709	8b-9a	*8b-9b	Immediate access to the meditation of a Tathagata
Stein 709	9a-11a	*9a-11a	The Madhyamika position and non-conceptual meditation
Lacuna C	X	*11b-?	?

* * *

of a work of Mo-ho-yen, or simply a brief compendium of Mo-ho-yen's ideas written by one of his followers.

Pelliot 812 is evidently a composite text, falling into three parts: (1) an introductory section of twelve short lines (recto 6a1-8a2 in a format of 7 X 12.5 cm), (2) a two-line pericope corresponding in part to Pelliot 117 (f.5b1) and 813 (f.8a2), and (3) a nine-line fragment with a truncated list of the five "means of approach" (thabs) (see Chart III). It becomes evident that (2) and (3) do not constitute part of (1) through two independent pieces of evidence. First, in Pelliot 812, section (2) is introduced with the phrase, "Mkhan-po Ma-ha-ya-na'i / bsam-btan ci la yaṅ..." (f. 8a2-3), which presumably could not be part of the preceding text, because it has been introduced before as a quotation from the teachings of Mo-ho-yen. Second, a passage parallel to section (1) can be found in Stein 706 verso, a valuable text of which, unfortunately, only one side of one folio is preserved (Stein 706 recto is in a different hand). The passage in question (five lines in a 19.5 X 8.7 format) begins with the third line of Pelliot 812, but continues without interruption beyond the end of section (1), showing that sections (2) and (3) of Pelliot 812, and the break appearing in f. 8a2-3 of the same ms. are not part of the original text of the "Essentials."

In light of the above I would rather consider the latter two fragments part of an independent text.[27] The same can be said of Pelliot 21 titled The Meaning of Non-conceptualization.[28] In spite of some correspondences to the Cheng-li chüeh, established by Okimoto,[29] this is not an abbreviated or truncated version of that text. The differences are greater

than the similarities. Furthermore, it is evidently
not meant to be a catechistic list or an account of a
polemic exchange, as the Cheng-li chüeh is.

In the latter genre falls another Tibetan fragment, Pelliot 823, whose correspondences with the
Cheng-li chüeh were established by Imaeda.[30] This
fragment, translated below from the Tibetan, corresponds to the Chinese in all but one of its sets of
questions and answers.

Two other short pericopes from Pelliot 116 have
been included in the translation. One of them
(Pelliot 116 verso, f. 167.4) is a quotation from Mo-
ho-yen's basic doctrine of no-mind found on Pelliot
813. The other fragment (Pelliot 116 verso f. 187.2)
--for which I have not been able to find a proper
location in the "hermeneutical grid" constructed in
the chart in Appendix I--introduces Mo-ho-yen's views
on the identity of saṁsara and nirvāṇa.

Finally, one must mention three pericopes from
the Bka'-thaṅ sde lṅa, at least two of which are of
doubtful attribution.[31] The longest one of the three
is a Tibetan translation of an unknown Chinese recension of the "Two Entrances and Four Practices" (Erh-ju
ssu-hsing lun 二入四行) traditionally attributed to
Bodhidharma.[32] The other two contain obscure allusions to theories that most probably were foreign to
our Chinese Ch'an Master--to wit, the distinction
between individual and universal characteristics of
entities (svalakṣaṇa and sāmānyalakṣaṇa),[33] and the
attribution of a depressed mind to the elements earth
and water, and an agitated mind to the elements fire
and wind.[34] I have omitted from my translation all
three of these passages as they are either not Mo-
ho-yen's teachings or expressive of aspects of his

doctrine for which we lack enough materials to understand their significance.[35]

* * *

On the basis of the documents examined and
translated here, we can assume that there were in the
late eighth century at least five works <u>attributed</u> to
Mo-ho-yen, or containing his sayings and teachings:
1) <u>Tun-wu Ta-sheng cheng-li chüeh</u> 頓悟大乘正
理決), compiled by Wang-hsi. Pelliot 4646, Stein
2672. Pelliot 823, although containing one passage
not found in the Chinese manuscripts, is most probably
a translation of parts of the <u>Cheng-li chüeh</u>, or at
least of one of its principal sources. Pelliot 21,
though in several respects close to Pelliot 4646, cannot be considered another fragment of the same work.[36]
The Tibetan portions in Pelliot 823 are translated
below under XI.

2) <u>Bsam-gtan cig-car 'jug-pa'i sgo</u> (*頓入禪
門). Stein 468, Stein 709, Pelliot 117, Pelliot 813,
and parts of the fragments attributed to Mo-ho-yen in
Pelliot 116 and Pelliot 812. This is the text we have
called <u>The Gate</u>. Its title is found in Pelliot
117.5b1: "Mkhan-po Ma-ha-yan-gyi // Bsam-bstan <u>chig-
car 'jug-pa'i sgo dan</u> // <u>bśad-pa'i mdo'</u> //" and in
Stein 468.1a1: "Mkhan-po Ma-ha-yan-gi <u>Bsam-gtan cig-
car 'jug-pa'i sgo</u> //." The available fragments of
this work are translated below under nos. I-VIII.

3) <u>Bsam-gtan-gyi sñin-po</u> (*禪要).[37] Stein 706
and part of Stein 709 and Pelliot 812, below IX.

4) <u>Myi-rtog-pa'i gźun</u> (*不觀義 or perhaps even
不觀語). Pelliot 21--I am not inclined to identify
this work with the fragments in Pelliot 116 and 117,
as suggested by others.[38] The similarities seem to me
to be superficial--see translation below, fragment X.

5) Finally, one important pericope in the set we have analyzed begins with an introductory phrase which could be construed as a title. The passage on the ten perfections in Pelliot 116 (f. 171b[1]) begins: "Mkhan-po Ma-ha-yan-gis // Bsam-brtan myi-rtog-pa'i naṅ-du pha-rol-tu phyind-pa drug daṅ / bcu 'dus-pa bśad-pa'i mdo //." Almost the same phrase occurs in the parallel passage from Pelliot 117 (6b4-6): "Mkhan-po Ma-ha-yan-gyi Bsam-brtan myi-rtog-pa'i naṅ-du / pha-rol-tu phyin-pa drug daṅ / bcu yaṅ 'dus-par bśad do //." This suggests to me the following hypothetical Chinese title: Ch'an-wu-kuan nei liu-shih-po-lo-mi she-lun 禪无觀內六十波羅密攝論 .

Other words used to allude to or quote from the sayings of Mo-ho-yen are probably not titles at all. The expression bsgom lun, for instance, is used in the Bsam-gtan mig-sgron (145.5) to quote a passage from Stein 468, a manuscript which, as discussed above, certainly contains part of The Gate. The Bsam-gtan mig-sgron (146.4) also refers to a passage from Stein 709--which we have also identified with The Gate--with the expression "Ma-ha-yan-gyi mdo-las." Do we have two works, lun and mdo, or do we have one work referred to by two different, but only generally descriptive names? I prefer the latter theory.[39]

Be that as it may, one point seems evident to me: Bu-ston's account, and therefore his knowledge, of the works of Mo-ho-yen is most probably inaccurate. The "titles" of five of Mo-ho-yen's works are mentioned by the Tibetan historian. None corresponds to the titles mentioned or suggested by the Tun-huang manuscripts.[40]

* * *

Chart III

Summary of Manuscript Correspondences

S. 486	S. 706 verso	S. 709	P. 116 verso	P. 117 verso	P. 812 recto	P. 813	Bsmi
1a1-b1							
1b1-2a3							145.5-146.3
2a3-b5							
		4a1-3					146.3-4
		4a3-b5					
		7a1-11a3					
	8b1-b4	42b1-5			6a1-2		121.4-122.2
	8b4-5				6a2-8a2		
				5b1-3	8a2-4	8a1-2	
				5b3-6b3	8a5-9a6	8a2-b1	164.6-165.3
				6b3-4	(9a6...)	8b1-2	165.3-4
			171b1-172b3	6b4-7b6			
			172b3-173b2				
			167.4				150.2-3

The total picture of Mo-ho-yen as a "Dhyāna Master" that we can derive from these fragments does not contradict the generally held view that he espoused a radical sudden enlightenment position (second only to figures such as Shen-hui and Ma-tsu).[41] The Ho-shang Mo-ho-yen affirms the immediate character of enlightenment--an immediacy that is reinforced by the simplicity of his teaching:[42]

The state of saṁsāra is merely the result of deluded thoughts (myi-bden-pa'i 'du-ses 妄想). Enlightenment is achieved by not grasping at these thoughts and not dwelling on them (ma-blans ma-chags: 不取不住), by not bringing them to the mind (myi-sems 不思), by not inspecting the mind (myi-rtog 不觀), but by merely being aware (tshor-ba 覺) of all thoughts as they arise.[43]

An important corollary of this teaching further reinforces the need for the simplest possible principles of conduct. For if all thought, good or bad, clouds the mind, then the cultivation of good thoughts is as counterproductive as the cultivation of evil ones. By necessity, then, one has to postulate a "spiritual life"--if so it may be called--that is not followed by cultivating any virtue or spiritual discipline.

All conceptual constructs are considered false, "from the hells below to the Buddhas above" (133b), but it would be a rather superficial interpretation of the teachings of Mo-ho-yen if one were to assume that this type of claim was meant merely as some kind of ontological or epistemological statement. It is

evident, from the context of the debates and from the
Tibetan fragments, that the central doctrines of Mo-
ho-yen are prescriptions for the practice of meditation and belong to the spheres of interest and discourse that so typically characterize the Ch'an/Zen
tradition. The sole effective method of spiritual
cultivation is an allopathic prescription, an antidote, the exact opposite of the cause of saṃsāra:

> (134a) Living beings cling to the dharmas of
> good and evil [created by] their false concep-
> tualizations (妄想), [only] because for ages
> without beginning they have made false dis-
> criminations (妄想分別). At times, good
> is on the increase; at other times it is evil
> that grows. Because of this, [living beings]
> are conditioned to birth and death and cannot
> escape. This is why the sutras insist that
> all conceptions (想) without exception are
> false. If one sees conceptions as no con-
> ception, one sees the Tathāgata.[44]

This is the one and only method to achieve liberation:

> (134a) To understand this single thought is in
> itself the greatest merit, surpassing by far
> all the merits that one could obtain by culti-
> vating good dharmas for innumerable cosmic
> periods. You claim that one should not follow
> this method if one is still in the stage of a
> common person; (134b) [but] all buddhas and
> bodhisattvas, after practicing the good dharma
> during innumerable cosmic periods and reaching

perfect awakening, have left behind their teachings to be practiced and cultivated by beings of future generations, who have been born in this latter period of the decay of dharma (末法). You claim that common persons should not follow this method. For whom, then, were these teachings left by the buddhas? And in what sutras is it taught that this method should not be followed by common people?...

The defect in conceptualization (想) is that it has the power to hinder the original omniscience (本來一切智) of all living beings, and thus make them turn about in the endless cycle of the three evil destinies. This is their defect. It is also taught in the Vajra[cchedikā Sūtra] that one calls buddha those who abandon all signs.[45]

The gradualist objects that one cannot become a Buddha merely by getting rid of discursive thought (129b).

(134b) There are certain occasions when one should produce and foster conceptual [processes] and there are occasions when one should not produce them. In the case of those who are still in the stage of common persons, or when they are only at the beginning of their practice, they should not try to do away with conceptual [processes].

Mo-ho-yen replies that his method is no different from that of all Buddhas--to remove the cause of suffering, for:

> (134b) all the sutras of the Great Vehicle say
> that all living beings are carried around by
> the currents of birth and death, because they
> cling to the false concepts of birth and
> death on account of the false concepts and
> distinctions they construct. (135a) [They
> also say that living beings] will be released
> the moment they stop clinging to the false
> concepts of birth and no-birth. From which
> sutra text do you conclude that common living
> beings should not try to do away with concep-
> tual thought?

Mo-ho-yen leaves no room for doubt regarding
the superiority of his method of liberation--it is the
only effective method, and the only one that is
required, a true panacea:

> (146b) According to the Mahāparinirvāṇa Sūtra,
> there is a certain medicinal herb that will
> cure all diseases in those who take it. It is
> the same with this absence of reflection and
> inspection. All false conceptualizations
> associated with the three poisons arise from
> modifications in the discriminatory faculty of
> reflection.... We ask you, therefore, to get
> rid of all wrong views and false conceptual-
> izations; in this way, by not engaging in any
> reflections, you will become free in one
> instant from all the habitual tendencies to
> engage in false conceptualizations born from
> the three poisons and the afflictions.

At this point the text returns to the question of the actual method to be followed in meditation—a point with which the first set of questions and answers had begun (129a), but which since then had been forgotten:

> (135a) [Gradualist] question: What do you mean when you speak of "contemplating the mind" (看 心)?
> Reply: To turn the light [of the mind] towards the mind's source, that is contemplating the mind. [This means that] one does not reflect on or observe[46] (不思不觀) whether thoughts (心) are in movement or not, whether they are pure or not, whether they are empty or not. It is also not to reflect on non-reflection.[47] This is why the Vimalakīrti Sūtra explains: "Non-observation is enlightenment."

Here Mo-ho-yen is trying to secure his position as a non-dualist by a dialectical procedure—logical and contemplative—common among his Indian predecessors. It is quite evident that he must have been aware of the fact that his preference for the pāramārthika point of view could be construed as some subtle form of dualism, for a second manuscript of the Cheng-li chüeh supplies us with the text of a lacuna in which the questioner presents what is perhaps the strongest argument of the gradualist. The questioner's reasoning is the following:[48]

Perhaps there might be someone who could argue: "[There is indeed a non-conceptual state, but] it must follow [the proper use of] concepts, as we have explained above.[49] Moreover, if the wisdom of the Saints is [totally] without concepts, it is not [truly] non-dual." If someone argued this way, what would you respond?

This passage reveals the polemical background of the section on the two truths in the First Bhāvanākrama, for the above quotation can be glossed with a charge of partiality to the absolute truth. That is to say, in the view of the gradualist, the defender of sudden enlightenment falls into a curious dualism--by rejecting conceptualization and favoring the non-conceptual realm, he could be reifying the latter.

A similar argument had been presented before (147b) by the gradualist, except that the emphasis there is more on the issue of the role of means (upāya)--a theme discussed repeatedly in the Bhāvanākramas. The question runs as follows (Cheng-li chüeh 147b):

In all the sutras of the Mahayana it is said that non-duality is reality; that non-duality is wisdom, and discrimination is means, but wisdom cannot exist in isolation [from means]. This the Vimalakīrti Sūtra explains in full detail.[50] One should not discriminate between the two by saying that one is indispensable and the other is not. If one were to make such discriminations, then

one would be discriminating between grasping
and relinquishing [something you yourself
admit to be contrary to Mahayana teach-
ings].51

The reply of the Ho-shang is of great interest as
behind its apparent tautology and petitio principii
it suggests that the sudden enlightenment of the Ho-
shang belongs to the type described by Tsung-mi as
sudden enlightenment followed by gradual cultivation.
In Mo-ho-yen's view the proper sphere for the cultivation of the discriminating mind is the practice that
follows enlightenment (prsthalabdhajñāna):

> (147b) After numberless kalpas, all Buddhas,
> the Tathāgatas, become free from false concep-
> tualizations associated with the three poisons
> and from discriminations associated with the
> afflictions. This is why they reach enlight-
> enment, (418a) and obtain non-dual, non-
> discriminating knowledge (无二无分别智). It
> is by means of this non-dual, non-discriminat-
> ing knowledge that they are able accurately to
> discriminate the marks of all dharmas. This
> is not the discrimination of false conceptual-
> izations, in which fools engage. For this
> reason, wisdom and means cannot exist in iso-
> lation from each other. If you claim that [in
> this] there is [still] grasping and relin-
> quishing, [I ask:] in the state of non-
> duality what [sort of] grasping and relin-
> quishing could there be?

Still, it is impossible to maintain consistently such a radical position, trying to keep it truly and uncompromisingly non-dual, without allowing at some point for the realities of human psychology. Unqualified suddenism is as impossible to maintain as unqualified gradualism. Master Mo-ho-yen must concede:

(158a) As long as one [is not capable] of practicing meditation (坐禪), one has recourse to the perfection of morality, the four immeasurable states of mind (āpramāṇya), and other such practices. Further, one cultivates meritorious [actions] and renders service to the Three Jewels. [One hears] the teachings of all the sutras and the instructions of the masters. Having heard them, one must practice according to these teachings. Only this is their goal--to cultivate all meritorious [actions]. As long as one is not able to practice non-examination one dedicates his merit to living beings, so that they all may attain buddhahood.

These statements could be construed as an honest attempt to grant a legitimate place to some form of gradualism in the plan of sudden enlightenment; but they could also be understood to be at best a reluctant concession to the social realities of the religious life. Mo-ho-yen's arguments in the Cheng-li chüeh would seem to indicate that the former is the case, although it is not at all clear how the gradualist elements--means, merit, etc.--can form an integral part of Mo-ho-yen's system.

For instance, in the <u>Cheng-li chüeh</u> Mo-ho-yen seems to assert and deny at the same time the need for gradualist practices. When his opponent asks (136b) whether the six perfections are or are not necessary, Mo-ho-yen replies that they are necessary, from the point of conventional truth, as means to the manifestation (顯) of ultimate truth. The gradualist presses the question further by expressing his doubts in a form that encapsules rather transparently one of the key bones of contention between the two parties (137b):

> Since these are means for the manifestation of ultimate truth, are they necessary [only] for beings of dull faculties (鈍根) or are they necessary for both beings of dull and sharp (利根) faculties?

The underlying assumption in the gradualist's question seems to be that at one time beings of sharp faculties also have access only to conventional truth, and then need the "means" that reveal or manifest the ultimate reality. Mo-ho-yen, however, does not see it that way. For him, it would seem, "sharp faculties" (利根) allow direct access to ultimate truth. Still he is not willing to concede that this creates a special class of persons for whom the six perfections and all other gradual practices become unnecessary. Accordingly, he claims (137a) that one cannot talk about (論) necessity or non-necessity when it comes to beings of sharp faculties.[52] Presumably, these superior beings, having understood that "need or the lack thereof, being and non-being, identity and difference, are all ungraspable" (不可得),[53] do not concern themselves with this issue of the role of means.

Still, this does not answer the objector's questions. The inconsistencies in the Ho-shang's position are quite evident. He tells us at one point that the question of the value or need of the pāramitās is a non-question from the viewpoint of ultimate truth (141a), that the duality of need or no-need--like other dualities--has meaning only in the relative realm (154a). This condition beyond need and no-need is explained in more than one way: it may mean that one could just as well practice or not practice virtue (141a), but it could also mean that there is no need to practice it! The latter interpretation is expressed as follows (137a):

> As regards beings of sharp faculties, one cannot talk about necessity or no-necessity. It is the same as medicine, which is necessary for the sick, and a boat which is necessary for someone who wishes to cross a river, but for a person in health one does not speak of need or no-need, and when one has crossed the river he needs no boat.

A fatal slip indeed! Clearly Mo-ho-yen has driven himself into a corner, and one is tempted to conclude that his last word is in fact an unconditional denial of the value of means for those who can have a direct access to ultimate truth. This is, in fact, the theme of several of the Tibetan fragments, most notably II.1.

It is also stated more than once in the Cheng-li chüeh that the gradual way is that of the common man, that the various practices of the path are only necessary for those who have not reached, or cannot achieve directly, the non-conceptual stage (154a-b, 156b, 158a). Yet Mo-ho-yen also insists that in the sutras the sudden approach has been taught for the common man (凡夫 pṛthagjana) as well (134a-b, 135a-136a, 137b-138a, 140a-b). Although his teaching is fundamentally pāramārthika, Mo-ho-yen claims, when he teaches the common man he makes use of means and enjoins the practice of the perfections (155b).

Demiéville has already pointed to the obvious contradiction between insisting on the primacy and accessibility of the direct, non-conceptual approach, and then proposing alternate paths for those who are not able to practice it;[54] but I am here interested in other, more fundamental implications of Mo-ho-yen's wavering. If the distinction between means and wisdom, relative and absolute, error and truth, is the pristine error (133b, 155b, 156a, 147b-148a), then it follows that the goal must be a state of freedom from these dualities, rather than any strengthening of the mental habits that they presuppose. In this Mo-ho-yen stands on firm ground. However, his position becomes no less dualistic by assuming that the direct access excludes the gradual elements of the path. To try to avoid the pitfall of a onesided view of "non-duality" Mo-ho-yen claims that there is an automatic or all-at-once attainment of all virtues when one gives up all conceptualizations (133b, 137b [=XI.6], 138a, 140b [=XI.10], VI.2a). This is Mo-ho-yen's idea of "the practice that is no practice" (131 bis b, 133b, 150a-b, 154a, etc.)--the opposition of practice to non-practice, virtue to non-virtue does not obtain, cannot be found (不可得) in the non-conceptual state (136a). Even the opposition between gradual and sudden becomes meaningless here (133b 2-4). What is more, the experience of the ungraspability of dualities is enlightenment--as the dualities are delusion.

If it were left at that, however, the position of the perfections as actual religious or ethical practices would still be obscure. Mo-ho-yen therefore has made a major concession to the gradualists: the perfections should be practiced--without expectation of reward--as long as one is not able to carry out the non-conceptual practice, but once there is no-thought the perfections are practiced without conscious effort (自然圓滿) (138a). However, the explanation of this "automatic practice" leaves much to be desired. From his short tract on the ten perfections (VIII) it becomes obvious that such a view requires a redefinition of the perfections, by virtue of which they are deprived of much of their specific moral contents.

The key to these issues may be in the Ho-shang's doctrine of "internal" and "external" perfection, which, unfortunately is only treated cursorily in the Cheng-li chüeh (137b = XI.6) and in one of the Tibetan fragments (Stein 709 = VI.2). The latter source identifies internal pāramitā with wisdom, and external with means. The internal is directed at liberation for oneself, the external at benefiting living beings (137b).[55] If both sources are combined, and their schemas represented in tabular form, one would have the following chart:[56]

external practice--benefiting others (upāya)

worldly

supramundane

supra-supramundane

internal practice--liberating self (prajñā)

all perfections subsumed or
achieved simultaneously in
non-conceptual practice

In spite of all the above, Mo-ho-yen's position
is ultimately that of the "absolute point of view"
(pāramārtha). The pair of external and internal is
not presented as a comprehensive or integral definition of correct practice, but as a distinction between
two independent types of practice. Mo-ho-yen's
preference among these is quite evident (VI.1-2,
especially 2b), but the fact that he makes allowances
for the other (IV, VIII) confirms the obvious demands
of human psychology and the scriptural tradition--to
say nothing of the political pressure that must have
been exerted on Mo-ho-yen after the arrival of the
Indian missionaries. Even the staunchest suddenist--
given the nature of human discourse and the nature of
the Buddhist tradition--must qualify his position so
that the continuity and the fruits of the mystical
process can be explained in some way, no matter how
rudimentary the explanation may be. Thus, Mo-ho-yen
cannot erase completely the six perfections. He must
account for them in his system. He must also concede
that not everyone can enter directly into the highest
stage of contemplation.

The Tibetan fragments translated below show
that his position is not as uncompromising as it would
seem from the polemical Cheng-li chüeh. In the latter
work most of Mo-ho-yen's gradualist statements appear
as reluctant concessions or grudging lip service to
the religious dressing of Buddhist meditation. In the
Tibetan fragments, on the other hand, Mo-ho-yen's

cultivation that is no-cultivation loses some of its
iconoclastic sting, when one sees the importance of
rigorous meditation (tso-ch'an/zazen) in his teachings
(I.2 and I.8).[57] His single method of no-reflection,
no-observation, and no-conceptualization seems more
complex once we examine a sample of the form in which
he would present it to his disciples, not in the heat
of debate.

Mo-ho-yen still simplifies the path to liberation by discarding the wisdom (prajñā) that grows from
study and reflection, and retaining only meditation
(VI.3). Yet, the practice of tso-ch'an is clearly
presented as spiritual discipline amenable to analysis
and explanation. In spite of its unique and ineffable
character, the experience that has no means of
approach (V) can be seen as a five-stage process
(IV.1-5).[58] It can be defined by contrast with the
teaching of non-buddhists (II.2) and Hinayanists (II.3
and VII.9), and evidently is not to be understood as
the mere suppression of thoughts (V).

It is also possible to see in these passages
the germs of a more subtle theory of the nature of
enlightenment as a religious goal--or a "Buddhology,"
if you will accept this barbarous neologism. In other
passages Mo-ho-yen begins a full development of a
theory of merit and the dharmadhātu (VI.10)--only to
be interrupted by the end of the fragment.

Another tantalizing and suggestive fragment
(VII.11), reminiscent of gradualist analyses, discusses the two basic defective states of concentration
that may hinder the normal course of meditation, and
how to overcome them. One sees in this passage the
difference between the Ch'an Master's day-to-day
advice on the practical problems of the spiritual

life, on the one hand, and, on the other, his _ex cathedra_ statements on the "true" nature of "the ineffable," and the experience of encountering it directly, without intervening methods or theories.

Separated from the polemical context of the _Cheng-li_ chüeh, it is therefore easier to see, from the internal perspective of the system itself, the dialectical necessities and limitations of a sudden enlightenment position. One is thereby freed from the caricature of Ch'an that both devotees and critics often draw. The inconsistencies and the tensions reveal a real human phenomenon, a religious ideal, and a spiritual practice more conscious of human needs than the rhetoric of the system itself is willing to recognize.

APPENDIX I

Synoptic Chart of the Tibetan Fragments

To clarify the interrelation between the various fragments and the translations, I have appended a table on which each translated text is identified by a roman numeral (topics), and an arabic numeral (paragraphs in the translation). These numbers are placed in separate columns corresponding to the manuscript fragment in which each text can be found. Numbers on the same horizontal line represent versions of the same text or, if quoted in parentheses, approximate parallels.

The order of the fragments on this chart corresponds to the numeration of the translations, and not to the order in the original manuscripts. The latter is indicated in Charts I-III, and by folio numbers inserted in parentheses in the translations.

This chart, like the translations that follow, is only meant as a provisional means of understanding the texts. It awaits revision following further study of these and other fragments from Tun-huang.

The Gate of Immediate Access to Meditation						On the Ten Perfections...	
(Identified by Title)			(No Title)				
S.468	P.117	S.709	P.813	P.812	Bsmi	P.116	P.117
1.1							
1.2					VII.3		
1.3					VII.4a		
1.4					VII.4b		
1.5					VII.4c		
1.6			(IV.2)				
1.7-8							
1.9							
		II.1			VII.5		
		II.2			VII.6		
		II.3					
			III.1	III.1	(VII.1)		
	III.2						
	IV.0				VII.9		
	IV.1		IV.1	IV.1	VII.9a		
	IV.2-4		IV.2-4	IV.2-4	VII.9b-d		
	IV.5		IV.5	(frag.)	VII.9e		
					V.=VII.9f		
		VI.1					
		VI.2a					
		VI.2b					
						VIII.1-6	VIII.1-6
						VIII.7-10	

The Essentials	The Meaning...	Other Fragments	Parallels in the Cheng-li chüeh
S̲.706 P̲.812	P̲.21	P̲.823 P̲.116	P̲.4646
			(134a3-b3)
			(135b4-5)
	(X.1)	(XI.3)	(129a4-6)
			(156a)
	(X.2)		(135a2-4)
			(134a,134b-135a)
			(142a-b)
			(132a)
		(XII.1)	
			(135b)
	(X.3)		(135b3-5)
			(136b2-5)
			(141a1-142b3)
			(137b6-138a3)
			(137b1-4,156a4-5)

APPENDIX II

English Translation of the Tibetan Fragments

Introductory Note:

The following translations of the fragments cannot claim anything more than a very provisional value. Many passages remain obscure, and, as explained above, the interconnections among the fragments are still problematic. However, this being a first attempt at translating the fragments as Chinese texts, and not as Tibetan works with an Indian prototype, I trust the exercise fills a need and will bear fruit in future researches.

All paragraph headings and divisions are the translator's. For the titles of each fragment or set of fragments, consult the main body of the article.

Reference to folia inserted in the translations are only for the convenience of the reader. They cannot but be approximate cross-references.

The Gate of Immediate Access to Meditation

Part 1: Fragment I. Stein 468:[1] "The Sudden Path."

I.1. The cause of transmigration.[2]

(1a1) The root of the wheel of birth and death in the world is the discriminating mind.[3] (1a2) Why is this? The discriminating mind arises from habitual tendencies [that have grown since] beginningless time.[4] (1a3) Because of this, one perceives [everything] in accordance with the [conceptualizations] that arise [in the mind], and one acts in accordance with that perception, producing fruits that agree with such actions.[5] (1a4) Therefore, from the highest

Buddha down to the lowest hell, (1a5) one perceives
only what is magically generated by one's own discriminating mind. [On the other hand], if the [discrimi-
nating] mind does not arise, one cannot find even an
atom of a dharma [on which to settle].[6] (1b1)

I.2. Sitting in meditation.

A person who understands that this is so should
give up other activities, sit alone in a place that is
isolated and free from noise, (1b2) cross his legs,
and keep his back straight, without sleeping morning
or evening.[7] (1b3)

I.3. No-mind.[8]

When he enters a state of deep contemplation,
he looks into his own mind.[9] There being no-mind,[10]
(1b4) he does not engage in thought. If thoughts of
discrimination arise, he should become aware of them.

I.4. Practice of no-mind: no-examination.[11]

How should one practice this awareness? (1b5)
Whatever thoughts arise, one does not examine [to
see][12] whether they have arisen or not, whether they
exist or not, (2a1) whether they are good or bad,
afflicted or purified.[13] He does not examine any
dharma whatsoever.[14] (2a2)

I.5. The "path of dharma."[15]

If he becomes aware in this way of the arising
[of thoughts, he perceives] the absence of self-
existence.[16] This is (2a3) called "The Conduct of
the Path of Dharma."

I.6. Erroneous meditation.[17]

If one fails to have this awareness of the arising of thoughts, or if the awareness is incorrect, one will act accordingly, (2a4) cultivate meditation in vain (or, cultivate an inexistent object!),[18] and remain as a common man.

I.7. Conceptualizations.[19]

When a person who cultivates meditation for the first time looks into the mind, (2a5) there arise conceptualizations. To this one should apply the same principles as above.

I.8. Awareness.[20]

After sitting [in this manner] for a long time, the mind will become tame, and one will realize that his awareness (2b1) is also discriminating mind. How does this occur? It is comparable to becoming blemished by bodily actions, (2b2) it is only on account of the blemish that one knows that one is blemished. In the same way, one has an awareness due to the blemish of the arising of thoughts. (2b3) It is on account of this [arising] that we know that we have an awareness.[21]

I.9. Awareness is to be abandoned too.

Awareness itself is without name or form, one cannot see the place whence it originally (2b4) came, nor can one discern whither it will finally go. The awareness and place where it occurs (2b5) cannot be obtained by any search.[22] There is no way of reflecting on the inconceivable.[23] Not to cling even to this absence of thought is [the immediate access of] the Tathagatas.[24]

The Gate of Immediate Access to Meditation

Part 2: Fragment II. Stein 709.   "Response to Several
        Objections."

II.1. There are no means of approach to sudden
enlightenment.[25]

(4a1) Still, if someone is not fit to enter
into contemplation without some means of approach,[26]
how then should he produce the means of approach to
contemplation?[27]   (4a2) To abide in no-mind[28] by giving up all states of contemplation is in fact the only
means of entering the contemplation of the Great
Vehicle. (4a3)

II.2. The sudden path is not like the meditation of the non-Buddhist.

Still, there may be some who raise doubts as to
whether there is here something of the contemplation
of the outsiders.[29]   (4a4) But all of the outsiders,
because they adhere to the view of a real self,[30] con-
fuse the permanent and the impermanent, (4a5) and fail
to accept the fact that the three world-realms are
only mind.   As they rely on their own great teachers,
(4b1) they hold views such as the rejection of causality, and they are grieved and terrified by their own
preconceptions.[31]   They find joy in nothingness, so
that they practice a contemplation which is nothing
whatsoever.   (4b2) In this way they create the view
that there is no form. Therefore, even after spending
many kalpas [practicing this type of contemplation],
still there arises in them the idea that they have not
reached nirvana, (4b3) so that they fall into hell
like any common mortal and suffer greatly.[32]

II.3. It is not like the meditation of the Auditors (śrāvakas).

(4b4) Still, there is also the suspicion that [non-conceptual practice] is like the contemplation of cessation of the auditors. Although the contemplation of the auditors has many forms, (4b5) in brief, it is based on [insight into] the absence of a self in the human person, the impermanence of all conditioned things, and...(lacuna).

The Gate of Immediate Access to Meditation

Part 3: Fragments III.1 and III.2. Pelliot 117, 812, 813: "Direct Access."

III.1. The "inconceivable."[33]

(Pelliot 812) One who does not examine any state of contemplation, when he is also free from reflection (8a4), is established in the inconceivable.

III.2. Immediate access to contemplation.[34]

(Pelliot 117) If one is able to practice it thusly, then it is called the direct access, the short-cut (5b2), the secret door, the door to the path of liberation.

The Gate of Immediate Access to Meditation

Part 4: Fragment IV. Pelliot 117, 812, 813: "The Five Means of Approach."

IV.0.   The five means of approach.[35]

(Pelliot 117) If one is not (5b3) able to practice   it   thusly,   then   there   are   five   means   of
approach.[36]   Which are these?   They are   the following:

IV.1.   First approach.[37]

(Pelliot 117)   At   the time   of   entering   non-
examination (5b4),[38] by direct awareness of   the arising of   deluded thoughts[39]   one does   not   have assurance[40] of enlightenment.

IV.2.   Second approach: the common man.

(Pelliot 117)   If   after becoming aware   of the
arising   of deluded   thoughts (5b5),   one   examines and
pursues   this   awareness,[41]   one   is   still   a   common
man.[42]

IV.3.   Third approach: cessation.[43]

(a) Pelliot 117 version:

If   one   [becomes]   aware   of   the   arising   of
deluded thoughts   (6b1) and,   because   one understands
the disadvantages of this arising, one   prevents (6b2)
their arising by this awareness, this is cessation.

(b) Bsmi version:

If, by becoming aware of the arising of deluded
thoughts and,   having understood the   disadvantages of
this   arising, one prevents [them from   arising], this
is the cessation of the auditors.

IV.4. Fourth   approach: serenity   and   emptiness.[44]

(Pelliot 117) If one becomes aware of the arising of deluded thoughts, and [perceives]   no intrinsic

being [in them], this is called the unity of serenity (6b3), and [also] propensity toward emptiness.

IV.5. Fifth approach: the highest contemplation.

(Pelliot 117) If after becoming aware of the arising of deluded thoughts, (6b4) one no longer examines or pursues this awareness, and every instant of thought is free,[45] this is the highest contemplation.

The Gate of Immediate Access to Meditation

Part 4: Fragment V. Bsmi: "Summary of the Method."

V.0. Conclusion.[46]

Therefore, one should not repress conceptualizations. Whenever they arise, if one does not contrive any [new thoughts],[47] but rather lets them go by, as one lets them go, though they may remain, they come to rest by themselves, (165.5) and one no longer pursues them.

The Gate of Immediate Access to Meditation

Part 5: Fragment VI. Stein 709: "Various aspects of the sudden path."
(Stein 709, second fragment)

VI.1. Non-duality applies to the antithesis of good and evil.

(7a1) (xxxx)[48] One should practice the six perfections as much as possible. At the time of sitting in contemplation, (7a2) if there is something like the propensity to discriminate even dualities such as avarice against [the perfection of] generosity, one should abandon, by way of non-attention,[49] even the duality [of the opposition between] the practical aspect of the six perfections[50] and contemplation (7a3). It is like the sun, which is equally obscured by white and dark clouds (7a4).[51]

VI.2. <u>Still, there are levels of perfection</u>.[52]

(a) <u>The three kinds of perfections</u>.

Fundamentally, there are three levels of perfection: the wordly, (7b5) the supramundane, and the supra-supramundane.[53]

The supra-supramundane perfections are devoid of apperception[54] (7b1), devoid of examination.[55] A mind that is free from examination accomplishes the six perfections simultaneously in an instant.[56]

Otherwise, if dualities are examined (7b2) and discriminated at the time of abiding in contemplation, one is overcome by feelings.[57]

(b) <u>The two kinds of perfection</u>.

(7b2) There are two kinds of perfections: first, (7b3) there are the practical perfections, which are practiced as means. Secondly, there is the perfection of wisdom, which is the inner state in which thoughts no longer arise (7b4).[58]

Therefore, even if one does not display the explicit conduct of the perfections of means (7b5), one can be effortlessly in possession of the perfection of wisdom.[59]

VI.3. <u>True seeing is no-seeing</u>.

Still, there are some who will say that one should cultivate great learning and only thereafter

(8al) enter contemplation.⁶⁰ Someone who is regarded as very learned may impress on his mind the non-arising of all dharmas (8a2). He may be called a man of great learning; but simply to study words and syllables is not true learning.

Why is this so? (8a3) One cannot see the Dharma by seeing, one cannot hear the Dharma by hearing, one cannot become aware of the Dharma by becoming aware, one cannot understand the Dharma by understanding (8a4). Therefore, those who seek by seeing, hearing, becoming aware, or understanding (8a5), though they seek, they are not really seeking the Dharma.[61]

VI.4. Response to another criticism.

(8a5) These [principles] are expressed by way of summary, but [our opponents] have reproached us for [practices that they claim can lead only to] doubt and lack of faith (8bl).[62] They say that there are numberless living beings who are not equal to the task of the path, and that these beings cannot understand this [immediate] cutting through the doubts caused by one's own conceptual examination (8b2). In the end, in every way, they will lose their faith and fall prey to doubts. [We reply that] if you are deceived by your own conceptualizations, there is no true cultivation of the meditation of former Tathagatas (8b3). Therefore one should not mind[63] any of these [conceptual examinations], (8b4) but [simply] be aware [of them].

VI.5. A simile for the sudden approach.

(8b4) When one enters directly into the contemplation of the Tathāgatas, one is not overpowered in any of the [sense] bases by the mere arising of thoughts (8b5).[64] If this is so, how much less is there cultivation of the unerring.[65]

This may be compared (9a1) to the lion cub that even before it has opened its eyes brings terror to other animals, or to the young of the kalaviṅka bird who upon leaving their eggs (9a2) are able to fly like their mother.[66]

The qualities of this contemplation cannot be easily compared with other things in this world (9a3). Its qualities are powerful and effective.

VI.6. Thinking is not mental cultivation.

(9a3) In this contemplation one ought to exert oneself in cultivating at all times faith in the Dharma of the Mahāyāna (9a4), and the conviction that all dharmas are mind only. If one expects to gain all its benefits without cultivating [these] (9a5), [one's efforts] will be fruitless--as one does not become wealthy by merely counting in the mind all the wealth of a rich man (9b1).

VI.7. The Dharmadhātu.

As for the means of the approach which consists in cultivating the [one] object of the Middle Way of the Great Vehicle, it is briefly stated:[67] From the point of view of relative truth (9b2) all dharmas, external or internal, are from the outset seen as illusions fashioned by one's own conceptual examination, or they are like magical productions, arisen by conditioned origination (9b3). Still, in an absolute sense, they are without any substantial reality. (9b4) Having no substantial reality, they do not arise; not arising, they do not cease. That which

neither arises nor ceases is the dharmadhātu.   (9b5)
The dharmadhātu is the body of dharma.[68]

VI.8. Effortless practice of non-examination.

(9b5) Therefore, since the inherent being of
all dharmas is like this, one should by all means
practice the cultivation (10a1) of non-examination.
The discriminating mind itself no real substance,[69] it
does not arise, it does not cease.   With this very
same body, which is the dharmadhātu, (10a3) one should
not contrive [conceptualizations], rather, one should
not pursue them, one should not oppose them.   (10a4)
It should be so that there is no artificial construction [of conceptualizations].[70]

≪Why is this?   When the mind abides in them no
more (10a5), it should then not be made not to abide.
When the mind does not examine, it should then not be
made not to examine. (10b1) To do so would be to contrive [further conceptualizations].≫

VI.9. Scriptural evidence.[71]

(10b1) In the sutras too it is said:
    Arising from dharmas without a self,
    Buddhas achieve buddhahood (10b2).
    They cultivate firmly the thought of
       awakening,
    Which cannot be apprehended by conceptual
       examination.
(10b3) It is also said in the sutras:
    Dharmas are a reflection in the mind.
    The mind too cannot be apprehended.
    (10b4) It arises not and ceases not--it is

> beyond understanding,
>> Like serene empty space, free from
>> concepts.

VI.10. Perfection of Buddhahood.

Cultivating in this way (10b5), he does not remain in saṃsara like the outsiders. Possessed of means and wisdom, he is said to be free from impurity and the afflictions.[72]

(11a1) He accumulates the double equipment of merit and knowledge and also perfects a variety of attainments for the benefit of himself and others (11a2). This is the body of merit. In the second level[73] he obtains the body of dharma, after which he enters supportless nirvāṇa, and (11a3) until the end of saṃsāra remains active for the sake of living beings.

Fragments from the Bsam-gtan mig-sgron

VII.1. Bsmi. 58.5.[74]

According to the teachings[75] of Master Mahayana, when one is free from reflection on the nature of all dharmas, he is established in non-reflection and non-examination.

VII.2. Bsmi. 122.3-4 = Bka'-than, Tucci p. 74/91.[76]

(Meditation Master) Mahāyāna says: "By correct vision one discerns (with the discernment of wisdom) the general (and the specific) characteristics of body and mind (--that is [what pertains to] the external and the internal, dharmas and self). One should understand that the specific characteristics are impermanence and sorrow, the general characteristics are emptiness and no-self.

VII.3.   Bsmi. 145.5-6 = I.2.[77]

VII.4.   Bsmi. 145.6-146.3 = I.3-5.

VII.5.   Bsmi. 146.3-4 = II.1, only fol. 4a2.[78]

VII.6.   Bsmi. 146.4-5.[79]
According to the sayings of Mahāyāna:

By relying on their masters, the outsiders fall prey to the view of a real self, thereby confusing the permanent and the impermanent, and assume that there is nothing to be done, thereby producing the idea of no-fruit.[80]

The whole sphere of no-thought should be abandoned. How is this to be done? While not thinking and not examining, one abides not in non-examination.[81]

VII.7.   Bsmi. 146.5-146.6.
Mahāyāna says:

For the mind to abide in bliss in this manner is for it to be free from[82] examination.

VII.8.   Bsmi. 146.6-147.2.
And in the same place:[83]

The proper method of holding the mind firmly is to look into the mind and its objects and, seeing that [there is] not [a thing] to be found [in them], cultivate correctly the non-apprehension [of all things]. If one examines non-apprehension itself without attachment to [the mental representations] that appear, [then] the person who examines in this way is skillful in means.[84]

VII.9. Bsmi. 164.6-165.5 = IV (Pelliot 117 verso ff. 5.3-6.4; Pelliot 812 recto ff. 8.5-10.1; Pelliot 813 ff. 8a2-8b2).

VII.10. Bsmi. 165.5-166.1.
The same [master] states that[85] one should not fall into the extreme of the peace of śrāvakas and pratyekabuddhas, which is attained by the practice of no apprehension and by visualizing an image of light.[86]

However, he does not apprehend this knowledge, he does not fall into [the extreme of] the non-existence of conceptualizations. When these do not arise, he will not examine with an absence of examination that conceives of perfect clarity. He will not fall into the [extreme of] dying away by abstaining from thoughts, he does not apprehend even the non-apprehension of a substantial reality of dharmas.[87]

VII.11. Bsmi. 166.1-166.3.
The same [master] states that,[88] if there are deluded thoughts when one is in a state of equanimity, and then one examines them,[89] one should understand them as lacking in any permanent intrinsic being. One should not pursue them by grasping at signs. If he sees a fault he should earnestly suppress it.[90] He is not to pursue awareness of arising. If one sets himself in apprehension by not abiding in self arising and self cessation, then one makes effort to bring about cessation.[91] When there is dullness or excite-

ment, he only cultivates [then] the clear comprehension that there is no dullness in dullness.

VII.12. <u>Bsmi</u>. 177.3-5.

According to the [Discourse on] Contemplation
of Mahāyāna,[92] if one practices contemplation in this
manner for an extended period of time, now and then
there will appear many Buddhas and Bodhisattvas. Now
and then one will produce various higher states of
consciousness--[such as] the five extraordinary faculties. Now and then, one will see great variety of
marvels associated with [higher states of] concentra-
tion--such as the light of a great lotus. All of
these are activities of conceptualization. At once,
one should not conceive of any of these, or become
attached to them.

<u>Short Treatise on the Six and the Ten Perfections in
Non-conceptual Practice</u>

Fragment VII. Pelliot 116: 171b1-173b2 and Pelliot
117: 6b4-7b6

VIII.0. <u>Title</u>.[102]
(171b1) Master Mahāyāna's <u>Sayings Summarizing
the Practice of the Six and the Ten Perfections in
Non-conceptual Contemplation</u>.

VIII.1. <u>Generosity</u>.
(171b2) When one enters non-examination, he
brings to perfection great generosity, because he has
renounced the three world realms.

VIII.2. <u>Morality</u>.

When one enters non-examination, (171b3) he brings to perfection great morality, because there is no arising of any faults in any of the three doors [of conduct].

VIII.3. <u>Patience</u>.

When one enters non-examination, (171b4) he brings to perfection great patient acceptance, because there is acceptance of the non-origination of concepts[93] in the mind.

VIII.4. <u>Energy</u>.

In non-examination, he brings to perfection great energy, (172b1) because there is no interruption [of effort], like a river that continues to flow.

VIII.5. <u>Meditation</u>.

(172b2) He brings to perfection great concentration,[94] because non-examination is concentration.

VIII.6. <u>Wisdom</u>.

(172b3) He brings to perfection great wisdom, because only non-examination is supramundane wisdom.

VIII.7. <u>Skillful Means</u>.

(172b4) He also brings to perfection great means, because non-examination is the only means to reach the highest condition.[95]

VIII.8. <u>Powers</u>.

When one enters non-examination, he brings to perfection great powers, because he is able to overpower the three world spheres.

VIII.9. Vows.

(173b1) He brings to perfection the great vows, because non-examination is the only vow, the vow to enter the Tathāgata's vows.

VIII.10. Knowledge.[96]

(173b2) He brings to perfection great knowledge, because only the non-conceptual is the sphere of the Tathāgata ['s knowledge].

The Essentials of Contemplation

Fragment IX. Pelliot 812: 6a2–8a2, Stein 706: b1–b5, and Stein 709:42b.

IX.0. Title.

(812: 6a1) Master Mahāyāna's Essentials of Contemplation (6a2) state that:[97]

IX.1. The Nature of Immediate Access.

Although there are many texts on meditation in the Great Vehicle, (6a3) the highest of all methods taught (6a4) is that of the immediate access to the Middle Way. (6a5) In immediate access there are no means of approach. One meditates [directly] (7a1) on the true nature of dharmas.

In this connection, "dharma" (7a2) means the mind, and the mind is without origination. What has no origination (7a3) is empty, like space. This emptiness is called "direct awareness," (7a4) because it is not the object of the six senses. (7a5)

By practicing direct awareness, direct awareness itself ceases. (8a1) Therefore, one should not dwell in the wisdom of study and reflection, (8a2) but rather meditate directly on the sameness of all dharmas.

IX.2. Non-dwelling.[98]

(706: 8b4) A Great Being,[99] when he cultivates this mind as non-production, (8b5) cultivates non-dwelling in any sign whatsoever. Being aware of this non-dwelling, he does not examine his non-dwelling in any way....

The Meaning of the Practice of Non-examination[100]

Fragment X. Pelliot 21 recto.

X.1. Neither accepting, nor rejecting thoughts.

It is not a matter of whether one should accept or reject all dharmas or anything else, rather it is a matter of not giving rise to concepts of acceptance or rejection. If one has understood this and turns the six gates [of the senses] to an approach to the culti-vation of contemplation and looks into the mind,[101] then whenever a single false concept arises, he [again] feels inclined to produce karma that will lead to transmigration.[102]

X.2. Non-duality in practice.[103]

If concepts arise, then one [should] not think[104] anywhere of being or non-being, purity or impurity, emptiness or the absence thereof, etc. One does not think of non-thinking either. Not to experi-ence this non-examination and to continue to act according to these thoughts is transmigration.

X.3. Liberation in every moment of thought.[105]

But if one were to experience non-examination and does not act according to these concepts, or accept them, or become attached to them, then every instant of mind is liberated at each moment. By cultivating the mind in this way, one awakens[106] perfectly as soon as one is free from all false concepts and all past habitual tendencies.

X.4. Colophon.

Thus concludes "The Meaning of Non-examination."

Parallels to the Cheng-li chüeh

Fragment XI. Pelliot 823 recto.

XI.1. Quotation from the Laṅkāvatāra.

fol. 1.1 = Pelliot 4646, 133b5-134a1 = Concile 75-6.

(1.1) Therefore, according to the Lankavatara, all dharmas have no self-nature, yet they are all perceived on account of false conceptualizations.[107]

XI.2. The defects of conceptual thought.

fol. 1.2-3 = Pelliot 4646, 134b3-5 = Concile 77

(1.2) Question: What is so wrong with conceptual thought?

Reply: The problem with it is that it carries omniscience[108] away from all living beings, and obscures it. (1.3) It is also a problem in many other ways, such as being the cause for rebirth in the three evil destinies, and for prolonged transmigration. The

Vajracchedika   also   says: "Abandon   conceptual thought."[109]

XI.3. Looking into the mind.
fol. 1.4-2.2 = Pelliot 4646, 135a2-4 = Concile 78-80.
(1.4) Question: What sort of activity is this "looking into the mind"?
Reply: It is to turn back the six sense doors and then look into the mind.   If concepts stir, one does not consider whether they exist or not, whether they are pure (2.1) or not, whether they are empty or not, etc., and one does not consider even one's state of non-examination and non-consideration.   In the Vimalakīrti it is (2.2) also said: "Non-examination is awakening."

XI.4. The means for removing conceptual thought.
fol. 2.2-4 = Pelliot 4646, 135b3-5 = Concile 82.
Question: If one removes conceptualization and the habitual tendencies, by what sort of means does one do so?
Reply: If one is aware of false conceptuali- zations when they arise, (2.3) being aware of birth and death, one does not carry out actions in agreement with these conceptualizations, one does not abandon them, nor does one remain attached to them.   The mind is free at every instant of thought.   In the Vajracchedikā, the Mahāratnakuṭa, (2.4) and other sutras it is said: "If one has no apprehension of even the minutest dharma, that is the unsurpassable awakening."

XI.5. The need to practice the perfections.

fol. 2.4-3.3 = Pelliot 4646, 136b2-5 = Concile 85.

Question: Is it or is it not necessary to practice other dharma-gates (3.1) such as the six perfections?

Reply: From the point of view of covering all of the six perfections, they are said to be means for the sake of teaching the ultimate truth, (3.2) and one should practice them in every way possible. [On the other hand], from the point of view of the ultimate truth, the true meaning is regarded as being beyond speech and thought. Therefore, one can neither say (3.3) that one should nor that one should not practice any other dharma-gates such as the six perfections; how much less can one speak about not practicing them. This has been explained in detail in the sutras.

XI.6. The two types of perfection.

fol. 3.3-4.3 = Pelliot 4646, 137b1-4 = Concile 87-88.

Question: If one engages in [the practice of] the six perfections and the like, how is he to practice these means?

(3.4) Reply: Even as one is engaged in the practice of the six perfections, there are two, the internal and the external. By the internal, one liberates himself. By the external one benefits living beings. (4.1) As to these means [which are] the practice [of the perfections], in the Perfection of Wisdom, the Lankavatāra, and the Viśesacintā, it is said that if one does not examine or consider any dharma at all in the practice of the six perfections

(4.2) and other [virtues], then the triple sphere[110] is purified, and one acts without thinking or appropriating anything, regarding [all dharmas] as a mirage. (4.3)

XI.7. Liberation.
fol. 4.3-5.1 = Pelliot 4646, 138a5-138b1 = Concile 89.

Question: If one practices this dharma-gate, how does one obtain liberation by means of it?

Reply: According to the Laṅkāvatāra and the Vajracchedikā, (4.4) if one abandons all conceptualizations, one is a Buddha.[111] When one cultivates like this, according to the sharpness or dullness of one's faculties, all false conceptualizations and habitual tendencies (5.1) are abandoned, and one obtains liberation.

XI.8. The perfection of wisdom and its merit.
fol. 5.1-8.2 = Pelliot 4646, 138b1-139a6 = Concile 93-98.

(a) Incalculable merit of the perfection of wisdom.

Question: By practicing the gist[112] of this dharma, is any merit gained?

Reply: The merit of non-examination and non-consideration, (5.2) cannot be counted by judgments resulting from consideration or examination, one should regard them as no different than the thought of a Buddha.[113] If one should speak of only a fragment of this....[114] Also, according to the Perfection of Wisdom, (5.3) all living beings, gods and men, śrāvakas and pratyekabuddhas, if they transfer (their merit) to the attainment of unsurpassable awakening, their merit is not worth a fraction of the merit of listening to and believing in the (5.4) gist of the Perfection of Wisdom. Why is this so? Men, gods, śrāvakas, (6.1) private buddhas, and unsurpassable awakening all arise from the perfection of wisdom, but the perfection of wisdom does not arise from awakening or from any human being, (6.2) no matter how many.

(b) Definition of the perfection of wisdom.

Now, what is this perfection of wisdom? Absence of signs, (6.3) non-apprehension, not abandoning, and not seeking, this is called the perfection of wisdom.

(c) Its merits again: two scriptural references.

According to the Tathāgatācintyaguṇāvatāra Sūtra, (6.4) if someone would worship as many Tathāgatas as there are atoms in three thousand great chilocosms for an incalculable kalpa with offerings and prayers, purifying for (7.1) these Buddhas, after their nirvāṇa, three thousand great chilocosms of stūpas adorned with the seven kinds of precious things, (7.2) and if they did this for an incalculable kalpa, the merit of cutting all doubts with regard to the dharma of no-thinking[115] (7.3) would be an incalculable thousand times more.

Also, according to the Vajracchedikā, if someone fills three thousand great chilocosms with the seven precious things (7.4) and offers them, and gives up his own body for as many times as there are sand in the Ganges, someone who keeps four lines [of this sūtra] has even more merit, (8.1) it cannot be compared. Similar expressions occur, in full detail, in all the Mahāyāna Sūtras, stating how it is impossible for anyone but a Buddha to have this merit.[116] (8.2)

XI.9. Non-examination and omniscience.
fol. 8.2-9.1 = Pelliot 4646, 140a2-5 = Concile 94-96.

Question: How can (8.3) omniscience be obtained by abandoning conceptualizations and practicing non-consideration and non-examination?

Reply: If false thoughts do not stir, and all conceptualizations have been abandoned, the knowledge that arises from the true self-nature appears by itself all at once. (8.4) In sutras such as the Gandavyūha and the Lankāvatāra it is said that it is like the sun appearing from behind the clouds, (9.1) turbid water becoming clear, a mirror wiped clean, or silver separated from its ore.[117]

XI.10. Benefiting living beings.
fol. 9.1-4 = Pelliot 4646, 140b5-6 = Concile 97-99.

Question: How is it possible to benefit living beings with non-conceptual knowledge? (9.2)

Reply: How one can act for the sake of living beings when one is free from reflection and examination has also been explained in full detail in the (9.3) Tathāgatācintyaguṇāvatāra. It is said that it is like the sun or the moon shining everywhere, or the wish-fulfilling jewel (9.4) that grants everything, or the vast earth from which everything is born.

XI.11. The three forms of grasping.
fol. 9.4-10.2 = Pelliot 4646, 141a1-2 = Concile 100.

Question: In your teaching you speak of grasping at objects, grasping at consciousness, (10.1) and

grasping at what is in between.   What is the basis[118]
for such talk?

Reply: This is said on the basis of the fundamental meaning[119] of the Mahāyāna (10.2) which   is the
unthinkable[120] Perfection of Wisdom, so that   there is
no grasping, even   at one   single thing, [how   can you
speak of three, then?]   any form, not even one.   This
is explained in detail in the Perfection of Wisdom.

XI.12.   The message of the sutras.
fol.   10.2-11.1   =   Pelliot 142a1-3   =   Concile
107.

Question: If this   is the fundamental meaning
of your doctrine, (10.3) how can you say that   this is
explained in full detail by the sutras?

Reply: Indeed   this   is all   that the   sūtras
speak about.   They only speak of the false conceptualizations of living beings. (10.4)   If one abandons all
conceptualization, there is no dharma about   which one
could   speak.   Therefore,   it   is   also   said in   the
Laṅkāvatāra that   all the sūtras speak about   the conceptualizations of living beings (11.1) and that there
is   nothing   in   a   single sutra   about   the   absolute
truth.

XI.13.   The Buddha's   freedom from conceptualization.[121]
fol.   11.1-4   and   lacuna;   no   equivalent   in
Pelliot 4646.

Question: How can a Buddha speak of the   conceptualizations of living beings?

Reply: A Buddha's (11.2) omniscience, and the
range   [of his knowledge] are inconceivable,   never to
be understood by understanding.   It cannot be grasped

by any form of human understanding, and cannot be
understood by [human] wisdom. (11.3) Thus, it is not
to be measured by examining what should be done or
pondered. According to the Mahāyāna sūtras, (11.4) if
one abandons all conceptualizations, he is a Buddha.
Therefore, by turning to look into the mind, one
abandons all conceptualizations and habitual tendencies. Why is it that you ask for the meaning [of
this]....

Miscellaneous Fragments

Fragments XII.1. (Pelliot 167.4) and XII.2 (Pelliot
116:186.4-187.2).

    XII.1. Non-examination.[122]
    According to the teachings of Master Mahāyana,
when one is free from reflection on the nature of
dharmas, he is established in non-reflection and non-
examination.

    XII.2. Identity of Saṁsāra and Nirvāṇa.
    In the texts on meditation of Master
Mahāyāna[123] it is said: Since birth and death, and
nirvāṇa are not two [separate realities], there is no
meeting or having to part, nothing pleasurable or
unpleasant. Why? The identity of saṁsāra and nirvāṇa
is [true] nirvāṇa.

APPENDIX III
Glossary

This glossary is meant as an aid to understanding the texts translated above, and the approach used in that translation. In addition to the materials presented below, I have relied heavily on the glossaries published by Ueyama Daishun as part of his "Chibetto-yaku Tongo shinshū yōketsu no kenkyū," Zenbunka Kenkyū Kiyō VIII (1976) 33-103.

The following list of Tibetan terms with Chinese equivalents is based exclusively on those fragments for which there are close Chinese parallels or equivalents, namely, part of Pelliot 21 (references indicated by the arabic numeral 21 followed by folio and line number) and Pelliot 823 (folio and line numbers alone). The Tibetan reference is followed by folio number in the Cheng-li-chüeh. Cross references to the translation and the notes appended to this article are meant to be illustrative and not exhaustive.

kun rdzob ltar (3.1; 136b / XI.5): 如世諦（法）
bkan̊ (7.4; 139a) 滿
bkod pa: see thug pa
skye śi (21:2, 21:5; 135b): 生死
skye śi tshor te (2.3; 135b): 生死覺意　　　(reading
　若　for 名　at the beginning of the phrase)
bskal pa (6.4; 139a): 却

'khor ba (1.2-3, 2.2-4; 134b, 135b): 生死・輪
'khor ba'i rgyur gyurd pa (1.3; 134b):輪迴故有
'khor sum (4.2; 137b): 三業

gaṅ ga (7.4; 139a): 恆河
graṅs myed pa (6.4; 139a): 无量
graṅs su smos pa (6.1-2; 138b): ?
grol thar (2.3, 21.5; 135b): 解脱
grol thar pa (4.3; 138a):
---see also s.v. thaṅ re
dgoṅs: see ma dgoṅs
dgos (3.1, 7.2; 136b, ??): 要
---see myi dgos
bgraṅ źiṅ (5.4; 138b): 數
sgo:
---chos kyi sgo (3.1; 136b): 法門
---sgo drug bzlog ste (1.4, 21.2; 135a // X.1, cf.
    sems la bltas in I.3): 返照心原
brgyan pa:
---bzaṅ du brgyan pa (7.1; 139a): 莊嚴
bsgoms (4.4, 21.5-6; 138b): 修習

naṅ soṅ gsum (1.3; 134b // XI.2): 三惡道

cha śas (5.2): ?
chags pa myed pa (6.3; 138b): 无著
---see also ma chags
chad myi gzuṅ (5.2; 138b) 不可測量
chu rñog (9.1; 140a): 濁水
chu bo (7.4; 139a): 河沙
chuṅ zad (kyaṅ) (2.4; 135b): 少
chos (2.4; 135b): 法
---chos kyi sgo: see sgo
---chos kyi gźuṅ: see gźuṅ
mchod (6.4; 139a): 供養
mchod rten (7.1; 139a): 塔

'jug pa (9.2; 140b): 入

nañ thos (passim): 聲聞

ñes pa (1.2; 135a): 過

mñan pa (7.2; 139a): 聞

sñed (7.4; 139a): 數

gtogs: see ma gtogs

gtoṅ: see myi gtoṅ ba

btaṅ ba:

---yoṅ su btaṅ ba (7.4; 139a): 布施

---see myi gtoṅ ba

rtog: see brtags pa, ma brtags, myi rtog, and myi
    brtag

---rnam par rtog pa ('i sems): seems to stand for 妄
    想分別 as in I.1 and 134a, but the term is not
    found in our two fragments

lta ba:

---see myi rtog

---ltos śig (5.2; 138b): 應 --- 見

---bltas pa: see sems la (b)lta(s) (pa)

staṅ zil:

---staṅ zil las dnul (9.1; 140a): 銀離鑛

stoṅ (6.4; 139a): 千

stoṅ ba

---stoṅ pa daṅ myi stoṅ pa (2.1, 21:4; 135a): 空不空

brtag:

---brtags pa (5.2; 138b): 觀照

---see also ma brtags and myi brtag

bstan pa (3.2; 136b): 顯

thag: see ma thag tu

thaṅ re:

---sems thaṅ re yaṅ grol thar re re (2.3, 21:5; 135b
    // Cf. X.2-3; XI.4 and Cheng-li chüeh 147b,

Concile p. 125, n. 6, 158, n. 7; Demiéville 1961, p. 22): 念念即是解脱般若

thabs (2.2, 3.1; 135b, 136b): 方便　(Cf. II.1, IV, n. 12 to article, n. 26, 67, 84 to translation)

---thabs ji ltar (3.3; 137b): 如何修行

---spyad pa'i thabs (4.1; 137b): 修行方便

thams cad (passim): 一切

---thams cad mkhyen pa'i ye śes (1.2; 135a): 未來一切智 (8.2-3; 140a): 一切種智

thar(d) (3.4; 137b):

---see: grol thar(d)

thug pa:

---thug pa bar du bkod pa ba (5.3; 138b): 盡證

thob (4.3; 138a // cf. I.1): 得

---(7.4; 139a): read thos: 聞

---thob pa myed (2.4; 135b): 不得

thos (5.4; 138b): 聞　(also 7.4; 139a where thob should be read thos)

dag pa (9.1; 140a): 淨

de bźin du (21.5; 138b): 如是

dogs (7.2) read dgos

don:

---don dam par (3.1-2; 136b): (如)勝義

---sems can gyi don...mdzad (9.1-2; 140b): 利益　---

bdag:

---bdag gi sems la bltas: see sems la bltas

---bdag thard (3.4; 137b): 自度

bden:

---bden pa: see myi bden pa and yaṅ dag pa'i bden pa

'das pa (3.2; 136b): 離

'du śes (1.2, 1.3, 2.2, 4.4, 8.2-3; ??, 134b, 135b, 138a, 140a): 想・妄想

---'du śes g-yos na (1.4; 135a): 想若動

---'du śes bźin (21:5; 135b): 隨妄想
---'du śes bźin du ma spyad (2.3; 135b): 不隨妄想作業

---see also <u>myi</u> <u>bden</u> <u>ba'i</u>--
'dra źiṅ (4.2; 137b): 如
rdul sñed (6.4; 139a): 微塵

rnam par rtog pa: see note under <u>rtog</u>
rnam par śes pa:
---rnam par śes pa 'dzin (9.4; 141a): 執識
rno rtul (4.4; 138a // cf. <u>Sba-bźed</u>: <u>rnon</u> <u>po</u> and
    <u>stul</u> <u>ba</u>): 利鈍
dpe:
---dpe daṅ chad myed (8.1; 139a): 不可比喻
spaṅ:
---spaṅs te (8.2; 140a): 離
---spoṅ (1.3; 134b): 離
spyad (3.3; 137b // I.1): 修行 (2.3; 135b): 作
    (5.1; 138b): 行 (21.5; 135b): 作業
---spyad pa'i thabs (4.1; 137b): 修行方便
---spyod (4.3; 138a): 修
---spyod pa na (4.2; 137b): ?
---see also <u>ma</u> <u>spyad</u>

pha rol du (tu) phyin(d) pa (passim): 波羅蜜
phan gdags:
---sems can la phan gdags (3.4; 137b): 利益
phyan pa (6.2): read <u>phyin</u> <u>pa</u>
phyi daṅ naṅ gi (3.4; 137b): 內外

bag chags (2.2, 4.4, 21:6; 135b, 138b // I.1): 習氣
bag tshags (4.4): read <u>bag</u> <u>chags</u>
byaṅ chub (6.1; 138b): 菩薩 (passim): 菩提

---bla na myed pa'i byaṅ chub la thug pa (5.3; 138b): 證无上菩提

byas pa (7.2; 139a): ??

byuṅ (6.2; 138b): 出

---see myi byuṅ

bye ma sñed (7.4; 139a): 沙數

bral (21:6; 138b): 互歇

bral na (4.4; 138a): 離

bla na myed pa'i byaṅ chub (passim): 无上菩提   see also byaṅ chub

blaṅ(s): see ma blaṅs

dbaṅ po (4.4; 138a): 根性

dbu ma 'dzin pa (10.1; 141a): 執中

sbyaṅ (2.2; 135b): 降

sbyin:

---sbyin ba byin pa (7.4; 139a): 用布施

ma:

---ma dgoṅs (9.2; 140b): 不思

---ma chags (2.3, 21:5; 135b): 不住

---ma gtogs par (8.2; 139a): 除

---ma brtags (9.2; 140b): 不觀

---ma thag tu (5.1; 138b): 歇即

---ma spyad (2.3; 135b): 不…作 (21:5; 135b): 不作業

---ma blaṅs (2.3, 21:5; 135b): 不取

---ma tshags (2.3): read ma chags

---ma tshor (21:4; 135b): 不覺

---ma g-yos (8.3; 140a): 不起

---ma bslabs (2.3; 135b): read ma blaṅs

mya ṅan las 'das (6.4, 7.1; 139a): 滅度

mya lstsogs (6.1; 138b)--read "myi la stsogs"??: ??

myi (passim): 人

myi:

---myi dgos (3.1-2; 136b): 不要

---myi gtoṅ ba (6.3; 138b): 无捨
---myi rtog (1.4; 135a): 不觀
---myi rtog pa (2.2; 135a): 不觀
---myi rtog pa'i ye śes (9.1; 140b): 若 (read 不觀智)
---myi rtog myi sems (4.2; 137b): 无思无觀
---myi rtog myi bsam pa (5.1; 138b): 无觀无想
---myi brtag (21:4; 135a): 不觀
---myi bden pa'i 'du śes (1.1, 2.2, 4.4, 10.3, 21:2, 21:6; 134a, 135b, 138b, 142a, 135a, 138b): 妄想

---myi bden ba'i sems (8.3; 140a): 妄心
---myi 'byuṅ ṅo (8.2; 139a): 无有
---myi laṅ bar che'o (5.4; 138b): 不能
---myi len pa (4.2, 6.3; 137b, 138b): 不取・无取
---myi sems (4.2; 137b): no Chinese equivalent
---myi sems myi rtog pa (8.2; 140a): 不思不觀
---myi bsam (1.4, 21:4; 135a): 不思
---myi bsam bar yaṅ myi bsam (1.4, 21:4; 135a): 不思者亦不思
mye loṅ:
---mye loṅ dag pa (9.1; 140a): 鏡得明淨
smos su yaṅ myed (3.3; 136b): 不可説言
smyug rgyu ba (4.2; 137b): 陽炎
smra:
---smra bsam las 'das pa (3.2; 136b): 離言説

gtsaṅ:
---gtsaṅ ba daṅ myi gtsaṅ ba daṅ (2.1, 21:3; 135a): 淨不淨
tsam śe:
---tsam śe dag byas te (7.2; 139a): ?
brtsir:
---brtsir myi laṅ bar che'o (5.4; 138b): 數所不能

stsog:

---(Imaeda, following mss., reads lstsogs for la
   stsogs) passim

---cf. also tshog

tshags: read chags

tshig:

---tshig gi naṅ na myed (11.1; 142a): 不名　(read 不、
   在)言説之中

tshigs:

---tshigs bźi pa'i le'u (7.4; 139a): 四句偈

tshog (4.2; 137b): 一切

---(Imaeda's so tshog is the mss.' so chog, and should
   read so cog, stshog, or stsog) chos stshog la
   (1.1; 134a): 諸 法　(Cf. X.1)

tshor (I.1, Concile pp. 125, 158 and notes; Demiéville
   1961, p. 22)

---tshor na (2.3, 21.5; 135b): 不覺　(correct 不 to
   若)

---see also ma tshor

mtshan ma:

---mtshan ma myed pa (6.2; 138b): 无想　(read 相 ?)

'dzim pa (9.4; 141a): 執

gźan:

---gźan su las kyaṅ myi 'byuṅ (8.2; 139a): 无有···者
   ---

gźuṅ (3.2; 136b): ?? (10.2; 141a): 義

---chos kyi gźuṅ (5.1, 7.2; 138b, 139a): 法義

---gźuṅ ltar na (3.2; 136b): ?? 如

---gzun thos (5.4; 138b): 聞 --- 義

gźun (10.1; 141a): 宗　(7.2; 139a): 義

bźin (21.4-5; 135b): 隨

---bzin du spyad na: see 'du śes--and bsam--

gzuṅ
---gzuṅ du myed (10.2; 141a): 不立
bzaṅ:
---bzaṅ du brgyan pa: see brgyan
bzlogs:
---sgo drug bzolgs (pa): see sgo

'og du (7.1; 139a): 後

yaṅ dag pa:
---yaṅ dag pa'i bden ba (11.1; 142a): 真如
---yan dag pa'i raṅ bźin ye nas (8.3; 140a): 真性非

yid:
---yid ches pa (5.4; 138b): 敬信
yun:
---yun riṅ por (1.3; 134b): 久遠
yul:
---yul 'dzin (9.4; 141a): 執境
ye śes (8.3-4; 140a): 一切種智
yoṅs su:
---yoṅs su dag pa (4.2; 137b): 清淨
yod:
---yod pa daṅ myed pa daṅ (1.4, 21.3; 135a): 有無
yon tan (6.3, 9.2; 139a, 140b): 功德.
yon gsol (6.4; 139a): ???
g-yos (2.2; 135b): 起
---cf. 133b5: 想者心念起動
---g-yos te tshor na (2.2-3; 135b): 起若覺
---g-yos na (1.4, 21.3; 135a): 若動
---see also 'du śes g-yos na and ma g-yos

raṅ bźin (8.3; 140a): 性
---raṅ bźin myed (1.1; 134a): 無自性

---see yaṅ dag pa'i raṅ bźin
raṅ saṅs rgyas (passim): 緣覺
rin po che (7.1; 139a): 寶
la la źig (6.4; 139a): 或有
laṅ:
---see myi laṅ
len: see myi len pa
lus (7.4; 139a): 身
saṅs rgyas (passim): 佛
sems (2.3; 135b): 心 (but sems can also stand for
　　念 and 思)
---see rnam par rtog pa'i sems, myi rtog myi sems,
　　myi bden ba'i sems, myi sems and myi bsam(s)
---sems thaṅ re yaṅ....: see thaṅ re
---sems la blta(s) (Cf. I.7, notes 43, 58 to article,
　　9, 101 to translation; also, Concile pp. 43,
　　51-2, 78, 125, and 125 n.6; 158, Demiéville 1961,
　　pp. 26-7):
---sems la blta ste (1.4, 21.2; 135a): 看心
sems can (3.4, 9.1-2; 137b, 140b): 眾生
bsam:
---see also ma bsam, myi rtog myi bsam (pa), and
　　myi bsam
---bsam gyis myi khyab par (6.3, 9.2-3; ??, 140b): no
　　Chinese equivalent
---bsam du myed pa (10.1; 141a): 无思 (7.2; 139a):
　　no Chinese equivalent, see n. 115 to translation
---bsam ba (5.2; 138b): 思
---bsam bźin du spyad na (21.4-5; 135b): 隨思·作業
bsod nams (5.1, 7.2, 7.4, 8.2; 138b, 139a): 功德·福德

bslabs: see ma bslabs
lhun:
---lhun kyi(s) 'byuṅ ba (8.4; 140a): 自然顯現

NOTES

1. This paper was not presented at the conference that gave rise to the present volume. A less developed version was read at the first meeting of the International Association of Buddhist Studies at Columbia University in September of 1978.

It would take too much space to express my appreciation for the support and assistance that I have received since then from various friends and colleagues, but I do want to mention J. Broughton, G. Houston, Mimaki Katsumi, G. Schopen, and Tokiwa Gishin for several bibliographic references or copies of essential articles. I also wish to express my gratitude and admiration for those indefatigable Japanese scholars who have opened this field for modern research, especially to the following, who kindly have provided me with off-prints of some of their articles: Prof. Ueyama Daishun of Ryūkoku University, Prof. Okimoto Katsumi of Hanazono College, and Prof. Obata Hironobu of Ryūkoku University.

2. Eugène Obermiller, History of Buddhism (Chos-hbyung) by Buston, 2 vols., Heidelberg, 1931-32, Part II (1932) pp. 191-196. _Eugene Obermiller, "A Sanskrit Ms. from Tibet--Kamalaśila's Bhāvanā-krama," (Journal of the Greater India Society, II.1 (1935) pp. 1-11). However, the Third Bhāvanākrama could not have been Bu-ston's only source; he is evidently indebted to sources similar to those of the Sba bźed, or he must have known at least some of the pericopes from the work of Mo-ho-yen; see below, notes 5, 6 and 50.

3. Paul Demiéville, Le concile de Lhasa: une controverse sur le quiétisme entre bouddhistes de l'Inde et de la Chine au VIIIe siècle de l'ère chrétienne, Bibliothèque de l'Institut des Hautes Etudes Chinoises, VII; Paris: Imprimerie Nationale de France, 1952. No critical edition exists, as Demiéville's work contains the Chinese text only in the form of a photographic copy of the Tun-huang manuscript. However, his extensive and erudite commentary and scholarly apparatus serve the purposes of an edition. Demiéville analyzes another Chinese fragment of this text (Stein 2672) in "Deux documents de

Touen-houang sur le Dhyāna chinois," Essays on the History of Buddhism Presented to Professor Zenryū Tsukamoto, Kyoto, 1961, pp. 1-27; reprinted in Choix d'études bouddhiques par Paul Demiéville, Leiden: E. J. Brill, 1973, pp. 320-346.

A Tibetan fragment from Tun-huang, Pelliot 823, contains twelve pericopes that correspond exactly to as many passages from Pc. 4646. This fragment has been edited and analyzed by Imaeda Yoshiro, in "Documents tibétains de Touen-houang concernant le Concile de Tibet," Journal Asiatique, CCLXIII.1-2 (1975) 125-146.

The field of the history of Ch'an in Tibet has expanded rapidly since the publication of Demiéville's Concile. I shall not attempt to outline here the bibliography on this subject. The reader will find an almost exhaustive discussion by consulting the following: (a) Paul Demiéville, "L'introduction au Tibet du bouddhisme sinisé d'après les manuscrits de Touen-houang (Analyse de récents travaux japonais)," in M. Soynié, ed., Contributions aux études sur Touen-houang--Centre de Recherches d'Histoire et de Philologie de la IVe Section de l'École pratique des Hautes Études, II. Hautes Études Orientales, 10--Genève-Paris: Librarie Droz, 1979, pp. 1-16, (b) Ueyama Daishun, "The Study of Tibetan Manuscripts Recovered from Tun-huang: A Review of the Field and its Prospects," in Early Ch'an in China and Tibet, ed. Lewis Lancaster and Whalen Lai, Berkeley Buddhist Studies Series, No. 4, forthcoming, and (c) L. O. Gómez, "Indian Materials on the Doctrine of Sudden Enlightenment," in the same volume.

4. See my "Indian Materials on the Doctrine of Sudden Enlightenment." Six years have now elapsed since I wrote that paper, and my views have changed significantly since then. I am less sanguine than I was on the main thesis of that paper, though I would still defend it in a less strong formulation. I also feel now that the correspondences between the Cheng-li chüeh and the works of Kamalaśila are greater than I suggested at that time, and merit a closer scrutiny.

5. Compare the English translation in Obermiller, History, II, p. 193. My translation is from The Collected Works of Bu-ston, ed. Lokesh Chandra, New Delhi: International Academy of Indian Culture, 1971, Part 24 (Ya), fol. 888.3. This passage corresponds to the second of the two opponent's theses presented in the polemical section of Kamalaśila's Third Bhāvanākrama (Sanskrit text, ed. by G. Tucci, in

Minor Buddhist Texts. Part III: Third Bhāvanākrama,
Serie Orientale Roma, XLIII; Rome: IsMEO, 1971;
henceforth IIIBhK), pp. 20-29. The passage in IIIBhK
has not been identified or marked properly by
Obermiller and Tucci. The same issues, though less
obviously marked, occur in several works of
Kamalaśīla, including, of course, the First and Second
Bhāvanākramas--see, L. O. Gómez, op. cit., especially
notes 10-11 and 24, also "Último tratado del cultivo
graduado," VIII.23 (1972) 85-137, and "Primer tratado
del cultivo graduado (Parte I)," Diálogos, XI.29-30
(1977) 177-224, and Parte II, forthcoming Diálogos,
XVII (1983).

It would be a mistake, however, to assume that
this summary of Mo-ho-yen's views is derived from the
IIIBhK. Here Bu-ston is evidently working on the
basis of a source very close to the extant version of
the Sba bźed. This and the following summary of Mo-
ho-yen's main doctrinal theses find close parallels in
the Sba bźed (R. A. Stein, Une chronique ancienne de
bSam-yas: sBa bźed, Publications de l'Institut des
Hautes Études Chinoises, Textes et Documents, 1,
Paris, 1961, ff. 57.16-58.7). Bu-ston's version seems
more rational than the rather confused passage of the
Sba-bźed, and may reflect an attempt to adapt the
traditional account of Mo-ho-yen's position to the
structure of the arguments in the IIIBhK.

This and the following of Bu-ston's summaries of
Mo-ho-yen's main doctrinal theses are extracted from
the Sba bźed (R. A. Stein, Une chronique ancienne de
bSam-yas: sBa bzed, Paris, 1961, ff. 57.16-58.7). It
may be useful to quote and translate the passage in
full (numbers identify the two topics into which Bu-
ston has divided the rather confused passage of the
Sba bźed):

thams cad sems kyis rnam par rtogs pas bskyed pa
/ dga' mi dga'i dbaṅ gis /

(1a)--las dge mi dges mtho ris daṅ naṅ soṅ gi
'bras bu myoṅ ziṅ 'khor ba na 'khor te-- /

(2a)--gaṅ źig ci la 'aṅ mi sems ci yaṅ yid la mi
byed pa de 'khor ba las yons su thar bar 'gyur ro / de
lta bas na ci yaṅ mi bsam mo-- / sbyin pa la sogs pa'i
chos bcu spyod pa ni / skye bo dge ba'i 'phro med pa
blo źan pa dbaṅ po stul ba rnams bstan pa yin / snon
blo sbyans pa (rnon po) dbaṅ po dag la /

(1b)--sprin dkar nag gan gis ni ma sgrib pa ltar
dge sdig gñis kas sgrib pas-- /

(2b)--ci yaṅ mi sems mi rtog / mi spyod pa ni mi
dmigs pa'o // gcig car 'jug pa ni sa bcu pa dan
'dra'o--gsuṅs....

"Everything is constructed by the conceptualization mind. Through the power of [our idea of] the pleasant and the unpleasant, (1a) there is karma, good and bad. One experiences its fruit in the heavens and the evil destinies, and one wanders in transmigration. (2a) Whoever does not reflect, whoever does not fix the mind on anything, will be completely liberated from transmigration. Therefore, do not reflect on anything.

"As to the practice of the ten [good] dharmas-- generosity and the rest--it has been preached for those persons who are of inconstant virtue, weak minds, and dull faculties. For those who already have purified their minds and have acute faculties, (1b) sin and virtue alike veil [the mind], just as clouds, whether they are white or dark, veil the sun. (2b) Consequently, they do not reflect on or examine anything, they do not practice anything, and do not apprehend anything. [This] immediate access is equal to the tenth stage (bhūmi)."

6. Op. cit., fol. 888.3-4, corresponding to IIIBhK pp. 13-20; see n. 5 supra.

7. Ueyama Daishun, "Donkō to Tonkō bukkyōgaku," Tōhōgakuhō, XXXV (1964), 141-214, and W. Pachow, "A Study of the Twenty-two Dialogues on Mahayana Buddhism," The Chinese Culture, XX.1 (Taipei, 1979)-- unfortunately I possess what appears to be a reprint (no place or date) of this study, and the pagination is not that of the journal article.

8. Analysis of Pelliot 116 in Okimoto Katsumi, "bSam-yas no shūron (1)--Pelliot 116 ni tsuite," Nihon Chibetto Gakkai Kaihō, 21 (1975) 5-8, following Ueyama Daishun, "Tonkō shutsudo chibettobun zen shiryō no kenkyū--P. tib. 116 to sono mondaiten," Bukkyō Bungaku Kenkyūjo Kiyō, 13 (1974) 1-11. Analysis of its connection to the Cig-car of Vimalamitra, by Harada Satoru, "bSam-yas no shūron igo ni okeru ton-mon-pa no ronsho," Nihon Chibetto Gakkai Kaihō, 22 (1976) 8-10.

The Cig-car is found in the Tanjur as no. 5306, vol. 102 of the Japanese reprint of the Peking version. Its full title there is Cig-car 'jug-pa rnam-par mi-rtog-pa'i bsgom don.

Also see Gómez, "Indian Materials," and "La doctrina subitista, de Vimalamitra," forthcoming in Estudios de Asia y África del Norte. The latter paper is in part a response to Harada's study, and reaches the following conclusions (quoting verbatim the English Summary at the end of the paper): "The

present paper argues against Harada Satoru's thesis
that the Cig-car 'jug-pa'i rnam-par mi-rtog-pa'i bsgom
don, attributed by the Tanjur to Vimalamitra is not a
treatise of the Sudden Enlightenment School, and
possibly not by Vimalamitra. It is proposed that we
take all Bhāvanākrama passages in the Cig-car as
interpolations, and not as instances of plagiarism or
concessions to the gradualists. It is also proposed
that, although the parallels from Pelliot 116 found in
the Cig-car are of obvious significance, it is still
too early to evaluate them."

9. I prefer "the Tibetan controversies of the
eighth century" as the most accurate description of
the historical realities behind these texts. In the
past I have exaggerated, however, the poor correspondence between the Cheng-li chüeh and the BhK. My
statements to that effect in "Indian Materials..."
should be qualified with a discussion of passages such
as....

10. "Tonkō shutsudo chibettobun Mahaen Zenji
ibun" in Indogaku Bukkyōgaku Kenkyū, XIX.2 (1971) 123-
126. These fragments were first brought to the
attention of Western scholars by Demiéville in a long
note on pp. 14-17 of Concile. The first pioneer in
this field, however, was Marcelle Lalou, who assisted
Demiéville in the preparation of this note, and
described the fragments cursorily, but accurately, in
her catalogue of the Pelliot collection--Inventaire
des manuscrits tibétaines de Touen-houang conservés à
la Bibliothèque Nationale (Fonds Pelliot tibétain),
Tome I, Paris: Adrien Maisonneuve, 1939, Tome II,
Paris: Bibliothèque Nationale, 1951, Tome III, Paris:
Bibliothèque Nationale, 1961. It was Lalou also who
first published and analyzed a Tibetan Ch'an text--
"Document tibétain sur l'expansion du dhyāna chinois,"
Journal Asiatique, CCXXXI (1939) 505-523.

11. Pelliot 117 verso ff. 5.1-7.5. The title of
the work is given in this fragment as "Mkhan-po Ma-ha-
yan-gyi Bsam-b(r)tan chig-car 'jug-pa'i sgo dan bsad
pa'i mdo,'" which Démieville (Concile, p. 14) recon-
structs in Chinese as shih tun-ju-men ch'an ching.
Okimoto Katsumi suggests: tun-ju ch'an-men ching, in
"Makaen no shiso," Hanazono Daigaku Kenkyūkiyō, 8
(1977) p. 15. In Stein 468 the work is titled "Mkhan-
po Ma-ha-yan-gi Bsam-gtan cig-car 'jug-pa'i sgo."
Only these two fragments give us a title. I have used
the shorter name as the standard title throughout this
paper. For the author I prefer the Chinese version of

his name. The earliest analysis of some (Pelliot 116, 117, 812, and 813) of these fragments is, of course, from the erudite pen of Demiéville--Concile pp. 14-17 note. For a synoptic view of the various fragments and their relationship, see the chart presented as Appendix I to this paper.

12. The method of no method. The word fang-pien is rendered in this paper by "approach" or "means of approach."   For the meaning of this term Demiéville suggests upāya, prayoga, and paryāya (Concile, pp. 17, note, 82, note, and pp. 85 and 357).   As will become obvious in the passages translated in the appendix to this paper, Mo-ho-yen's use of the term is not as far removed from Indian usage as is the meaning given to it in the Northern School of Ch'an. Both Demiéville (loc. cit.) and Takasaki Jikidō ("Some Problems of the Tibetan Translations from Chinese Materials," L. Ligeti, ed. Proceedings of the Csoma de Körös Memorial Symposium, (Bibliotheca Orientalis Hungarica, 23), Budapest: Akadémiai Kiadó, 1978, pp. 459-67) have observed that fang-pien can translate terms such as yoga and prayoga, but they have not noted the fact that one of the meanings of upāya is precisely the "methods and practices" that lead to enlightenment (see, for instance, the passage from Bodhisattvabhūmi analyzed by E. Lamotte in his translation of the Vimalakīrti, pp. 116-117, n. 68 (L'enseignement de Vimalakīrti, (Bibliothèque du Muséon, 51), Louvain: Publications Universitaires--Institut Orientaliste, 1962).

13. Mark Tatz, "T'ang Dynasty Influences on the Early Spread of Buddhism in Tibet," The Tibet Journal, III.2 (1978) 3-32.

14. Okimoto Katsumi, "bSam-yas no shuron (3)-- nishū no Mahaen ibun," Nihon Chibetto Gakkai Kaiho, 23 (1977) 5-8.

15. Strictly speaking there is no basis for claiming conclusively that rnam par rtog pa'i sems stand in the works of Mo-ho-yen for any Sanskrit term (cf., e.g., Demiéville, Concile, p. 22, 127 n.1, 128- 135). In light of the equivalences in Pelliot 823 and Pc. 4646, one can ascertain that the Chinese original must have been either wang-hsin or wang-hsiang, both standard equivalents for the Sanskrit term. Insofar as possible, I have tried to base my interpretation on equivalences such as these--see notes and vocabulary to the translations in Appendix II.

16. See note 14 above.

17. Kimura Ryūtoku, "Tonko shutsudo chibetto-bun shahon Stein 709," Nihon Chibetto Gakkai Kaihō, 22 (1976) 11-13.

18. Cf. Bu-ston's summary of the "debate," above, notes 11 and 12.

19. Okimoto, "bSam-yas no shūron (3)," argues on the basis of the calligraphic and material similarity of the manuscripts (p. 7, column b). The leaves are approximately identical in size (26 x 8.7 cm. for Stein 468, and 26 x 9 cm. for 709). Both manuscripts are written in the same hand.

20. Kimura, op. cit.

21. Op. cit., p. 7, column a.

22. Gnubs-chen Saṅs-rgyas-ye-śes, Rnal-'byor mig-gi bsam-gtan or Bsam-gtan mig-sgron, (Smanrtsis Shesrig Spendzod, 74--Leh, Ladakh: S. W. Tashigangpa, 1974), ff. 145.5-146.4. This work is also known under the following two variant titles: Rdzogs-chen-gyi man-ṅag bsam-gtan mig-sgron and Sgom-gyi gnad-gsal-bar phye-ba bsam-gtan mig-sgron. Japanese and Western scholars prefer the shorter title Bsam-gtan mig sgron, sometimes abbreviated SMG. Below we have used the shorter title or the abbreviation Bsmi.

23. This is either a general term for works such as the "Gate" ("sayings on mental cultivation"), or a variant title for the work. In the latter case lun would be a different translation for the original of mdo, and bsgom for bsam gtan. The latter seems unlikely to me.

24. Bśad-pa'i mdo in Pelliot 116 suggests to me that bśad-do in Pelliot 117 is a mistake for bśad-mdo. Note also the title of The Gate in Pelliot 117: -sgo daṅ bśad-pa'i mdo (daṅ perhaps for par).

25. The similarities between the actual and the hypothetical folia numbers of Pelliot 117 are purely accidental, the mss. being materially and contextually different.

26. Concile, p. 17. This passage may be by 'Gal-yan.

27. Cf. Ueyama, "Tonkō shutsudo chibetto-bun Makaen Zenji ibun."

28. Rnam-par myi-rtog-pa'i gźuṅ, reading the last word in the title as synonymous with gsun or lun (Chinese: lun). Cf. the Brda-dag miṅ-tshig gsal-ba of Dge-bses Chos-kyi Grags-pa (rev. ed., Peking: 1957), sub voce. But it is possible to see in this word an equivalent for Chinese yi--see Okimoto in "Makaen," p. 15, and translation notes 112 and 119.

29. Okimoto Katsumi, "bSam-yas no shūron (3)," pp. 5-6.

30. Op. cit.

31. Chapter Thirteen, "The Ston-mun-pa." I have used the edition of the relevant sections in Tucci, Minor Buddhist Texts, Part II, pp. 68-81. There is a very rough, and often misleading translation in pp. 81-101.

32. Tucci, pp. 79-80. Studied by Okimoto in "Chibetto-yaku Ninyū Shigyō ron ni tsuite," Indogaku Bukkyōgaku Kenkyū, 24.2 (1976) 992-999. John Jorgensen's study of the "Long Scroll"--The Earliest Text of Ch'an Buddhism: the Long Scroll, M.A. Thesis, Australian National University--which has been unavailable to me, presumably deals with this text.

33. Tucci, p. 74.

34. Tucci, p. 77. Okimoto Katsumi in his "Makaen no shisō," p. 17, accepts the attribution of this passage on the basis of what he considers corre- spondences with Stein 468, but the only parallel is in the fact that both passages describe the method of tso-ch'an, and many texts relating to the Tibetan controversies--including the Bhāvanākramas--have very similar descriptions. In fact, it is only on the physical posture of dhyāna that all of these texts seem to agree.

35. I have also omitted from all consideration four other fragments relevant to the study of the ideas of Mo-ho-yen, but belonging to a different genre. These are Pelliot 121, 699 and 827, and Stein 689. Part of Pelliot 121 (ff. 36-40) seems to be traceable to Mo-ho-yen and his circle. Stein 689 is a fragment of Pelliot 121, and Pelliot 699 a complete commentary of the same work. These materials seem to

be of some importance, unfortunately, I still have not
been able to secure photographic copies of the manuscript fragments. Cf. Okimoto, "Mahaen no shisō," p.
17, and "Tonkō shutsudo...(1)," p. 461, and Kimura
Ryūtoku, "Le dhyāna chinois au Tibet ancien après
Mahāyāna," Journal Asiatique, CCLXIX (1981), pp. 190-
91. Also, cf. the corresponding entries in the catalogues of Lalou (cited above, n. 10) and Louis de la
Vallée Poussin--Catalogue of the Tibetan Manuscripts
from Tun-huang in the India Office Library, London:
Oxford University Press, 1962.

36. Okimoto, "Mahaen no shisō," p. 16, suggests
this identification.

37. Ueyama, in "Tonkō shutsudo," p. 123 suggests: "shuo ch'an hsin sui."

38. Okimoto, loc. cit., Harada, op. cit.

39. Okimoto, loc. cit., lists lun (sic), mdo as
possible titles, but does not seem to distinguish lun
from lon.

40. Bu-ston, ff. 887.6 (p. 192 in Obermiller)
mentions five works as Mo-ho-yen's. His list can be
traced to earlier sources, such as Sa-paṇ's Skyes-bu
dam-pa rnams-la spriṅs-ba'i yi-ge--see Samten G.
Karmay, "A Discussion on the Doctrinal Position of
rDzogs-chen from the 10th to the 13th Centuries,"
Journal Asiatique CCLXIII.1-2 (1975) pp. 152-54. The
five titles are: (1) Bsam-gtan ñal-ba'i khor-lo, (2)
Bsam-gtan-gyi lon, (3) yaṅ lon (Is it simply "another
lon," or another Bsam-gtan-gyi lon?), (4) Lta-ba'i
rgyab śa, (5) Mdo-sde brgyad cu khuṅs.
Obermiller attempts to interpret these titles as
Sanskrit terms (cf. Karmay pp. 153-54). The same
mistake is made by G. W. Houston in his Sources for a
History of the Bsam Yas Debate, Ph.D. thesis, Indiana
University Uralic-Altaic Department, 1976.
Similar lists occur in the Mkhas-pa'i dga'-ston
and the New Red Annals--respectively, Mkhas-pa'i dga'-
ston of Dpa'-bo-gtsug-lag, ed. Lokesh Chandra, New
Delhi, 1962, Part 4 (Ja), f. 116a, and as Deb T'er
Dmar Po Gsar Ma: Tibetan Chronicles by bSod nams
grags pa, ed. G. Tucci, Vol. I, Serie Orientale Roma
XXIV, Rome, 1971, f. 27, translation p. 155.
Only (2) and (3) could represent one of the works
we have identified above (perhaps The Gate). As to
the rest, Kimura, in "Le dhyāna chinois..." pp. 185-
186, has shown that (5) is not one of Mo-ho-yen's

works. Also, in the light of Karmay's "A Discussion..." p. 153, title (1) probably should be attributed to a different author. As observed also by Karmay loc. cit., Pelliot 117 recto, folia 1-6, ends (623-4) with the colophon "Bsam-brtan-gyi lon rdzogs so"--however, this is no reason for assuming that the fragment is by Mo-ho-yen.

41. On Mo-ho-yen's affiliations see the survey of the literature by Demiéville in "L'introduction au Tibet..." (supra n. 4), and the article by Broughton in this same volume.

42. The following is a paraphrase of paragraphs I.1, X.1 and XI.4 in Appendix II. Throughout this section references are made to the translations in Appendix II by a Roman numeral (sometimes followed by an Arabic numeral), and to the Cheng-li chüeh by only an Arabic numeral (often followed by the letters "a" or "b" to indicate recto and verso).

43. A number of terms in this summary present major translation problems--see notes 12, 15, and 46. The Tibetan-Chinese equivalents for these terms are available to us in Pelliot 21 and 823 (see translation X.2, and XI.4 and 12, and cf. Cheng-li chüeh 134a): (a) myi bden pa'i 'du śes--clearly synonymous with the myi bden pa'i sems and ma rig pa'i sems of IV.1 ff.-- stands for wang-hsin which can be considered an approximate equivalent of vikalpa, but which evidently overlaps with nimitta and mithya-samjñā or the like. The occasional expansion of the term in Chinese (e.g., 134a) with the addition of two characters--into wang-hsiang fen-pieh--is primarily an attempt to focus the meaning of the term, as suggested by Demiéville, Concile p. 76 n. 5: "...ce double composé ne doit répresenter, en fait, qu'une ideé unique...," but it may also be a way of indicating the mental activity as distinguished from the object or result of discrimination. (Cf. op. cit. p. 132 n. 5) (b) ma blaṅs and ma chags are quite straightforward and represent concepts shared by all Buddhists. Although it would be difficult, if not impossible, to reconstruct Sanskrit equivalents, the concepts themselves would present no difficulty to the gradualist were it not for the way they are applied in the context of meditation--for ma bslabs and ma chags are meant to define myi sems (or myi bsam(s)) and myi rtogs, respectively. (c) myi sems (pu-ssu) myi rtog (pu-kuan) can only stand for concepts such as vitarka and vicāra--respectively, "to consider, to bring to mind" and "to look into, to

examine." They could correspond to smrti and manasikāra only in a very general sense. (Cf. Concile pp. 78-9 n. 3, and "Indian Materials..." n. 7,8.) (d) tshor ba, which translates vedanā in the classical terminology after the Mahāvyutpatti, stands in the fragments of Mo-ho-yen for chüeh. The concept is implicitly defined in Cheng-li chüeh 147a-b:

> Question: From which sutra text [do you derive the idea of] looking into the mind, and becoming aware of false notions when these arise?
> Reply: In Section 18 of the Nirvāna Sutra it is said: "What do we call Buddha? We call Buddha one who is aware (or awake), that is to say, one who awakens himself, as well as being able to awaken others. ...it is like someone who becomes aware that there is a thief, the thief then cannot [enter his home]. The Bodhisattva Mahāsattva is able to become aware of all the innumerable per-turbations (kleśa), the moment he is fully aware of them, there is nothing that these can do to him...." This is why if one looks into the mind while sitting in meditation, and every time that false conceptualizations and thoughts arise he becomes aware of them and [does not] hold onto or abide in them, and does not act according to the perturba-tions, then this is called liberation in each thought [moment].

Note that in this passage the Sūtra and Mo-ho-yen both play on the ambiguity of the term chüeh ("under-stand," "realize," but also "wake up"). Thus, he wakes up and realizes that there is a thief in the house, etc. (Cf. Translation IV.5 and IX.2.)

44. On the sources and the reading of these two sentences, see notes 6, 7, and 8 in Concile, p. 76.

45. Tibetan parallel below, XI.2.

46. We have chosen to translate kuan and pu-kuan at face value, although the former's Tibetan equiva-lent (rtog) and the contexts of its usage in the gradualist's arguments in the Cheng-li chüeh would indicate that it stands for vikalpa. Whereas whenever the gradualist speaks of pu-kuan as the ultimate end of the practice (e.g., in 132b--cf. 135a) we can sur-mise that this refers to nirvikalpa. When the context

is the proper method, pu-kuan must stand for a denial
of pratyaveksana (kuan-ch'a in 148a). (Cf. the notes
in Concile 73, 79, 81, 97, and 130.)   Since Sanskrit
has two words for what Chinese expresses with only
one, it seems reasonable to assume that--in spite of
the obvious overlap which made the dispute possible--
the terms do not correspond fully.   This terminolog-
ical ambiguity was no doubt an important contributing
factor--if not a major cause--for the controversy.
See my "Indian Materials..." n. 6.

47.   Tibetan parallels below, I.4, X.2.

48.   Demiéville, "Deux documents...," p. 12.

49.   See Cheng-li chüeh 132b-133a, and Concile
pp. 72-74, 130-140.

50.   Compare the use of the Vimalakirti in this
same connection in the BhK--this is another example of
an implicit dialogue between the Cheng-li chüeh and
the BhK.

51.   Concile pp. 91 n. 1, 109 n. 5, and 127 n. 1.

52.   More literally, "persons of sharp faculties
do not discuss whether they are necessary or not."   In
Concile p. 86, Demiéville translates, "pour ceux qui
ont des facultés aiguës, la question de leu nécessité
ou de leur non-nécessité ne se pose pas," and in p.
87, "pour ceux dont les facultés sont aiguës, la
question de nécessité ou de non-nécessité ne se
discute pas."   Evidently the passage means that "need"
is applicable only in the sphere of the relative.   One
should compare, however, the Tibetan rendering in
Appendix II, XI.5, for what appears to be a different
understanding.

53.   "Pu-k'e-te" corresponding to Sanskrit anupa-
labhya, or the like; that is, they cannot be found
anywhere, they cannot be obtained or attained.

54.   Concile 157 n. 3; cf. 76-77.

55.   Cf. Concile 87 n. 3 and 158 n. 13.   In the
first of these notes Demiéville assumes that the
"inner perfection" of Mo-ho-yen is "définie justement
comme celle du Petit Véhicule, 'utile à soi.'"   If
this were the case then the passage would contradict
Cheng-li chüeh 156a (Concile 158) where it is said
that the precepts and perfections of the bodhisattvas

are internal(ized) virtues. Demiéville sees such a contradiction ("les épithètes sont inversées"). I suspect, however, that Mo-ho-yen's distinction of internal and external is less scholastic than it seems, and the categories more inclusive than the terms chosen by Demiéville as a key to understanding the concept. Mo-ho-yen may be accused of using the terms loosely, but there is no contradiction: the selfcentered practices of the śrāvakas are "external," though they benefit only oneself, and the altruistic practices of the bodhisattva are also "external" (that is, "mere externals") if they lack in wisdom.

56. Cf. the discussion in Okimoto, "Makaen."

57. The physical aspects of sitting in meditation are among the few elements shared by both gradualists and suddenists. In this emphasis Mo-ho-yen differs from the Southern School.
For the critique of ts'o-ch'an in the Southern School see: T'an-ching section 19 in P. Yampolsky, The Platform Sutra of the Sixth Patriarch, New York and London: Columbia University Press, 1967, also pp. 117, 135-36, 140-81 of the same; for Shen-hui see Hu Shih, Shen-hui ho-shang yi-tsi, Shanghai: Oriental Book Co., pp. 97-98, 116-17, 134, 175-77; and the Vajrasamādhi, Taisho 273, vol. IX, 368a.

58. These are not the "five upāya" of the Northern School, and Mo-ho-yen may be purposefully separating himself from that tradition. Notice also his use of k'an instead of kuan to describe the process by means of which one becomes aware of the mind. See n. 9 to translation, I.3.

NOTES TO APPENDIX II

1. Since my discussion of this fragment and its translation was presented at the IABS meeting, I have been apprised of the publication of a translation of this fragment, Stein 468. It was an edition and translation of the fragment by my friend Gary W. Houston, published in the Central Asiatic Journal, XXI.2--special volume, In Honor of the 65th Birthday of Prof. Helmuth Hoffman (ed. by G. W. Houston, Wiesbaden, 1977). Houston's work, however, does not take into account the fact that the fragment is a translation from the Chinese, not from the Sanskrit, nor does it place the fragment in the context of other fragments attributed to Mo-ho-yen. Houston also does not seem to be aware of Japanese scholarship on the subject.

2. Fundamental statement of Mo-ho-yen's position as represented in the III BhK pp. 13-14, 15 ff.; cf. translation XI.2-4 and Cheng-li chüeh 134a-135b, etc.

3. In spite of my general agreement with Demiéville's interpretation of wang-hsiang fen-pieh (see note 43 to article, above), there is no doubt in my mind that this or a similar term is being translated by the rnam-par rtog-pa'i sems of our fragment, and is to be distinguished, strictly speaking, from sems (I.4, etc.) and 'du śes or myi bden 'du śes (I.7 and IV passim, respectively), though ultimately--in terms of the practice of meditation and the theory of liberation--"discrimination," "thoughts," "conceptualizations" are synonymous.

4. Thog ma myed pa'i bag chags kyi rgyu las: more literally, "from a torrent of habitual energies without beginning." The bag chags are, of course, the vasanā of Indian tradition.

5. Literally: "as they arise so does one perceive, as one perceives so does one act, as one acts so are the fruits produced." It is not clear here that what arises are thoughts and not the habitual tendencies, but what follows and the parallel passages quoted in n. 2 above confirm our interpretation.

6. Chos rdul tsam yaṅ thob par ruṅ ba myed do: "atom" is not to be taken here technically, the expression follows the Chinese (see glossary), and the

object of comparison comes closer to a fine, minute particle of dust than to an atom.

7. The whole paragraph is found, verbatim, in Bsmi 145.5-6, and said there to be from "Ma-ha-yan-gyi Bsgom-lun," which suggests, once more, that the expressions lun and mdo (bsad mdo)--and possibly lon- -are used interchangeably as equivalents to ching or, preferably, lun.

8. Verbatim in Bsmi 145.6-146.1; cf. also Pelliot 21 (VIII.2a).

9. "Contemplation" will be our standard equiv- alent for bsam-gtan (dhyāna, ch'an) throughout this translation. Its limitations notwithstanding I find it preferable to "trance" (too "psychic") and "medita- tion" (too discursive) in the context of Ch'an. In Mo-ho-yen's method, dhyāna seems to entail basically a looking into the mind (k'an-hsin), which he evidently calls "k'an" and not "kuan" to distinguish it in at least two respects from what he considers to be his opponents' view (Northern Ch'an or Kamalaśila, or both). First, this is looking directly into the mind, not inspecting, examining, or analyzing thoughts Second, it is a mere being aware of thoughts and not an absorption into the mind's substance or ground.

10. This point continues from the previous sentence the implicit critique of those who believe that dhyāna reveals the mind substance. I see in the sems dpa' of Stein 468 a mistake for sems pa (as in Bsmi 146.1), lit. "the thinking one," the subject. Notice that in spite of his position Mo-ho-yen does not seem to be aware of, or at least to favor expres- sions such as wu-nien, and li-nien.

11. The same in Bsmi 146.1-3; cf. Pelliot 21 (VIII.2b). Also Chen-li 135a (Concile 78-80), Pelliot 823 (XI.3).

12. Myi brtag: cf. Cheng-li 135a and Pelliot 823:2.1, myi bsams. Regarding the concept of the "arising" ("stirring" or "arousal") of conceptual thought it should be noted that Tibetan has one word (g-yo ba) where Chinese has two--see glossary, and Shen-hui p. 119 (cf. 117, 149, 193 for the concept of tung so central to Chinese Buddhism and Taoism--as in the T'an-ching (section 48), and in the apocryphal Śurangama Sutra). See also the discussion of no- thought in T'an-ching section 17-19.

13. Free rendering for ñon moṅs pa daṅ rnam par byaṅ bar, which in Tibetan stands for kleśa-vyavadāna but here probably represents a simple Chinese ching pu-ching as in Cheng-li chüeh 135a.3.

14. Lit., "he does not examine all dharmas in any manner whatsoever" (ci lta bur yaṅ).

15. Parallel with minor variants in Bsmi 146.3.

16. Stein 468: raṅ bzin myed pa. Bsmi: raṅ med.

17. Cf. trans. IV.2. Here, as in IV, Mo-ho-yen recognizes the fact that there are varying qualities of experience; there is no reason why one should assume that this concession to the gradualist entails stages of progress, or aspects in ultimate reality.

18. Don ma yin pa--problematic. The proper expression for "pointless" or "in vain" should be don med; for an inexistent or unreal object, ma yin pa'i don (more commonly yan dag pa ma yin pa'i don). I am inclined to the latter rendering, though I cannot guess what the underlying Chinese was.

19. It seems that I.6 and I.7, like IV, are trying to introduce specific circumstances or conditions which in practice may require special caution or methodology, but it is not clear that this is the purport of these passages.

20. Perhaps here, in considering the difference between I.7 and I.8, one can speak of degrees of realization.

21. With this somewhat forced metaphor Mo-ho-yen seems to reiterate the implicit arguments outlined above (n. 10) by indicating that awareness of passing thoughts is just that, without any implication of an unmoving reality behind or beyond the thoughts. See also n. 78 below.

22. Perhaps the gnas is a clumsy rendering of suo, in which case the meaning is "awareness and its object (that is, that of which one is aware)." Btsal du myi rñed ciṅ is literally, "not found in searching [for it]"--a standard Buddhist and Ch'an expression, in other grammatical garb.

23. Bsam gyis myi khyab pas myi bsam ste:
perhaps "the inconceivable does not carry out
reflection" would be grammatically more correct, but I
suspect the meaning is more like "in" or "with" (the
suffix -s for yü ?) "the inconceivable one does not
reflect." On the "inconceivable" see n. 28 below.

24. Lit., "Not clinging even to not thinking (or
"to the one who does not think") is"...with the rest
supplied on the assumption that the sentence does not
end here but continues into a folio now lost.

25. The last sentence of this first paragraph is
found verbatim in Bsmi 146.3-4.

26. My translation of upāya (thabs) attempts to
combine the non-Indian shades of fang-pien, as well as
the standard Indian concept of upāya as means for
one's own advancement in the path (see n. 12 to
article). Insofar as the means are special strategies
or methods, they stand between the person and his or
her realization of the non-dual, inconceivable truth.
As long as the method is in operation, its object
cannot be realized. [Upāya is a form of vikalpa
(Cheng-li chüch 147b).] Again, Mo-ho-yen assumes here
a characteristic stance. However, he makes concessions in IV, etc. Cf. Shen-hui 111, 121, 127, and
150-152.

27. A hint that some provision must be made for
those who have not yet attained sudden realization.

28. Myi sems par 'dug pa: perhaps better to be
interpreted as "to sit without thinking." Three types
of terms for no-mind cannot be taken to be synonymous.
As pointed out above, pu-ssu and pu-kuan are Mo-
ho-yen's terms. In the Vajrasamādhi and the T'an-
ching, it is wu-nien or wu-hsin--cf. also the Wu-hsin
lun attributed to Bodhidharma. The Northern School,
on the other hand, speaks primarily of li-nien.
However, Demiéville, Concile 14-15, has suggested that
terms such as bsam gyis myi kyhab pa (as above n. 23,
and in Pelliot 812 and 117, translated in III.1) are
really clumsy ("maladroite") translations of Chinese
expressions such as wu-hsin. Yet the Chinese fragments speak only of wu-ssu, seemingly unaware of or
ignoring the concept of wu-nien and wu-hsin. Also,
see the concept of the inconceivable in Shen-hui 100
and 131.

29. Our standard rendering for mu-stegs (tīrthika), following the Chinese wai-tao and recognizing the inapplicability of the more common "heretic."

30. Gźi bdag du lta ba.

31. Conjectural translation. Also, "preconceptions" translates here 'du śes, which may mean not only their particular form of pet conceptions but conceptions in general.

32. Conjectural translation.

33. Pelliot 812:8a3-4, 813:8a2. Only the last phrase ("bsam gyis myi khyab par gźag go") in Pelliot 117:5b1. On the "inconceivable" or "unthinkable," see n. 23 and 28 above.

34. Pelliot 117:5b1-2 only.

35. This passage is found almost in its entirety in each of the three mss. Only Pelliot 813 is missing part of the last of the five upayas. Bsmi 164.6-165.1, Pelliot 117: verso ff. 5.3-6.4, 812: recto 8.5-10.1, 813:8a2-b2.

36. From this one must surmise that, appearances to the contrary, what follows are a series of methods and hints to be used in the practice of meditation by those who fail to enter the absolute directly.

37. I am at a loss as to what heading to give to this passage (see n. 40).

38. This first phrase in Pelliot 117 only.

39. Note ma rig pa as the Bsmi equivalent of the myi bden pa of the Tun-huang fragments. In spite of these phrases it is evident that for Mo-ho-yen every thought is a deluded one. See, e.g., Cheng-li chüeh 134a, and 134b (= XI.2). Cf. Shen-hui 118, 121, 127-29 and 132.

40. Luṅ du mi ston normally vyākarana or "prediction of enlightenment," but I take it here to be closer to samyaktvaniyāma in the sense of "assured enlightenment." This passage baffles me. Either we assume that he means to say that the first encounter with "awareness" (still "a mind" in opposition to "no-mind") is not true ("assured," "recognized" or "full")

enlightenment, or simply that Mo-ho-yen does not guarantee or certify any kind of practice (as in Cheng-li chüeh 150b ?), or, better, that enlightenment and its assurance come only after all practices are abandoned (op. cit. 135ab). Mo-ho-yen's views on this point are rather obscure. Cf. Cheng-li chüeh 143b, 150b, Concile 64-5, 81, 114, 143, 145-6.

41. This tends to confirm the first of the alternatives suggested in n. 40.

42. Sems can phyal ba (or phal): prthagjana (?) --elsewhere it is myi tha mal; e.g., I.1).

43. The Bsmi version makes it clear that this is "cessation" in a "hīnayāna" sense.

44. This line presents a number of interesting features: seeing that there is no substance in mind (ran med), one achieves samadhi (źi ba phyogs gcig), and "comes close to emptiness" (stoṅ pa bgal nal: presumably a first insight).

45. See n. 43 to article; also cf. translation IX.2, and Cheng-li chüeh 135b, 147ab, and 156a. On liberation of every instant of thought see Demiéville and his references to the T'an-ching in Concile 82, 125 and 158.

46. Found only in Bsmi 165.4-5, but evidently must follow the preceding without interruption.

47. My rendering of the obscure mi bcos par gyi na. The same concept recurs below in VI.8, see n. 70.

48. The first eight syllables of this leaf complete a sentence from the previous folio (6b), now lost. I have not been able to reconstruct the sentence or make much meaning of the remaining syllables: "...kyi rgyur myi stsogs pa ma yin kis/..."

49. Yid la myi bya ba: amanasikāra, a term missing in the Cheng-li chüeh but common in Shen-hui (pp. 118, etc.)--see my "Indian Materials...."

50. Lit., "the practice of the six perfections."

51. Therefore, the issue of the "adventitious kleśas" is irrelevant (Demiéville, Concile 108 n. 1 to the contrary--cf. his n. 1 p. 95). I have discussed

elsewhere ("Purifying Gold..." in the forthcoming
second volume of this series) the metaphors chosen by
Mo-ho-yen to illustrate his point. Suffice it to say
that the idea is that any vikalpa is an obscuration.
This will become transparent to anyone who reads this
passage from Stein 709--which, by the way, must be the
original source for Bu-ston's paraphrase of the position of Mo-ho-yen (see n. 5 to article).

52. See analysis in the main body of the
article.

53. 'jig rten las 'das pa'i mchog go clearly
stands for the ch'u-shih-chien shang-shang of Cheng-li
chüeh 138a.

54. Myi dmyigs pa which stands for the technical
Sanskrit anupalambhya, and the less technical, but
equally consecrated Chinese (especially Ch'an) term
pu-k'e te.

55. Rtog pa myed for wu-kuan.

56. Possibly for the tzu-jan yüan-man of Cheng-
li chüeh 138a, but more likely an intentional emphasis
on the sudden or instantaneous aspects of Mo-ho-yen's
immediate path. See the discussion in the main body
of this article. Both aspects of the process are
emphasized here by the juxtaposition of skad cig la,
"in one instant," and char (var.: car) "simultaneously."

57. Obscure. Perhaps tshor is to be taken in
its usual value in these fragments ("overcome by
[excessive] awareness [of dualities]" ??), or tshor
bas ("awareness is overcome [by dualities]" ?).

58. Lit., "First, there is the practice of the
perfections.... Secondly, when there is no arising of
thoughts within...."

59. Ran bźin gis ldan no: "naturally" or "spontaneously" in possession of.

60. Man du thos pa, "great learning," refers to
the study of scripture recommended by the gradualists.
See, e.g., IBhk 198-99. The criticism is repeated
below, IX.1.

61. A standard Ch'an phrase. Its formulation in
terms of the tetrad "seeing," "hearing," "becoming

aware" and "understanding" appears in the Wu-hsin lun and in the Long Scroll or Dharma's Yü-lu. It is one of those phrases of Ch'an that can be easily connected to early Indian tradition (e.g., in the Suttanipata).

62. Conjectural translation.

63. Free rendering of myi bsam, translated before as "not reflect" or "not consider."

64. Sems bskyed pa tsam gyis kyaṅ khams su ma zil kyis gnon par 'gyur na: that is, no matter which sense field the thought is associated with, it is left to pass by without clinging--largely a conjectural translation and interpretation.

65. Not clear; conjectural translation. The meaning seems to be something like this: if the Tathāgata's dhyāna is free from clinging to thoughts in all its usual forms, how much less should one expect the practitioner of dhyāna to attach himself to some kind of "unerring practice" (ma nor bar sgom pa ??).

66. The simile of the lion is common, but the object of comparison is usually the jackal or fox--as in the Cheng-tao ke of Yeng-chia, stanza 43. See also the forthcoming article by J. Broughton in The Sudden-Gradual Polarity (a later vol. of this series).

67. Another upāya or, shall we say, an alternative approach to the unapproachable, a point of view on the unseen? Here Mo-ho-yen approaches the gradualist almost to the letter--see, e.g., IBhk 218, III BhK 11, etc.

68. Here in the Ch'an sense of the equation dharmadhātu = dharmakāya = the man himself (see T'an-ching section 20).

69. Dṅos po: here, as elsewhere, to be distinguished from its near synonym, raṅ bźin, which I render--e.g., in this same paragraph--as "inherent being."

70. Bcos pa: which elsewhere is rendered as "contrive." The term here seems to indicate the conscious generation of "good thoughts" or "liberating states of mind" in meditation, in contradistinction to spontaneous distracting thoughts. See also note 47 above.

71. I have not been able to identify the source of these quotations.

72. Bsgrib pa dan ñon mons pa: sgrib pa is normally āvaraṇa, in which case the term would be a mistake for kleśāvaraṇa--likely given the centrality of this concept in the arguments of the gradualist.

73. The second bhūmi (sa)! The attribution of this whole passage would be suspect if it were not placed as clearly as it is in the context of Stein 709.

74. No exact parallel, but close to cf. I.4-5, 9, and IX.1.

75. Bśad pa las, seemingly not a title, unless bśad-pa stands for yü, or the like.

76. Here the translation is conflated from Bsmi and Bka'-thaṅ, using single parentheses to indicate phrases from the latter missing in the former, and double parentheses for the material found only in Bsmi. I have serious doubts regarding the attribution of this passage to Mo-ho-yen.

77. Stein 468 verbatim, with the indication here that the passage is from the "Ma-ha-yan-gyi Bsgom lun."

78. Stein 709 only in part, but its placement is confirmed by de ñid las at the beginning of the Bsmi fragment.

79. "Ma-ha-yan-gyi Mdo-las." The passage is somewhat reminiscent of Stein 709:4a3-4, and may be related to it.

80. Conjectural translation. Mo-ho-yen seems to be accusing the tīrthikas of nihilism--a common criticism.

81. Mi rtog pa la' aṅ mi gnas so: cf. I.9, etc.

82. Spaṅs pa, lit., "to abandon examination."

83. De ñid las: that is the same source as that of VII.7. The doctrine of looking into the mind (k'an-hsin) occurs in X.1 (n. 101) and in XI.3 (= Cheng-li chüeh 135a2-4).

84. Thabs la mkhas pa: context requires this departure from my normal rendering.

85. Simple yaṅ. Could refer to the same work.

86. Conjectural translation. I cannot attempt to understand this sentence without some notion of what is meant by the gsal bar śes pa of the "hīnayāna." Perhaps it is ālokasamjñā?

87. Again, conjectural translation. Perhaps the point at issue is whether no-thought is the literal absence of thought (perfectly pure and clear mind), or simple awareness of thoughts.

88. Simply yaṅ, as above.

89. It would seem that here we have a recommendation to examine the mind!

90. Again, an apparent contradiction to previous recommendations.

91. Conjectural translation.

92. "Ma-ha-yan-gyi Bsam-gtan-las."

93. 'du śes, here as the object of the dharma-anutpatti-ksanti.

94. Mo-ho-yen, or his translator, here uses samādhi for the dhyānā-pāramitā.

95. Bla na myed pa'i gnas: anuttara-pada (?).

96. Ye śes: jñāna.

97. Attribution to Mo-ho-yen is questionable.

98. Cf. Pelliot 21 (X.2) and Stein 468 (I.9).

99. 'gro ba ches pa for mahāsattva (?).

100. In spite of a few obscure constructions, this fragment is the most organic (perhaps complete ?) of all.

101. Sems la bltas na. Cf. VII.8, etc. n. 83 above.

102. Conjectural.

103. Cf. I.4, XI.3, Cheng-li chüeh 147b, etc.

104. Or "consider," "ponder," "reflect on"--myi bsam.

105. See note 45 above, and XI.4 below.

106. Tshor ba here in the more common meaning of chüeh, which the Tibetan term lacks.

107. A favorite phrase with the gradualists too. See VI.7 above.

108. In the Chinese texts this is pen-lai i-ch'ieh chih, a significantly different idea.

109. See Concile, ad locum.

110. The trimandala-pariśuddhi.

111. See Concile, ad locum.

112. Gźuṅ, assuming its sense of "essential meaning."

113. Bsam pa: a Buddha's conceptual thought? An intentional paradox. See n. 121 below.

114. Problematic in both Tibetan and Chinese: de las cha śas śig smos na see Demiéville, ad locum.

115. Conjectural for bsam du myed pa'i chos kyi gzun 'di la dgos bźin du mñam pa. The Chinese here indicates a meaning closer to that of the Sutra ("no doubting thoughts" instead of simply "no thoughts").

116. It is difficult to see what point Mo-ho-yen expects to make here.

117. Again the similes mentioned above, n. 51. Some of these, and others occur in XI.10, with a different meaning.

118. Gźun (tsung), "the fundamental principle or idea," but here translated freely to allow for a smoother translation in this context.

119. Gźuṅ (i), see above n. 112.

120. Bsam du myed pa theg pa chen po'i gźuṅ las: the Chinese here does not correspond syntactically to

the Tibetan. The former has to be read "the fundamental unthinkable meaning of the dhyana-gate of the
Mahāyāna."

121. Although this passage is not found in Cheng-
li chüeh one should compare the passage on the
Buddha's conceptual thoughts in folia 147b-148a of the
same work.

122. Suspiciously close to Bsmi 58.5 (VII.1), and
perhaps part of I.

123. "Mkhan-po Ma-ha-yan-gyi Bsam-brtan-gyi mdo-
las." The same as I?

A note of gratitude:

To Belinda Bicknell for persistent effort in
typing and retyping the main body of the article and
its tables through several stages of revision.
To Joan George for courageous effort in the final
and rushed stages of typing--for those hours she gave
for the sake of a few notes on some forgotten scraps
of a spiritual menu, forsaking the actual meal.

THE OX-HEAD SCHOOL OF CHINESE CH'AN BUDDHISM:
FROM EARLY CH'AN TO THE GOLDEN AGE
by
John R. McRae

　　　　The Ox-head (Niu-t'ou 牛頭宗) School has occu-
pied rather a unique position within modern research
on early Chinese Ch'an Buddhism.　On the one hand, it
has not received anything like the attention accorded
the Southern School of Hui-neng 慧能 　, Shen-hui
神會 ,　and the Liu-tsu t'an-ching 六祖坦經
(Platform Sūtra of the Sixth Patriarch, hereafter simply Platform Sūtra).　The "sudden" teachings of this
latter school have generally been considered the main-
stream and, at the same time, the most innovative,
even revolutionary, expression of the entire Ch'an
tradition.　On the other hand, neither has the Ox-head
School been treated with the obvious disregard
accorded the so-called Northern School of Shen-hsiu
神秀 ,　and P'u-chi 普寂 　, et al., which has almost
invariably been interpreted according to the originally perjorative description of "gradualism" that
derives from the vituperative attacks of Shen-hui and
the comprehensive, if biased, analysis of Tsung-mi
宗密 .　The Ox-head lineage is supposed to have been
a transmission ancillary to that of the Ch'an School
per se, but to have had teachings closely akin to that
of the Southern School.　As such the Ox-head School
has been analyzed, admired, and argued about, but
never with quite the thoroughness or intensity associated with the study of the other two Schools of
North and South.　Although some of the early research
on the Ox-head Ch'an, specifically, that by Kuno Hōryū

久野芳隆 , is remarkable for its suprising degree
of sophistication, it is only recently, with the work
of Yanagida Seizan 柳田聖山 , that the true significance of this school has become apparent.

Although this situation is understandable in
view of the more spectacular and more thoroughly documented discoveries from the Northern and Southern
Schools, it is no longer possible to consider the Ox-
head School as merely an intriguing but unimportant
footnote to the development of the Ch'an tradition as
a whole. My own research in early Ch'an--which has
been inspired by that of Professor Yanagida--indicates
that it was the Northern School, not the Southern,
which formed the mainstream of Ch'an throughout the
first half of the eighth century and that the teachings of the Northern School were fundamentally different from the simplistic gradualism of traditional
ascription. These findings are significant here
because of the following corollary: Far from being
only an interesting tradition of meditation practice
and doctrine ancillary to the true transmission of
"Bodhidharma Ch'an," the Ox-head School may actually
constitute a bridge between the "early Ch'an" of the
Northern and Southern Schools and the "golden age" of
spontaneous repartee or "encounter dialogue" typified
most clearly by Ma-tsu Tao-i 馬祖道一 and his
associates.

This article constitutes the first step in the
investigation of this hypothesis about the Ox-head
School and will include: (1) a short review of previous scholarship on Ox-head Ch'an, (2) a critical
analysis of the biographies of the major Ox-head
masters, and (3) a brief discussion of the School's
teachings. The ultimate goal of this study is to

establish meaningful correlations between the available biographical and doctrinal information concerning
the Ox-head School. Since the hypothesis stated above
can only be fully tested after a similar investigation
of the Hung-chou 洪州 School associated with Ma-tsu
Tao-i, the reader must be forewarned that only the
most general and basic introduction to the study of
the Ox-head School can be made in the present context.
The detailed investigation of all available doctrinal
materials relating to the Ox-head School, not to
mention the examination of Ma-tsu's Hung-chou School
and the earliest forms of true "encounter dialogue,"
must be left to a later date.

1. The Modern Study of the Ox-head School

        Modern research on the Ox-head School began
with, and until recently has been almost entirely
limited to, the study of its most important text, the
Chüeh-kuan lun 絕觀論 (Treatise on the Transcendence of Cognition). Knowledge of this text began with
the publication of D. T. Suzuki's 鈴木大拙
Shōshitsu issho 少室逸書 (Lost Works from
Bodhidharma's Cave) in 1935.[1] Several additional
manuscripts and critical editions of the Chüeh- kuan
lun were published in the next few years by Suzuki and
Kuno Hōryū.[2] The best early analysis of the teachings
and historical significance of the Ox-head School were
a long article by Kuno and a chapter in the first
volume of the great Ui Hakuju's 宇井伯壽 Zenshūshi
kenkyū 禪宗史研究 (Studies in the History of the
Ch'an School), both published in 1939.[3] Kuno's article includes a long introductory discussion of the
various Schools of early Ch'an and an analysis of the

doctrinal relationship of the Chüeh-kuan lun to various texts of the Chinese Mādhyamika tradition, while Ui's work includes a critical discussion of the biographies of many of the Ox-head masters, cites the various listings of Ox-head works taken to Japan by ninth-century pilgrims, and concludes with a short anthology of material attributed to Ox-head School masters, not including the Chüeh-kuan lun. Although new findings have rendered many of their specific conclusions obsolete, these two contributions by Kuno and Ui were written with such technical and analytical sophistication that they are both eminently worthy of consultation even today.

Comprehensive editions of all the extant Tun-huang 敦煌 manuscripts of the Chüeh-kuan lun were published by Suzuki in 1945 and Yanagida in 1970.[4] The latter includes three separate, critically edited versions of the treatise printed together on different registers of the same page, each version being based on two of the six extant manuscripts. The authoritative edition of the text is to be found in a volume published in 1976 by the Institute for Zen Studies at Hanazono College in Kyōto. This volume includes an introductory statement by Yanagida, photo-reproductions of all the six Tun-huang manuscripts, a single Chinese text edited by Yanagida, the same scholar's translation into modern Japanese (a real translation, not just a mechanical transposition into Japanese grammar), and an English translation by Tokiwa Gishin 常盤義伸 .[5] Would that all the major early Ch'an documents from Tun-huang could be treated in such admirable fashion!

Meanwhile, the study of the Ox-head School progressed apace, the most common topic of discussion

being the authorship of the Chüeh-kuan lun. Suzuki's
published works indicate that he vacillated on this
question, at different times favoring attributions to
either Shen-hui or Bodhidharma or someone in their
immediate lineages.[6] Suzuki argued vigorously against
the attribution of the text to Niu-t'ou Fa-jung 牛頭
法融, the legendary figurehead of the Ox-head School,
an attribution that was supported first by Kuno and
then by Sekiguchi Shindai 関口真大 .[7] Sekiguchi's
work on the subject consolidates all the available
evidence regarding the traditional attribution of the
Chüeh-kuan lun to Fa-jung, in the process thoroughly
confuting the attributions to Bodhidharma and Shen-
hui. Although he fails in his attempt to prove the
attribution to Fa-jung (rather than to a later anonymous member of the Ox-head School), Sekiguchi's combined output on the subject of the Ox-head School's
history and doctrines constitutes the most comprehensive treatment yet attempted by any scholar.[8]

The year 1967 saw the publication of what is
unquestionably the single most important volume in the
modern study of early Ch'an: Yanagida's Shoki Zenshū
shisho no kenkyū 初期禅宗史書の研究 (Studies in
the Historical Texts of the Early Ch'an School).[9] The
importance of this book lies in the fact that it goes
beyond the simple questions of textual and biographical authenticity and analyzes the contents of the
most influential and explicit of the early works in
order to show how each one derived from and contrib-
uted to the growing Ch'an tradition. Professor
Yanagida is the first scholar within the field of
Ch'an studies to diagnose the relative merits of both
historical "fact" and legendary fabrication, clinging
to neither but rather showing how each affected the

other. Yanagida's overall purpose was to show how the Ch'an School and its religious ideology developed between the publication of two milestone texts, the Hsü kao-seng chuan 續高僧傳 (Supplement to the "Lives of Eminent Monks," or HKSC) of 645/667 and the Sung kao-seng chuan 宋高僧傳 (Lives of Eminent Monks [compiled during the] Sung [Dynasty], or SKSC) of 998. The conclusions made by Yanagida which are most relevant to the present study are as follows:

1. the basic conception of the "transmission of the lamp" theory of the history of Ch'an was first stated in several Northern School works;

2. the ideas on which Shen-hui based his attack upon the Northern School did not derive directly from Hui-neng, but were developed by Shen-hui himself in the course of his own religious development;

3. the Ox-head School developed not as a seventh-century offshoot of the tradition of Bodhidharma, but rather as an eighth-century reaction to either the Northern School or the combination of the Northern School and Shen-hui's Southern School;

4. the Chüeh-kuan lun was probably written during the Ox-head School's greatest period of activity, i.e., during the third quarter of the eighth century; and

5. it was a member of the Ox-head School named Fa-hai 法海 --neither Hui-neng, Shen-hui nor one of their students--who was responsible for the first recension of the Platform Sūtra.[10]

The most striking of the points listed above is indubitably the last. Although the genesis of the Platform Sūtra is a subject of great complexity which cannot be treated here in any detail, suffice it to say that Yanagida has shown the first version of this text to have been an Ox-head School compilation that included some direct criticism of Shen-hui's teachings as well as other samples of that master's teachings introduced under the name of Hui-neng. To date there has been no critical challenge to this unique interpretation of the identity of the Ox-head School and the origins of the Platform Sūtra. There have been other contributions to the study of the Ox-head School after the appearance of Yanagida's work, but, with one exception, they need not concern us here.[11] The exception is an article by Yanagida himself on the teachings of the School, to which we shall refer at the very end of this paper.[12]

2. The History of the Ox-head School

The starting point of this brief outline of the history of the Ox-head School, as is invariably the case in the study of early Ch'an, is the statement and criticism of the traditional version of the School's transmission. This traditional account begins with a meeting between Fa-jung and Tao-hsin道信 (580-651), the Fourth Patriarch in succession from Bodhidharma, in which the depth of the former's experience was supposedly verified by the latter.[13] From this point the Ox-head lineage is generally traced through six generations, with Fa-jung at the beginning and either of two individuals at the end:

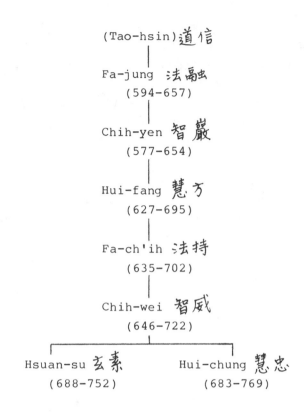

(Tao-hsin) 道信

Fa-jung 法融
(594-657)

Chih-yen 智巖
(577-654)

Hui-fang 慧方
(627-695)

Fa-ch'ih 法持
(635-702)

Chih-wei 智威
(646-722)

Hsuan-su 玄素   Hui-chung 慧忠
(688-752)   (683-769)

It is obvious that the very notion of a list of six
generations is drawn from the Bodhidharma tradition;
we may even note the similarity in the bifurcated
nature of the sixth generation of each. Also, a brief
glance at the dates of the first two patriarchs given
above indicates a problem, one that is rendered even
greater by investigation of the biographies of the men
involved. That is, not only was Chih-yen some seven-
teen years older than his supposed teacher, but he
also died a year or two before his supposed student's
(Hui-fang's) first ordination. The only available
data for Hui-fang's biography, the admittedly
unreliable Ching-te ch'üan-teng lu 景德傳灯錄
(Records of the Transmission of the Lamp [compiled

during the] Ching-te [Period], hereafter CTL) of 1004,
has him studying with Chih-yen after his full ordination, so this implies a definite contradiction.
Actually, close attention to specific dates and ages
given in the CTL suggests that Fa-jung, Hui-fang, and
Fa-ch'ih were all together in the same location at one
point in their careers--a most unlikely situation in
the context of a supposedly lineal succession.[14]

The most that can reliably be said about the
earliest Ox-head School "patriarchs" is that Fa-jung
and Chih-yen each had some individual impact on the
general tradition of Buddhist Studies and meditation
practice at Mt. Niu-t'ou and the surrounding area.
The possibility of their being teacher and student
notwithstanding, it is of course quite out of the
question that one transmitted any kind of patriarchate
to the other. Both of these men were figures of some
prominence and the subjects of HKSC biographies. Fa-
jung[15] was from the very prominent Wei 韋 family[16] in
Yen-ling 延陵 (Tan-yang 丹陽 hsien, Kiangsu) who
became a monk at age nineteen, or in the year 612. He
studied for an unknown length of time with a Mādhyamika master of some repute[17] and spent over three
months in Ch'ang-an 長安 in 624 attempting to induce
the T'ang authorities to relax certain local restrictions against Buddhism.[18] The rest of Fa-jung's life
was devoted to meditation practice and scriptural
study, perhaps for a time under another Mādhyamika
master in Yüeh-chou 越州 (Shao-hsing 紹興 hsien,
Chekiang). He resided at two different temples on
Mount Niu-t'ou from at least 637 until the very last
years of his life, when he gave public lectures on
the Lotus, Perfection of Wisdom, and Great Collection
(Ta-chi 大集) sūtras. The beginning of the Ox-

head School is usually traced to his founding of a
meditation center at Yü-hsi 幽栖 Temple on Mount
Niu-t'ou in 642, and there may be some truth in this
assertion. That is, the HKSC does say that Fa-jung's
new center attracted ever greater number of students,
and there may have been some continuity with later Ox-
head School figures. Various hagiographical anecdotes
that occur in Fa-jung's lengthy biography will be
omitted here, but please note that there is no mention
of either Tao-hsin or Chih-yen. Ui and Sekiguchi take
opposite views on the historicity of the meeting
between Fa-jung and Tao-hsin, the negative conclusion
of the latter scholar being definitely preferable.
Fa-jung's HKSC biography does not mention any written
works.

Chih-yen,[19] who was from the Hua 華 family of
Ch'ü-a 曲阿 (also Tan-yang hsien, Kiangsu) in Tan-
yang, spent the early part of his life as a military
officer. He became a monk at age 45,[20] after which he
became known for the practice of the contemplations of
"impurities" (pu-ching kuan 不淨觀 , i.e., on the
body and corpses), compassion (tz'u-pei kuan
慈悲觀), and "birthlessness" (wu-sheng kuan
无生觀 , i.e., on the essentially unconditioned
nature of all things). He resided at different locations in what is now Chiang-ning 江寧 hsien, Kiangsu,
the home of many of the later Ox-head figures, as well
as on Mount Huan-kung 峴公 (Ch'ien-shan 潛山 hsien,
Anhwei), a location connected with the Third Patriarch
of Ch'an, Seng-ts'an 僧璨. In spite of later assertions, there is no known link between him and either
the Ox-head School or Seng-ts'an.[21] No written works
are known.

The biographies of Hui-fang and Fa-ch'ih are based on such late sources, and even there are so lacking in detail, that it is impossible to ascertain their true relationships with predecessors and successors.[22] There are no doubts about the succession from Fa-ch'ih onward, but there is some question about when that succession became associated with Ch'an. The SKSC and CTL claim that Fa-ch'ih studied under Hung-jen, the Fifth Patriarch of the Bodhidharma tradition, and that he was one of that master's ten major disciples. Nevertheless, there are enough problems with this assertion to infer that the connection with Hung-jen was not of major importance to the development of the Ox-head School.[23]

As Yanagida points out, it was during Chih-wei's life that we must look for the real beginnings of the Ox-head School. Although Chih-wei's specific teachings are unknown, he seems to have taken deliberate actions aimed at expanding the purview of his following: After spending many years on Mount Niu-t'ou or "Ox-head Mountain" (Chiang-ning hsien, Kiangsu), this being the origin of the Ox-head Schools' peculiar name, he deputed supervision of his community there to Niu-t'ou Hui-chung and moved into Yen-tso延祚 Temple in Chin-ling金陵 (the modern Nanking, in the same hsien in Kiangsu). Even while there he continued to teach, the transmission to Hsuan-su occurring at this new location.[24] Chih-wei is also supposed to have had several other students, and an excerpt of one of his students' teachings is still extant. The biography of this student, An-kuo Hsuan-t'ing 安國玄挺 , is unknown.

Certainly the example of the Northern School's recent success would have been a major inspiration for this Southern tradition, but there is no evidence that any specific theory of an Ox-head School transmission was known during Chih-wei's life. Chih-wei's position as the Fifth Patriarch of the Ox-head tradition is analogous to that of Hung-jen 弘忍 in the Bodhidharma tradition, in the sense that each tradition achieved its first real growth during the lives of their students. This similarity only makes it more reasonable to assume that the lineage innovations which define the Ox-head School as independent from the Northern and Southern Schools may have developed in nuclear form during Chih-wei's life, but were only crystallized during the sixth generation and later.[25]

The later development of the Ox-head School is generally described in terms of four factions or sub-lineages, which are named after the figures standing at the head of each: (a) the "Mount Niu-t'ou faction" headed by Niu-t'ou Hui-chung; (b) the "Fo-k'u faction" headed by Hui-chung's disciple Fo-k'u I-tse 仙窟 遺則 ; (c) the "Ho-lin faction" headed by Ho-lin Hsüan-su 鶴林玄素 ; and (d) the "Ching-shan faction" headed by Hsuan-su's disciple Ching-shan Fa-ch'in 徑山法欽 . Let us first summarize the biographies of these major figures and some of their students and then add some closing comments about the historical identity of the "school" with which they were associated.

(a) The Mount Niu-t'ou Faction: Niu-t'ou Hui-chung[26] was from Shang-yuan 上元 (also Chiang-ning hsien, Kiangsu) in Jun-chou 潤州 and of the surname Wang 王 . He was ordained at Chuang-yen 莊嚴 Temple in Chin-ling in the year 705 at the age of twenty-three. The SKSC and CTL give slightly different accounts of the dialogue between him and his soon-adopted teacher Chih-wei, and it is impossible to tell how long he stayed at Mount Niu-t'ou or whether he left for a period of wandering before taking over there. After deputing control of Mount Niu-t'ou to Hui-chung, Chih-wei moved to Yen-tso Temple in Chin-ling, where he taught for at least a short while before his death. Hui-chung remained in charge at Mount Niu-t'ou until his own death, but in 742, at the request of the prefectural magistrate, he moved back to Chuang-yen Temple, the site of his ordination. He labored to repair the temple, which had fallen into disuse since its high point in the Liang 梁 Dynasty, adding a new Dharma Hall (fa-t'ang 法堂), a very important component of Ch'an temple construction in later years. His death, which is described with the sort of hagiographical detail that is typical of these texts, occurred there in 769. Hui-chung is said to have written two works, one called the Chien-hsing hsu 見性序 (Preface on Seeing the [Buddha]-nature) and another called the Hsing-lu nan 行路難 (How Diffi-cult, the Traversing of the Path!). As Sekiguchi sug-gests, the first of these may have been the source of the long citation of Hui-chung's teachings found in the Tsung-ching lu 宗鏡錄 (Records of the Mirror of Truth, hereafter TCL) by Yung-ming Yen-shou 永明延壽 (904-975), while the second may be represented in other materials from Tun-huang and elsewhere but not bearing Hui-chung's name.[27] The CTL says that he had thirty-six major disciples, who taught at quite a few different locations throughout southeastern China. Biographical details are available for only three of these, as well as for three others not listed in the CTL, but there is nothing that would be gained from sifting through these rather sparse, stereotypical accounts here. Only one of Hui-chung's students is known through a roughly contemporary epitaph: T'ai-po Kuan-tsung 太白觀宗 (731-809). His epitaph is of some value in the study of Ox-head School history and doctrine.[28] It is unfortunate that no such document exists for Hui-chung himself.

(b) The Fo-k'u Faction: The fact that Fo-k'u Wei-tse (751-830)[29] is placed at the head of a sub-lineage independently of his teacher's derives from his alleged success in establishing his own thriving center at Mount T'ien-t'ai 天台山 (T'ien-t'ai hsien, Chekiang). The SKSC even contains allegations that the "Fo-k'u learning" flourished there no less than did the T'ien-t'ai School of Chih-i and that it attained a status independent of the Northern, Southern, and Ox-head Schools. Whatever the validity of these assertions, there are only a few passages and documents left with which to gauge the nature of this faction's teachings and virtually no information at all about the lives of its members. What is known is that Fo-k'u himself was a gifted individual whose calligraphy and writings were widely praised and sought after even during his own lifetime.[30]
Fo-k'u I-tse was of the Ch'ang-sun 長孫 family from the capital of Ch'ang-an, where his grand-father had been an official in the central government. Fo-k'u's father, however, had retired from public life and moved to Chin-ling. The youth supposedly became a student of Hui-chung's after becoming a Buddhist and being ordained at age twenty-two, but the fact that Hui-chung is said to have died when Fo-k'u was only nineteen (by the Chinese method of reckoning) renders

this assertion problematic.   After achieving enlightenment he moved to Fo-k'u cliff on Mount T'ien-
t'ai--hence his name[31]--where he stayed for some forty
years until his death in 830.   If Fo-k'u did stay at
Mount T'ien-t'ai for some forty years--and such
figures are often exaggerated--then there was a gap of
twenty years or more between Hui-chung's death and the
beginning of this long residency.   In view of this gap
and Fo-k'u's young age at the time of his master's
death, it seems reasonable to doubt the extent of the
relationship between the two.   It is impossible to
ascertain any particulars at this late date, but it
would seem likely that other teachers had an influence
on Fo-k'u as well.   Nevertheless, the SKSC and the
catalogues of the Japanese pilgrims to China indicate
that he compiled at least one specifically Ox-head
work, as well as several others of uncertain nature:

1. Hsu-chi jung tsu-shih wen 序集融祖
    師文 (Writings of the Patriarch [Fa]-
    jung, with Preface), in three fascicles

2. Pao-chih shih-t'i erh-shih-ssu chang 寶誌
    釋題 二 十 四章 (Explanation of the
    Titles of Pao-chih's [Works] in Twenty-
    four Sections)

3. Nan-yu fu ta-shih i-feng hsu 南遊傅大
    士遺風序 (Preface to the Religious
    Legacy of Bodhisattva Fu [Hsi], Who Roamed
    the South)

4. Wu-sheng teng i 無生等義 (The Meaning
    of Birthlessness and Other [Doctrines])
    (Given in the Japanese catalogues as Wu-
    sheng i, or The Meaning of Birthlessness),
    in two fascicles

5. Fo-k'u chi 仏崛集 (<u>Anthology</u> <u>of</u> <u>Fo-</u><u>k'u's</u> [<u>Teachings</u>]), in one fascicle

6. Fo-k'u ch'an-yuan ho-shang hsing-chuang 仏崛禪院和尚行狀 (<u>Outline</u> <u>of the</u> <u>Actions</u> <u>of</u> <u>the</u> <u>Preceptor</u> <u>of</u> <u>Fo-k'u</u> <u>Medita-</u><u>tion</u> <u>Chapel</u>), in one fascicle

7. Fo-k'u ta-shih hsieh-chen ts'an 仏崛大師 寫真讚 (<u>Eulogy</u> <u>on a</u> <u>Portrait</u> <u>of the</u> <u>Great</u> <u>Master</u> <u>Fo-k'u</u>), in one fascicle

8. Huan-yuan chi 還源集 (<u>Anthology</u> <u>on</u> <u>Returning</u> <u>to</u> <u>the</u> <u>Source</u>), in three fascicles[32]

In the absence of the original texts, the English equivalents given above must be considered tentative. Some of the works listed were obviously not written by Fo-k'u himself but were about him (numbers seven and eight), some were anthologies compiled and prefaced by him (one, three, and possibly two), leaving only four works that were entirely his own (four, five, six, and nine). Of course, it is impossible to tell what part Fo-k'u had in the compilation of the poems and sayings attributed to such early figures as Pao-chih and Fu Hsi.[33] At the moment, the only remnants of Fo-k'u's works that still exist are excerpts from the <u>Wu-sheng</u> <u>i</u> and the <u>Huan-yuan</u> <u>chi</u> (numbers four and nine) found in the <u>TCL</u> and another work by Yen-shou. Incidentally, the <u>Wu-sheng</u> <u>i</u> was perhaps the earliest of the lot, since Saichō took it and not the others back to Japan upon his return there in 805.[34] Finally, it may be noted that the <u>CTL</u> claims the Fo-k'u's temple on Mount T'ien-t'ai was destroyed during the persecution of 845 and eventually taken over by Taoists. Only his stele was saved, to be removed to safety by a Buddhist monk in 865.[35]

In contrast to Hui-chung's "Mount Niu-t'ou faction," which included well over thirty named monks and nuns, the name of only one of Fo-k'u's students is known. Even here, there is no biographical information whatsoever, although excerpts from his works occur in the TCL.[36]

(c) The Ho-lin Faction: Whereas the "Mount Niu-t'ou faction" and the "Fo-k'u faction" allow virtually no insight into their historical realities and only the slightest glimpse at their teachings, the other two sub-lineages of the Ox-head School are known in much greater detail. Indeed, the lives of both Ho-lin Hsüan-su and Ching-shan Fa-ch'in are known through lengthy epitaphs preserved in the Ch'üan T'ang wen (Complete Writings of the T'ang [Dynasty], hereafter CTW) and elsewhere. The first of these in particular is an extremely important document for its doctrinal contents and biographical detail. In addition, several of the students of each man are known through epitaphs and other contemporary material. Although there are internal contradictions and other problems that make some of these sources unusable for the present purposes, the very existence of these contradictions and other problems is in itself an important clue to the eventual role of the Ox-head School.

The biography of Ho-lin Hsüan-su is known primarily through an epitaph by Li Hua 李華 (d. ca. 766), a figure who is himself of no little importance in the development of early Ch'an.[37] Hsüan-su is said to have been from Yen-ling (Tan-yang hsien, Kiangsu) in Jun-chou and of the surname Ma 馬 . Like the Vinaya

Master Yin-tsung 印宗 (627-713) and the famous Ma-tsu
Tao-i (709-88), Hsüan-su was often referred to as Ma-
tsu 馬祖 ("Patriarch Ma"), or even by the amalgam of
his family and religious names, Ma-su 馬素 . As one
might expect, the former usage has led to some confusion between him and Ma-tsu Tao-i, who is more often
referred to in contemporary sources by the title Ta-
chi 大寂 .38   At any rate, in 692 Hsüan-su was
ordained and registered at Ch'ang-shou 長壽 Temple in
Chiang-ning 江寧 (also Chiang-ning hsien, Kiangsu).39
Sometime thereafter he went to Yü-hsi Temple on Mount
Niu-t'ou and received the teachings from Chih-wei.
During the years 713-714 Hsüan-su was invited to a
place named Ching-k'ou 京口 (Tan-t'u 丹徒 hsien,
Kiangsu) and installed in Ho-lin Temple there.40
Later, during the years 742-755, he moved temporarily
to Kuang-ling 廣陵 or Yang-chou 揚州 (Chiang-tu 江都
hsien, Kiangsu),41 but the people of Ching-k'ou peti-
tioned strongly for his return, which led to a bitter
struggle between the two communities. In fact, the
epitaph describes the reception received by Hsüan-su
from people in various areas all around Yang-chou as
having been so effusive that one is inclined to think
that the stature of this septagenarian monk was very
great indeed. In any case, he eventually returned to
Ho-lin, where he died at midnight on the eleventh day
of the eleventh month of the eleventh year of the
T'ien-pao period (752).42

In addition to the above outline of Hsüan-su's
life and some extremely important material on the
doctrines and lineage theories of Ox-head Ch'an, there
is one item recorded in his epitaph that bears consideration here. This is Chih-wei's prediction upon
first meeting him:

The Great Master [Chih]-wei rubbed [Hsüan-su's] head and said: "The true teaching of the Southeast awaits your propagation. I will have you teach the students who come to you in a separate situation."

It is tempting--and probably accurate--to interpret the phrase "true teaching of the Southeast" (tung-nan cheng-fa 東南正法) as a reference to the Ox-head School's independent status apart from the Northern and Southern Schools. As Sekiguchi suggests, the term "separate situation" (as the troublesome expression pieh-wei 別位 has been translated here) is probably based on Chih-wei's prior delegation of control of the Mount Niu-t'ou center to Hui-chung.[43] Of course, it is not certain that the statement above was actually made by Chih-wei. It may have been supplied retrospectively in order to explain the equivalent status of his two major successors. One hypothetical interpretation is that Chih-wei and Hsüan-su left Mount Niu-t'ou at the same time, in 713 or shortly thereafter. According to this interpretation, the established and relatively stable center at Mount Niu-t'ou was left to the gifted but still comparatively inexperienced Hui-chung, whereas Chih-wei and Hsüan-su, who was much older than Hui-chung but still had not finished his training, moved on to Yen-tso Temple in Chin-ling. As mentioned above, it was only at this temple that Hsüan-su received the final transmission of the Dharma from Chih-wei.

Hsüan-su's epitaph lists five students: Fa-ching 法鏡 of Wu-chung 吳中 , Fa-ch'in 法欽 of Ching-shan 徑山 , Fa-li 法勵 , Fa-hai 法海 , and

Hui-tuan 慧端. In addition, it lists the names and titles of eleven prominent lay supporters, several of whom--perhaps all--held office at one time or another in Jun-chou. Finally, we should not forget the two other monks and one layman mentioned previously in the epitaph, as well as the author Li Hua, who lists himself as a personal disciple of Hsüan-su.[44]

Regarding Hsüan-su's ordained students, there exists biographical information for Fa-ch'in, Fa-hai, Lung-an Ju-hai 龍安如海 , Lung-ya Yüan-ch'ang 龍牙圓暢 , and Ch'ao-an 超岸. The last of these studied under Hsüan-su and then under Ma-tsu Tao-i, and, probably earlier in his career, perhaps also under a Northern School monk named T'ung-kuang 通光 .[45] The next-to-last, Lung-ya Yüan-ch'ang, has been mistakenly listed in the CTL as a student of Tao-i rather than Hsüan-su, no doubt through the use of the name Ma-tsu for each teacher.[46] Lung-an Ju-hai, on the other hand, "studied under Hui-yin 惠隱 in the North and sought (the Dharma) from Ma-su of the South." Hui-yin was perhaps a student of the Northern School figures Chiang-ma Tsang 降魔藏 and/or I-fu 義福 , but no biographical details about him are available. It is known, however, that Ju-hai first became a monk at Hsi-ming 西明 Temple in Ch'ang-an after the travails of 755 (his family had originally pressured him into a civil career). He eventually lived at Ch'ang-sha 長沙 (Ch'ang-sha hsien, Hunan) and Mount Kou-lou 岣嶁山 (Heng-shan 衡山 hsien, Hunan), where Lung-an Temple was built. Very little beside this is known about his life, the importance of which is over-shadowed by some of the statements about Ch'an found in his epitaph, a document written by the great literatus Liu Tsung-yüan 柳宗元 .[47]

Considering the particular perspective of this study, it is possible to argue that these sketchy details about Hsüan-su's lesser-known disciples constitute at least partial support for the contention that the Ox-head School formed a bridge between early Ch'an, specifically the Northern School, and the golden age of "encounter dialogue."[48] Even so, more extensive and substantive evidence is obviously necessary. Ultimately, this evidence will have to be extracted from doctrinally-oriented material, but the following discussion of Hsüan-su's two most important disciples is also relevant.

Fa-hai was not originally considered Hsüan-su's most favored disciple, being listed only fourth in his master's epitaph, but in terms of individual historical impact it is possible to describe him as one of the most important figures in all of early Ch'an Buddhism. This assertion is based on the elaborately documented suggestion by Yanagida that Fa-hai was the original compiler of the Platform Sūtra. Fa-hai's SKSC biography, which refers to him as Wu-hsing 吳興 Fa-hai, says that his lay surname was Chang 張 , his style Wen-yün 文允 , and his native place Tan-yang 丹陽 (Chen-chiang 鎮江 hsien, Kiangsu).[49] He left home to become a monk at Ho-lin Temple (thus the connection with Hsüan-su) while young, after which he studied the scriptures and achieved what is called a unique level of understanding. During the years 742-755 he studied under a Vinaya Master named Fa-shen 法慎 in Yang-chou, being listed as a disciple of this teacher elsewhere in the SKSC. Fa-hai was thus a part of the movement of combined meditation and Vinaya studies so popular then in the vicinity of the lower Yangtze River.[50] His primary filiation, however, was to Hsüan-su, whose epitaph states that Fa-hai was exceptional among the group of disciples in his efforts at building the departed master's stūpa and keeping his memory alive. Fa-hai's dates are unknown, but it may be inferred that he was still alive around the year 780, the approximate date of the compilation of the Platform Sūtra.

The SKSC also mentions that Fa-hai "wandered in the forests and had a formless communion" with the poet-monk Chiao-jan 皎然 .51 This monk, also known as Ch'ing-chou 清畫 , had a remarkably large oeuvre of poetry, only a small portion of which is on religious subjects. Some of these works are directly relevant to the study of early Ch'an--particularly his short eulogies to such figures as Shen-hsiu and Hui-neng, Lao-an 老安 and P'u-chi 普寂 (two important Northern School masters), and Hsüan-su. At present, however, it is his participation in a large coopera-tive literary project organized by Yen Chen-ch'ing 顏真卿 (709-785), an official known to posterity as a great literatus and calligrapher, that is of inter-est here. During the slightly more than four years of his appointment as magistrate of Hu-chou 湖州 (Wu-hsing 吳興 hsien, Chekiang) from 773 to 777, Yen enlisted the cooperation of more than fifty local literati and monks to complete a 360-fascicle encyclo-pedia of poetic usages and rhymes. Although Yen had begun work on this project many years before, it was only completed with Chiao-jan's assistance using his temple (Miao-hsi 妙喜 Temple on Mount Chu 杼 in K'uai-chi 會稽 , which is in the present-day Shao-hsing hsien, Chekiang) as a base of operations. The basic description of this project, which was published under the name Yün-hai ching-yüan 韻海鏡源 (Mirror-origin of the Sea of Rhymes), placed Fa-hai's name at the very top of the list of those involved.[52] In other words, not only did Fa-hai's experience in the combined study of meditation and the Vinaya give him the sort of religious background one might expect of the author of the Platform Sūtra, he also had the literary ability necessary to compose such a gem of dramatic prose.

(d) The Ching-shan Faction: At last we come to Ching-shan Fa-ch'in (714-792), who was without question Hsüan-su's major disciple, who became very prominent at the Court of Emperor Tai-tsung (r. 762-779), and whose students are notable for their extensive contact with Ma-tsu Tao-i and Shih-t'ou Hsi-ch'ien 石頭希遷 (700-790).[53] Fa-ch'in's lay surname was Chu 朱 and his native place Wu-chün k'un-shan 吳郡 崑山 (Wu 吳 hsien, Kiangsu). Having mastered the Chinese classics in his youth, at age twenty-eight he happened to be passing through Tan-yang on his way to Ch'ang-an when he heard of Hsüan-su at Ho-lin Temple. He went to visit the great master and experienced a "complete transmission of the secret seal of the Tathāgata in a single moment" during his very first encounter, shaving his head and becoming a disciple that very day. Hsüan-su is supposed to have been extremely impressed with his new disciple, but Fa-ch'in apparently stayed with his teacher for only a short time. According to his epitaph, he arrived at Hsüan-su's temple at age twenty-eight, i.e., in 741, then left and took up residence at Mount Ching 徑山 to the south (Yü-hang 餘杭 hsien, Chekiang), not taking the complete precepts until 743, at the age of thirty.

The _SKSC_ suggests that he took the full precepts before leaving Hsüan-su, but it says nothing about the length of this study under that teacher. At any rate, when Fa-ch'in did set out on his own, the only advice that Hsüan-su would give him was: "Follow your own intuition and stop when you reach a by-way (_ching_ 徑)." As one might suspect, he eventually took up residence on a mountain described to him by a wood-cutter as such a "by-way"--hence his name, Ching-shan (Fa-ch'in).

In 766 or 768 (the latter according to the _SKSC_) Fa-ch'in was summoned to court by Emperor Tai-tsung.[54] Fa-ch'in's entry into court is somewhat reminiscent of the treatment accorded the great Shen-hsiu some two-thirds of a century before: After the master was carried into the palace on a palanquin amid lavish pomp and circumstance, Tai-tsung respectfully inquired of his teachings. Almost a thousand members of the ruling class were supposed to have visited him every day. Indeed, three short oral exchanges of a very novel sort between Fa-ch'in and such extremely prominent lay-people are recorded in an early ninth-century work.[55] Taking no pleasure in the lavish gifts bestowed on him, Fa-ch'in requested and received permission to return to his temple, but only after he had been given the title Kuo-i 國一 ("First in the Land") ta-shih and his temple the official name of Ching-shan Temple. Fa-ch'in's title was supposedly coined by none other than one of Hui-neng's successors, Nan-yang Hui-chung 南陽慧忠 (d. 775, not to be confused with Niu-t'ou Hui-chung).

During his journey from Ch'ang-an back to his temple, Fa-ch'in was besieged by supplicants and over-whelmed by donations (all audiences with him had been prohibited by the emperor during the monk's trip to Ch'ang-an). All the offerings he received were given away, so that he supposedly received the nickname of Kung-te shan 功德山 or "Merit Mountain."[56] According to the SKSC, Emperor Tai-tsung invited him to court again in 789, but Fa-ch'in declined the offer. At the end of his life, in 780-783 according to the epitaph or 790 according to the SKSC, Fa-ch'in moved from Ching-shan Temple to the Lung-hsing 龍興 Temple in Hang-chou,[57] where his death occurred on the evening of the twenty-eighth day of the twelfth month of 792. The magistrate of Hang-chou immediately notified the Emperor, who granted the title Ta-chüeh 大覺 ("Greatly Enlightened") ch'an-shih. There is no mention of any written works.

Of all of Fa-ch-in's disciples (that is, of the few whose biographies are known), Ch'ung-hui 崇慧 of Chang-hsin 章信 Temple in Ch'ang-an was no doubt the most prominent during his own lifetime.[58] This is not to say that he was Fa-ch'in's most intimate successor (the biography of the man who is said to fit this description is unknown), but that his activities attracted the greatest public atention. What is surprising is how atypical of Ch'an these activities were: A native of Hang-chou, Ch'ung-hui first studied meditation under Fa-ch'in and then spent several years in mountain retreat reciting a dhāraṇī or incantation of Esoteric Buddhism. Ching-hui moved to Ch'ang-an in 766 and two years later became involved in a sorcerer's competition with a Taoist priest. Ching-hui's ultimate success in this competition was based on his ability to walk barefoot up a ladder of knives and through fire, thrust his hands into boiling oil, and chew up pieces of iron with his teeth. All this

greatly pleased Emperor Tai-tsung, who showered various privileges upon Ch'ung-hui. Verses describing the
event were widely circulated in China and taken back
to Japan by two of the Buddhist pilgrims from that
country. Note that the year in which this event
occurred, 768, was either the very year that Fa-ch'in
was invited to the imperial court or just a couple of
years afterward. Although the entire incident constitutes an interesting example of syncretism between
Ch'an and Esoteric Buddhism, the closeness of the
relationship between Fa-ch'in and Ch'ung-hui is
unclear. It is entirely possible that the latter
exaggerated the importance of his much earlier contact
with the former after learning how highly the great
Ch'an monk was regarded at court.[59]

In contrast to Ch'ung-hui's example, virtually
every other monk known to have studied under Fa-ch'in
was also connected in some way with more "orthodox"
Ch'an figures such as Ma-tsu Tao-i and Shih-t'ou Hsi-
ch'üan. In the first place, some of these famous
masters' students spent time with Fa-ch'in, e.g., Ma-
tsu's disciples Hsi-t'ang Chih-tsang 西堂智藏 and
Chia-shan Ju-hui 夾山如會 and Shih-t'ou's student
Tan-hsia T'ien-jan 丹霞天然 . On the other hand,
some practitioners became students of Fa-ch'in only to
study under these other famous masters at a later
time: Fu-niu Tzu-tsai 伏牛自在 , T'ien-huang 天皇
(or T'ien-wang 天王) Tao-wu 道悟 , and, perhaps, Yao-
shan Wei-yen 藥山惟儼. Actually, this tendency was
not limited to the Ching-shan faction of the Ox-head
School, for Hsüan-su's student Chao-an and Hui-chung's
student Fu-jung T'ai-yü 芙蓉太毓 both studied
under Ma-tsu Tao-i. (Chao-an was the first known Ox-
head figure to do so.) Even though some of these

individuals' biographies are contained in the SKSC, which lacks the relentless editorial bias of the CTL, there is little that would be gained by enumerating the details here. The study of such figures must await a better understanding of the rise of "encounter dialogue," a task that must be carried out, as far as possible, with reference to material other than those filtered through the Sung Dynasty editors.[60]

3. The Historical Identity of the Ox-head School

The most convenient way to approach the problem of the historical identity of the Ox-head School is to consider the various segments of its lineage diagram:

(a) The First Four Generations:

(Tao-hsin)

Fa-jung

Chih-yen

Hui-fang

This part of the lineage is an obvious fabrication. It is unlikely that Fa-jung ever met Tao-hsin, while Fa-jung, Chih-yen, and Hui-fang were almost certainly not lineal successors. Nevertheless, Fa-jung and Chih-yen were men of some status in the Chinese Buddhist world of the late seventh century. Both were meditation specialists, Fa-jung in particular being closely connected with Mount Niu-t'ou. As such, they may well have had an actual, direct effect on the

development of the Ox-head School. Whether or not
this was the case, it is undeniable that their names
and reputations had a strong appeal for the later
members of that School. In Ch'an, the force of such
legendary reputations was often very great, sometimes
greater than that of the actual historical roles of
the individuals in question.

(b)   The Fifth through Seventh Generations:

(Hui-fang)

Fa-ch'ih

Chih-wei

It was at this stage that the awareness of the Ox-head
School as a single, discrete entity probably developed. Fa-ch'ih is something of an unknown entity--his
study under Hung-jen and his attachment to Pure Land
practices need not be denied,[61] but it is difficult to
assess how much impact they had upon the subsequent
development of Ox-head Ch'an.   Chih-wei's teachings
are unknown, but it is certain that he actively strove
to expand the influence of his own faction in southeastern China. Yanagida's suggestion that the germ of
the Ox-head lineage scheme developed under the influence of the Northern School during Chih-wei's lifetime
seems eminently reasonable.

(c) The Eighth and Ninth Generations:

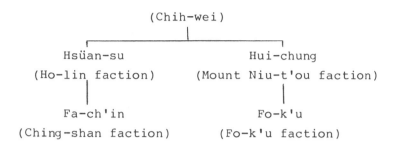

(Chih-wei)

Hsüan-su
(Ho-lin faction)

Hui-chung
(Mount Niu-t'ou faction)

Fa-ch'in
(Ching-shan faction)

Fo-k'u
(Fo-k'u faction)

Although it is clear that the period of greatest Ox-
head School activity was the second half of the eighth
century, it is difficult to assess precisely the
relative strengths of the School's different factions.
Certainly, the Ho-lin and Ching-shan factions seem to
have been more numerous, but this may be a result of
the epigrapher Li Hua's close association with Hsüan-
su and other similar factors. Acknowledging this
possible bias, we may still note the different characters of each of the four factions:

Mount Niu-t'ou: The absence of epitaphs and
other contemporary materials is most keenly felt here,
for there is really nothing special that can be said
about Hui-chung and his students. We will have to
await consideration of the brief doctrinal comments
attributed to Hui-chung in the TCL to detect any
possible unique identity of this faction.

Fo-k'u: The most striking feature of the Fo-
k'u faction is that it is composed of Fo-k'u and
virtually no one else. It is hard to believe that the
"Fo-k'u learning" flourished on Mount T'ien-t'ai as
much as the T'ien-t'ai School of Chih-i, but even so,
Fo-k'u himself seems to have had a very special reputation among his contemporaries.

Ho-lin: Two characteristics of the Ho-lin faction stand out. These are the great number of its members for whom significant biographical information is still available and the high percentage thereof who had some contact with Ma-tsu Tao-i and Shih-t'ou Hsi-ch'üan. The biographies of the members of this faction suggest the very transition hypothesized above, i.e., from early Ch'an to the classical or golden age.

Ching-shan: The contact with Ma-tsu and Shih-t'ou is continued here, but Ching-shan's successful visit to the imperial court is also of great significance. Several decades earlier, such a visit would have been of cardinal importance in the establishment of a Buddhist School; one can only wonder how drastically the new regionalism of Chinese society after the An Lu-shan rebellion had changed the impact of imperial support.

There are two general characteristics that apply to all, or all but one, of the above lineages. The first of these is the evidence of literary creativity. Hui-chung, Fo-k'u, and Fa-hai are all known for their endeavors in the field of religious literature. The number of passages from the works of other Ox-head masters preserved in Yen-shou's works suggests that this tendency probably obtained in all the different factions.[62] The second general characteristic is the very weakness of the links from one teacher to the next. Hui-chung died when Fo-k'u was still a boy, and Hsüan-su and Fa-ch'in were together only a brief while during the latter's youth. This is different from the problems involved in the alleged transmission from Fa-jung to Chih-wei, since it cannot be doubted that Fo-k'u and Fa-ch'in believed themselves to be, or at least presented themselves as, successors to Hui-chung and Hsüan-su. It seems unreasonable, a priori, to suppose that Hui-chung and Hsüan-su were the sole influences on the religious development of their successors--the general environment of the day must have had a significant impact, even if there were no other individual teachers involved. What, then, was the validity of their identity as successors to Fa-jung within the Ox-head School?

It should go without saying that his was not a "school" in any organizational or institutional sense. Even though Chih-wei and others strove actively on its behalf, there never was any strictly defined unit to which some monks clearly belonged and others did not. On the contrary, even more than in the cases of the earlier schools of Northern and Southern Ch'an, the term "Ox-head School" (Niu-t'ou tsung) represented a religious ideal with which one might empathize, a loose sense of fellowship rather than a precisely defined clique. This was the real function of the School's lineage of early Patriarchs--not a historical explanation of the development of the Ox-head Ch'an, but a set of names of men who collectively represented a certain religious ideal that developed in a certain part of China. Even the association with Mount Niu-t'ou soon became largely sentimental, for by the middle of the eighth century members of the Ox-head School were present at Mount T'ien-t'ai, in Hang-chou, Kuang-ling, and a dozen other locations throughout southeastern China. Indeed, this is the implication of the reference in Lung-an Ju-hai's epitaph to the "true teaching of the Southeast."

Although some of the links in its genealogy may seem tenuous, there was nothing understated about the way in which its members perceived the message of the Ox-head School. Li-Hua's epitaph for Hsüan-lang 玄朗 (673-754), a T'ien-t'ai monk who was not involved directly with Ch'an, contains the earliest list of the factions of Ch'an. These include two separate Northern School factions, the Southern School associated with Hui-neng (and Shen-hui, although he is not mentioned), and the Ox-head School of Fa-jung and Ching-shan Fa-ch'in.[63] Another epitaph that was written by Li Chi-fu 李吉甫 for Fa-ch'in contains the following statement on the identity of the Ox-head School:

> After the extinction of the Tāthagata the mind-seal was transmitted successively through twenty-eight Patriarchs to Bodhidharma, who propagated the great teaching widely and bequeathed it to later students. At first those later students formed themselves into the two schools of "North" and "South." Also, in the third [sic] generation from [Bodhi]-dharma, the Dharma was transmitted to Dhyāna Master [Tao]-hsin. [Tao]-hsin transmitted it to Dhyāna Master Niu-t'ou [Fa]-jung, [Fa]-jung transmitted it to Dhyāna Master Ho-lin Ma-su [= Hsüan-su], and [Ma]-su transmitted it to Ching-shan [Fa-ch'in] or Dhyāna Master Kuo-i. This is a separate teaching outside of the two schools [of North and South].[64]

It is especially significant that the teaching transmitted from Fa-jung to Fa-ch'in was a "separate teaching outside of the two schools."

This is a standard position of Ox-head Ch'an, which could not establish its own identity as a unique school of Ch'an without clearly differentiating itself from the earlier schools associated with Shen-hsiu and P'u-chi, Hui-neng, and Shen-hui.

Contrary to what one might expect, there is no evidence that the members of the Ox-head School considered either Northern or Southern Ch'an superior to the other. Instead, they wished to place a certain distance between themselves and the entire dispute between those two that had been instigated by Shen-hui. Three passages should be sufficient to prove this point. The first is by the poet-monk Chiao-jan:

> Eulogy on the Two Patriarchs
> [Hui]-neng and [Shen]-hsiu
>
> The minds of these two men
> were like the moon and sun.
> With no clouds in the four directions
> did they appear in space.
>
> The Three Vehicles share the same path;
> the myriad teachings are one.
> The "division into Northern and Southern
> Schools" in an error of speech.[65]

It is significant that Chiao-jan offers eulogies to Bodhidharma, Chih-i, Lao-an, and P'u-chi of the Northern School, Hui-neng and Shen-hsiu, Pao-chih, Shen-hsiu (individually), and Hsüan-su--but none survives that is dedicated to Hui-neng or Shen-hui alone.

Liu Tsung-yüan's epitaph for Lung-an Ju-hai is even more outspoken in its rejection of small-minded sectarianism:

> The Buddha's birthplace is only twenty thousand _li_ away from China, while his death was only two thousand years ago. Thus the greatest aberration in the diminution of the religion is the term "Ch'an": Grasping, it defiles things; misleading, it becomes separate from the truth. This separation from the truth and increase of deception is greater than the [entire realm of] space of [both] present and past. Such stupid errors and deluded self-indulgence [only] debase oneself, misrepresent _ch'an_ [here meaning "$\bar{d}$hy$\bar{a}$na"?], and do injury to the teachings [of Buddhism. Those who make this error] are characterized by stupidity and moral dissolution.

> He who is different from this is the master of Lung-an to the south of Ch'ang-sha. The master has said: "Twenty-two generations separated Kāśyapa and Siṁha [Bhiksu]. It was further to [Bodhi]-dharma and five generations further to [Hung]-jen. It was further to [Shen]-hsiu and [Hui]-neng. North and South reviled each other like fighting tigers, shoulder-to-shoulder, and the Way became hidden.[66]

Although the above is just a paraphrase of the original Chinese, it should serve to give some impression of the strength of Ju-hai's feelings in the matter.

A simpler statement by Chih-wei's student An-
kuo Hsüan-t'ing is preserved in the TCL:

> A lay supporter asked: "Are you [a follower]
> of the Southern School or the Northern
> School?" [Hsüan-t'ing] answered: "I am not
> [a follower of either] the Southern School or
> the Northern School. The mind is my
> School."[67]

Here we confront a problem of translation: Although
the English version above implies that Hsüan-t'ing was
talking about a school in the sense of a sectarian
entity, the Chinese character tsung 宗 is better taken
as a reference to a teaching or doctrinal principle.
The question is thus whether he follows the teachings
of the Northerners or the Southerners, the answer
being that the true teaching of Buddhism concerns the
mind and transcends any "teachings" to which one might
adhere. Similar exchanges on the rejection of both
Northern and Southern Schools occur in the epitaph of
a monk who died in 751[68] and the Li-tai fa-pao chi
歷代法寶記 (Records of the [Transmission of the]
Dharma-Treasure through the Generations), a product of
the Szechwan Schools that was written in 774 or
shortly thereafter.[69] Obviously, a major problem of
Ch'an Buddhism in the second half of the eighth
century was the need to move beyond the division into
Schools of North and South.

Although Ox-head Ch'an wished to supersede the
Northern and Southern Schools, it still had to build
upon the foundation laid by those earlier Schools.
The Li-tai fa-pao chi manifests consideration of the
same problem, which it solves by adopting Shen-hui's

version of the transmission from Bodhidharma to Hui-
neng, then concocting an outlandish story about the
transmission of Hui-neng's robe from Hui-neng to
Empress Wu and eventually to Wu-chu 無住 (714-774),
for whom the text was written.[70] In the case of the
Ox-head School, the same problem produced a different
sort of peculiarity. This occurs in Fa-hai's composition of the Platform Sūtra, which is devoted to Hui-
neng even though the Ox-head lineage was traced
through Tao-hsin.[71] Technically, Hui-neng and the Ox-
head tradition were unrelated, but, in actual fact,
that tradition grew out of the earlier era of the
Northern and Southern School and had to define itself
in relation to them. The nature--and even the
weakness--of the Ox-head tradition may be seen in the
fact that Fa-hai's work never makes any intimation of
its own origins. This is the ultimate identity of the
Ox-head School: an ideal with which to identify, an
ideal which sought to go beyond simple sectarianism,
but one which of its very nature required the suppression of its own identity.

In order to define the nature of the Ox-head
ideal more precisely, it will be necessary to turn to
strictly doctrinal matters. As it turns out, the
Platform Sūtra will be a very useful guide in this
endeavor as well.

4.   The Teachings of Ox-head Ch'an

In the discussion of the historical development
of the Ox-head School above, it was necessary to begin
with a statement of the traditional explanation of the
School's lineal development. In a somewhat analogous
fashion, it will be convenient here, at the

beginning of our brief analysis of the School's doctrines, to sketch the basic positions of modern
scholarship on the development of early Ch'an. The
following three points define the general consensus of
modern scholarship prior to 1967:

1) The Northern and Southern Schools
represent two different factions or interpretations that developed under the tutelage of
Hung-jen, the teacher of both Shen-hsiu of the
North and Hui-neng of the South. The Northern
School, which was clearly dominant at first,
taught a basically "gradualistic" doctrine of
spiritual practice, while the Southern School
maintained the more advanced and authentic
"sudden" teaching of Ch'an.[72] (The terms
"sudden" and "gradual" will be explained
below.)

2) The beginning of the Southern School's
march to its rightful ascendancy was the vigorous anti-Northern School campaign by Hui-
neng's disciple Shen-hui. This campaign
initiated a battle which was hard-fought on
both sides, but which eventually induced the
followers of Ch'an to desert the
Northern School in favor of the banner of
Hui-neng.[73]

3) The Ox-head School preceded and thus
stood apart from the events just mentioned.
It was derived from the Mādhyamika tradition
of South China, but its teachings were fundamentally similar to those of the Southern
School of Ch'an.

The newer interpretation of the development of early Ch'an, which is based on the research of Professor Yanagida and myself, is as follows:

1) The Northern School represents the first flowering of early Ch'an. This School was responsible for the basic formulation of Ch'an--its pseudo-historical theories, its approach to meditation, and its doctrinal expression. The exceptional treatment accorded Shen-hsiu by Empress Wu in Lo-yang and Ch'ang-an at the very beginning of the eighth century was an important source of the School's momentum and, eventually, both a standard of comparison for subsequent factions of Ch'an to emulate and a target for them to criticize. Although the teachings of the Northern School included many different elements, some of them "gradualistic" and some "sudden," the primary or ultimate position of the School was that enlightenment should be manifest <u>constantly</u> in all activities. This was called the "perfect teaching" (<u>yüan-tsung</u> 圓宗 or <u>yüan-chiao fa-men</u> 圓教法門).[74]

2) Shen-hui's campaign was not only partly designed to correct perceived excesses on the part of Shen-hsiu's successors, but also to establish Hui-neng as the legitimate Sixth Patriarch of Ch'an and to advance Shen-hui's own personal status as his successor. Shen-hui's attacks were made vigorously and persistently and, although the Northern School apparently never saw fit to respond to them directly, they irrevocably stigmatized both

attacker and victim. On the one hand, Shen-hui's ideas were incorporated into the works of later factions, even though his own lineage was not accepted as orthodox. No doubt the self-serving nature of Shen-hui's campaign and his penchant for personal invective before large public audiences rendered association with him relatively undesirable. The sub-lineages of the Northern School, on the other hand, continued to flourish numerically, but the teachings of the School itself came to be thought of in some circles as simplistic and superficial. It had never really existed as a single, discrete "school" in the institutional sense, so that in the second half of the eighth century it lost most of its former appeal and creative momentum.[75]

3) That momentum shifted to the several other factions of Ch'an that emerged in the second half of the eighth century: the Szechwan Schools, the Ox-head School, and the Hung-chou School of Ma-tsu Tao-i. The last of these occupies a very special place in the development of Ch'an, being the first phase of Ch'an's classical or golden age. Like the Szechwan Schools, however, the Ox-head School was clearly transitional in nature in its attempt to transcend the sectarianism of North versus South and to create a doctrine and style of practice fit for the new age.

Previous scholarship on the Ox-head School has emphasized its anti-contemplative, anti-Northern School stance and its Mādhyamika ties. Note, for

example, the following lines drawn by Kuno from the
Hsin ming 心銘 (Inscription on the Mind), a work that
is attributed (no doubt falsely) to Niu-t'ou Fa-jung:

> If you wish to attain purity of mind,
> then make effort [in the context of] no-mind
> (wu-hsin 無心).
> To maintain tranquility with the mind is
> still not to transcend the illness [of
> ignorance].
> One's numenous penetration [of wisdom]
> responds to things and is always [focused on]
> the immediate present.[77]
> Do not struggle to maintain an infantile
> practice.
> Enlightenment (bodhi) is fundamentally
> existent and needs no maintenance; the illu-
> sions (kleśa) are fundamentally non-existent
> and need no eradication.
> Without refuge and without accepting [the
> influence of other entities] transcend contem-
> plation (chüeh-kuan, literally, to "cut-off"
> or "extirpate contemplation")[76] and forget
> maintaining [awareness of the mind].

Kuno concludes that these and other lines from
Hsin ming clearly display the Ox-head School's opposi-
tion to the contemplative tendencies of the Northern
School--specifically, the doctrine of shou-hsin
or "maintaining [awareness of] the mind" found in the
Hsiu-hsin yao lun 修心要論 (Treatise on the
Essentials on Cultivating the Mind) attributed to
Hung-jen.[78] Although we cannot undertake a detailed
analysis of the Hsin ming here, at least one modern

authority would have the last line introduced above
translated differently. Nakamura Hajime's dictionary
of Buddhist terminology defines the phrase chüeh-kuan
wang-shou 絕觀忘守 as the rejection of the
"examination of truth" (i.e., kuan) and the
"conscientious practice of the path" (shou).[79]
Further examination of the term chüeh-kuan indicates
that Nakamura's definition is essentially correct.

The first known usages of the term chüeh-kuan
occur in the Ta-sheng hsüan-lun 大乘玄論 (Treatise
on the Mysteries of the Mahāyāna) by the great
Madhyamika scholar Chi-tsang 吉藏 (549-623). Before
introducing these usages themselves, we should first
note his explanation of the term kuan in the same
text. It is clear from the equivalents that he uses--
"comprehension" (liao-ta 了達), "illumination" (lü-
chao 履照), "investigation" (chien-chiao 檢校),
and "examination" (kuan-ch'a 觀察)--that Chi-tsang is
not referring specifically to the practice of
vipaśyanā or insight meditation, but rather to the
function of perceptual cognition in general. To
paraphrase his explanation, just as light illuminates
both good and bad, so does cognition (kuan) perceive
(also kuan) both success and failure. Chi-tsang
mentions but ignores the use of kuan in the terminology of meditation. Instead, he approaches the term by
way of the "view of the middle" (chung-kuan 中觀),
saying that the meaning of kuan is understood con-
currently with the understanding of the middle, i.e.,
the middle truth that lies between the extremes of
phenomenal and ultimate reality.[80] To refer once
again to Nakamura, kuan is to "cognize the truth of
things with wisdom."[81]

Although Nakamura's definition is based on the Mādhyamakākarikā, he could just as well have referred to the following statement by Chi-tsang:

> The myriad transformations [of phenomenal reality] are not without their own truth (tsung), but that truth is their character-lessness. The truth of emptiness (hsü-tsung 虛宗 , presumably śūnyatā) is not without correspondence [in the mind of the sage], but that which corresponds is [the sage's] no-mind (wu-hsin 無心). Therefore, the sage uses the wondrous wisdom of no-mind to correspond to that characterless truth of emptiness. Internal and external are both effaced; condi-tions (i.e., the objects of perception) and wisdom are both serene. Wisdom is a name for the illumination of knowing (chih-chao 知照). How could it be equivalent to the prajñā that transcends cognition (chüeh-kuan, i.e., of things with wisdom.)[82]

This passage occurs in the context of a discus-sion about the meaning of the Sanskrit term prajñā and its various translations into Chinese. The difference between prajñā and the native term chih-hui 智慧 or "wisdom," Chi-tsang is saying, is that the latter involves the perception of objects. True prajñā, on the other hand, is beyond all types of discrimination and is thus without any specific objects. Wisdom is thus the understanding of the superficial veneer of phenomenal reality, while prajñā reaches the ultimate truth of śūnyatā and is entirely beyond all phenomenal distinctions. As we shall see, the "Chüeh-kuan lun"

refers to the illumination of wisdom, but only in the
sense of the sage's no-mind embracing the non-
substantial or "empty" character of reality. Hence
the title of this Ox-head text must be translated, not
as the Treatise on the Eradication of Contemplation,
but as the Treatise on the Transcendence of
Cognition.[83]

(a)   The "Chüeh-kuan lun" or Treatise on the
Transcendence of Cognition: The Chüeh-kuan lun is
presented as a dialogue between two openly hypothetical individuals. One is a teacher named Ju-li hsien-
sheng 入理先生 , "Mister Entered-into-the-Absolute"
or, for a simpler interpretive reading, "Professor
Enlightenment." The other is a student named Yüan-
men 緣門 , "Teaching of Conditionality" or just
"Conditionality." Here are the opening and closing
sections of the main part of the text:

> Professor Enlightenment was silent and
> said nothing. Conditionality then arose sud-
> denly and asked Professor Enlightenment: "What
> is the mind? What is it to pacify the mind
> (an-hsin 安心)? [The master] answered:
> "You should not posit a mind, nor should you
> attempt to pacify it--this may be called
> 'pacified.'"
> Question: "If there is no mind, how can
> one cultivate enlightenment(tao 道)?" Answer:
> "Enlightenment is not a thought of the mind,
> so how could it occur in the mind?"
> Question: "If it is not thought of by
> the mind, how should it be thought of?"
> Answer: "If there are thoughts then there is

mind, and for there to be mind is contrary to enlightenment. If there is no thought (wu-nien 無念) then there is no mind (wu-hsin 無心), and for there to be no mind is true enlightenment."

Question: "Do all sentient beings actually have mind or not?" Answer: "If there are thoughts then there is mind, and for there to be mind is contrary to enlightenment. If there is no thought (wu-nien) then there is no mind (wu-hsin), and for there to be no mind is true enlightenment."

Question: "Do all sentient beings actually have mind or not?" Answer: "[To say that] all sentient beings actually have minds is a mistaken view. To posit mind within [the realm of] no-mind is to generate wrong ideas."

Question: "What 'things' are there in no-mind?" Answer: "No-mind is without 'things.' The absence of things is the Naturally True (t'ien-chen 天真). The Naturally True is the Great Enlightenment (ta-tao 大道)."

Question: "How can the wrong ideas of sentient beings be extinguished?" Answer: "If you perceive [i.e., "think in terms of"] wrong ideas and extinction, you will not transcend (li 離) wrong ideas."

Question: "Without extinguishing [wrong ideas], can one attain union with the principle of enlightenment?" Answer: "If you speak of 'union' and 'non-union' you will not transcend wrong ideas."

Question: "What should I do?" Answer: "You should do nothing."

Question: "I understand this teaching now even less than before." Answer: "There truly is no understanding of the Dharma. Do not seek to understand it."

Question: "What is the ultimate?" Answer: "There is no beginning and no end."

Question: "Can there be no cause and effect [i.e., training and enlightenment]?" Answer: "There is no fundamental (pen 本) and no derivative (mo 末)."

Question: "How is this explained?" Answer: "The true is without explanation."

Question: "What is knowing and perception (chih-chien 知見)?" Answer: "To know the Suchness of all dharmas, to perceive the sameness of all dharmas."

Question: "What mind is it that knows, what eye is it that perceives?" Answer: "This is the knowing of non-knowing, the perception of non-perception."

Question: "Who teaches these words?" Answer: "It is as I have been asked."

Question: "What does it mean to say that it is as you have been asked?" Answer: "If you contemplate [your own] questions, the answers will be understood [thereby] as well."

At this Conditionality was silent and he thought everything through once again. Professor Enlightenment asked: "Why do you not say anything?" Conditionality answered:

"I do not perceive even the most minute bit of anything that can be explained."

At this point Professor Enlightenment said to Conditionality: "You would appear to have now perceived the True Principle."

Conditionality asked: "Why [do you say] 'would appear to have perceived' and not that I 'correctly perceived' [the True Principle]?" Enlightenment answered: "What you have now perceived is the non-existence of all dharmas. This is like the non-Buddhists who study how to make themselves invisible, but cannot destroy their shadow and footprints."

Conditionality asked: "How can one destroy both form and shadow?" Enlightenment answered: "Being fundamentally without mind and its sensory realms, you must not willfully generate the ascriptive view [or, perception] of impermanence."

*　*　*

Question: "If one becomes [a Tathāgata] without transformation and in one's own body, how can it be called difficult?" Answer: "Willfully generating (ch'i 起) the mind is easy; extinguishing the mind is difficult. It is easy to affirm the body, but difficult to negate it. It is easy to act, but difficult to be without action. Therefore, understand that the mysterious achievement is difficult to attain, it is difficult to gain union with the Wondrous Principle. Motionless is the True, which the three [lesser types of] are only rarely attained."

At this Conditionality gave a long sigh,
his voice filling the ten directions.
Suddenly, soundlessly, he experienced a great
expansive enlightenment. The mysterious
brilliance of his pure wisdom [revealed] no
doubt in its counter-illumination. For the
first time he realized the extreme difficulty
of spiritual training and that he had been
uselessly beset with illusory worries. He
then lamented aloud: "Excellent, excellent!
Just as you have taught without teaching, so
have I heard without hearing. Hearing and
teaching being unitary is equivalent to serene
non-teaching...."84

Other scholars have analyzed the contents of
the Chüeh-kuan lun by focusing on individual lines and
terms from the text,85 but I believe that it is the
transformation experience by Conditionality that is
its most important and revealing aspect. The stages
in this transformation are as follows:

1. From the very beginning through the
greater part of the text, Conditionality asks
one question after another without ever really
understanding the point of Enlightenment's
answers. The questions are not always particularly profound, but they serve as a useful
aid in the presentation of the Ox-head
approach to religious practice. The impact of
the Mādhyamika on this approach is quite evident in Enlightenment's consistent refusal to
allow the conscious postulation or willfull

generation of any religious ideal or
activity.

2. At the end of the second segment presented above, Conditionality achieves what he
thinks is a major breakthrough: the complete
disappearance of all discriminative perception. This is not sufficient for his teacher,
who greets this attainment with pointedly
faint praise and rejects it as a form of
cognitive nihilism.

3. Although Enlightenment continues to
talk in negative terms about extinguishing the
mind and body, his student's final experience
of enlightenment is described in very positive
terms. That is, "the mysterious brilliance of
his pure wisdom [revealed] no doubt in its
counter-illumination."

Although one might quibble that this dramatiza-
tion of Conditionality's enlightenment is not very
realistic, it is more important to notice that it adds
substantially to the literary effect of the Chüeh-
kuan lun at the same time that it helps to underscore
an important point of Ox-head religious doctrine. The
Ox-head School, if we are to judge by the Chüeh-kuan
lun was not entirely against the notion of meditative
contemplation per se. On the contrary, it sought to
promote the practice--but demanded a certain sophistication that was all too frequently lacking in the
beginning student. Throughout the course of the
Chüeh-kuan lun, Professor Enlightenment struggles
diligently to bring his student to this level of
religious sophistication. In the process he deflects
Conditionality's interests in pacifying the mind,

achieving the extraordinary abilities associated with meditative endeavor (telepathy, levitation, and the like), and maintaining the letter rather than the true spirit of the precepts, etc. When Conditionality succeeds in eliminating all these tendencies, his teacher carries him still further, so that he ultimately achieves a state of perfect wisdom. The point of all the negation and denial, then, is not that there was no positive goal to be reached, but that the discrimination or conceptualization of goals, techniques, and moral standards was absolutely rejected. This is no different from the most fundamental message of the Prajñā-pāramitā or Perfection of Widsom texts: that one should practice the Bodhisattva path, but never perceive there to be any path or any person practicing it. The distinctive feature of the Chüeh-kuan lun is thus not its ultimate message, but the form in which it presents that message.

The final state of wisdom reached by Conditionality is described in terms that are essentially identical both to Chi-tsang's definition of prajñā and the religious ideal of the Northern School. Concerning the former, Conditionality's penultimate achievement represents the transcendence of all discriminatory cognition, while his final achievement represents a breakthrough into the pure, non-discriminating illumination of śūnyatā. Before considering the relationship between this achievement and the teachings of the Northern School, let us first consider the very informative example of the Platform Sūtra. The question of immediate antecedents to Ox-head School doctrine can then be introduced and discussed in a more integrated and meaningful way.

(b) The Platform Sūtra: The Platform Sūtra, which is now thought to have been written around the year 780, begins with a very charming narrative about the transmission of the Dharma from Hung-jen, the Fifth Patriarch, to Hui-neng. In this account Shen-hsiu is depicted as a highly learned and sincere, but unenlightened, chief student of the Fifth Patriarch. Hui-neng, on the other hand, is represented as an illiterate barbarian from the far South who is not even a monk, but who is nonetheless intuitively enlightened to the true meaning of Buddhism.   Realiz-ing that the time of his death is approaching, Hung-jen gives his students the following assignment: Each of them was to write a verse describing his own under-standing of Buddhism, the one with the best verse to receive transmission of the Dharma and become his successor, the Sixth Patriarch. The majority of Hung-jen's students do not even attempt to enter this com-petition, since they are convinced that victory will go to Shen-hsiu.   After all, had he not been their own instructor over the years?   Shen-hsiu himself, however, is intensely aware of his own lack of true understanding.   Finally, in great consternation, he writes:

The body is the Bodhi Tree.
The mind is like a bright mirror's stand.
Laboring all the time to wipe [the mirror],
one should not let there be any dust.

The Fifth Patriarch inwardly realizes the limitations of this verse, but exhorts his students to recite it and practice accordingly. When Hui-neng, who has been serving as a lowly temple menial since his arrival

eight months previously, hears about the competition
and Shen-hsiu's verse, he composes the following:

> Bodhi fundamentally has no tree.
> The bright mirror likewise has no stand.
> The Buddha-nature is always clear and pure--
> where could there be any dust?[86]

Although this verse is the key to Hui-neng's accession
to the status of Patriarch, thereby upsetting the
favorite candidate, Shen-hsiu, it is not the final
statement of the Platform Sūtra's teachings. This
final statement must be sought in the long sermon that
completes the core portion of this important text.
Although it is difficult to select one segment that is
in itself representative of the entire sermon, the
following verse is "Hui-neng's" last pronouncement
before accepting questions from his listeners:

> The ignorant person practices seeking future
> happiness, and does not practice the Way,
> And says that to practice seeking future hap-
> piness is the Way.
> Though he hopes that almsgiving and offerings
> will bring boundless happiness,
> As before, in his mind the three [types of]
> karmas are created.
> If you wish to destroy your crimes by practic-
> ing seeking future happiness,
> Even though in a future life you obtain this
> happiness, the crime will still be left.
> If you can, in your mind cast aside the cause
> of your crimes,

Then each of you, within your own natures,
will truly repent,

If you awaken to the Mahāyāna and truly
repent,

Evil being removed and good achieved, you will
truly attain to crimelessness.

If students of the Way observe their own
selves well,

They will be the same as those already
awakened.

I am causing this Sudden Teaching to be transmitted,

And one who aspires to learn it will become
one with me.

If in the future you wish to seek your
original body,

Wash out the evil abuses of the three poisons
from within your minds.

Work hard to practice the Way; do not be
absent-minded.

If you spend your time in vain your whole life
will soon be forfeited.

If you encounter the teaching of the Mahayana
Sudden Doctrine,

Join your palms in devotion and sincerity,
and strive earnestly to reach it.[87]

Although the Chüeh-kuan lun and the Platform
Sūtra are obviously two very different works, there is
a certain parallelism in the structure of their arguments. Each work begins with the statement or implication of a relatively unsophisticated doctrine of
religious training, i.e., Conditionality's questions
and implicit preconceptions and "Shen-hsiu's" verse.

This relatively primitive doctrine is then rejected, by Professor Enlightenment's relentless negations and "Hui-neng's" verse, respectively. The final or ultimate position of each text is then stated in positive terms, in Conditionality's final experience of enlightenment and "Hui-neng's" sermon. In other words, both texts relate their message by means of a thesis, antithesis, and synthesis.

On the surface, such a tripartite structure should not seem surprising in the context of any major religious tradition, especially Buddhism. Considering the Mādhyamika affiliations of the Ox-head School, we could compare this structure to the doctrine of the Two Truths, the samvṛti-satya or Conventional Truth and the paramārtha-satya or Ultimate Truth. In Mādhyamika texts, the conventional apprehension of the world by ordinary, discriminative consciousness is never granted ultimate validity, but it is only through the investigation of the contradictions inherent in that unenlightened perception of reality that the higher truth is indicated.

This being the case, it would be a relatively simple matter to search for similar styles of presentation in texts written well before the advent of the Ox-head School. Nevertheless, I have not observed this particular structure of argument in any text of early Ch'an, which is after all the subject at hand. Shen-hui, of course, indicates his own teachings with the aid of comparison to a well-criticized version of Northern School teachings, but his approach was more inclined to simple comparison than integrated dialectical progression. Other early texts will state different series of teachings with the implication of ascending hierarchies of profundity, but I recall no

example where the lower doctrines are actually
repudiated in favor of the higher. It would seem that
this type of argument is a trademark of the Ox-head
School.

Even more than the Chüeh-kuan lun, the Platform
Sūtra has long been associated with Shen-hui and his
teachings. In this case, the suspicion that it was
actually written by a member of his lineage received
much greater credence because of the text's numerous
borrowings from his works. Yanagida's analysis of the
Ox-head origins of the Platform Sūtra was based
principally on issues other than those under consideration here. Briefly, then, how do the verses attributed to Shen-hsiu and Hui-neng relate to the long sermon that follows?

The traditional interpretation of "Shen-hsiu's"
verse is that it represents a gradual teaching. That
is, the practitioner is supposed to strive constantly
to purify and perfect himself, progressively ridding
himself of illusions just as a mirror might be cleaned
of dust. According to this interpretation, one
achieves enlightenment upon completely ridding one's
mind of illusion, just as a mirror that is made completely clean will reflect or "illuminate" all things
perfectly.

This interpretation of "Shen-hsiu's" verse is
consistent with the other references to Northern
School doctrine in the sermon that follows. In particular, the practice of "viewing purity" (k'an-ching
看淨), a well-known mainstay of Northern School
meditation practice, is rejected because it supposedly
implies a dichotomy between what is pure and what is
impure.[88] The sudden teaching, of course, refuses to
stipulate any difference between purity and impurity.

Hence "viewing purity" is incorrect because it implies the attempt to reject impurity and embrace purity, just as polishing the mirror of the mind is incorrect because the dusts of illusion are fundamentally non-existent.

Two questions of real significance here are, first, whether or not these interpretations of the metaphor of the mirror and the practice of "viewing purity" are accurate representations of Northern School doctrine and, second, whether or not Fa-hai was aware of the authentic teachings of the Northern School at the time of his compilation of the <u>Platform Sūtra</u>. The answer to the first of these questions is definitely negative, but that to the second is uncertain.

A simple key to the understanding of the teachings of the Northern School and the original intent of the metaphor of the mirror as found in the <u>Platform Sūtra</u> verse is provided by the following excerpt from Shen-hsiu's <u>Kuan-hsin lun</u> 觀心論 (<u>Treatise on the Contemplation of the Mind</u>):

> Further, lamps of eternal brightness (<u>ch'ang-ming teng</u> 長明灯, i.e., votive lamps) are none other than the truly enlightened mind. When one's wisdom is bright and distinct, it is likened to a lamp. For this reason all those who seek emancipation always consider the body as the lamp's stand, the mind as the lamp's dish, and faith as the lamp's wick. The augmentation of moral discipline is taken as the addition of oil. For wisdom to be bright and penetrating is likened

to the lamp's flame (or, in an alternate version, "brightness"). If one constantly burns
such a lamp of truly such-like true enlightenment, its illumination will destroy all the
darkness of ignorance and stupidity. If one
can [inspire others to] become enlightened by
using this teaching, then one lamp lights a
hundred or a thousand lamps. Since the lamps
are bright successively, the brightness is
never exhausted. In the past there was a
Buddha named "Burning Lamp" (Dīpaṃkara), the
meaning of which is the same as this.[89]

This passage does not describe a doctrine of gradual
practice, but rather one that the Northern School
texts variously refer to as "perfect and sudden"
(yüan-tun 圓頓) or "perfectly accomplished"
(yüan-ch'eng 圓成).[90] It defines a style of religious practice that is to be maintained constantly.
There is no mention of any instantaneous flash of
insight, a single moment in which one is transformed
from ignorant to enlightened person , simply because
there is no essential difference between these two
states. The congruence between the metaphor of the
lamp in the passage above and that of the mirror in
the Platform Sūtra verse hardly needs explication; the
latter reads like a fragment of the former. Omitting
the reference to the Bodhi Tree for a moment, wiping
the surface of the mirror and never allowing any dust
to alight thereon is not the key to the mirror's first
attainment of its reflective capacity (i.e., a moment
of enlightenment), but rather a standard maintenance
operation necessary for the on-going functioning of
the mirror. Analogous elements in the metaphor of the

lamp are the addition of oil and trimming of the wick, both of which are necessary to the lamp's continued function of illumination.

The mirror is, in fact, a better metaphor than the lamp for the never-ending brilliance of the mind's inherent capacity for wisdom: A lamp can go out, but a mirror always shines, whether obscured by dust or not. As the Northern School texts themselves point out, the mirror's reflective capacity is inherent, a fundamentally existent capacity. The dust that might obscure it, however, is quintessentially illusory and non-existent and thus has no real impact on the mirror at all. There are, in fact, a number of passages within Northern School texts that indicate basically the same idea as that found in "Hui-neng's" verse, i.e., that the illuminative capacity of the mirror (the mind) is so fundamental that dust (the illusions) either have no impact whatsoever or do not even really exist.[91]

The original meaning of "viewing purity" is a bit more subtle and, therefore, more difficult to explain quickly than the metaphor of the mirror. There are numerous references in Northern School works to the correct type of "viewing" to be undertaken in the course of meditation, but the most revealing one is the very simple statement attributed to Shen-hsiu: "View purity in the locus of purity (<u>ching-ch'u</u> <u>k'an</u> <u>ching</u> 淨處看淨)."[92] The implication of this and other references to the same subject is not that one should reject impurity in favor of purity, but that one's entire existence, both subjective and objective, self and environment, is essentially pure. To paraphrase the <u>Ta-sheng</u> <u>ch'i-hsin</u> <u>lun</u> 大乘起信論 (<u>The</u> <u>Awakening</u> <u>of</u> <u>Faith</u> <u>in</u> <u>the</u> <u>Mahāyāna</u>), this is not the

purity of pure and impure, but a higher sort of purity
that transcends all dualities. In addition, the
notion that one should willfully generate or "activate" (ch'i 起) the mind in order to view purity--or
to do anything, for that matter--was specifically pro-
scribed in the Northern School texts. Indeed, the
early Northern School devotion to the ideal of pu-ch'i
不起 or "non-activation" of the mind is one of the
best-documented facts about the School's teachings and
practices.[93]

Next, did Fa-hai know the real Northern School
interpretations of the metaphor of the mirror and the
practice of "viewing purity?" Were it not for the
discussion of the latter subject in the Platform
Sutra, the answer to this question might well be
affirmative. This is only in part because of the
remarkable coincidence between that metaphor and the
passage introduced above from Shen-hsiu's Kuan-hsin
lun. In addition to this, the reference to the Bodhi
Tree in the same verse can also be keyed to passages
within Northern School literature.[94] If Fa-hai had
been aware of the authentic interpretation of this
metaphor, we could argue as follows: Instead of
positing a relatively primitive doctrine of spiritual
training, Fa-hai chose the most sophisticated doctrine
known to him. "Hui-neng's" verse would thus have even
greater impact as the repudiation of something previously considered to be extremely profound and valuable. Naturally, this would have important implications regarding the relative importance of Northern
School teachings in the formation of Ox-head
doctrine.

However interesting this possibility might be,
the entire scenario does not fit with the contents of

the rest of the _Platform Sūtra_. First of all, the verse from "Hui-neng's" sermon introduced above quite openly criticizes the quest of ignorant people for future happiness. Within a Buddhist context there can hardly be any more primitive approach to religious activity. This willingness to criticize quite elementary doctrines prevails throughout the entire sermon. In addition, there is repeated evidence that Fa-hai's understanding of Northern School doctrines (and it should be pointed out that the most characteristic of Northern School doctrines discussed in the _Platform Sūtra_ are never labeled as such) was based primarily on the polemical positions of Shen-hui.

We now come to the question of Northern Ch'an influence on the doctrines of the Ox-head School. Before beginning, it is necessary to point out that it will be impossible in the present context to include the sort of elaborate cross-referencing of primary sources that will ultimately be necessary to prove the assertions made here. Such documentation will accompany a new translation of the _Chüeh-kuan_ _lun_ to be published sometime in the future. Further, all discussion of Shen-hui's influence on the development of Ox-head doctrine will also be deferred to a later occasion. Although the precise dimensions of Shen-hui's contribution to the development of early Ch'an are, in my opinion, still to be delineated, the fact of that contribution is beyond question. It is the matter of the Northern School's influence that is much more obscure and, perhaps for that very reason, of much greater importance to our own search for understanding. What we are looking for here is not the obvious impact of Shen-hui's high-profile campaign,

but the more pervasive influence of over a century of
Ch'an activity.

What, then, are the areas of similarity between
Northern and Ox-head School doctrine as demonstrated
in the Chüeh-kuan lun and the Platform Sūtra? Certain
minor indications of commonality are almost immediately evident--such as the presence of quotations from
the Leng-ch'ieh ching 楞伽經 or Lankāvatāra Sūtra
in the former and a reference to the i-hsing san-mei
一行三昧 or the Samādhi of Oneness, to use
Yampolsky's translation, in the latter.[95] In other
cases the Ox-head doctrines are clearly built upon
earlier Northern School formulations--such as the
equivalence of meditation and wisdom. (Shen-hui's
teachings on the subject played a part in the development of this doctrine as well.)[96] A complete listing
of such matters would be excessively intricate and
tedious, so that at present it will be best to focus
on the following three points:

1. The Metaphor of the Sun and Clouds: The
Platform Sūtra contains a description of the Buddha
nature existent within all sentient beings that is
couched in terms of an ever-shining sun obstructed by
the clouds of ignorance. Part of this description
reads:

The sun and the moon are always bright,
yet if they are covered by clouds, although
above they are bright, below they are dark-
ened, and the sun, moon, stars, and planets
cannot be seen clearly. But if suddenly the
wind of wisdom should blow and roll away the
clouds and mists, all forms in the universe
appear at once. The purity of the nature of

man in this world is like the blue sky; wisdom
is like the sun, knowledge like the moon.
Although knowledge and wisdom are always
clear, if you cling to external environments,
the floating clouds of false thoughts will
create a cover, and your own natures cannot
become clear.[97]

This is an elaboration of a metaphor that first occurs
in two very important early Ch'an works, the Hsiu-hsin
yao lun attributed to Hung-jen and Shen-hsiu's Kuan-
hsin lun.[98] Please note that it is not acceptable to
consider this metaphor to be part of some common
legacy received by both Shen-hsiu Hui-neng from Hung-
jen. The point is not so much that the date of composition of the Hsiu-hsin yao lun is in doubt, but
that the "Hui-neng" who appears in the Platform Sūtra
is not the same as the historical figure of the same
name.

It is interesting that his metaphor, or rather
the conception of latent enlightenment shared by all
people that it describes, formed the basis for the
practice of shou-hsin or "maintaining [awareness of]
the mind." Shou-hsin has already been mentioned above
as the apparent object of criticism by the Ox-head
School's Hsin ming. If both the Platform Sūtra and
the Hsin ming are to be accepted as products of the
Ox-head School, then we must infer that the lines
introduced above from the latter work cannot be interpreted as a simple repudiation of meditation
practice.

2. The Importance of Pu-ch'i or "Non-activation": We have already discussed this concept above.

its importance in the following statement by
-neng":

Men of the world, separate yourselves
from views; do not activate (ch'i) thoughts.
If there were no thinking, then no-thought
(wu-nien) would have no place to exist.... If
you give rise to thoughts (ch'i-nien 起念.)
from your self-nature, then, although you see,
hear, perceive, and know, you are not stained
by the manifold environments, and are always
free.[99]

The concept of pu-ch'i may best be explained
with reference to the metaphor of the mirror, not the
specialized example that occurs in the Platform Sūtra
verse, but the more general understanding that abounds
in the works of Northern Ch'an and other Buddhist
schools. According to this metaphor, the sage's mind
is supposed to perceive all things perfectly, just as
a mirror perfectly reflects its objects. As in Chi-
tsang's concept of wisdom, the enlightened person's
mind "illuminates" all things. Illuminating or per-
ceiving all things perfectly, the enlightened person
is supposed to react immediately to the needs of sentient beings. Just as the mirror displays an image
when an object is placed in front of it but does not
create images on its own, so the sage reacts perfectly
to the world around him but generates no independent
activities of his own. This avoidance of the intentional generation of any activity, physical or mental,
is known as pu-ch'i. Although not as prominent in the
Platform Sūtra as other concepts such as wu-nien or
"no-thought," the presence of pu-ch'i here indicates a

direct continuity between the Northern Ox-head Schools.

3. The Use of Kuan-hsin-shih or "Contemplative Analysis": The Platform Sutra gives some very interesting definitions for the term tso-ch'an 坐禪 or "sitting in meditation" and ch'an-ting 禪定 or "Ch'an meditation":

> In this teaching "sitting" means without any obstruction anywhere, outwardly and under all circumstances, not to activate thoughts (nien pu-ch'i). "Meditation" is internally to see the original nature and not become confused.
>
> And what do we call Ch'an meditation (ch'an-ting)? Outwardly to exclude form is "ch'an"; inwardly to be unconfused is meditation (ting).
>
> ...Separation from form on the outside is "ch'an"; being untouched on the inside is meditation (ting). Being "ch'an" externally and meditation (ting) internally, it is known as ch'an meditation (ch'an-ting).[100]

These explanations are obviously far removed from the primary meanings of the compounds involved. Although not immediately manifest in the Chüeh-kuan lun, this style of interpretation occurs in other fragmentary writings associated with the Ox-head School, so that Yanagida has called it a characteristic practice of that School.[101] Before it became associated with Ox-head Ch'an, however, this style of "contemplative analysis" was originally associated with the Northern School and, in particular, with Shen-hsiu.

The original tendency of "contemplative analysis" as practiced by the Northern School was to
redefine standard Buddhist terms and doctrines as
direct metaphors for the practice of meditation. The
metaphor of the lamp introduced above from Shen-hsiu's
Kuan-hsin lun is one example of this practice; other
examples, including those in which two-character compounds are split up and defined separately, abound in
the literature of his school. The Platform Sūtra discussion of tso-ch'an and ch'an-ting is interesting
in that it applies this process to a term for meditation itself.[102]

5. Conclusion

This article has been the first step in the
investigation of a hypothesis about the Ox-head
School: that it represents a link between the early
and classical phases of Chinese Ch'an Buddhism.
Obviously, the precise dimensions of the School's
historical role are still far from clear. The following types of research endeavor are still necessary:

    a. a more detailed examination of the
writings of Ox-head masters, including extensive cross-referencing between their ideas and
those of earlier and later figures in other
schools;
    b. study of the biographies of those
monks known to have trained under teachers of
both the Ox-head and later factions of Ch'an;
and

c.   The   search in early "encounter dialogue" material for any specific Ox-head
influence.

Several preliminary conclusions may be stated
as a result of study to date:
1.   The Ox-head School was a uniquely Southern
tradition, all of its members being from the South.
In fact, all of its major figures--the very early Fa-
jung and Chih-yen included--came from or were active
in a small area of what is now Kiangsu.
2.   The bonds that joined the Ox-head masters
were not based on long years of study together.
Although the limits of existent documentation may have
concealed a more extensive network of teacher-student
relationships, we must still infer that the School
represented some sort of an abstract religious ideal
with which personal identification was both attractive
and easily accomplished.
3.   Biographical data has suggested that the
Ox-head School was indeed related to both earlier and
later phases of Ch'an.   Two or three Ox-head monks are
known to have studied under Northern School masters,
and even more are associated with Ma-tsu Tao-i and
Shih-t'ou Hsi-ch'üan.   It is notable that there is so
little association of Ox-head monks with figures from
Shen-hui's lineage.   In addition, it is curious that
all of the monks associated with the later Ch'an
figures are members of the Ho-lin and Ching-shan factions of the Ox-head School.
4. A major part of the Ox-head School's unify-
ing religious ideal was the sense of its identity as
something separate from both the Northern and Southern
Schools.   There was no clear statement of any hierar-

chical judgment applied to these two earlier factions of Ch'an, only the express desire to transcend the sectarian division between the two.

     5.   Two of the Ox-head School's most important works state their message by means of a common structure of thesis, antithesis, and synthesis. Although the length, complexity, and textual problems of "Hui-neng's" sermon in the Platform Sūtra make comparison with the conclusion of the Chüeh-kuan lun difficult, it is clear that both texts are indebted to the much earlier contributions of the Northern School. That is, even though Shen-hui's perjorative interpretation of the Northern School's teachings was accepted and used, the ultimate teaching of the two Ox-head School texts remained in basic conformity with some of the most basic tenets of Northern School religious theory.

     The most interesting aspect of the Ox-head School is the way in which its teachings mirror its historical identity. The opening narrative of the Platform Sūtra, for example, can be read as historical allegory. Although the story itself is palpably false--Shen-hsiu and Hui-neng were never at Hung-jen's side at the same time and neither of them was there at the time of the master's death[103]--Shen-hsiu was a learned individual who taught great numbers of disciples within Hung-jen's lineage and Hui-neng was an obscure figure from the far South. The fact that Hui-neng is made to disappear for a time after his acquisition of the Dharma, as well as the popularity among Hung-jen's disciples of practice according to "Shen-hsiu's" verses, parallels the early ascendancy of the Northern School. Although Hui-neng's accession to the status of Sixth Patriarch implies an alignment of the

Platform Sūtra with Shen-hui's Southern School, note
that the virulence of Shen-hui's anti-Northern School
campaign is entirely missing. The Platform Sūtra
espouses the "sudden teaching" of the "Southern
School," but the content of each is different from
that of Shen-hui.

Even more than the allegorical interpretation
of the Platform Sūtra, the shared logical structure
and specific contents of it and the Chüeh-kuan lun are
entirely appropriate to the historical identity of the
Ox-head School. The use of thesis, antithesis, and
synthesis imply a legitimate association with the
Mādhyamika tradition. In addition, the School's
criticism of the ascribed teachings and use of the
authentic teachings of the Northern School and its
acceptance of Shen-hui's doctrinal innovations at the
same time as it rejected the polemical virulence of
his anti-Northern School campaign both demonstrate
that the Ox-head School was indeed an integral part of
the burgeoning Ch'an movement. As such, it was
indebted to previous developments at the same time as
it embraced its own unique and fully independent
ideal. Certain aspects of this unique ideal seem to
foreshadow the new spirit of Ch'an that was developing
in southeast China, but the discussion of such matters
is best left for a later occasion.

NOTES

1. The full title is Tonkō shutsudo shōshitsu issho (Ōsaka: Ataka Bukkyo bunko, 1935). This volume included photo-reproductions of the Tun-huang texts found by Suzuki in Peking; printed editions and Suzuki's comments were published by the same publisher the following year under the title Kōkan shōshitsu issho oyobi kaisetsu. The place-name shōshitsu, which literally means "small room," refers to a cave on Mount Sung which is traditionally associated with Bodhidharma, hence the English paraphrase used here. Please note that the English equivalents for Chinese and Japanese titles given in this article are offered for the reader's convenience and are not always literal translations.

2. Suzuki published his "Tonkō shutsudo Daruma oshō zekkanron ni tsuite" in Bukkyō kenkyū I:1 (1937). This included a critical edition based on three Tun-huang manuscripts and comments on the authorship of the treatise. This article is reproduced, with some revisions, in the Suzuki Daisetsu zenshū, II (Tōkyō: Iwanami shoten, 1968), 161-168. See note 6 below. Kuno had introduced these three manuscripts, which each man had independently discovered in the Pelliot Collection at Paris, and his own critical edition just a few months earlier in his "Ryūdōsei ni tomu Tōdai no Zenshū tenseki--Tonkō shutsudobon ni okeru Nanzen-Hokushū no daihyōteki sakuhin," published in Shūkyō kenkyū, new series XIV:1 (1937), 117-144.

3. See Kuno's "Gozu Hōyū ni oyoboseru Sanronshū no eikyō," Bukkyō kenkyū III:6 (1939), 51-88, and Ui's Zenshūshi kenkyū, I (Tōkyō: Iwanami shoten, 1939), 91-134. The second volume of Ui's Zenshūshi kenkyū (1941), pp. 511-519, includes a discussion of Fa-jung's relationship with five Chinese Mādhyamika masters.

4. See Suzuki and Furuta Shōkin, eds., Zekkanron (Kyōto: Kōbundo, 1945), or the Suzuki Daisetsu zenshū, II, 188-200, and Yanagida's "Zekkanron no hombun kenkyū," Zengaku kenkyū LVIII (1960), 65-124.

5. This volume has both Japanese and English titles: Tokiwa Gishin and Yanagida Seizan, Zekkanron--Eibun yakuchū, gembun kōtei, kokuyaku (Kyōto: Zen Bunka Kenkyūjo, Chūgoku zenroku kenkyūban, 1976) and Tokiwa Gishin, tr., A Dialogue on the Contemplation-Extinguished--A Translation based on Professor Seizan Yanagida's modern Japanese translation and consultations with Professor Yoshitaka Iriya (Kyōto: Institute for Zen Studies, 1973). The Institute referred to is connected with Hanazono College, which is itself affiliated with the Rinzai Zen School. Of the two dates given, the later one represents the date of the book's actual publication, although its preparation may have taken place much earlier.

6. Sekiguchi Shindai's Daruma daishi no kenkyū (Tōkyō: Shōkokusha, 1957; rpt. Toykō: Shunjūsha, 1969), pp. 85-93, contains a very convenient summary of the various arguments made in various articles by Suzuki, Kuno, and Sekiguchi himself. In addition to the works mentioned in notes 1, 2, and 4 above, Suzuki also discussed the Chüeh-kuan lun and the Ox-head School in his Zen shisōshi kenkyū, dai-ni--Daruma kara Enō ni itaru--which was actually written in 1943-1944, but published by Iwanami shoten in Tōkyō in 1951 and reprinted in the Suzuki Daisetzu zenshū, II, 161-208. Pages 161-168 contain a reproduction of Suzuki's article of 1937, pages 168-187 represent his comments to the edition of 1943, while pages 188-209 are devoted to editions of portions of two Tun-huang manuscripts. For the contributions of Kuno and Sekiguchi, see notes 2, 3, and 8.

7. Actually, Kuno first suggested the attribution to Shen-hui, but soon abandoned it in favor of that to Fa-jung. Suzuki never made any explicit response to Sekiguchi's arguments, which were published in "Zekkanron (Tonkō shutsudo) sensha kō," Taisho Daigaku gakuho XXX and XXXI (1940).

8. In addition to the article mentioned in the previous note, Sekiguchi has also written the following: "Tonkō shutsudo Zekkanron shōkō," Tendai Shūkyōgaku Kenkyūjo hō I (1951), which includes further evidence on the Ox-head affiliations of the Chüeh-kuan lun; Daruma daishi no kenkyū, already cited above, which includes long sections on the Chüeh-kuan lun (pp. 82-185) and the closely related Wu-hsin lun (Treatise on No-mind, pp. 186-212); "Gozuzen no rekishi to Darumazen," Shūkyō bunka XIV (March 1959), 1-118, republished in his Zenshū shisōshi (Tōkyō:

Sankibō busshorin, 1964), pp. 240-402, which includes
a painstaking examination of every available shred of
information about the lives of all the known Ox-head
masters; "Gotaisan to Gozusan," Tōhō shūkyō XVI
(November 1960), 21-39; and Daruma no kenkyū (Tōkyō:
Iwanani shoten, 1967), 344-356, which adds interesting
speculation about the apparent connection between Fo-
k'u Wei-tse and Fu Hsi.   (Note that Daruma Daishi no
kenkyū and Daruma no kenkyū are completely different
works.)   Sekiguchi's failure to prove the attribution
of the Chüeh-kuan lun to Fa-jung is based on a methodological oversight: He showed the text to be associated with Fa-jung's name in ninth-and tenth-century
sources and Fa-jung to lack any historical relationship to the Ch'an School, but this does not prove that
the Chüeh-kuan lun itself was also created independently of the Ch'an School.   Rather, it is most likely
that the Chüeh-kuan lun was a later compilation by a
member or members of the Ox-head School and attributed
to the legendary founder, who himself had had no
contact with the Ch'an School per se and nothing to do
with the Chüeh-kuan lun.

9.   Yanagida's book was published by Hōzōkan in
Kyōto.

10.   Yanagida discusses the establishment of the
"transmission of the lamp" (dentōshi or tōshi in
Japanese) genre within the Northern School on pp. 33-
100; other examples of Northern School precedents to
various facets of Southern School thought occur on pp.
102, 148-149, 153, and 182-184.   On the Ox-head
School's being a reaction or alternative to the
Northern and/or Southern Schools, see pp. 127, 132-
133, and 181-182.   On the date of authorship of the
Chüeh-kuan lun, see p. 143.   The probable authorship
of the Platform Sutra by Fa-hai is discussed on pp.
101-212, most specifically on pp. 195-209.

11.   Kamata Shigeo has written the following on
the subject of the Ox-head School: "Chōkan ni okeru
zenshisō no keisei--gozuzen no sōjō--," Indogaku
Bukyōgaku kenkyū IX:2 (1961), 73-78; Chūgoku Kegon
shisōshi no kenkyū (Tōkyō: Tōkyō daigaku shuppansha,
1965), pp. 390-393 and 475-500; Chūgoku Bukkyō
shisōshi kenkyū (Tōkyō: Shunjūsha, 1969), pp. 6, 61,
115, 132, 225, 237-258, and 394; and "Sanronshū-
Gozuzen-Dōkyō o musubu shisōteki keifu--sōboku jōbutsu
o tegakari to shite--," Komazawa Daigaku Bukkyō Gakubu
kenkyū kiyō, XXVI.   Kamata's contributions are interesting and skillfully done, especially on the

doctrinal relationship between the ideas of Ox-head Ch'an and Taoism, but they are too specialized to be of use here. Nakagawa Taka has written two articles on the Chüeh-kuan lun: "Zekkanron kō," Indogaku Bukkyōgaku kenkyū VII:2 and "Zekkanron o chūshin to shite mitaru shoki Zenshushi no mondaiten, "Tōhoku Yakka Daigaku kiyō V (November 1958). Unfortunately, her attempts to make Bodhidharma's disciple Hui-k'o and Fa-jung the primary and secondary authors of the Chüeh-kuan lun and Fo-k'u Wei-tse its editor are quite unacceptable.

12. "Gozuzen no shisō," Indogaku Bukkyōgaku kenkyū XV:2 (1967), 16-23.

13. On the supposed meeting between Tao-hsin and Fa-jung, see Ui, pp. 91-96. The historical summary presented here has been compiled with close reference to Sekiguchi's long article in Zenshūshi kenkyū. Some information from additional sources will be introduced, but all arguments based on "encounter dialogue" material from the CTL and other late sources will be omitted.

14. The point that Fa-jung, Hui-fang, and Fa-ch'ih were all together at one time is made by Ui, p. 100. The other observations made here are taken, with some modification, from Sekiguchi, Zenshū shisōshi, pp. 265-268.

15. See T50.603c-605b and Sekiguchi, Daruma daishi no kenkyū, pp. 134-147.

16. It is possible that Fa-jung was thus related to Ching-chüeh of the Northern School and some of the prominent lay supporters of Buddhism (the Ox-head School included) active during the second half of the eighth-century. See Yanagida, Shoki Zenshū shisho no kenkyū, pp. 203-204.

17. Fa-jung's teachers are discussed by Ui. See note 3 above.

18. These restrictions, which involved limitations on the number of temples, etc., in areas of the South which the T'ang authorities felt were supporting rebels against the newly-established state, were imposed in 621. See the HKSC, T50.633c.

19. See T50.602a-c and Sekiguchi, Zenshū shisōshi, pp. 251-258.

20. The text reads age forty, but Sekiguchi, p. 252, shows that the correct figure is forty-five.

21. See Yanagida, Shoki Zenshū shisho no kenkyū, pp. 36 and 45, note 4.

22. See the CTL T51.228c, for their biographies.

23. This assertion is made in the SKSC at T50.757c and the CTL at T51.228c. The SKSC, which is the earlier and longer of the two accounts, devotes more space to this alleged connection with Hung-jen than to Fa-ch'ih's studies under Hui-fang. The wording of the assertion presumes knowledge of the description of Hung-jen's last words as found in the Leng-ch'ieh jen-fa chih (Account of the Men and Teachings of the Lankā [vatāra School]), but Fa-ch'ih's name is not included in the list contained in this work--only in one of the lists in Tsung-mi's voluminous writings. See Yanagida, Shoki no Zenshi I-- Ryōgashijiki, Den'hōbōki--, Zen no goroku, Vol. 2 (Tōkyō: Chikuma shobō, 1971), p. 273 or T85.1289c and Kamata Shigeo, Zengen shosenshū tojo, Zen no goroku, Vol. 9 (Tōkyō: Chikuma shobō, 1971), p. 289. Furthermore, the age at which the SKSC has Fa-ch'ih studying under Hung-jen corresponds to the year 647--four years before the death of Hung-jen's own teacher Tao-hsin and fully a decade before that of Niu-t'ou Fa-jung. If, on the other hand, one accepts the CTL version that Fa-ch'ih studied under Hung-jen at age thirty or in 664, this is only one year before Chih-wei is supposed to have studied under Fa-ch'ih. Yanagida, who points out these details on p. 129 of his Shoki Zenshū shisho no kenkyū, suggests that Fa-ch'ih's study under Hung-jen was relatively brief and not enough to inspire his inclusion in the list of that master's major disciples. Although Yanagida acknowledges that he is using late materials, he further suggests that the attempt to link the Ox-head School with the Ch'an tradition of Bodhidharma through Hung-jen and Fa-ch'ih was an early enterprise that had already disappeared by the 750's (p. 130, his emphasis). Although it is impossible to corroborate this hypothesis, it does agree with the general tendency of early Ch'an to elaborate matters relating to the patriarchs in the reverse order of their presumed succession. Thus it would have been quite natural for the Ox-head School to identify itself first with Hung-jen and then with Tao-hsin.

24. Chih-wei's SKSC biography is at T50.758b-c.
His move from Mount Niu-t'ou to Chin-ling was supposedly modeled after a similar move by Fa-ch'ih, but
one tends to wonder whose biography was modeled after
whom. Obviously, the emergence of the Ox-head School
as an alternative to both the Northern and Southern
Schools must have been a post-732 phenomenon, but even
before that year, in which Shen-hui opened his attack
upon the so-called "Northern School," there may have
been some feeling of community identity shared by
Chih-wei and his students in southeast China.
Yanagida's suggestion about Chih-wei occurs on p. 180
of Shoki Zenshū shisho no kenkyū.

25. See Sekiguchi, Zenshū shisōshi, pp. 270-272,
for the several brief references to An-kuo Hsüan-t'ing
in primary sources. The TCL contains a passage
attributed to him, T48.944b.

26. See T50.834c-835b, T51.229a-230b, and Sekiguchi, Zenshū shisōshi, pp. 275-281.

27. See Sekiguchi, p. 279. For the excerpt of
Hui-chung's teachings that occurs in the TCL, see
T48.945b. The title Hsing-lu nan is taken from a
fixed refrain in the text--that is, in the Tun-huang
manuscript of the text, which is not necessarily that
by Hui-chung. For a discussion of this refrain, see
Iriya Yoshitaka, "Chōshin kōro nan--teikaku renshō no
kakyoku ni tsuite--," Tsukamoto hakase juki kinen
Bukkyō shigaku ronshū (Kyōto: Tsukamoto hakase juki
kinen kai, 1961), pp. 82-83. For information about
the text itself and the extant Tun-huang manuscripts,
see Yanagida's "Zenseki kaidai," Nishitani Keiji and
Yanagida Seizan, eds., Zenke goroku, sekai koten
bungaku zenshū, No. 36B)(Tōkyō: Chikuma shobō, 1974),
II, 465.

28. The CTL's list of Hui-chung's disciples
occurs at T51.223c-224a. For a discussion of their
biographies, see Sekiguchi, pp. 282-292. T'ai-po
Kuan-tsung's epitaph may be found in the Ch'üan T'ang-
wen (Complete Writings of the T'ang, hereafter abbreviated CTW), in the fascicle 721.

29. See T50.768b-c, T51.231a, and Sekiguchi,
Zenshū shisōshi, pp. 328-335. By all rights this monk
should be referred to as Wei-tse, but the toponym Fo-
k'u has been used throughout to minimize the possibility of confusion. Fo-k'u is also the more common
in the primary sources.

30. See Sekiguchi, p. 334.

31. The same place-name is also used in reference to a location on Mount Niu-t'ou, but this fact is not mentioned in the primary sources vis-à-vis Fo-k'u Wei-tse.

32. See T50.768c, T55.1106b-c, and Sekiguchi, Zenshū shisōshī, p. 332. Some of the same works are also listed in other catalogues by Saichō (T55.1059b), Eun (1089a and 1091b), and Enchin (1093c, 1095a, and 1100c-1101b). These listings are generally made without attribution. The poems listed here as Fo-k'u's fifth work were not necessarily one integrated whole, but a number of different poems circulated either together or separately.

33. The Ch'an works that exist under the names of Pao-chih and Fu Hsi--which are, of course, totally spurious attributions--should be examined for their possible connection with the Ox-head School. Sekiguchi's Daruma no kenkyū, pp. 350-356, contains some interesting material in this regard, as already noted above.

34. For a complete list of the materials related to the Ox-head School that Saichō took back to Japan, see Sekiguchi, pp. 353-354. Also see his Zenshū shisōshi, pp. 333-334. Saichō's listing of the Wu-sheng i was mentioned in note 23 above; note that he also lists the CKL.

35. The SKSC lists the author of the inscription on this stele, but the work itself does not survive.

36. See T48.946b. The excerpts from his (no specific works are listed) occur at T48.910a and 947a. The student in question is known as Yün-chü Fu-chih. He is associated with both Mount T'ien-t'ai (which toponym is often prefixed to his name) and Yün-chü Temple on Mount Chung, just north of Chin-ling. The Japanese catalogues list a collection of his writings in juxtaposition with Fo-k'u's Huan-yüan chi. See T55.1089a, 1091b, and 1106b, cited in Sekiguchi, Zenshū shisōshi, p. 336.

37. Li Hua wrote some very interesting and useful epitaphs for members of several different Ch'an and non-Ch'an factions. See the brief discussion of his life and contributions by Yanagida, Shoki Zenshū shisho no kenkyū , pp. 136-137 and 144, note 1. The

epitaph for Hsüan-su occurs in the CTW, fascicle 320. The SKSC account (T50.761c-762b) is obviously based on this epitaph. That in the CTL (T51.229b-c) is quite limited. See Sekiguchi, Zenshū shisōshi, pp. 293-299.

38. Unfortunately, this is not the only potential source of confusion surrounding Hsüan-su's names and titles. Not only is he also commonly referred to by the name of his temple, Ho-lin, he is known within his epitaph as Ching-shan ta-shih, a name one would have expected to find in reference to his student, Ching-shan Fa-ch'in. The epitaph also refers to Hsüan-su as Yuan-su, but this is merely a reflection of the ritual avoidance of the first character of Emperor Hsüan-tsung's name. The epitaph mentions Hsüan-su's style of Tao-ch'ing, which is apparently not used elsewhere. Neither does his official title, which will be mentioned just below, seem to have been widely used.

39. The name Yuan-su occurs in the inscription for the Shao-lin Temple written by one P'ei Ts'ui (CTW, 279). Since the individual in question is described as a Vinaya Master who lived after the Chen-kuan era (627-649) and is discussed before Fa-ju, who died in 689, it seems unlikely that he might be the Hsüan-su under consideration here. If Hsüan-su had actually lived at Shao-lin Temple, even for a brief period of time, it would be a significant indication of a link between the Northern and Ox-head Schools.

40. Ho-lin Temple was prepared for Hsüan-su by the magistrate of Jun-chou, an individual named Wei-Hsien. See Yanagida's discussion of this and other persons of the same surname active in the Ch'an movement during the latter half of the eighth century, pp. 203-204. See note 16 above.

41. See Sekiguchi, pp. 301 and 309, for comments about the official who supported Hsüan-su in Yang-chou.

42. Hsüan-su and his temple were both eventually granted official titles, his being Ta-lü ("Greatly Regulated") ta-shih. See Sekiguchi, pp. 296-297, for comments on the circumstances of this bequest.

43. See Zenshū shisōshi, p. 296.

44. Li Hua's close connection with Hsüan-su and the Ox-head School is discussed by Yanagida, Shoki

Zenshū shisho no kenkyū, pp. 136-137 and 144-145, notes 1-2. Of the laymen listed in the epitaph, the only one of interest is Li Tan, who could through orthographic error be the same as the Li Chou mentioned in a Sung Dynasty work as the author of a biography of Hui-neng. Although there is no way to test this quite tenuous speculation, if correct it would supply an additional link between the Ox-head School and the biography of Hui-neng (additional, that is, to the Platform Sūtra). See Yanagida, p. 99, note 16. Another layman is known as the author of an epitaph for a southeastern Vinaya Master; see Yanagida, pp. 198, 210 note 13, and 255. The CTL (T51.223c and 225b) lists only two other students of Hsüan-su's; their biographies are unknown.

45. See Ui, Zenshūshi kenkyū, I, 328, for the occurrence of Chao-an's name among T'ung-kuang's students, and Sekiguchi, Zenshū shisōshi, pp. 319-320 and 371-372.

46. See Sekiguchi, pp. 313-319.

47. Ibid., pp. 320-322. On Ju-hai's teacher Hui-yin, the CTL lists a Hui-yin of Nan-yüeh as a student of the Northern School monk Chiang-ma Tsang (T51.226b). The identification of this monk with Nan-yüeh could have developed after Ju-hai's studies with him, if such were the case. In fact, Ju-hai could have studied under him at Nan-yüeh, which was something of a Northern School center at the time, if one takes the epitaph to refer to the Northern School rather than the northern part of China. (An earlier line in the epitaph implies that this is the case.) In addition, Ui, Zenshūshi kenkyū, I, 295, notes a Ta-yin of Ch'ang-an listed in the CTL as a student of I-fu (T51.224c). A passage from Liu Tsung-yüan's epitaph for Ju-hai will be quoted below.

48. The term "encounter dialogue" is a convenient usage that I selected during the translation of an article by Yanagida. It corresponds to the Chinese chi-yüan wen-ta, but this pair of compounds does not generally appear as a single unit in the original texts. See "The 'Recorded Sayings' Texts of Chinese Ch'an" in Lewis Lancaster and Whalen Lai, eds., Early Ch'an in China and Tibet, Berkeley Buddhist Studies Series, Vol. III (Berkeley: University of California Press, forthcoming).

49. See T50.738c-9a and Yanagida, Shoki Zenshū shisho no kenkyū, pp. 195-212.

50. The SKSC reference is at T50.796c. See Sekiguchi, Zenshū shisōhi, pp. 308-312, and Yanagida, Shoki Zenshū shisho no kenkyū, pp. 197-198, on the probable identity of Fa-shen and Huai-jang. See pp. 197-200 for Fa-hai's place within the combined meditation and Vinaya movement.

51. Chiao-jan's dates are unknown, but see the epitaph for him by Shen-hui's disciple Fu-lin (CTW 918) and various short works as well as an epitaph by Chiao-jan himself (CTW 917 and 918). Besides several references to Chiao-jan in Yanagida's Shoki Zenshū shisho no kenkyū, see the article by Ichihara Kōkichi on T'ang Dynasty poet-monks, "Chūtō shoki ni okeru kōsa no shisō ni tsuite," Tōhō gakuhō, Kyōto series XXVIII (March 1958). The discussion below is based chiefly on Yanagida, pp. 200-203.

52. See the inscription by Yen Chen-ch'ing cited in Ichihara, p. 228.

53. Fa-ch'in's epitaph (CTW, 512) was written by Li Chi-fu (760-814), who was Prime Minister during part of Emperor Te-tsung's reign (779-805). The closing lines of the SKSC account (T50.764b-765a) mention epitaphs by four other prominent officials, but only Li's is still extant. Shih-t'ou has traditionally been paired with Ma-tsu as one of the first leaders of the new "encounter dialogue" style of Ch'an. See Ui, Zenshūji kenkyū, I, 396-418.

54. See the purported text of this invitation in the CTW, 48, and Sekiguchi, Zenshū shisōshi, p. 342.

55. This work is the T'ang kuo-shih pu by Li Chao, written in the second decade of the ninth century. It includes events from circa 713-824. See the Shih-chieh shu-chü yin-hang edition (publisher's number 0155, Yang Chia-lo, general editor), pp. 21 and 24. The existence of this evidence concerning the Ox-head School is mentioned at the very end of Yanagida's "Gozuzen no shisō," p. 23.

56. The source mentioned in the previous note gives a different derivation of this name (p. 24).

57. The SKSC gives some specific information about this move, i.e., that the magistrate of Hang-

chou wished Fa-ch'in to occupy the temple so that it would not be destroyed by an overly-aggressive regional military commander. The epitaph points out that Hang-chou was a major cultural and mercantile center. Fa-ch'in's center at Ching-shan eventually grew into one of the most important of all Chinese Ch'an temples, being considered one of the "five mountains" (wu-shan), but the growth that led to this status did not really begin until some three-quarters of a century after Fa-ch'in's death.

58. See T50.816c-817a and Sekiguchi, Zenshū shisōshi, pp. 349-353.

59. This was not, of course, the first example of contact between the Ch'an and Esoteric Buddhist traditions. The Northern School monks Ching-hsien (660-723) and I-hsing (685-727) are associated with Subhākarasiṃha and Vajrabodhi, I-hsing in particular being one of the most important figures in the entire Chinese Esoteric School. See Yanagida's "Zenseki kaidai," p. 468, and Ui, Zenshūshi kenkyū, I, 299-300.

60. Sekiguchi, Zenshū shisōshi, pp. 291-292, 319-320, and 371-394 (see the table of contents on pp. 242-243), discusses the biographies of the men mentioned in the paragraph above. In general, the study of the development of encounter dialogue is made difficult by the fact that almost all the texts available from the period in question are extant only because they were edited and published in woodblock form during the Five Dynasties period and Sung Dynasty. There are exceptions to this treatment—Ma-tsu's recorded sayings are known through a later but potentially more authentic Ming Dynasty edition, for example—but there is no equivalent of the Tun-huang cache for this particular period. (Virtually nothing from the post-Ma-tsu years of Ch'an literature is represented at Tun-huang.) See Yanagida's "Zenshū goroku no keisei," Indogaku Bukkyōgaku kenkyū XVIII:1 (35) (1969), or my translation mentioned in note 48 above.

61. See Yanagida, Shoki Zenshū shisho no kenkyū, pp. 130-131.

62. The entire catalogue of Ox-head doctrinal statements preserved in Yen-shou's works is listed in Yanagida's "Gozuzen no shisō." Note that he inadvertently overlooks one such citation at T48.910a. Several of the quotations from works attributed to

Fa-jung must be considered later anonymous contributions.

63. See the convenient summary in Yampolsky, The
Platform Sūtra of the Sixth Patriarch (New York and
London: Columbia University Press, 1967), pp. 38-39.

64. CTW, fascicle 512. The mistaken reference to
Tao-hsin as the third, rather than the fourth, generation successor to Bodhidharma also occurs in the CTW
texts of other epitaphs by Li Hua.

65. CTW, 917.

66. CTW, 817. The last sentence of the first
paragraph reads, literally: "Capped with stupidity,
released in dissolution."

67. T48.944b.

68. See Li Hua's epitaph for Hui-chen (673-751),
CTW 319. Although Hui-chen is not really a member of
the Northern School per se (see the lineage diagram in
Yanagida, pp. 199-200), his epitaph contains material
very reminiscent of Northern School teachings.

69. See Yanagida's critical edition and annotated
translation, Shoki no zenshi II--Rekidai hōbō ki--,
Zen no goroku, Vol.3 (Tōkyō: Chikuma shobō, 1976), p.
231, or T51.190c. The term "Szechwan Schools" is used
as a convenient means of reference to the factions
headed by the Korean Reverend Kim (Chin ho-shang or
Wu-hsiang in Chinese) and his self-proclaimed Chinese
successor, Wu-chu. See Jeffrey Broughton's article
elsewhere in this volume.

70. See Yanagida, Shoki no zenshi, II, 129-130,
137, 140, and 142-143, or T51.184a-185c.

71. The implicit contradiction between the Ox-
head School's own lineage claims and Fa-hai's authorship of the Platform Sūtra was first pointed out to me
by Robert Gimello. See Yanagida's Shoki Zenshū shisho
no kenkyū, pp. 253-278, for a discussion of the complex origins of the contents of the Platform Sūtra.

72. Kuno, p. 56, and Ui, Zenshūshi kenkyū, I,
271-272, are each careful to reject the traditional
bias of orthodox Ch'an sources against the Northern
School. This simplified account may do these two

scholars a slight injustice, but it is useful for the present.

73. The main exponent of the importance of Shen-hui's role in the development of the Ch'an School was Hu Shih. See the first page of the introduction to his Shen-hui ho-shang i-chi, originally published in 1930 by the Ya-tung t'u-shu kuan in Shanghai and reprinted along with additional material in 1968 by the Chung-yang yen-chiu yüan Hu Shih chi-nien kuan in Taiwan. Also see his biographical study of Shen-hui in the same volume, pp. 5-90. The most convenient and accessible article by Hu Shih in English is his "Ch'an (Zen) Buddhism in China: Its History and Method," Philosophy East and West II:1 (1963). See pp. 4-9. Immediately following this article is D. T. Suzuki's "Zen: A Reply to Hu Shih," and it is interesting to note that, in spite of his fundamental disagreement with Hu Shih's approach to the study of Ch'an, Suzuki was in essential agreement with him on strictly historical matters. See pp. 27-28. A more sophisticated analysis, if not the final word on the subject, occurs in Paul Peachey's translation of Heinrich Dumoulin, S.J., A History of Zen Buddhism (New York: Random House, 1963; repr., Boston: Beacon Press, 1969), pp. 83-85.

74. See lines 13 and 216 of the Tun-huang manuscript, Pelliot number 3559. Also note the use of yüan-tun, "perfect and sudden," in the Ch'üan fa-pao chi (Annals of the Transmission of the Dharma-Treasure). See Yanagida, Shoki no zenshi I, 346.

75. See my doctoral dissertation on the Northern School of Ch'an, being written under the direction of Professor Stanley Weinstein at Yale University.

76. The translation given here is intended to fit with Kuno's understanding of the text. The meaning of this term will be discussed below.

77. See Kuno, p. 57. The original text occurs in the last fascicle of the CTL, T51.457b-58a.

78. Hung-jen's treatise may be found at T48.377a-379b and in the Suzuki Daisetsu zenshū, II, 303-307. My dissertation includes a new edition, English translation, and analysis of this text.

79. Nakamura Hajime, Bukkyōgo daijiten (Tōkyō: Tōkyō shoseki, 1975), p. 833a.

80. T45.76a-b.

81. Nakamura,   p.   195b   (third   definition).
Nakamura gives the Sanskrit equivalent for this usage
of kuan as pariksa.

82. T45.50a.

83. The subtle difference between these two readings of chüeh-kuan is manifest in a passage from
Tsung-mi's shorter commentary on the Yüan-chüeh ching
(Sūtra on Perfect Enlightenment). In this passage
chüeh-kuan   is indeed   juxtaposed   to kuan-hsing,
"contemplative practice," but it is further identified
as   the   attainment of complete mental quiescence.
Clearly, meditative practice is only one part of that
which is transcended or eradicated in chüeh-kuan.
Although it is not certain that Tsung-mi's passage was
written with specific reference to the CKL, it
exhibits a similar type of dialectical argument to
that outlined below. See the Yüan-chüeh ching lüeh
shu and Yanagida, "Zekkanron no hombum kenkyū," p.
75.

84. The portions translated here are from sections 1, 14, and 15 of Yanagida's Institute for Zen
Studies text, pp. 87 and 97-99. All notes to the
translation will be deferred until a later occasion.

85. This statement applies not only to the work
of Kuno, Suzuki, and Sekiguchi, but to that of Kamata
as well. The most frequent focus of attention has
been the term wu-hsin or "no-mind."

86. See Yampolsky's translation of the Platform
Sūtra, pp. 128-132 in particular, for the complete
account of this fictional exchange. For the present
purposes we will ignore "Hui-neng's" second verse in
the Tun-huang version and the famous third line,
"Fundamentally there is not a single thing" (pen-lai
wu i wu), from later versions of the Platform Sūtra.
Apparently, this anecdote and the exchange of verses
circulated independently of the Platform Sūtra.
Tsung-mi was obviously aware of the verses, but he
never mentions the Platform Sūtra. See Yanagida,
Shoki Zenshū shisho no kenkyū, pp. 203-204. In addition, the ninth-century Japanese catalogues list works
that were almost certainly devoted to the exchange
between Hung-jen's two successors. See T55.1094a,
1095a, 1101a (two different titles), and 1106b. The
Platform Sūtra itself is listed in the same context at

0

T55.1095a, 1100c, and 1106b. Assuming that no other
material was involved, these works either formed the
nucleus of what eventually became the Platform Sūtra
or were extracted from that text itself.

87. This is Professor Yampolsky's translation.
See pp. 154-155 for his notes on several textual problems. The verse that is translated on pp. 159-161 of
his book might have been a better choice as the grand
conclusion of the Platform Sūtra's message, but it is
too long and so completely riddled with textual problems that authoritative interpretation seems impossible.

88. See Yampolsky, p. 137. K'an-ching is one of
the basic elements in Tsung-mi's description of the
teachings of the Northern School. See Z1, 14-277c.

89. See T85.1272a and the Suzuki Daisetsu zenshū,
suppl. Vol. I, pp. 622-623. This text occurs, under a
different title, at T48.368c.

90. See note 74 above.

91. The most explicit of these passages occurs in
a work called Liao-hsing chü (Stanzas on the
Comprehension of the [Buddha]-Nature), which reads:

> It is like a bright mirror on which there
> is dust. How could [the dust] damage its
> essential brightness? Although [the dust] may
> temporarily obstruct [the mirror], rubbing
> will return the brightness. The brightness is
> fundamentally bright....

See the Suzuki Daisetsu zenshū (Tōkyō: Iwanami
shoten, 1968), II, 450.

92. This line occurs in the Tun-huang manuscript,
Pelliot number 3559, line 614 (plate 26, line 9).

93. The Esoteric Buddhist master Śubhākarasimha
seems to be criticizing the practice of pu-ch'i when
he says in a discussion with Ching-hsien of the
Northern School: "You beginning students are quite
afraid of activating the mind and moving the
thoughts...and single-mindedly maintain no-thought as
the ultimate." See T18.945a. The term pu-ch'i occurs
more than once in the Wu fang-pien or Five Expedient
Means material of the Northern School. See the Suzuki
Daisetsu zenshū, III, 170, for example.

94. See *ibid.*, p. 233.

95. The lines from the Leng-ch'ieh ching used (without attribution) within the text of the Chüeh-kuan lun are noted by Kuno, pp. 72-73, and again by Yanagida, p. 148, note 21. For the I-hsing san-mei, see Yampolsky, p. 136, and Yanagida, Shoki no zenshi, I, 186-298.

96. This is one of the major points of the Platform Sūtra's message, one that distinguishes it from Shen-hui's teachings. See, for example, Yampolsky, p. 135; Suzuki Daisetsu zenshū, III, 224, and Yanagida, Shoki Zenshi shisho no kenkyu, pp. 156-157.

97. See Yampolsky, p. 142.

98. See T48.377a-b and 367a.

99. See Yampolsky, p. 139.

100. *Ibid.*, p. 140.

101. "Gozuzen no shisō," pp. 20-21.

102. In part, the Northern School practice of "contemplative analysis" may be understood as a means of overcoming the great weight of Chinese Buddhist tradition and legitimizing a new emphasis upon individual spiritual endeavor. The metaphors of Shen-hsiu's Kuan-hsin lun are perfect examples of this process. By the time of the Platform Sūtra, however, the practice of "contemplative analysis" was no longer limited to the re-interpretation of general Buddhist jargon as metaphors for the practice of meditation, but was also applied to the terminology of meditation itself.

103. The Ch'üan fa-pao chi has Shen-hsiu studying under Hung-jen for six years beginning at the former's age 46, of the year 651. See Yanagida, Shoki no zenshi, I, 396. The earliest source for Hui-neng's biography to include any dated information is attached to a work of Shen-hui's. This has him first traveling to Hung-jen's temple at age 22, or 659. This is at least two years after Shen-hsiu is said to have left. See Suzuki and Kuda Rentarō, Tonkō shutsudo Kataku Jinne zenji goroku (Tōkyō: Morie shoten, 1934), p. 60. Later sources have Hui-neng arriving at Hung-jen's side even later, so that the transmission to him

occurred closer to the end of the master's life. The fact that Shen-hsiu and Hui-neng did not study under Hung-jen at the same time was first pointed out to me by Robert Zeuschner.

THE TEACHING OF MEN AND GODS:
THE DOCTRINAL AND SOCIAL BASIS OF LAY BUDDHIST
PRACTICE IN THE HUA-YEN TRADITION

by

Peter N. Gregory

When we compare the doctrinal classification scheme (p'an-chiao 判教) elaborated by Tsung-mi 宗密 (780-841) in his Inquiry into the Origin of Man (Yüan-jen lun 原人論) with the classical five-fold scheme formulated by Fa-tsang 法藏 (643-712) in his Treatise on the Five Teachings (Wu-chiao chang 五教章), one of the most striking differences is Tsung-mi's inclusion of the Teaching of Men and Gods (jen-t'ien-chiao 人天教) as the first and most elementary level of Buddhist teaching. Fa-tsang's only mention of the Teaching of Men and Gods in the Treatise on the Five Teachings occurs in his discussion of a subsidiary enumeration of Buddhist doctrines, the so-called Ten Tenets (shih-tsung 十宗), where it is merely cited as the first of two subdivisions of the first tenet that both self and dharmas exist (wo-fa chü-yu 我法俱有).[1] Not only is the Teaching of Men and Gods not accorded the status of a separate category of teaching in Fa-tsang's classification scheme, it is also conspicuously absent in the classification schemes of Hui-yüan[2] 慧苑 (ca. 673-743) and Ch'eng-kuan 澄觀 (737-838). These two later Hua-yen masters only make passing reference to the Teaching of Men and Gods in their historical surveys of previous classification schemes[3]--a context which only serves to underline the insignificance with which they viewed this teaching. Given this long history of disregard on the part of his predecessors in the Hua-yen school, why did Tsung-mi break with tradition and include the Teaching of Men and Gods as a major feature of his classification scheme in the Inquiry into the Origin of Man?

The present paper is an attempt to answer this question, which will be addressed from several perspectives. It is divided into five sections, encompassing 1) a discussion of the Teaching of Men and Gods, 2) an examination of how this teaching functions in the Inquiry into the Origin of Man, 3) a brief sketch of the historical context in which Tsung-mi wrote the Inquiry, 4) a consideration of the development of lay Buddhist Hua-yen societies as providing the social context for Tsung-mi's inclusion of this teaching in the Inquiry, and 5) an annotated translation of the Teaching of Men and Gods section of the Inquiry into the Origin of Man.

1. The Teaching of Men and Gods

The Teaching of Men and Gods refers to the simple moral teaching of karmic retribution. It is so called because it teaches men how they can gain a propitious birth as a man or a god by maintaining the five precepts prescribed for laymen and by practicing the ten good deeds.[4]

The Teaching of Men and Gods generally corresponds to the teaching for laymen as found in such early Indian Buddhist scriptures as the Discourse on the Lesser Analysis of Deeds (Cūlakammavibhangasutta) and Discourse on the Greater Analysis of Deeds (Mahākammavibhaṅgasutta).[5] In the first of these scriptures, for example, a young Brahmin asks the

Buddha why human beings live in such a variety of circumstances, some being short lived while others are long lived, some suffering many illnesses while others enjoy good health, some being impoverished while others are wealthy, some being born into families of low station while others are born into families of high station, etc. The Buddha answers that the discrepancies seen in human life are all due to karma. The Buddha then elaborates, saying that those who kill other living creatures, if they are reborn as humans in their next life, will be short lived and those who abstain from killing other living creatures, if they are reborn as humans in their next life, will be long lived. Similarly, in their next life, those who mistreat living creatures will suffer many illnesses, those who are kind to living creatures will enjoy good health, those who are stingy will be impoverished, those who are generous will be wealthy, those who are arrogant will be born into families of low station, and those who are humble will be born into families of high station.

While the teaching of karma was basic to all forms of Buddhism, it seems to have formed the central focus of the teaching directed to laymen, especially as it dealt with the casual link between various actions or types of action and specific forms of rebirth. While lay practice centered around the maintenance of the five precepts, it was always justified in terms of the good consequences to be experienced in a future rebirth, as well as in the present lifetime.[6] We find the Buddha in numerous other early scriptures, for instance, exhorting laymen to practice almsgiving (dāna) with the promise that their generosity will lead to a desirable rebirth in a heavenly realm.[7]

Although the Teaching of Men and Gods thus seems to correspond to the teaching for laymen in the Indian Buddhist tradition, it was not referred to as a particular category of teaching by this name in Indian Buddhism. Rather, the term "the Teaching of Men and Gods" seems to have been invented by Chinese Buddhists during the second half of the fifth century in an effort to accommodate Buddhism to the needs of its growing number of lay adherents by adapting it to the more socially oriented concerns of Confucianism. The first mention of the Teaching of Men and Gods occurs in the doctrinal classification scheme of Liu Ch'iu 劉虬 (438-495), a lay Buddhist recluse in the south. He divided the Buddha's teachings into two general types, the sudden and the gradual. The sudden teaching consists of the teaching of the Hua-yen (Avataṁsaka) Sutra, which directly expressed the content of the Buddha's enlightenment. Since this teaching was too profound for any but the most advanced bodhisattvas to understand, the Buddha then expounded a series of gradual teachings to prepare his disciples for the ultimate truth by stages. Liu Ch'iu divided the gradual teachings into five teachings and seven stages. The first teaching is that of men and gods, as taught in the T'i-wei Po-li ching 提謂波利經 (The Sutra of Trapuśa and Bhallika). The second teaching is that of the Three Vehicles and is comprised of three stages, one for each vehicle, i.e., that of śrāvaka, pratyekabuddha, and bodhisattva. The third teaching is that of emptiness, as taught in the Prajñāpāramitā sutras. The fourth teaching is that of the One Vehicle, as taught in the Lotus Sutra. The fifth teaching is that of eternity, as taught in the Nirvana Sutra.[8]

The T'i-wei Po-li ching,[9] the scripture on
which the Teaching of Men and Gods is based, is a text
which was fabricated in northern China around 460 by
T'an-ching 曇靖 . At the end of the biography of
T'an-yao 曇曜 , the famous Superintendent of Monks
who set the course for the revival of Buddhism after
the Northern Wei persecution of 446, Tao-hsüan 道宣
adds a brief note on T'an-ching, which links the composition of the T'i-wei Po-li ching with the restoration of Buddhism. He writes that since the former
translations had been burned up during the persecution, some basis for guiding the people was urgently
needed, and that T'an-ching thus composed the T'i-wei
Po-li ching to make up for this deficiency.[10] The
T'i-wei Po-li ching fit in well with the widescale
ideological use of Buddhism on the part of the
Northern Wei state in its efforts both to control a
people of mixed ethnic stock for whom Confucian moral
teachings had not yet been deeply ingrained as well as
to mobilize the general population for the restoration
of Buddhism on a scale whose massiveness was symbolized, more than anything else, by the colossal Buddha
images carved in the guise of the first five Northern
Wei emperors in the rock caves at Yün-kang.

The T'i-wei Po-li ching purports to have been
taught on the seventh day after the Buddha's enlightenment to a group of five hundred merchants led by
Trapuśa (T'i-wei 提謂) and Bhallika (Po-li 波利).
It exhorts them to take the Triple Refuge in the
Buddha, Dharma, and Saṃgha, to maintain the five
precepts, and to practice the ten good deeds so as to
insure a good future birth as a man or a god. The
five precepts are given special emphasis and are even

accorded cosmological significance. They are said to be

> the root of Heaven and Earth and the source of all spiritual beings. When Heaven observes them, yin and yang are harmonized; when Earth observes them, the myriad creatures are engendered. They are the mother of the myriad creatures and the father of the myriad spirits, the origin of the Great Way and the fundamental basis of nirvana.[11]

The five precepts are homologized with other sets of five in Chinese cosmology--such as the five phases, five planets, five emperors, five sacred peaks, five internal organs, five colors, five virtues[12]--and the failure to maintain them consequently has cosmic reverberations throughout the various spheres with which they correspond. Most significantly for Chinese lay Buddhist practice, the Buddha, in this spurious sutra, matches the five Buddhist precepts for laymen with the five constant virtues of Confucianism. Thus, the Buddhist precept not to take life is paired with the Confucian virtue of humanity (jen 仁); not to take what is not given, with righteousness (i 義); not to engage in illicit sexual activity, with propriety (li 禮); not to drink intoxicating beverages, with wisdom (chih 智); and not to lie, with trustworthiness (hsin 信).[13]

While there is nothing, in terms of content, comparable to the T'i-wei Po-li ching in Indian Buddhist literature, the Aṅguttara-nikāya does contain a Tapussasutta,[14] whose resemblance to the T'i-wei Po-li ching, however, does not go beyond its title. The earliest account of Trapuśa and Bhallika occurs in the

Vinaya section of the Tripitaka,[15] where they offer
the Buddha his first meal after his enlightenment,
take refuge in the Buddha and Dharma (the Samgha still
not having been formed), and become the Buddha's first
lay disciples.

Whereas the T'i-wei Po-li ching couches
Buddhist moral injunctions within the framework of
Chinese cosmological thought, Tsung-mi's version of
the Teaching of Men and Gods in the Inquiry into the
Origin of Man rationalizes the teaching of karmic
retribution with Buddhist cosmology as systematically
developed in the Abhidharma literature. In Tsung-mi's
account all of the practices whose karmic fruits still
involve beings in the various realms of birth are
encompassed within the purview of the Teaching of Men
and Gods. Thus, while the Teaching of Men and Gods
generally refers to the lay teaching within Buddhism,
the more advanced stages of meditation included within
Tsung-mi's version of this teaching do not fall within
the usual sphere of lay Buddhist practice.

Tsung-mi gives a condensed account of this teaching in his Ch'an Preface (Ch'an-yüan chu-ch'uan-chi
tu-hsi 禪源諸詮集都序):

> The Teaching of the Causes and Effects of Men
> and Gods, teaching the karmic retribution of
> good and bad, enables [men] to know that there
> is no discrepancy between cause and effect, to
> dread the suffering of the three [evil] des-
> tinies, to seek the joy of men and gods, to
> cultivate all good practices--such as giving,
> maintaining the precepts, and practicing
> meditation--and thereby gain birth in the

Realm of Men and Gods up to the Realm of Form
and the Realm of Formlessness.[16]

In the Inquiry into the Origin of Man, Tsung-mi
gives a more detailed explanation of the workings of
karmic retribution, connecting various types of moral
and spiritual action with birth in specific realms
described in Buddhist cosmology. Accordingly, the
commission of the ten evils leads to birth in the
three evil destinies. The commission of the ten evils
in their highest degree leads to birth in hell; in
their lesser degree, to birth as a hungry ghost; and
in the lowest degree, to birth as a beast. The maintenance of the five precepts, on the other hand,
enables men to avoid birth in the three evil destinies
and to gain birth as a man, and the practice of the
ten good deeds leads to birth as a god in one of the
six heavens of desire. All of the destinies enumerated so far fall within the Realm of Desire
(kāmadhātu, yü-chieh 欲界), the first and lowest of
the three realms of birth. Birth into the next two
realms is only possible through the practice of meditation. While the early Indian Buddhist scriptures do
contain examples of laymen who succeeded in being born
into these higher realms through the practice of meditation,[17] such cases are the exception rather than the
rule. In general, the moral practices usually taught
to laymen would only lead to birth in the higher
spheres of the Realm of Desire. Birth into the next
realm, the Realm of Form (rūpadhātu, se-chieh 色界),
is attained through the mastery of the four stages of
meditation, and birth into the highest realm, the
Realm of Formlessness (arūpadhātu, wu-se-chieh 無色

界), is attained through the mastery of the four formless attainments.

Such, in outline, is the system of karmic retribution that Tsung-mi sets forth in the Inquiry into the Origin of Man. The details of this system will be dealt with in the final section of this paper, in which an annotated translation of Tsung-mi's Teaching of Men and Gods from the Inquiry will be given. Since the scheme of karmic retribution that he outlines is most easily grasped visually, it should, for now, suffice to present the diagram on the following page.

A point that is especially noteworthy in Tsung-mi's account of the Teaching of Men and Gods in the Inquiry is the fact that he says that the Buddha matched the five Buddhist precepts with the five Confucian constant virtues in order to encourage beginners to maintain the five precepts and so succeed in gaining birth as a human. In his own note on this passage, Tsung-mi goes on to pair the five precepts with the five constant virtues in the same manner in which they had been paired with one another in the T'i-wei Po-li ching passage referred to before.

As a final comment on the Teaching of Men and Gods in the Ch'an Preface, Tsung-mi adds a critical note on this teaching which points to the way in which this teaching is superseded by the next level of Buddhist teaching, that of the Small Vehicle. He says that the Teaching of Men and Gods only explains "worldly causes and effects" and not "the causes and effects of transcending the world."

It merely causes [beings] to have an aversion for the lower [realms] and to take delight in

DIAGRAM OF THE OPERATION OF KARMIC RETRIBUTION

ACTION (karma)	DESTINY (gati)		REALM (dhātu)
Four Formless Attainments	God	Four Formless Heavens	Realm of Formlessness (arūpadhātu)
Four Stages of Meditation	God	Four Meditation Heavens	Realm of Form (rūpadhātu)
Ten Good Deeds	God	Six Heavens of Desire	Realm of Desire (kāmadhātu)
Five Precepts	Man		
Ten Evils — { lowest degree — beast / lesser degree — hungry ghost / highest degree — hell }	} Three Evil Destinies		

the higher [realms], not yet teaching that
the three realms are all afflictions which
should be renounced. It also has not yet
destroyed [the belief in] the self.[18]

2. The Function of the Teaching of Men and Gods in
the Inquiry into the Origin of Man

Before taking up the question of the function
of the Teaching of Men and Gods within the overall
context of the Inquiry into the Origin of Man, it is
first necessary to consider briefly the nature and
scope of p'an-chiao, as this will provide the proper
perspective from which to gauge Tsung-mi's
uniqueness.

For Chinese Buddhists p'an-chiao served two
broad functions, one integrative and one sectarian.
It was, first of all, a hermeneutical device whereby
the entire spectrum of teachings alleged to have been
taught by the Buddha could be harmonized into an
integral whole. The main rubric for this enterprise
was provided by the doctrine of expedient means
(upāya, fang-pien 方便). According to this doctrine, which assumed cardinal importance in Mahāyāna,
the Buddha geared the content and style of his teaching to the spiritual capacity of his audience. The
Buddha is often spoken of as a great physician, and,
by extension, his various teachings were each seen as
serving as an antidote for a specific ailment.
Accordingly, the bewildering welter of teachings to
which the Chinese Buddhists were heir--all of which
were equally sacred as the Buddha Word (buddhavacana)
--could thus be unified into a hierarchical series
beginning with the most elementary and progressing to

the most profound. In this fashion, each level of teaching serves to overcome the particular shortcoming of the teaching which precedes it, while, at the same time, laying the foundation for the next and higher level of teaching. The manner in which the teachings were arranged, however, was a matter of interpretation, depending on the scripture or body of texts that was taken as authoritative in a given tradition. By thus providing a methodology for ranking the various teachings of the Buddha on a scale of their relative profundity, p'an-chiao also furnished the basis on which each school of Buddhism established its claim as embodying the paramount teaching of the Buddha, many of the schools of Chinese Buddhism--such as the Hua-yen--being known by the name of the scripture to which they accorded supremacy.

In any case, whatever the particular scheme by which the teachings were classified, p'an-chiao was an enterprise that applied exclusively to the Buddha's teachings. One of the principal objections that Ch'eng-kuan leveled against the four-fold classification scheme developed by Fa-tsang's most eminent disciple, Hui-yüan, was that his first category was comprised of non-Buddhist teachings, thus confusing Buddhism with false teachings.[19] The charge was serious, and was one of the prime reasons for which Hui-yüan was posthumously excised from the Hua-yen lineage and branded as a heretic.

The case of Hui-yüan highlights the innovative character of Tsung-mi's Inquiry into the Origin of Man. While the precise status of Confucianism and Taoism within his p'an-chiao scheme is problematical, their role in setting the overall tenor of the essay is undeniable. Even though Tsung-mi does not include

them within his five-fold categorization--suggesting
that they should, strictly speaking, be seen as falling outside the purview of p'an-chiao, which would
only apply to the "inner" teachings--he does, nonetheless, extend the Problematik of p'an-chiao to the two
teachings. He writes: "Confucius, Lao-tzu, and
Śākyamuni were consummate sages, who, in accord with
the times and in response to beings, made different
paths in setting up their teachings."[20] Tsung-mi here
uses the Buddhist rubric of expedient means to account
for the differences between the three teachings. The
three sages should all be regarded as equally enlightened. The differences between their teachings are due
to the limitations set by the particular historical
circumstances in which they lived and taught rather
than to any qualitative difference in the level of
understanding achieved by them. Tsung-mi continues:

> The inner and outer [teachings] complement one
> another, together benefiting the people. As
> for promoting the myriad practices, clarifying
> cause and effect from beginning to end,
> exhaustively investigating the myriad phenom-
> ena, and elucidating the full scope of birth
> and arising--even though these are all the
> intention of the sages, there are still pro-
> visional and ultimate [explanations]. The two
> teachings [of Confucianism and Taoism] are
> just provisional, [whereas] Buddhism includes
> both provisional and ultimate. Since
> encouraging the myriad practices, admonishing
> against evil, and promoting good contribute in
> common to order, the three teachings should
> all be followed and practiced. [However], if

it be a matter of investigating the myriad
phenomena, exhausting principle, realizing the
nature, and reaching the original source, then
Buddhism alone is the ultimate judgment.[21]

While Tsung-mi naturally regards Buddhism as a
higher level of teaching than either Confucianism or
Taoism, what is especially noteworthy is that his
attitude towards them is sympathetic and inclusive.
Even though his designation of them as provisional
teachings places them in a category inferior to the
Buddhist teachings, it also--and far more
significantly--places them within the same realm of
discourse: although its concrete forms of expression
differ, the Truth realized by the three sages is universal. Tsung-mi's originality thus does not lie in
the mere reshuffling of the traditional repertoire of
Buddhist teachings to come up with a new p'an-chiao
arrangement; it lies in extending the scope of p'an-
chiao itself.

Tsung-mi's syncretic approach stands in sharp
contrast to that of Ch'eng-kuan and Hui-yüan. Not
only was Ch'eng-kuan critical of Hui-yüan for incorporating non-Buddhist teachings into his p'an-chiao
scheme, he also excoriated those who maintained that
the three teachings were one. He said: "Those who go
too far and equate [false teachings] with Buddhism are
all outside the Buddhadharma."[22] He goes on to liken
the Buddha's teaching to cow's milk, from which the
ghee of liberation can be obtained; the teachings of
non-Buddhists, however, are likened to donkey's milk,
from which ghee can never be obtained: they lack the
taste of liberation and can only be made into urine
and ordure.[23] Further, he says that the gap between

Buddhism and the two teachings is "so vast that even a thousand leagues would not seem far."[24] He concludes this invective with the following admonition:

> Do not seek after the trivial reputation of a single age and confuse the three teachings as one. Studying the poisonous seeds of false views is a deep cause for being born in hell, opens up the wellspring of ignorance, and blocks off the road to omniscience. Take heed! Take heed![25]

While the first category of Hui-yüan's four-fold classification is comprised of non-Buddhist teachings (i.e., the ninety-five heretical views of the Indian philosophers), he uses his discussion of them as an opportunity to criticize those who identify Buddhist teachings with those of Confucianism and Taoism. He says that those who claim that the Buddhist tathā gatagarbha is the same as the Taoist Non-Being's engendering of the manifold universe, for instance, "not only do not understand the garbha [i.e., embryo, womb, matrix] of the Tathāgata, but have also not yet even discerned the true meaning of Nothingness."[26] Hui-yüan, in other words, charges those who try to elucidate Taoist ideas by drawing from the doctrinal repertoire of Buddhism not only with demonstrating their failure to understand Buddhism, but also, more damagingly, with revealing their ignorance of the meaning of the principal ideas of their own tradition, which they only distort in their efforts to explain.

Nowhere is Tsung-mi's syncretic approach more apparent than in the concluding section of the Inquiry

into the Origin of Man, where he incorporates
Confucianism and Taoism, together with the five levels
of Buddhist teaching, into an overarching explanation
of the origin of man. By creating a framework in
which Confucianism, Taoism, and Buddhism could be
synthesized, Tsung-mi not only transcended the polemical intent of the earlier debates between the three
teachings, but he also laid out a methodology by which
Confucian terms--infused with Buddhist meaning--were
later to be resurrected in the Confucian revival of
the Sung dynasty.

Having considered the overall approach of the
Inquiry into the Origin of Man, we are now in a position to see how the teaching of Men and Gods functions
within the dynamics of Tsung-mi's p'an-chiao scheme.
However, since it is precisely the teaching of karmic
retribution that answers the dilemma which Tsung-mi
poses for Confucianism and Taoism, it is first necessary to understand the thrust of his critique of these
two teachings.

After giving a brief synopsis of the gist of
Confucianism and Taoism, followed by a general critique, Tsung-mi singles out four major concepts to
subject to more detailed scrutiny and criticism.
These are: the Way (tao 道), Spontaneity (tzu-jan
自然), the Primal Pneuma (yüan-ch'i 元氣), and the
Degree of Heaven (t'ien-ming 天命).

His major critique of Confucianism and Taoism
consists in his raising, mutatis mutandis, the issue
of theodicy. Whereas the question of theodicy, in a
Christian context, asks how there can be evil in a
world where God is at once good and omnipotent, the
question, in a Confucian context, devolves around the
existence of social inequity and injustice in a

universe which functions in accord with the Confucian
moral order. According to Confucian political myth-
ology tracing back to the Classic of History (Shu
ching), Heaven--whether conceived as a personal god-
like agency or as an impersonal natural force--is that
which monitors the socio-political world of human
endeavor to insure that it resonates with the larger
rhythms of a universe functioning in natural harmony
with Confucian moral principles. Translated into
historical terms as a theory of dynastic cycles, this
myth held that when a ruler became tyrannical or
otherwise morally unfit to exercise rule, Heaven dis-
played its disfavor in the occurrence of ominous
portents and natural disasters. If the situation
became severe enough, Heaven would withdraw its mandate, disorders would increase, and the political
order would fall into chaos. Out of the ensuing
turmoil and strife, Heaven would select the most
worthy upon whom to confer a new mandate to rule, and
peace and order would once again be restored.

Thus, according to this myth, Heaven was seen
as a cosmic moral force; or, in the more straightforward words of the Classic of History, "The Way of
Heaven is to bless the good and punish the bad."[27] At
the same time, other Confucian texts of equally
hallowed provenance maintained that the individual's
lot in life was determined by Heaven. The Analects
(Lun-yü), for instance, quotes Confucius as saying:
"Death and life have their determined appointment,
riches and honor depend upon Heaven."[28] If this is
so, Tsung-mi reasons, then Heaven must also be responsible for the manifold examples of injustice so apparent in the world. How then, he asks, can it be moral?
As he eloquently puts the case in his own words:

As for their statement that poverty and
wealth, high and low station, sageliness and
ignorance, good and evil, good and bad fortune, disaster and bounty all proceed from the
Decree of Heaven, then, in Heaven's endowment
of destiny, why are the impoverished many and
the wealthy few, those of low station many and
those of high station few, and so on to those
suffering disaster many and those enjoying
bounty few? If the apportionment of many and
few lies in Heaven, why is Heaven not fair?
How much more unjust is it in cases of those
who lack moral conduct and yet are honored,
those who maintain moral conduct and yet are
debased, those who lack virtue and yet enjoy
wealth, those who are virtuous and yet suffer
poverty, or the refractory enjoying good fortune, the righteous suffering misfortune, the
humane dying young, the cruel living to an old
age, and so on to the moral being brought down
and the immoral being raised to eminence. How
can there be the reward of blessing the good
and augmenting the humble and the punishment
of bringing disaster down upon the wicked and
affliction upon the full? Furthermore, since
disaster, disorder, rebellion, and mutiny all
proceed from Heaven's Decree, the teachings
established by the sages are not right in
holding man and not Heaven responsible and in
blaming things and not destiny.[29]

Tsung-mi makes the same point in regard to the Way:

Their statement that the myriad things are all
engendered by the Great Way of Nothingness
means that the Great Way itself is the origin
of life and death, sageliness and ignorance,
the basis of fortune and misfortune, bounty
and disaster. Since the origin and basis are
permanently existent, disaster, disorder, misfortune, and ignorance cannot be extirpated,
and bounty, blessings, sageliness and goodness
cannot be increased. What use, then, are the
teachings of Lao-tzu and Chuang-tzu?[30]

Although Tsung-mi's critique of tzu-jan (Spontaneity) takes a different tack, his essential criticism focuses on its moral implications. Interpreting
tzu-jan as an acausal principle, Tsung-mi points out
that if the universe did operate in accordance with
tzu-jan, moral cultivation would be impossible. "For
what use then," he asks, "did Lao-tzu, Chuang-tzu, the
Duke of Chou, and Confucius establish their teachings
as invariable norms?"[31] The question is, of course,
rhetorical. Tsung-mi never calls into doubt the need
for moral cultivation. His posing of the question
merely serves to make obvious the absurdity of tzu-jan
as an explanatory principle.

Tsung-mi's main objection to the Primal Pneuma
(yüan-ch'i) is that it cannot, on the one hand,
account for the predispositions inherited at birth,
nor, on the other hand, can it account for the existence of spirits of the dead (kuei-shen 鬼神).
Advancing what to himself and his contemporaries were
empirical arguments, Tsung-mi adduces a number of
examples of the existence of spirits of the dead,

drawing from a body of Confucian historical literature, to support his contention that death is not a
mere cessation of existence. After all, without the
mechanism of rebirth supplied by the teaching of
karmic retribution, there would be no impelling reason
for men to behave morally. Ample cases of wicked men
prospering with impunity and good men suffering
unjustly could be cited from both history and the contemporary world. If, upon death, their "spirits"
simply dispersed into nothingness and there were no
punishment or reward in a future state, then why
should men behave morally, especially in cases where
moral behavior demanded that they act contrary to
their own immediate interests?

What is especially significant about Tsung-mi's
critique of Confucianism and Taoism is that it is
carried out within the framework of the moral vision
of Confucianism. This moral vision itself is not
challenged; it is only the ability of Confucianism and
Taoism to provide a coherent ontological basis for
that vision that is disputed. It is in this context
that the Teaching of Men and Gods takes on importance
as its teaching of karmic retribution provides a way
in which the Confucian moral vision can be preserved,
for it is precisely the teaching of karmic retribution
that is needed to explain the apparent cases of
injustice in the world. If the good suffer hardship
and die young, it is because they are reaping the
consequences of evil committed in a former life. If
the bad prosper with impunity, it is because they are
enjoying the rewards of good deeds done in a former
life.

In terms of the overall structure of the
Inquiry into the Origin of Man, the Teaching of Men

and Gods thus serves as the crucial link relating the
teachings of Confucianism and Taoism to those of
Buddhism. On the one hand, it serves a polemical purpose by subordinating the two teachings to even the
most elementary and superficial teaching of Buddhism.
On the other hand, it also serves a broader and more
syncretic purpose. The teaching of karmic retribution, by resolving the dilemma of theodicy, preserves
the Confucian belief in a moral universe. It also
opens the way for Confucian moral practices to be
incorporated into Buddhism by assimilating the five
constant virtues of Confucianism into the five precepts of Buddhism. Even though Confucianism cannot
provide a convincing metaphysical rationale for the
moral functioning of the universe, the moral practices
that it advocates--being, in essence, no different
from those advocated in Buddhism--are still meritorious and can lead to a good future birth in the human
realm.

3. The Historical Context of the Inquiry into the
    Origin of Man

     The importance of Confucianism and Taoism in
setting the tenor and direction of the Inquiry into
the Origin of Man raises the question of why these two
teachings were of such concern for Tsung-mi. What, in
short, was the historical context in which Tsung-mi
wrote?
     Despite the creative achievement of authenti-
cally Chinese modes of Buddhist thought and practice
that reached mature form during the T'ang, Buddhism
found itself on the defensive throughout much of the
period. Fu I's memorial calling for the extirpation

of Buddhism,[32] presented to Kao-tzu shortly after the founding of the dynasty, precipitated a heated round of polemical responses and counterresponses among Buddhists and Taoists.[33] These attacks were accompanied by a renewed attempt to require Buddhist monks to pay obeisance to the emperor and their parents--a highly charged and symbolic issue reflecting on the status of Buddhism as a separate and autonomous institution in Chinese society. Thus, at the inception of the T'ang period, Buddhism once again found itself in the position of having to defend itself against the traditional array of Chinese social, political, economic, moral, and cultural objections to its existence as an institution within Chinese society.

Politically, with the exception of the reign of Empress Wu (684-705), Buddhism found its freedom to operate in Chinese society constantly checked by the government's attempts at control and regulation. The supervision of the saṃgha, for example, was placed under the jurisdiction of various government bureaus which restricted the number of men and women who could become monks and nuns, the liberty of monks and nuns to move freely in secular society, the number of temples that could be built, the repair of existing temples, the construction of private temples by individuals, the extent of temple holdings, etc.[34] Moreover, the imperial family, bearing the same surname as that traditionally ascribed to Lao-tzu, claimed descent from that hallowed Taoist sage and consistently subordinated Buddhism to Taoism in various symbolic ways, such as according Taoists priority over Buddhists in matters of state ceremony. Imperial support of Taoism reached its apogee during

the reign of Hsüan-tsung (713-756), who, in addition
to promulgating a spate of measures imposing fresh
restrictions on Buddhism, also personally wrote a
commentary on the Lao-tzu, which every household was
required to have in its possession, and set up special
schools for Taoist studies as part of the state
university system to help aspiring students prepare
for a special civil service examination based on
Taoist scriptures.[35]

Along with the favoritism accorded Taoism on
the part of the court, the Taoist church grew into a
powerful institution rivaling Buddhism for both
imperial patronage and popular support. Religious
Taoism also came to have an increasingly sophisticated
body of doctrine, much of which was built on Buddhist
ideas and modes of thought.[36] Such doctrinal preda-
tion, set against the background of the imperial support of Taoism, framed the context in which Ch'eng-
kuan so virulently denounced the claim that the three
teachings were fundamentally of one essence.

Although never entirely satisfactory, Buddhism
did reach a modus vivendi with the state, and the
vehemence of the early debates between Buddhists and
Taoists gradually cooled as the dynasty wore on. The
early controversies eventually became formalized into
debates between the three teachings, which were often
held to celebrate the birthday of the reigning
emperor. While these were ritual affairs conducted
largely for the emperor's entertainment, they nevertheless served to underline the symbolic subordination
of Buddhism to Taoism and Confucianism and were thus
taken seriously by Buddhists.[37] One such debate was
held on the occasion of the imperial birthday in

827,[38] around the time that Tsung-mi authored the Inquiry into the Origin of Man.

Perhaps the most important factor forming the immediate intellectual context in which Tsung-mi wrote the Inquiry into the Origin of Man was the revival of Confucianism, which began in the late eighth century and gained momentum in the early ninth. In 819 its most strident spokesman, Han Yü 韓愈 (758-824), presented his famous anti-Buddhist memorial to the throne, written in remonstrance against the emperor's having sponsored and taken part in a spectacular parade of a relic of the Buddha through the capital, where it was received and honored in the imperial palace. While Han Yü's arguments were neither original nor philosophically profound, they were presented in a rhetorical style that carried a forceful emotional impact. In a more philosophical vein, Han Yü had also authored a series of five essays in response to what he read as the overly Buddhistic sympathies expressed by his disciple Li Ao 李翱 in his Essay on Returning to the Nature (Fu-hsing shu 復性書). Significantly, this series of essays were all entitled Inquiry into the Origin of (Yüan 原)-- the Way (tao 道), the Nature (hsing 性), Man (jen 人), Ghosts (kuei 鬼), and Slander (hui 毀).[39] The title of Tsung-mi's Inquiry into the Origin of Man (Yüan-jen lun 原人論) strongly suggests that it was, at least in part, stimulated by Han Yü's criticism of Buddhism.

As a response to renewed attacks against Buddhism, the Inquiry into the Origin of Man can be seen as the product of a long history of Buddhist polemical literature extending back to the introduction of Buddhism in China. Yet, unlike earlier

polemics--such as those written in the debates between
Buddhists and Taoists at the beginning of the T'ang
dynasty--Tsung-mi's essay is not an apologetic concerned with refuting the traditional array of Chinese
objections against Buddhism. Rather, viewed with
hindsight from the perspective of the subsequent
development of Neo-Confucianism in the Sung, Tsung-
mi's essay gains importance because it does go beyond
the polemical intent of earlier works and, in so
doing, shifts the field of controversy to a new and
more philosophical level, putting Buddhism, for the
first time, in the position of determining the intellectual context in terms of which Confucianism was
called upon to respond.

The historical background outlined above, while
important in delineating the overall context in which
Tsung-mi lived and thought, still does not fully
explain his unusually sympathetic attitude towards
Confucianism and Taoism, seen most dramatically in his
attempt to incorporate their teachings into a single,
overarching explanation of the origin of man. Rather,
his syncretic approach must be seen as an expression
of his own psychological need to reconcile the
Confucian moral values that he had learned as a youth
with the teachings of the religion that he later
adopted as an adult. Tsung-mi, in an autobiographical
passage, informs us that he studied Confucian texts
from the age of six to fourteen or fifteen. For the
next three years he turned to Buddhist works. He then
renewed his concentration on Confucian texts--
presumably in preparation for the civil service
examinations--studying at the I-hsüeh Academy in Sui-
chou. He reached the turning point in his life at the
age of twenty-four when he met the Ch'an priest Tao-

yüan道圓 .[40] The two had an immediate rapport and Tsung-mi became his disciple.[41] Even though Tsung-mi abandoned his ambition to serve the world as a Confucian scholar-official, his earlier study of Confucian texts had made a deep impression on his character and thought, as can be seen in the style and focus of the Inquiry into the Origin of Man.

In fact, it does not seem improbable to suppose that the very questions which Tsung-mi poses for Confucianism and Taoism in that essay were much like those which first turned his attention to Buddhism as a young man. Even though he looked to Buddhism for the answer, his underlying question, having to do with the meaning of moral action in the universe, still reflects a deep Confucian concern with the overriding importance of moral activity.

4. The Social Context of the Teaching of Men and Gods: The Development of Lay Buddhist Hua-yen Societies

So far we have seen that Confucianism and Taoism played an important role in determining the tone and focus of the Inquiry into the Origin of Man and that the Teaching of Men and Gods played an important role in that essay by providing the context in which the teachings of Confucianism and Taoism could be related to those of Buddhism. On the one hand, the Teaching of Men and Gods served the polemical function of subordinating the most profound teachings of Confucianism and Taoism to the most superficial teaching of Buddhism. On the other hand, by resolving the dilemma of theodicy, it also supplied the context in which the Confucian moral vision could be preserved within Buddhism. This syncretic function of the Teaching of Men and Gods was furthered by its equation of the five Buddhist precepts with the five Confucian constant virtues, thus incorporating Confucian moral practice into the Buddhist cosmological framework of karmic retribution. Moreover, the polemical purpose of the Inquiry can be seen both within the general historical context of the imperial support of Taoism throughout much of the T'ang dynasty, the growing strength of the Taoist Church as an institution with an increasingly sophisticated body of doctrine, and the survival of the early controversies between Buddhists and Taoists in the form of debates between the three teachings held on the emperor's birthday, as well as within the more immediate historical context of the new challenge posed by the revival of Confucianism, as expressed most forcefully in Han Yü's attacks on Buddhism. The more syncretic purpose of the Inquiry can be seen within the context of Tsung-mi's own need to reconcile the Confucian moral values that he had learned in his youth with the teachings of the religion that he had adopted as an adult.

Tsung-mi's inclusion of the Teaching of Men and Gods in the Inquiry also reflects the growing impor-tance and popularity of lay Buddhist societies in the later part of the T'ang dynasty. Whereas the movement which culminated in the Hua-yen societies that flour-ished in Tsung-mi's day had its origin in the fifth century, it did not occur as a widespread social phenomenon until the beginning of the ninth century.[42] Tsung-mi's inclusion of the teaching prescribed for laymen as the first category of Buddhist teachings in the Inquiry can thus be set against the broader social

context of the rising importance of lay Buddhist societies in late T'ang Buddhism.

Not only did the spurious T'i-wei Po-li ching
provide the necessary scriptural basis for the inclusion of the Teaching of Men and Gods as a category in
Chinese Buddhists' classification schemes, it also
gave both form and impetus to Chinese lay Buddhism by
defining the course of moral practice and religious
observance for the householder. In easy to understand
language, the T'i-wei Po-li ching blended elements of
Chinese folk belief, yin-yang cosmology, and simplified Confucian moral teachings with the Buddhist
teaching of karmic retribution. It emphasized the
karmic merit of taking the Triple Refuge in the
Buddha, Dharma, and Saṃgha, maintaining the five precepts prescribed for laymen, and practicing the ten
good deeds. It also prescribed periods of religious
observance, called chai 斋 or "fast days," to be held
on the first, fifth, and ninth month and on the
eighth, fourteenth, fifteenth, twenty-third, twenty-
ninth, and thirtieth day of each month--these were the
so-called three long months and six fast days.[43]
During these times the pious householder was supposed
to abstain from eating meat as well as from eating
after the forenoon meal.

The term "chai" was a translation of the
Sanskrit "upavasatha" (Pali, uposatha), which had its
roots in ancient Indian religious practice. The Vedas
prescribed a ritual sacrifice to the new and full moon
for the householder. These were preceded by a day of
religious observance--called upavasatha or "fast-
day"--during which the householder was to abstain from
food, work, and sex. These upavasatha days gradually
became observed as general holy days, which were, in

the Buddha's time, observed by the assorted communities of wandering ascetics, who used them as occasions
for the study, recital, and discussion of their sacred
texts.[44] The Buddha, according to the account contained in the Mahāvagga,[45] decided to adopt the practice of upavasatha on the urging of King Bimbisāra,
who pointed out that other groups of ascetics used the
convocation of their followers on the eighth, fourteenth, and fifteenth day of each fortnight for
attracting adherents. The Buddha, however, modified
the observance of the upavasatha by making it a fort-
nightly ceremony in which the monks gathered to recite
their monastic code, the Prātimoksa. The upavasatha
ceremony was also important for the spread of Buddhism
throughout lay society by providing a ritualized occasion in which laymen could come into contact with
monks and gain merit by providing meals for them.

While the chai in the T'i-wei Po-li ching refer
to designated times of fasting, the term came to be
used in China to have the more general meaning of
maigre feast. As Yamazaki Hiroshi and other scholars[46] have pointed out, chai, or maigre feasts, were
held on a wide variety of occasions. On their most
elaborate scale, huge maigre feasts were organized by
the state to celebrate the birthday of the reigning
emperor or to mourn the anniversary of the death of an
imperial ancestor. They were likewise held on a more
modest scale by individuals to express gratitude for
some good fortune that might have befallen them or to
observe the memorial of a deceased family member.
They were also held on religious holy days, such as
the day when Buddha was born or the day when he passed
into nirvana, as well as on a host of other occasions.
The diary of the Japanese pilgrim monk Ennin, who

traveled in China during the last part of Tsung-mi's lifetime, contains many detailed descriptions of such chai.[47] Whereas laymen played an ancillary role as donors in the original Indian context by providing meals for the monks, in China laymen became partici- pants in the feasts. Sometimes, in fact, the tradi- tional roles were reversed and we find cases of monasteries providing maigre feasts for the people.

Societies were also formed for sponsoring chai on a periodic basis. Often these would convene quar- terly or once a month to chant a sutra which was held in particular reverence by the group. In the Continued Biographies of Eminent Monks (Hsü kao-seng chuan 續高僧傳), Tao-hsüan mentions that in the K'ai-huang era (581-600) of the Sui dynasty the T'i- wei Po-li ching enjoyed great popularity among the people and societies formed to promote its study held maigre feasts on a monthly basis.[48] In the T'i-wei Po-li ching we find the Buddha recommending the read- ing of that sutra for those who seek riches, honor, and long life in a future birth; birth among the gods; avoidance of the three evil destinies; escape from birth, old age, sickness, and death; the Way of the Buddha; the Way of the Arhat; the Way of nirvana; etc.[49] While Tao-hsüan does not furnish us with any details on such T'i-wei Po-li societies, they presum- ably would have used their monthly convocation as an occasion for chanting the T'i-wei Po-li ching. This is suggested by another entry in the Continued Biographies of Eminent Monks, which tells us that a certain Pao-ch'iung 寶瓊 (d. 634) formed numerous societies of thirty members each to gather together every month to recite the Mahāprajñāpāramitā Sūtra and have a maigre feast. Tao-hsüan comments that "societies such as these numbered over a thousand."[50]

One of the major ways in which a popular cult began to form around the Hua-yen Sutra had to do with the belief in the efficacy of chanting the sutra, as the continual recitation of the sutra was held to be an especially effective means for generating supernormal powers. This practice was first carried out by monks who took the continual recitation of the Hua-yen Sutra as their form of meditation practice. The early biographical literature--such as Tao-hsüan's Continued Biographies of Eminent Monks or Fa-tsang's Record of the Transmission of the Hua-yen Sutra (Hua-yen ching chuan chi 華嚴經傳記)--contains numerous examples of monks who demonstrated thaumaturgical powers gained through this practice. These monks are typically depicted as eschewing the centers of political power and prestige, preferring to live an austere and obscure life in the countryside ministering to the people. While the people could not be expected to understand the recondite philosophical content of the sutra, they could give their unconditional reverence to miracle-working monks who chanted the Hua-yen Sutra as their religious practice. These monks thus provided the first focus around which a popular Hua-yen cult could coalesce. They played an active role in organizing the laity into communal religious confraternities, the ritual context of which was provided by maigre feasts in which the monks and laymen participated together. Historically, such gatherings had the important function of supplying the ritual framework in which the awe that the people felt for such charismatic monks could be transferred to the Hua-yen Sutra as an object of religious devotion.

Many of the features of the early stages of the development of a popular Hua-yen cult are illustrated in the biography of P'u-an 普安 (530-609),[51] a monk who is described as "always taking the Hua-yen Sutra as his object of religious practice, chanting and meditating upon it, and relying upon it as his standard."[52] At the time of the Northern Chou persecution of Buddhism (574-579)--which, among other measures, decreed the laicization of all monks and nuns--P'u-an fled to Mt. Chung-nan,[53] a short distance southwest of the capital. There he was later joined by other prominent monks likewise seeking to escape the proscription against the practice of their religion. While these monks were all reinstated in their former positions with the Sui revival of Buddhism a few years later, P'u-an chose to disregard the imperial summons and remained in the mountains, where he continued to live an ascetic life among the people.[54]

P'u-an's biography relates a number of miracles that occurred as a result of his deep faith in the Hua-yen Sutra. An admirer, for instance, built P'u-an a hermitage in a cliff by the side of a gorge where two valleys converged. The first day that P'u-an spent there he noticed a large boulder precipitously perched overhead. He was anxious that it might fall on top of his dwelling and, when he prayed that it move somewhere else, it immediately flew away. The people marveled at P'u-an's powers, but he assured them that it was all due to the power of the Hua-yen Sutra and was nothing extraordinary.[55]

Another incident involved an ascetic named Su, who was secretly jealous of P'u-an's powers and plotted to kill him. He enlisted the aid of three

accomplices, and, carrying bows and knives, they went
to P'u-an's hermitage. They bared their arms, drew
back their bowstrings, and were ready to release their
arrows, but the arrows would not leave the bowstrings
and their fingers would not let go of them. They thus
stood there frozen in position throughout the night.
They were unable to speak and could only utter hor-
rible cries. Hearing them, passers-by gathered from
near and far like clouds. The villagers bowed down to
P'u-an and paid their sincere thanks. P'u-an told the
would-be assassins that what had happened to them
could only have been due to the power of the Hua-yen
Sutra and that, if they wanted to be set free, they
should repent. Only after they had done as P'u-an had
instructed were they released.[56]

After relating several other similar miracles,
all of which P'u-an ascribed to the power of the Hua-
yen Sutra, the biography recounts an incident in which
P'u-an restored a dead man to life. He had a devoted
follower named Ho, who constantly came to him for
instruction. Once, when P'u-an was away, the man
became severely ill and died. He had been dead for
two days and his body had been bound in preparation
for burial when P'u-an returned. When P'u-an reached
a nearby village, he called out repeatedly for Ho. On
asking some of the villagers why Ho had not come out
to greet him, he was informed that Ho had died. P'u-
an, however, refused to believe them and hastened
to Ho's village. As he approached Ho's home, he
shouted loudly for him. Inside Ho's body stirred, and
the people standing by cut his funerary bindings.
When P'u-an entered, he again called out, and Ho arose
and crawled towards him. The biography adds that Ho
went on to live for another twenty years.[57]

The biography goes on to say that P'u-an's reputation spread as a result of such events, and many laymen and monks came to pay their respects and hold merit gatherings (<u>fu-hui</u> 福會), at which there were many further miraculous occurrences.[58] On one occasion, for instance, an old woman in one of the villages became sick, having lost her voice and been confined to bed for a hundred days. She had her son ask P'u-an to come to her home. As soon as the sick woman saw P'u-an, she spontaneously got out of her bed, greeted him, inquired after his health, and in no time at all she was behaving as usual and had completely recovered from her illness.

In order to celebrate this event, the village decided to hold a great maigre feast, and the people went around to the different households to solicit contributions. There was one extremely poor family in the village. The eldest daughter--aptly enough named Hua-yen--wanted to give her bare piece of coarse cloth--her sole item of clothing and only material possession--as an offering. However, when the villagers came to her house, P'u-an had them pass it by out of pity for the family's poverty. But the daughter was struck with remorse. Realizing that her dire poverty had thus prevented her from gaining the merit of contributing to the feast and fearing that, if she could not make some offering, her future lot might be even worse, she looked all around for something else to give, but was unable to find anything. When she raised her head to cry out in despair, she noticed a bundle of rice stalks that had been used to plug up a hole in the roof. She retrieved them and shook out some ten grains of rice, which she determined to take, together with her piece of coarse cloth, to the offering site. When she got there, she prayed that through her practice of giving in spite of her utter poverty, she might hope for some future reward. She then threw her ten grains of yellow rice into the communal pot, praying that, if her prayer were truly sincere, all the rice in the pot would turn yellow. The following day the villagers were all surprised to find that the rice had turned yellow. P'u-an assured them that it was a result of the girl's prayer.[59]

Whatever we make of such "miracles"--we should remember that they certainly were taken literally by their recorders, including such a sophisticated thinker as Fa-tsang--they must be taken seriously as dramatically revealing the climate of religious belief in which a popular cult based on the Hua-yen Sutra could grow. If nothing else, they are eloquent testimony to the tremendous spiritual power with which figures such as P'u-an were seen as being endowed.

P'u-an's biography is also significant in revealing his active participation in and vital concern with the communal life of the people. Unfortunately, neither Tao-hsüan nor Fa-tsang provide us with any details on the ritual content and format of the merit gatherings (fu-hui) and maigre feasts (chai) which P'u-an promoted, and we can only speculate as to their nature. Given that the people to whom P'u-an ministered must have been almost totally illiterate, it is doubtful that these communal religious gatherings could have involved the recitation of the Hua-yen Sutra. Nor do they seem to have been held on a regular basis. Rather, from the example cited in the biography, they seem to have been ad hoc affairs which were organized to celebrate some specific miraculous occurrence. Nevertheless, considering the whole tenor of P'u-an's life and practice of devotion to the Hua-yen Sutra--together with the fact that most of the miracles recounted in his biography conclude with P'u-an's assertion that "it was due to the power of the Hua-yen Sutra"--such occasions would certainly have provided P'u-an with a perfect opportunity for instilling a profound veneration for the sutra among the people.

The final section of P'u-an's biography gives us a further clue as to the social organization of the early Hua-yen cult. It says that in the area in which P'u-an lived there were many groups which performed the bi-annual sacrifices to the god of the soil, which was held every spring and autumn. These sacrifices were part of the popular religion which had deep roots in archaic Chinese religious observances. During these sacrifices animals would be slaughtered and offered to the god, after which the meat would be eaten by the participants as part of a communal ritual feast, which would also involve the drinking of wine, dancing, and a general air of celebration. The biography says that P'u-an made it a practice to buy back the animals to be sacrificed on these occasions. He urged the people to practice the Dharma--which meant, in this context, not taking life--and was eventually successful in converting the groups engaged in these sacrifices into "societies for not killing living creatures" (pu-sha-sheng-i 不殺生邑).[60]

The altar to the god of the soil (she 社) provided a natural focus around which rural social groupings constellated; the people who participated together in the bi-annual sacrifices at a given altar constituted a natural basis of social organization.

Although our biographers are again reticent on the matter of the organization of such societies for not killing living creatures, we can suppose that the original sacrificial groups, converted to Buddhism, would have formed a natural social basis for holding maigre feasts periodically, in place of the former animal sacrifices. Moreover, these chai, as Buddhist communal feasts, would have been festive occasions which would have naturally taken the place of the communal feasts held as part of the earlier sacrifices. That these ancient social groupings based on the sacrifices to the god of the soil might, in fact, have provided a basis out of which the later Hua-yen societies were to grow is suggested by the fact that these later societies were designated by the term "she." The role that a popular cult played in the formation of the Hua-yen school is symbolized by the later tradition's designation of Tu-shun 杜順 (558-640) as the first patriarch and founder of the school. Despite the enormous contribution that his Meditation on the Dharmadhātu (Fa-chieh kuan-men 法界觀門) made to the subsequent development of Hua-yen thought, it was primarily as a charismatic miracle-working monk, and not as a profound philosophical thinker, that Tu-shun was known. Tao-hsüan, for instance, places Tu-shun's biography in the section dealing with thaumaturges (kan-t'ung 感通), and not that dealing with exegetes (i-chieh 義解), in his Continued Biographies of Eminent Monks. In contrast to the learned monks in the large metropolitan temples who devoted their energies to the scholastic exegesis of the Hua-yen Sutra, Tu-shun, like P'u-an, lived among people in the countryside, where he gained a reputation as a miracle-working monk skilled in exorcizing

demons and curing the sick. Although his biography
says nothing about the content of his religious practice, it presumably involved the recitation of the
Hua-yen Sutra, as we find him urging this practice on
one of his disciples.[61] He also actively participated
in the communal religious life of the people, as can
be seen in the following excerpt from his biography.

> He eventually went to preach in Ch'ing-chou
> and exhorted the people there to hold a
> [maigre] convocation. The offerings were to
> be for no more than five hundred persons,
> [but] on the occasion of the maigre feast
> twice that number came. The host was appre-
> hensive over this, but [Tu-]shun said, "Just
> distribute [the food] all around and turn none
> away from the site of the offerings." Thus
> were a thousand persons all satisfied.[62]

In addition to illustrating Tu-shun's involvement in
organizing chai, this story is also noteworthy in
illustrating his miracle-working powers, many other
examples of which are attested to in his biography.
The first reference to explicitly Hua-yen chai
is the Record of the Hua-yen chai (Hua-yen-chai chi
華嚴齋記) written by Hsiao Tzu-liang 蕭子良 ,
the second son of Emperor Wu of the Southern Ch'i
dynasty (479-501). This work contained prescriptions
for the performance of Hua-yen chai. Although Hsiao
Tzu-liang's work is no longer extant, Fa-tsang's comments on it in his Record of the Transmission of the
Hua-yen Sutra give us an inkling of what these gatherings must have been like. He says that Hsiao Tzu-
liang's Record of the Hua-yen chai served as a guide

for the observance of the numerous Hua-yen chai that had been organized from Ch'i and Liang (502-557) times down to the present (i.e., the beginning eighth century). He adds that in his own time Dharma Master Hung also took the Hua-yen Sutra as the object of his devotions, urging laymen and true believers to form merit societies (fu-she 福社) of fifty to sixty people. These societies would meet on the fifteenth day of each month, when one household would sponsor a maigre feast and have the ceremonial hall prepared. After the sponsor took his seat, the others would assume their places, and each member would take a turn reciting a roll of the sutra. Only after everyone had finished chanting would the group disperse. Fa-tsang notes in conclusion that this was all carried out in accordance with the prescriptions contained in the Record of the Hua-yen chai.[63]

Kamata Shigeo has argued that the merit societies formed by Dharma Master Hung can be seen as representing a more developed stage in the evolution of the Hua-yen cult than the type of communal religious gatherings depicted in P'u-an's biography. Since they mark a crucial shift in lay practice in which the recitation of the sutra, along with its attendent ritual, overshadows the maigre feast as the main focus of religious observance, he concludes that they should thus be seen as occupying a transitional stage in the development of the Hua-yen societies that were to assume their mature form in the latter part of the T'ang.[64]

The fully developed form that Hua-yen societies were to take in the late T'ang is best illustrated by the one founded in Hang-chou in 822 by the monk Nan-ts'ao 南操 . In 826 the famous poet Po Chü-i 白居易

(772-846), upon the request of Nan-ts'ao, wrote an account of the society, which gives us a good idea of its ritual and organization.

Monk Nan-ts'ao of the Lung-hsing Monastery in Hung-chou during the second year of Ch'ang-ch'ing (822) invited monk Tao-feng of the Ling-yin Monastery to lecture on the Hua-yen Sutra. When he heard about Vairocana in the section of the Lotus-womb World, Ts'ao became so elated that he uttered an earnest wish, hoping that he could urge a group of one hundred thousand people, monks and laymen, to recite the Hua-yen Sutra. Each of the one hundred thousand people would in turn urge a thousand others to recite one chapter of the same sutra. The entire assemblage would meet together quarterly. Ts'ao carried out his earnest wish and organized the group into a society, and regulated the proceedings through quarterly maigre feasts. From the summer of 822 to the present autumn, fourteen such maigre feasts have been held. At each feast, Ts'ao offered incense respectfully and knelt before the image of the Buddha, making the following supplication, "May I and every member of the society be reborn before Vairocana in his paradise within the Golden Wheel of the Precious Lotus, floating on the Great Ocean of Fragrant Waters in the Lotus-womb World. Then I will be satisfied."

Ts'ao solicited enough funds from the members to purchase an estate of ten ch'ing of land, the income from which was used to defray

the expenses of the maigre feasts.... I have
heard that the merit of donating one strand of
hair or one grain of rice will never be lost;
how much greater is the merit gained in preparing with ceaseless energy the boundless
offering of four maigre feasts annually, supplied by the income of a thousand mou? I have
heard that the power of one earnest wish and
the merit of one verse will never be lost; how
much greater then is the merit accruing from a
thousand mouths uttering the twelve divisions
of the canon? Moreover, how much greater also
when hundreds or thousands of ears are listening to myriads of sutras?[65]

While the number of members that Po implies as
belonging to the society is surely exaggerated, the
fact that Nan-ts'ao was successful in raising the
money necessary to purchase enough land to act as an
endowment to support its quarterly convocation and
insure its continuation indicates the solidarity and
extensiveness of its membership, as well as its high
degree of organization. Both the extent of the
society's membership and its level of organization go
far beyond the earlier Hua-yen societies organized on
the basis of the Record of the Hua-yen chai. The
sheer magnitude of the society founded by Nan-ts'ao
also suggests that its membership must have cut across
class lines to include people from a wide cross section of Chinese society.

While societies such as the one found by Nan-
ts'ao can be seen as having developed out of the Hua-
yen chai which trace back to at least the end of the
fifth century, they did not occur as an organized and

widespread social phenomenon permeating different
strata of Chinese society until the early ninth
century.   The shift in the political structure and
economic base of the dynasty that had occurred in the
wake of the An Lu-shan Rebellion no longer permitted
the existence of a purely philosophical Buddhism
patronized by the imperial court.[66] The rebellion had
not so much been brought to an end by the vigorous
reassertion of imperial authority as by a grudging
accommodation to the very process of political frag-
mentation that had been its cause. The dynasty's loss
of centralized political control, witnessed in the
creation of a growing number of virtually autonomous
satrapies under the control of military governors,
also meant the loss of enormous tax revenues to a
government whose coffers had alredy been drained by
the cost of the campaigns and whose available tax
resources had been further strained by the devastation
of civil war.   While the dynasty did make a concerted
effort to reverse this centrifugal movement--
especially during the reign of strong emperors such
as Te-tsung (779-805) and Hsien-tsung (805-820)--it
was still never able to regain its former centralized
grip on the empire as a whole.

Along with the decline in imperial power in the
aftermath of the An Lu-shan Rebellion, Hua-yen societies spread throughout Chinese society as later Hua-
yen masters were forced to turn to other and more
reliable areas of Chinese society for support.
Ch'eng-kuan, for instance, in addition to enjoying
long and intimate ties with the imperial court, also
had close connections with a number of important
scholar-officials, as well as with some of the powerful military governors--men of action who preferred

the more direct teaching of Ch'an to the highly philosophical abstractions characteristic of Fa-tsang's
thought.[67] Fa-tsang, by contrast, had lived during a
time when the imperial institution was at the height
of its power and commanded vast resources, which it
used to patronize Buddhism on a lavish scale. Moreover, he was active during the reign of Empress Wu
(684-705), who had raised Buddhism to a position of
pre-eminence in her efforts to make it serve as an
ideological support for the legitimation of her rule,
and he had little need to gear his teaching down to a
more popular level. While Ch'eng-kuan's writings are
still scholastic in tone, their incorporation of Ch'an
terms and ideas gives them a practical dimension that
cannot be found in Fa-tsang.

Tsung-mi also had close ties with a number of
prominent scholar-officials, most notable of whom were
P'ei Hsiu 裴休 [68] (?787-860), Li Hsun 李訓 [69] (d.
835), and Po Chü-i.[70] He had gained entry to court
circles through his association with Ch'eng-kuan. In
828, for instance, Emperor Wen-tsung awarded him the
purple robe and later bestowed on him the title of
Great Worthy (ta-te 大德).[71] While the tribute thus
accorded Tsung-mi was a clear token of the esteem with
which he was regarded by the court, it was still a
strictly honorary recognition and does not seem to
have entailed the kind of financial support that Fa-
tsang had enjoyed in an earlier period.

Tsung-mi's writing also went much further in
popularizing Hua-yen thought than did that of Ch'eng-
kuan. And when compared to the complexity and sophistication of Fa-tsang's Treatise on the Five Teachings,
Tsung-mi's discussion of Buddhist teachings in his
Inquiry into the Origin of Man was simple and

straightforward, and could be understood without a detailed knowledge of the intricacies of Buddhist doctrine. Furthermore, the style and content, as well as the overall thrust, of the essay suggest that Tsung-mi intended it as a popular tract addressed to a broad intellectual audience. The vocabulary and allusions with which Tsung-mi defines the central focus of the essay in the Preface, for example, would have struck a resonant chord with the scholar-official of his day familiar with Confucian and Taoist classics. Many of these same scholar-officials, such as Po Chü-i, would also have made up an important segment of the lay Buddhist societies that were popular when Tsung-mi wrote, and his inclusion of the Teaching of Men and Gods--as the teaching which the Buddha was believed to have specifically addressed to his lay followers--in the Inquiry into the Origin of Man reflects the spread and growing importance of lay Buddhist societies throughout different strata of Chinese society during the latter part of the T'ang dynasty.

APPENDIX

An annotated   translation of "The Teaching of   Men and
Gods" from   Tsung-mi's Inquiry into the Origin   of Man

The Buddha, for the sake of beginners, at first
set forth the karmic retribution of the   three periods
of time[1] and the   causes and   effects of good   and bad
[deeds].   That is   to say, [one who] commits   the ten
evils[2] in   their highest degree[3] falls into   hell upon
death, [one who commits the ten evils] in their lesser
degree becomes   a hungry   ghost, and [one   who commits
the ten evils] in their lowest degree becomes a beast.
Therefore, the Buddha grouped [the five precepts] with
the five constant virtues[4] of the worldly teaching and
caused [beginners] to maintain the five   precepts,[5] to
succeed   in avoiding the three [evil]   destinies,[6] and
to be born into   the human realm. (As for   the worldly
teaching of India, even though its observance   is distinct, in its admonishing against evil and its exhorting to   good,   there is   no difference   [from   that of
China].   Moreover, it   is not separate from the   five
constant virtues of humanity, righteousness,   etc. and
there is virtuous conduct which should be cultivated.[7]
For example, it   is like   the clasping[8]   of   the hands
together   and   raising them   in this   country   and the
dropping of the   hands by the side in   Tibet--both are
[examples of] propriety.   Not killing is humanity, not
stealing is righteousness, not committing   adultery is
propriety,   not   lying   is   trustworthiness,   and,   by
neither drinking   wine nor eating meat, the   spirit is
purified   and one   increases in   wisdom.)   [One who]
cultivates the ten good deeds[9] in their highest degree
as   well as bestowing alms, maintaining   the precepts,
etc.[10] is   born   into   [one   of]   the   six   heavens   of

desire;[11] [one who] cultivates the four stages of meditation[12] and the eight attainments[13] is born into
[one of] the heavens of the realm of form[14] or the
realm of formlessness.[15]   (The reason why gods,
[hungry] ghosts, and the denizens of hell are not
mentioned in the title [of this treatise] is because
their realms, being different [from that of man], are
beyond ordinary understanding.   Since the secular
person does not even know the branch, how much less
could he presume to investigate the root thoroughly.
Therefore, in response to the secular teaching, I too
have also entitled [this treatise] "An Inquiry into
the Origin of Man."   [However], in now relating the
teachings of the Buddha, it was, as a matter of principle,[16] fitting that I set [the other destinies]
forth in detail.)   Therefore, [this teaching] is
called the Teaching of Men and Gods.   (And, as for
karma, there are three types: 1) good, 2) bad, and 3)
neutral.   As for retribution, there are three periods
of time, that is to say, retribution in the present
life, in the next life, and in subsequent lives.)
According to this teaching, karma constitutes the
origin of bodily existence.

Now I will assess [this teaching] critically.
Granted that we receive a bodily existence in [one of]
the five destinies[17] as a result of our having generated karma, it is still not clear who generates karma
and who experiences its retribution.   If the eyes,
ears, hands, and feet are able to generate karma, then
why, while the eyes, ears, hands, and feet of a person
who has just died are still intact, do they not see,
hear, function, and move?   If one says that it is the
mind which generates [karma], what is meant by the
mind?   If one says that it is the corporeal mind,[18]

then the corporeal mind has material substance and is embedded within the body. How, then, does it suddenly enter the eyes and ears and discern what is and what is not of externals? If what is and what is not are not known [by the mind], then by means of what does one discriminate them? Moreover, since the mind is blocked off from the eyes, ears, hands , and feet by material substance, how, then, can they pass in and out of one another, function in response to one another, and generate karmic conditions together? If one were to say that it is just joy, anger, love, and hate which activate the body and mouth and cause them to generate karma, then, since the feelings of joy, anger, and so forth abruptly arise and abruptly perish and are of themselves without substance, what can we take as constituting the controlling agent and generating karma? If one were to say that [the parts of the body] should not be investigated separately like this, but that it is our body-and-mind as a whole which is able to generate karma, then, once this body has died, who experiences the retribution of pain and pleasure? If one says that after death he has another body, then how can the commission of evil or the cultivation of merit in the present body-and-mind cause the experiencing of pain and pleasure in another body-and-mind in a future life? If we base ourselves on this [teaching], then one who cultivates merit should be extremely disheartened and one who commits evil should be extremely rejoiceful. How can the holy principle be so unjust?[19] Therefore we know that those who merely study this teaching, even though they believe in karmic conditioning, have not yet reached the origin of their bodily existence.

NOTES

1. See T45.481c11; cf. Francis Cook, "Fa-tsang's Treatise on the Five Doctrines, An annotated Translation" (unpublished Ph.D. dissertation: University of Wisconsin), 1970, p. 177.

2. Although a neglected and often maligned figure, Hui-yüan was the foremost of Fa-tsang's numerous disciples. It was he who, upon his master's death, took over and completed his unfinished commentary on Śikṣānanda's new translation of the Hua-yen Sutra. This work, known as the Hsü Hua-yen ching lüeh-shu k'an-ting chi, superseded Fa-tsang's commentary on Buddhabhadra's earlier translation of the Hua-yen Sutra, the Hua-yen ching t'an-hsüan chi, and served as the orthodox interpretation of the sutra until the late eighth century when Ch'eng-kuan wrote his commentary and subcommentary on the sutra, in which he discredited Hui-yüan. For a reassessment of Hui-yüan's importance see Part I of Sakamoto Yukio's Kegon kyōgaku no kenkyū (Kyoto: Heirakuji, 1964).

3. See Ch'eng-kuan's Hua-yen ching shu, T35.508c26-27 and Hua-yen ching sui-shu yen-i ch'ao, T36.43a8-9 and Hui-yüan's K'an-ting chi, HTC 5.8b18-c8.

4. The close resemblance between the name of this teaching and the Buddha's epithet, the Teacher of Gods and Men, suggests that the term "the Teaching of Men and Gods" might have been inspired by this famous epithet of the Buddha. "The Teacher of Gods and Men" (t'ien-jen shih, śāstā deva-manuṣyāṇām) occurs as a member of a stock formula of ten epithets of the Buddha in the early scriptures--see, for example, Anguttara-nikāya 3.314, translated by E. M. Hare, The Book of Gradual Sayings (London: Pali Text Society, 1961) 3.224, where the ten epithets are enumerated as the first of six recollections to be observed by the Buddhist disciple (see T2.143b24-26 for the corresponding passage in the Chinese collection of the Āgamas). The term is explained as follows in the Ta-chih tu-lun (T25.72c4-8):

[The Buddha] is also called śāstā deva-
manuṣyānām. Śāstā means teacher; deva,
gods; manuṣyanam, men. The term thus means
Teacher of Gods and Men. Why is [the
Buddha] called Teacher of Gods and Men?
Because the Buddha taught [gods and men]
what they should do and what they should not
do, what is good and what is bad. Those who
followed his teaching without abandoning the
Path gained the reward of deliverance from
the passions. Therefore [the Buddha] is
called the Teacher of Gods and Men.

The Buddha's epithet, the Teacher of Gods and Men, is
thus defined in terms of the beings whom the Buddha
taught and therefore has an entirely different point
of reference than the Teaching of Men and Gods, which
is defined in terms of the destinies in which beings
are reborn as a result of their following that teaching. Moreover, the Buddha is spoken of as the Teacher
of Gods and Men because he taught gods and men how to
gain deliverance from the passions, i.e., how to
escape from the cycle of rebirth. The Teaching of Men
and Gods, however, teaches beings how to gain a better
birth within the cycle of rebirth. Since the meaning
of the two terms is so different, it would seem that
the derivation of the name of the Teaching of Men and
Gods had little, if anything, to do with this epithet
of the Buddha.

5. Majjhima-nikāya 3.202-206 and 207-215, translated by I. B. Horner, The Middle Length Sayings
(London: Pali Text Society, 1967), 3.248-253 and 254-
262. For the Chinese version of these texts see Ying-
wu ching and Fen-pieh ta-yeh ching, nos. 170 and 171
of the Chung-o-han, T1.703c23-706b10 and 706b14-
708c28.

6. A. K. Warder notes that the standard course
of instruction for lay disciples comprised discourses
on giving (dāna), morality (śila), and heaven
(svarga); the disadvantage, vanity, and depravity of
sense pleasures; and the advantage of renunciation
(see Digha-nikāya 1.110, translated by T. W. Rhys-
Davids, Dialogues of the Buddha [London: Pali Text
Society, 1977], 1.134-135 and Majjhima-nikāya 1.379,
translated by I. B. Horner, The Middle Length Sayings
[London: Pali Text Society, 1975], 2.45). Warder
goes on to point out that in the Mahāsamghika version
of these texts "merit" and "the result of merit" are
substituted for the last two items (Indian Buddhism

[Delhi, Varanasi, and Patna: Motilal Banarsidass, 1980], p. 187).

7. The idea that one may obtain birth as a man, in one of the six heavens of desire, or in the Brahma Heavens (the lowest sphere in the Realm of Form) by giving alms can be found in the early Buddhist literature; see, for example, Digha-nikāya 3.258-260, translated by T. W. Rhys-Davids, The Dialogues of the Buddha (London: Pali Text Society, 1977), 3.40-241 and Aṅguttara-nikāya 4.239-241, translated by E. M. Hare, The Book of Gradual Sayings (London: Pali Text Society, 1965), 4.163-164 for a description of the eight types of rebirth due to giving.

8. For a discussion of Liu Ch'iu and early doctrinal classification schemes see Ito Giken, "Tendai izen no kyōhan ni tsuite," Ryūkoku daigaku ronsō, no. 284 (February 1929), pp. 46-77 and no. 285 (July 1929), pp. 71-97; Fuse Kogaku, Nehanshū no kenkyū (Tokyo: Kokusho kankōkai, 1973), 2.283-310; Leon Hurvitz, Chih-i (538-597): An Introduction to the Life and Ideas of a Chinese Buddhist Monk (Bruxelles: l'Institut Belge des Hautes Études Chinoises, 1962), pp. 214-229; Leon Hurvitz and Tsukamoto Zenryū, Wei Shou, Treatise on Buddhism and Taoism (Kyoto: Jimbun-kagaku kenkyūsho, 1956), pp. 33-35; and Kenneth Ch'en, Buddhism in China: A Historical Survey (Princeton University Press, 1972) pp. 180-183.

9. Tsukamoto Zenryū has gathered together the various fragments of the T'i-wei Po-li ching which are quoted in other sources and has published them in his Shina bukkyōshi kenkyū, Hokugi hen (Tokyo, 1942, pp. 293-353 (reprinted in Tsukamoto Zenryū chosaku shū [Tokyo: Daitō shuppansha, 1974], 2.189-240). The second fascicle of this text (Stein #2051) was among the works found at Tun-huang and has been published by Makita Tairyō in his "Tonkōbon Daiikyō no kenkyū," Bukkyō daigaku kaigakuin kenkyū kiyō (1968), pp. 137-185. Discussions of this text can also be found in Mochizuki Shinkō, Bukkyō daijiten (Tokyo: Sekai shoten kankō kyōkai, 1958), 4.3193c3195a; T'ang Yung-t'ung, Han Wei liang-Chin Nan-pei-ch'ao fo-chiao shih (Taipei: Ting-wen shu-chü, 1975), pp. 811-817; and Kenneth Ch'en, The Chinese Transformation of Buddhism (Princeton: Princeton University Press, 1973), pp. 55-60.

10. Hsü kao-seng chuan, T50.428a10-12.

11.   Fragment #6, quoted in Tsukamoto   chosaku shu 2.203.

12.   See fragment #8, ibid., 2.204.

13.   See fragment   #9, ibid., 2.204.   The way   in which the five precepts are paired with the   five constant   virtues differs   in the different   fragments of this text quoted by Tsukamoto.   For a   discussion and translation of these see Ch'en, The   Chinese Transformation of Buddhism, pp. 57-59.

14.   See Hare, The Book of Gradual   Sayings 4.293-295.

15.   See   I. B.   Horner, The   Book   of   Discipline (London: Pali Text Society, 1970), 1.5-6.   For mention of this encounter in the Chinese sources see Ssu-fen lü,   T22.103a; Jui-ying pen-ch'i   ching, T3.479a; Pen-hsing   chi   ching,   T3.801a;   and   P'u-yao   ching, T3.526b.

16.   T48.403a18-21; cf. Jeffrey   Broughton, "Kuei-feng   Tsung-mi: The   Convergence   of   Ch'an   and the Teachings" (unpublished Ph.D. dissertation: Columbia University, 1975), pp. 157-158.

17.   In   the   Dhānañjānisutta   of   the   Majjhima-nikāya (translated by I. B. Horner, The   Middle Length Sayings [London: Pali Text   Society, 1975],   2.372-379), the Brahmin Dhananjani succeeds in gaining birth in the Heaven of Brahma as   a result of   having practiced   the meditation   of suffusing the   universe with friendliness,   compassion, sympathetic joy,   and equanimity.   In the Anāthapiṇḍikovādasutta (translated by Horner,   The   Middle Length   Sayings 3.309-315),   the pious layman   and dānapati   Anāthapiṇḍika succeeds in being born in the Tusita Heaven as a result   of having heard Sariputta discourse on the course of mental discipline usually taught to monks.   As a final example, Ananda,   following   the instructions of   the   Buddha, explains the four   stages of meditation to a   group of laymen   in the   Sekhasutta (translated by   Horner, The Middle Length Sayings, 2.18-25), concluding his sermon with the assertion that householders can   also achieve nirvana.   For a discussion of the role of   meditation in the Buddha's teaching for laymen see Warder, Indian Buddhism, pp. 187-200.

18.   T48.403b7; cf. Broughton, p. 161.

304

19. See Yen-i ch'ao, T36.17a26. Elsewhere in the same work Ch'eng-kuan says that Hui-yüan's inclusion of non-Buddhist teachings within his p'an-chiao scheme constitutes "the error of confusing the true and the false.... If one does not know what is false, then how can he understand what is true?" (51c23-24). Altogether Ch'eng-kuan levels ten criticisms against Hui-yüan in the beginning of the Yen-i ch'ao (see T36.16b15-18c7; for a discussion of these see Sakamoto, Kegon kyōgaku no kenkyū, pp. 58-91).

Hui-yüan's four-fold classification scheme, it should be said in his defense, was based on solid canonical authority, deriving from a passage in the Pao-hsing lun (Ratnagotravibhāga) (T31.839b18-21), itself based on a passage from the Śrīmālā Sutra (T12.222b19-21), categorizing the different types of sentient beings who do not have access to the tathāgatagarbha (see K'an-ting chi, HCT 5.12a18-12b2).

20. T45.798a8.

21. Ibid., 708a8-13. This passage is of partic-ular interest because it shows the ease and skill with which Tsung-mi was able to draw from his early educa-tion in Confucian classics. The phrase "exhausting principle, realizing the nature, and reaching the ultimate source," for instance, is based on an almost identical passage from the I ching, which James Legge translates as: "They (thus) made an exhaustive dis-crimination of what was right, and effected the com-plete development of (every) nature, till they arrived...at what was appointed for it (by heaven)" (Z. D. Sung, The Text of the Yi King [Taipei: Ch'eng-wen Publishing Co., 1971], pp. 338-339). Tsung-mi's phrase "contribute in common to order" (t'ung-kuei-yü-chih) is drawn from the Shu ching passage, which Legge translates as: "Acts of goodness are different, but they contribute in common to government. Acts of evil are different, but they contribute in common to disorder" (The Shoo King [The Chinese Classics, Vol. 3] [Oxford: Clarendon Press, 1893], p. 490). Tsung-mi's use of the phrase t'ung-kuei, moreover, recalls another passage from the I ching, which Legge trans-lates as: "In all (the processes taking place) under heaven, what is there of thinking? What is there of anxious scheming? They all come to the same (success-ful) issue, though by different paths; there is one result, though there might be a hundred anxious schemes" (Sung, p. 316). The I ching passage is of further importance because it connects Tsung-mi's use

of the phrase t'ung-kuei with the phrase shu-t'u,
which he used in the previous quotation when he said
the three sages "made different paths in setting up
their teachings." Taken together, the phrase shu-t'u
t'ung-kuei--which we could render freely as "the different paths ultimately lead to the same goal"--was
used by Chinese Buddhists to express the teaching of
the Universal Vehicle (i-sheng, ekayāna) found in the
Lotus Sutra, according to which the teachings of the
three vehicles (i.e., those of the śrāvaka, pratyekabuddha, and bodhisattva) were all subsumed into one
all-inclusive vehicle of salvation. Dharma Master Chi
of the Liu-Sung dynasty (420-479), for instance,
classified the teaching of the Lotus Sutra as the
Universal Teaching (t'ung-kuei chiao) because "it sub-
sumes the three into the One" (hui-san kuei-i) (see
T35.508c21-23). The phrase "the different paths ultimately lead to the same goal" thus provided Chinese
Buddhists with a convenient formula for establishing
the ultimate identity of all the different teachings
of the Buddha. By the same token, the phrase was also
used to assert the ultimate identity of the Three
Teachings (san-chiao i-chih), and seems to have gained
currency in this usage by at least the second half of
the eighth century; see, for example, Chan-jan's Chih-
kuan fu-hsing chuan-hing chüeh, T46.441a8-9. Tsung-
mi's use of the phrases shu-t'u and t'ung-kuei thus
indicates that he thought of the teaching of
Buddhism--or, more accurately, the Ultimate Teaching
of Buddhism--as embodying the Universal Truth towards
which all other teachings ultimately lead and into
which all other teachings are ultimately subsumed. It
also reveals the sophistication with which he utilized
classical allusions to establish a syncretic framework
in which the teachings of Buddhism, Taoism, and
Confucianism could be seen as but different expressions of one Universal Truth.

22. Hua-yen ching shu, T35.521b15-16. Ch'eng-
kuan goes to some length in the Yen-i ch'ao to elaborate ten major points of difference which distinguish
the teaching of Buddhism from that of Taoism and
Confucianism (see T36.106a27-107a13).

23. Yen-i ch'ao, T36.106a7-12. Ch'eng-kuan's
remark is based on a parable from the Nirvana Sutra
(see T12.381c-382b8) which he cites in full in the
passage immediately preceding this one (see 105b17-
106a5). In this parable, which is related to illustrate the difference between the Buddha's teaching and
the worldly teachings, the Buddha recounts the story

of a man who had a herd of cows. He kept them and saw
that they were well tended in order to have ghee made
out of their milk. When the man died, the whole herd
was stolen by a band of thieves, who also wanted to
make ghee from their milk. However, since they did
not know how to churn the milk to make cream, they
could not make it thicken. They then added water to
it, hoping thereby to make ghee, but only ruined the
milk. The Buddha then explains that even though the
common man has access to the Buddha's most excellent
teaching, he does not know how to use it to attain
liberation, just as the thieves did not know how to
use the cow's milk to make ghee.

Ch'eng-kuan's remark also recalls the well-known
analogy of the Five Flavors, which is also found in
the Nirvana Sutra (see T12.690c27-691a6). The Buddha
uses this analogy to compare the different levels of
his teaching to milk, cream, butter, melted butter,
and ghee--all of which are made from cow's milk.
Since Ch'eng-kuan likens the teachings of Taoism and
Confucianism to donkey's milk, he puts them in an
entirely different soteriological class than the
teachings of Buddhism.

24. Ibid., 107a7-8.

25. Ibid., 107a11-13.

26. K'an-ting chi, HTC 5.13a9-10. In his comment
on this passage, Sakamoto (p. 273) has speculated that
Hui-yüan might be referring to Ch'eng Hsüan-ying
(active early to middle seventh century), whom Ch'eng-
kuan singles out for censure for confusing the three
teachings (see Yen-i ch'ao, T36.105b13-16). Ch'eng-
kuan remarks that Ch'eng Hsüan-ying, in using Buddhist
ideas to elucidate the meaning of the Lao-tzu and
Chuang-tzu in his commentaries on these two Taoist
classics, merely saw that there was some similarity in
their expression without recognizing that their meaning differed greatly. Tao-hsüan, in discussing the
imperial edict ordering Hsüan-tsang to translate the
Lao-tzu into Sanskrit, says that the two Taoists of
stature commensurate to debate with Hsüan-tsang were
Ts'ai Hung and Ch'eng Hsüan-ying, and that it was
their custom to quote Buddhist works (such as the
Middle Treatise and the Hundred Treatise) to explain
the meaning of Taoist ideas (see Chi ku-chin fa-tao
lun-heng, T52.386c2-7). Yoshioka Yoshitoyo has shown
that Ch'eng Hsüan-ying made use of Buddhist methodology (especially the Mādhyamika logic of negation) in
his interpretation of the Lao-tzu (see Dōkyō to

bukkyō, Vol. 1 [Tokyo: Gakujutsu shinko kai, 1959], pp. 109-115). Since, on the basis of the above evidence, it would seem that Ch'eng Hsüan-ying relied on Mādhyamika concepts and methodology in his elucidation of Taoist texts, it is unclear whether he would also have drawn on tathāgatagarbha thought to explain the ontological function of the Tao as Non-being in the creation of the phenomenal world. For a discussion of Ch'eng Hsüan-ying and his use of Buddhism see Kamata Shigeo, Chūgoku kegon shisōshi no kenkyū (Tokyo: Tokyo daigaku shuppankai, 1965), pp. 274-276. Ch'eng Hsüan-ying's commentary on the Chuang-tzu can be found in the Taoist Canon (Tao-tsang #507). His commentary on the Lao-tzu was among the works discovered at Tun-huang (Pelliot #2353) and its Preface has been published by Yoshioka in his Dōkyō to bukkyō, 1.110-115.

27. Legge, The Shoo King, p. 186. Tsung-mi cites this passage in his own commentary on the corresponding section of his critique of the Decree of Heaven found in the Yüan-chüeh ching ta-shu (see Yüan-chüeh ching ta-shu ch'ao, HTC 14.415dl-2).

28. James Legge, Confucian Analects, The Great Learning and the Doctrine of the Mean (The Chinese Classics, Vol. 1) (Oxford: Clarendon Press, 1893), p. 253. Tsung-mi cites this passage in the corresponding section of the Yüan-chüeh ching ta-shu, HTC 14.163b3-4.

29. T45.708b28-c7. In his Yüan-chüeh ching ta-shu ch'ao (HTC 14.415c17-d6) Tsung-mi points out that "the reward of blessing the good and augmenting the humble and the punishment of bringing disaster down upon the wicked and affliction upon the full" alludes to the passage from the Shu ching already cited in note 7, as well as a passage from the I ching, which Legge renders: "It is the way of heaven to diminish the full and augment the humble" (Sung, p. 71).

30. Ibid., 708b4-8.

31. Ibid., 708b13.

32. See Arthur Wright, "Fu I and the Rejection of Buddhism," Journal of the History of Ideas, 12.33-47.

33. These debates can be found in the Chi ku-chin fo-tao lun-heng (T#2104) and Kuang hung-ming chi (T#2103), both of which were compiled by Tao-hsüan.

The best study of them still remains Tokiwa Daijō's Shina ni okeru bukkyō to jukyō dōkyō (Tokyo: Tōyō bunko, 1930), pp. 115-138, Kubota Ryōon's Shina ju dō butsu sangyō shiron (Tokyo: 1931), pp. 299-386, and the same author's Shina ju dō butsu kōshōshi (Tokyo: Daitō shuppansha, 1943), pp. 172-193.

34. For a discussion of the state's continual efforts to keep the Buddhist institution under its bureaucratic control see Chapter 3 of Ch'en's The Chinese Transformation of Buddhism, especially pp. 78-81 and 84ff.

35. See Denis Twitchett, "Hsüan Tsung (reign 712-756)," Chapter 7 of Denis Twitchett, ed., Sui and T'ang Ching, 589-906, Part I (The Cambridge History of China, Vol. 3) (Cambridge, London, New York, and Melbourne: Cambridge University Press, 1979), pp. 361-362 and 411-412.

36. From the Sui through the early T'ang a number of Taoist texts such as the T'ai-hsüan chen-i pen-chi ching, Ta-sheng miao-lin ching, and Hai-k'ung chih-tsang ching were written under the direct influence of Buddhist works. While this early group of texts is often no more than a crude plagiarism of Buddhist works, the process of doctrinal appropriation had become more sophisticated by the mid T'ang, as evidenced by the Tao-chiao i-shu (a systematic compendium of Taoist doctrine), which skillfully adapted Buddhist terms and categories to express genuinely Taoist ideas. For a study of this literature see Part I of Kamata Shigeo's Chūgoku bukkyō shisōshi kenkyū (Tokyo: Shunjūsha, 1969).

37. See Kamata, Chūgoku kegon shisōshi no kenkyū, pp. 257-258.

38. A brief account of this debate can be found in Arthur Waley's The Life and Times of Po Chü-i (London: George Allen and Unwin Ltd., 1970), pp. 169-171.

39. See J. K. Rideout, "The Context of the Yüan Tao and the Yüan Hsing," Bulletin of the School of Oriental and African Studies 5.403.408.

40. Tsung-mi is our sole source of information on this monk. According to his Chung-hua ch'uan-hsin-ti ch'an-men shih-tzu ch'eng-hsi t'u (HTC 110.435a), Tao-yüan inherited the teaching of Ho-tse Shen-hui through

Tz'u-chou Chih-ju and I-chou Nan-yin. Since there is also a Nan-yin in the Ching-chung line of Ch'an founded by Chih-hsien, a controversy has arisen among Ch'an scholars as to whether Tsung-mi should not be placed in the Ching-chung lineage instead of the Hotse lineage with which he identified himself. For a summary of the debate see Jan Yün-hua, "Tsung-mi: His Analysis of Ch'an Buddhism," T'oung Pao, Vol. 58 (1972), pp. 9-10.

41. See Yüan-chüeh ching ta-shu, HTC 14.190c12-15 and Ta-shu ch'ao, HTC 14.222a11-223b11; virtually identical passages can also be found in Tsung-mi's Yüan-chuan ching lüeh-shu, T39.524b20-23 and Lüeh-shu ch'ao, HTC 15.105d8-107b9.

42. The present section is much indebted to Kamata Shigeo's pioneering study of the role of the early Hua-yen cult and Hua-yen societies in the formation of the Hua-yen school; see Chūgoku kegon shisōshi no kenkyū, pp. 42-47 and 235-248.

43. See fragment #17, quoted in Tsukamoto chosaku shū, 2.206-208, and the related discussion on pp. 217-225.

44. See S. Dutt, Buddhist Monks and Monasteries of India (London: George Allen and Unwin, Ltd., 1962), pp. 71-74 and Charles Prebish, Buddhist Monastic Disciple (University Park and London: Pennsylvania State University Press, 1975), pp. 24-27.

45. See T. W. Rhys-Davids and Hermann Oldenberg, trs., Vinaya Texts, Part I (The Sacred Books of the East, Vol. 13) (Oxford: Oxford University Press, 1881), p. 239ff.

46. See Yamazaki Hiroshi, Shina chūsei bukkyō no tenkai (Kyoto: Hōzōkan, 1971), pp. 732-763 and Ch'en, The Chinese Transformation of Buddhism, pp. 276-281.

47. See Edwin Reischauer, trs., Ennin's Diary: The Record of a Pilgrimage in Search of the Law (New York: Ronald Press, 1955), pp. 218-222 for an example of a detailed description of one such maigre feast. See also Reischauer's companion volume, Ennin's Travels in T'ang China (New York: Ronald Press, 1955), pp. 177-183.

48. T50.428a19-20.

49.　See the T'i-wei Po-li ching passage quoted in Makita, "Tonkōbon Daiikyō no kenkyū," p. 149.

50.　T50.688a13-15.

51.　P'u-an's biography can be found in both the Hsü kao-seng chuan, T50.681a9-682b4 and Hua-yen ching chuan chi, T51.167c4-168c17.

52.　Hsü kao-seng chuan, T50.681a12-13.

53.　From at least the last quarter of the sixth century, Mt. Chung-nan was one of the early and most important centers in which the Hua-yen cult flourished. The mountain figures in the biographies of many of the monks noted for their devotion to the Hua-yen Sutra, and both Tu-shun and Chih-yen, the persons later singled out as the first and second patriarchs of the Hua-yen tradition, resided there. Tsung-mi also spent a considerable portion of his life there, much of it passed at the Ts'ao-t'ang ("thatched hall") temple situated near Kuei Peak (kuei-feng), by whose name he was often designated.

54.　See T50.681a13-b16 and T51.167c8-168a5.

55.　See T50.681b16-22 and T51.168a5-9.

56.　See T50.681b22-27 and T51.168a9-16.

57.　See T50.681c7-18 and T51.168a22-b4.

58.　See T50.681c18-20 and T51.168b4-5.

59.　See T50.681c20-682a12 and T51.168b5-26.

60.　See T50.682a14-16 and T51.168b28-c1.

61.　See Hua-yen ching chuan chi, T51.166c10.

62.　Hsü kao-seng chuan, T50.653b26-29, translated by Robert Gimello, "Chih-yen and the Foundations of Hua-yen Buddhism" (unpublished Ph.D. dissertation: Columbia University, 1976), p. 122.

63.　T51.172a23-b1.

64.　See Chūgoku kegon shisōshi no kenkyū, p. 238.

65. _Po-shih ch'ang-ch'ing-chi_ (_Ssu-pu ts'ung-k'an_ edition), 59.7a-8b. The translation has been adapted from that of Kenneth Ch'en, _The Chinese Transformation of Buddhism_, pp. 210-211.

66. See Kamata, _Chūgoku kegon shisōshi no kenkyū_, p. 235.

67. See _Ibid._, pp. 221-230.

68. P'ei Hsiu was Tsung-mi's closest and most prominent lay disciple. He wrote prefaces to many of Tsung-mi's works, as well as composing his funerary inscription (see _Ch'üan T'ang-wen_ 743). His standard biography can be found in _Chiu T'ang-shu_ 177 and _Hsin T'ang-shu_ 182. Henri Maspero gives a brief sketch of his life in "Sur Quelques Textes Anciens de Chinois Parlé," _Bulletin de l'École Française d'Extrême-Orient_, Vol. 14 (1914), pp. 1-36 (cf. the unpublished emended English translation by Iriya Yoshitaka, Ruth Fuller Sasaki, and Burton Watson, "On Some Texts of Ancient Spoken Chinese," pp. 11-15). See also Broughton, pp. 57-59 and Jan Yün-hua, p. 10.
In addition to P'ei Hsiu, Tsung-mi's biography in the _Ching-te Ch'üan-teng lu_ (T51.305c-308b) also indicates his association with three other lay figures: Hsiao Mien, Wen Tsao, and Shih Shan-jen. Although nothing is known about Shih Shan-jen, both Hsiao Mien and Wen Tsao were scholar-officials of some note. Hsiao Mien served as Chief Minister in 820-821 (see _Chiu T'ang-shu_ 172 and _Hsin T'ang-shu_ 101) and Wen Tsao served as President of the Board of Rites in his later years (see _Chiu T'ang-shu_ 165 and _Hsin T'ang-shu_ 91). See also Yamazaki Hiroshi, _Zui tō bukkyōshi no kenkyū_ (Kyoto: Hōzōkan, 1967), pp. 231-234. Tsung-mi was also friends with Chia Tao (779-843), a poet belonging to Han Yü's circle (see Broughton, p. 26).

69. Li Hsün is famous as one of the conspirators in the Sweet Dew Incident, an abortive attempt in 835 to oust the eunuchs from power. His standard biography can be found in _Chiu T'ang-shu_ 169 and _Hsin T'ang-shu_ 179. Yamazaki discusses his relation to Tsung-mi in his _Zui tō bukkyōshi no kenkyū_, pp. 225-231. See also Broughton, pp. 58-62 and Jan, pp. 17-19.

70. For Tsung-mi's connection with Po Chü-i see Waley, _The Life and Times of Po Chü-i_, p. 188 and Ch'en, _The Chinese Transformation of Buddhism_, pp. 218-220.

312

71. See Kamata Shigeo, _Shūmitsu kyōgaku no shisōshi-teki kenkyu_ (Tokyo: Tokyo daigaku shuppansha, 1975), p. 68.

APPENDIX NOTES

1. The three periods of time refer to the past, present, and future.

2. The ten evil deeds (dasākuśala) are 1) killing, 2) stealing, 3) adultery, 4) lying, 5) slander, 6) harsh speech, 7) frivolous chatter, 8) covetousness, 9) malice, and 10) false views. A standard description of the ten evils can be found in the Saleyyakusutta (translated by I. B. Horner as "Discourse to the people of Sālā" in The Middle Length Sayings [London: Pali Text Society, 1976], 1.343‑ 349), the Sevitabba‑asevitabba‑sutta (translated by I. B. Horner as "Discourse on What Is To Be Followed and What is Not To Be Followed" in The Middle Length Sayings [London: Pali Text Society, 1970], 2.94‑104), and elsewhere in the Pali Canon. For a similar description in the Chinese Āgamas, see Hsing ching in the Chung‑o‑han, T1.437b‑438b.

3. Yüan‑chüeh's commentary on this passage (Hua‑ yen yüan‑jen lun chieh, HTC 104.120b‑c) says that all good and evil deeds have three degrees, which, in turn, can be analyzed from three perspectives, i.e., in regard to the object, the state of mind of the perpetrator, and the three periods of time. In regard to the object, the killing of a person is a case of an evil in its highest degree; the killing of an animal is a case of an evil in its lesser degree; and the killing of an insect is a case of an evil in its lowest degree. In regard to the state of mind of the perpetrator, the commission of an evil deed with malicious intent is a case of an evil in its highest degree; the commission of an evil deed with only some deliberation is a case of an evil in its lesser degree; and the commission of an evil deed unintentionally is a case of an evil in its lowest degree. Finally, in regard to the three periods of time, the commission of an evil deed without any sense of contrition in any of the three periods of time (i.e., before, during, and after) is a case of an evil in its highest degree; the commission of an evil deed with a sense of contrition in any one of the three periods of time is a case of an evil in its lesser degree; and

the commission of an evil deed with a sense of contrition in two of the three periods of time is a case
of an evil in its lowest degree.

The idea that there are degrees of good and evil
can be found in the Daśabhūmika chapter of the Hua-yen
Sutra. In the section dealing with the second bhūmi,
the Śikṣānanda translation says, "The course of the
ten evil deeds is the cause of being born in [the
realm of] hell, beasts, and hungry ghosts. The course
of the ten good deeds is the cause of being born in
[the realm of] men and gods up to the pinnacle of
existence" (T10.185c1-3). And further, "As for the
course of the ten evil deeds, the highest [degree] is
the cause of [being born as] a denizen of hell, the
lesser [degree] is the cause of [being born as] a
beast, and the lowest [degree] is the cause of [being
born as] a hungry ghost" (185c16-18). For the corresponding passages in the Buddha bhadra translation see
T9.549a14-15 and 26-28. It should be noted that
whereas the passage from the Hua-yen Sutra says that
evils of a lesser degree are a cause for being born as
a beast and that evils of the lowest degree are a
cause for being born as a hungry ghost, the passage
from the Inquiry into the Origin of Man says that
evils of a lesser degree are a cause for being born as
a hungry ghost and that evils of the lowest degree are
a cause for being born as a beast. The Abhidharmakośa
also ranks birth as a beast below that as a hungry
ghost.

Ch'eng-kuan, in his commentary (T35.774c25-27)
and subcommentary (T36.475a13-23), on this passage
from the Hua-yen Sutra, gives an analysis of the
various degrees of good and bad deeds that is similar
to that of Yüan-chüeh cited above.

Hakeda's translation of the passage of the
Inquiry into the Origin of Man under discussion
("...if a man of high grade commits the ten evils, at
death he falls into hell; if a man of medium grade
commits the ten evils, he becomes a hungry ghost; and
if a man of low grade commits the ten evils, he
becomes a beast") is not only mistaken doctrinally--as
should be clear from the discussion above--but is also
grammatically untenable. In the Chinese, "highest
degree" (shang-p'in), "lesser degree" (chung-p'in),
and "lowest degree" (hsia-p'in) clearly modify "the
ten evils." For Hakeda's translation to work,
"highest degree," etc. would have to precede the verb
"to commit." See William T. de Bary, ed., The
Buddhist Tradition in India, China and Japan (New
York: Random House, 1972), p. 185.

4. The five constant virtues are humanity (jen), righteousness (i), propriety (li), trustworthiness (hsin), and wisdom (chih).

5. The five precepts (panca-sila) are not to kill, not to steal, not to commit adultery, not to lie, and not to drink intoxicating beverages.

6. The three evil destinies are those of the denizens to hell (naraka), hungry ghosts (preta), and beasts (tiryagyoni).

7. The punctuation of the Taishō text is in error. The punctuation should come after hsiu, as should be clear from Yüan-chüeh's commentary (121b). Li ("for example") begins the next sentence. This is also the way that the text is read by the Japanese commentators.

8. The Taishō text has han; following Kamata Shigeo (Genninron [Tokyo: Meitoku shuppansha, 1973], p. 60), I have emended han to read lien. Morohashi also notes that han is often written for lien (Daikanwa jiten [Tokyo: Daishūkan shoten, 1964], 6.6362c).

9. The ten good deeds (dasakusala) are not to commit the ten evils. See note 2 above.

10. I.e., he practices the six perfections (pāramitā) of giving (dāna), morality (sila), patience (ksānti), vigor (vīrya), meditation (dhyāna), and wisdom (prajñā).

11. The six heavens of desire constitute the upper levels of the kāmadhātu. They are, according to the Abhidharmakośa (T29.41a; cf. Louis de la Vallée Poussin, L'Abhidharmakośa de Vasubandhu [Bruxelles: l'Institut Belge des Hautes Études Chinois, 1971], 2.1), 1) the heaven of the retainers of the four great kings (caturmahārājakāyika-deva), 2) the heaven of the the thirty-three gods (trayastrimśa-deva), 3) the heaven of the yāmas (yāma-deva), 4) the heaven of the satisfied (tusita-deva), 5) the heaven of those who have pleasure in creation (nirmānarati-deva), and 6) the heaven of rulers over things created by others (paranirmitavaśavartin-deva). The same enumeration can be found in earlier texts; cf. Majjhima-nikāya 2.194 and 3.100 (translated by Horner, The Middle Length Sayings 2.377 and 3.139-140) and Dīgha-nikāya 1.216 (translated by T. W. Rhys Davids, The Dialogues

of the Buddha [London: Pali Text Society, 1977],
1.280-281). For a more detailed discussion of these
six heavens, see Mochizuki 4.3770b-3771b and Louis de
la Vallée Poussin, "Cosmogeny and Cosmology
(Buddhist)," in James Hastings, ed., Encyclopedia of
Religion and Ethics (Edinburgh: T. & T. Clark and New
York: C. Scribner's Sons, 1908-1926), 4.134-135.

12. The standard description of the four stages
of meditation (catur-dhyāna) says that having become
free of sense-desires and unwholesome states, one
enters the first stage of meditation, which is accompanied by applied and discursive thought, born of
detachment, rapturous and joyful. From the appeasing
of applied and discursive thought, one enters the
second stage of meditation, where the inward heart is
serene and uniquely exalted, and which is devoid of
applied and discursive thought, born of concentration,
rapturous and joyful. Through distaste for rapture,
one dwells evenmindedly, mindful and clearly conscious, and enters the third stage of meditation,
experiencing with his body that joy of which the
Aryans declare, "joyful lives he who is evenminded and
mindful." From the forsaking of joy, from the forsaking of pain, from the going to rest of one's former
gladness and sadness, one enters the fourth stage of
meditation, which is neither painful nor pleasurable,
and which is the utter purity of evenmindedness and
mindfulness (I have adapted the rendition of the four
stages of meditation found in Edward Conze's Buddhist
Meditation [New York: Harper and Row, 1969], pp. 113-
118). This standard description of the four stages of
meditation can be found in numerous places throughout
the Pali Canon; cf. Digha-nikāya 1.73-75 and 2.314
(translated by Rhys Davids, The Dialogues of the
Buddha 1.84-86 and T. W. Rhys Davids, The Dialogues of
the Buddha [London: Pali Text Society, 1977], 2.345),
Majjhima-nikāya 1.174 (translated by Horner, The
Middle Length Sayings 1.218), and elsewhere. The
paramount importance of the four stages of meditation
in Buddhism is established by the fact that it was
only after passing through all four stages that the
Buddha experienced enlightenment; see the
Bhayabheravasutta (translated by Horner, The Middle
Length Sayings 1.27-29) and the Cūlasaccakasutta
(translated by Horner, The Middle Length Sayings
1.301-303). For a standard scholastic analysis of the
four stages of meditation, see Visuddhimagga 4, translated by Bhikkhu Ñanamoli, The Path of Purification
(Kandy, Sri Lanka: Buddhist Publication Society,
1975), pp. 144-175.

13. The eight attainments are comprised of the
four stages of meditation and the four formless
attainments (catasra arupya-samapattayah). The four
formless attainments are those of infinite space
(akasanantyayatana), infinite consciousness
(vijnanantyayatana), nothingness (akincannayatana),
and neither consciousness nor non-consciousness
(naivasamjna-nasamjnayatana). For a detailed discussion of the four formless attainments, see
Visuddhimagga 10 (Nanamoli, pp. 354-371), Mochizuki
3.2039b-2040c, and H. R. Perera, "Aruppa," in
Malalasekera, ed., Encyclopedia of Buddhism (Ceylon:
Government of Ceylon, 1961-), 2.104-105.

The eight attainments form part of the heritage
of yogic practices that were incorporated by the
Buddha into his teaching. According to the Majjhima-
nikaya 1.164ff., the teachings of two of the Buddha's
teachers, Alara Kalama and Uddaka Ramaputta, culminated, respectively, in the seventh and eighth attainments. Since the attainment of neither one of these
states frees one from the cycle of rebirth, they were
rejected as being ultimate by the Buddha (see Horner,
The Middle Length Sayings 1.208-210). Sometimes a
ninth state, that of the cessation of consciousness
and sensation (samjna-vedayita-nirodha-samapatti), is
added to the eight attainments to comprise an ascending series of meditational stages known as the attainments of the nine successive stages (navanupurva-
vihara-samapatti), which are enumerated in the
Anguttara-nikaya 4.409 (translated by E. M. Hare, The
Book of Gradual Sayings 4.276-277) and elsewhere in
the Pali Canon.

14. The realm of form (rupadhatu), located above
the six heavens of desire, is comprised of four main
heavens which correspond to the four stages of meditation. The number of heavens within these four main
heavens, however, varies with different texts.
According to the Abhidharmakosa (T29.41a; cf. Poussin,
2.2-4), the first three meditation heavens are each
comprised of three heavens while the fourth is comprised of eight. The first meditation heaven is
inhabited by gods in the retinue of Brahma
(brahmakayika-deva), the Brahma chaplains
(brahmapurohita-deva), and the Great Brahmas
(mahabrahmana-deva). The second meditation heaven is
inhabited by gods of limited splendor (parittabha-
deva), of immeasurable splendor (apramanabha-deva),
and of radiance (abhasvara-deva). The third meditation heaven is inhabited by gods of limited beauty
(parittasubha-deva), of immeasurable beauty

(apramānāśubha-deva), and of complete beauty (śubhakṛtsna-deva). The fourth meditation heaven is inhabited by gods who are cloudless (anabhraka-deva), merit born (puṇya-prasava-deva), of abundant fruit (bṛhātphala-deva), effortless (abṛha-deva), of no heat (atapa-deva), beautiful (sudṛsā-deva), well-seeing (sudarśana-deva), and sublime (akaniṣṭha-deva). All of the gods dwelling in the heavens of the realm of form, being wholly beyond sense-desires, are without sexual characteristics and are born by apparitional birth without the intermediacy of parents; their bodies are luminous and of a subtle substance, which feeds on joy. For a more detailed discussion of these heavens and their inhabitants, see Mochizuki 4.3771b-3772a and Poussin, "Cosmogeny and Cosmology," pp. 135-136.

15. See note 13 above.

16. The punctuation of the Taishō text seems to be in error; the editors of the Ching-yüan commentary (98c) as well as all of the Japanese commentators that I have consulted place the punctuation after "ching." Moreover, Kishigami Kairyo (Kachu genninron kogi [Osaka, 1901], 3.9), Atsuta Ryochi (Genninron kogi [Kyoto, 1896], p. 66), and Kamata (p. 60) all emend "ching" to read "chiao"; accordingly, I have translated "fo-ching" as "the teachings of the Buddha."

17. The five destinies are those of the denizens of hell, hungry ghosts, beasts, men, and gods. Sometimes a sixth destiny, that of titans (asura), is added.

18. Yüan-chüeh (123b), condensing a passage from Tsung-mi's Ch'an Preface (T48.401c17ff), says that the corporeal mind is one of four types of mind commonly taught in Buddhism. The other three are the object-perceiving mind (i.e., the mind of the eight consciousnesses), the mind which accumulates and produces (i.e., the ālayavijñāna), and the true mind (i.e., the mind which is unchanging and untainted by defilements and which is seen as Suchness). Since the corporeal mind is the lowest of the four types, Yüan-chüeh observes that Tsung-mi is implicitly criticizing the superficial understanding of the followers of the Teaching of Men and Gods who do not know of the three higher types of mind.
In the Ch'an Preface passage, Tsung-mi says of the first type of mind: "The first is the ho-li-ta-ye [Skt., hṛdaya]; this is the corporeal mind; this is

the mind of the five internal organs." For a more detailed discussion of Tsung-mi's four types of mind, see Kamata Shigeo, <u>Zengen</u> <u>shosenshū</u> <u>tojo</u> (Tokyo: Chikuma shobō, 1971), pp. 74-76; Broughton, pp. 133-136; and Mochizuki 1.475c.

19. Tsung-mi's point is that if the body and mind are taken as a single totality, then the body-and-mind in this present existence is entirely different from the body-and-mind in another existence in the future. If this is so, then there can be no personal continuity and it is someone else who reaps the benefits and misfortunes caused by my actions.

LI T'UNG-HSÜAN AND THE PRACTICAL
DIMENSIONS OF HUA-YEN
by
Robert M. Gimello

There is little doubt among modern scholars of
the Hua-yen tradition of Buddhism that the once
standard view of it as having consisted essentially in
the thought of five great "patriarchs" is a drastic
over-simplification of the actual complexity of its
history.[1] We now realize--perhaps more clearly than
at any other time since the eighth century coinage of
the term Hua-yen tsung 華嚴宗 [2]--that what may
legitimately be called "Hua-yen" began considerably
before the time of its purported "first patriarch,"
Tu-shun 杜順 (557-640); that it numbered among its
creators many more than just five thinkers; and that
it continued to develop long after the time of its
purported "fifth" or last major "patriarch," Tsung-mi
宗密 (780-841). Of course, on certain premises,
there is some measure of truth to the traditional
"five patriarch" conception of Hua-yen. If one
defines Hua-yen as only a system of doctrine of the
sort one finds outlined in Fa-tsang's 法藏 (643-711)
Wu-chiao-chang 五教章 , then I think it true to say
at least that the doctrinal innovations most characteristic of the tradition, as well as the larger
patterns of their systematic interrelation, were for
the most part realized during that period of time
marked by the lives of the so-called "patriarchs"--
i.e., during the seventh, eighth, and early ninth
centuries. Before then, it would seem, the lineaments
of a separate Hua-yen mode of Mahāyāna were still

indistinct. And after that period, such continuing development as Hua-yen did undergo would seem to have consisted largely in the further refinement and gradual elaboration of ideas that had taken their essential shapes in the first two and a half centuries of T'ang China.

However, it is now apparent--thanks primarily to the labors of modern Japanese scholars--that if we can alter our premises and entertain a broader, more supple definition of Hua-yen as something more than just a static architecture of ideas--if, for instance, we can give the name Hua-yen as readily to certain lineages of religious practice as to any particular systems of thought, or if we can locate the tenor of Hua-yen history in the use through time of certain images and symbols, even if they be divorced from any single conceptual system--then the history of Hua-yen can be shown to be a richer and more various thing than traditional views have suggested it was.

Consider, for example, the question of Chinese Hua-yen after Tsung-mi. What is to be counted as the next stage in its history? Traditional approaches to the subject might lead one to identify for this role certain figures of the Sung--perhaps the so-called "four masters" (i.e., Tao-t'ing 道亭 , Kuan-fu 觀復 , Shih-hui 師會 and Hsi-ti 希迪).[3] But the writings of these men were, for the most part, only commentaries on the original works of their predecessors, such T'ang "patriarchs" as Fa-tsang and Ch'eng-kuan 澄觀 . If we are to count such as these as the true successors of Tsung-mi, then we must content ourselves with the prospect of a rather barren later Hua-yen history, for their thought offered little that was truly new. Rather, they were concerned almost exclusively with preserving and explaining, in ever greater detail, the texts and ideas of earlier generations.

But what if one were to choose as the next phase in the history of Hua-yen after Tsung-mi, say, the "five-ranks" (<u>wu-wei</u> 五位) thought of men like Tung-shan Liang-chieh 洞山良价 (807-869)[4] or Ts'ao-shan Pen-chi 曹山本寂 (840-901)[5] and their successors? "Five-rank" thought, of course, is usually treated under the rubric of Ch'an禪, Ts'ao-tung 曹洞 Ch'an particularly.[6] But need it be assigned to that category alone? After all, some of the basic motifs of "five-rank" thought are of Hua-yen origin, and "five-rank" theory is a genuinely innovative use of those motifs. Moreover, even the traditional view allows that much of the essence of Hua-yen was absorbed by Ch'an during that period when the Hua-yen "school," strictly defined as an institution, was in decline. We need not be so respectful of sectarian distinctions as to omit from future surveys of "Hua-yen" so fascinating a variation on, or transmutation of, Hua-yen themes as "five-rank" theory.

Considerations of this sort lead me to suggest that we would be better served by a definition of a tradition like Hua-yen which stresses its variety, its malleability, even its discontinuity, and which allows us to see it as a sequence of changes and diversifications. Such a revisionary definition would be much more useful to us than continued adherence to the view that it is but a heritage of preservation, continuous evolution, and "orthodox" exegesis. Seen as the former, Hua-yen can be studied as a vital religious and intellectual tradition, responsive through history to the changing needs of its adherents. Seen as the

324

latter, it is neither vital nor responsive; rather it
is only a conceptual abstraction, an artful pattern of
indifferent and lifeless doctrines.

The Place of Li T'ung-hsüan in East Asian Buddhism

The thought and later influence of the T'ang
dynasty Buddhist layman Li T'ung-hsüan 李通玄
stands, I believe as strong testimony to the validity
and usefulness of an approach to Hua-yen that emphasizes its great diversity and the many changes it
underwent, rather than only its invariant essential
ideas. Li T'ung-hsüan is a mysterious, eccentric
figures, said to stand somewhat apart from the main-
stream of Hua-yen. Thus, the very little scholarship
that has been devoted to him (and there is very little
indeed[7]) has tended to concentrate on discrepancies
between his thought and that of allegedly "more orthodox" Hua-yen thinkers like Fa-tsang. Yet, when one
adopts an approach like the one I have suggested above
and explores the later (i.e., the post-T'ang) Hua-yen
tradition with attention particularly to its episodes
of innovation and disjuncture, it is surprising how
often one encounters the influence of Li T'ung-hsüan.
What seems to emerge from the records as one begins to
investigate them is the curious fact that a thinker
judged by the so-called "orthodox" tradition (and by
earlier modern scholarship still beholden to that
orthodoxy) to have been marginal and idiosyncratic has
often proved more influential, just at those periods
when Hua-yen underwent significant change or renewal,
than have any of the more "orthodox" Hua-yen masters.
The appendix to this essay includes an annotated translation of one of the most detailed and one

of the earliest hagiographical accounts of Li's life, but the highlights of that account can be sketched here as follows. Li T'ung-hsüan lived from 635 to 730.[8] He was, therefore, an elder contemporary of Fa-tsang, the best known of all Hua-yen thinkers. Very little, I regret to say, is known about his life. He is said to have been related to the T'ang imperial house, but of course we are not told how he was so related, and the tradition seems to be forever unverifiable. All that we know of roughly the first 50 years of his long life is that he was educated, as most aristocrats would have been, in the secular traditions of his native culture, i.e., in the classics of Confucianism and Taoism. The hagiographical tradition tells us this, and it is corroborated by displays of his non-Buddhist learning in his own later writings.[9] During the reign of Empress Wu, we are informed, he conceived an interest in the Avataṁsaka-sūtra, which was then, under the auspices of the imperial court, being expounded by Fa-tsang and re-translated by Śikṣānanda.[10] Apparently, he spent most of the sixth and seventh decades of his life (i.e., c. 685–705) studying this scripture and familiarizing himself with much of the earlier exegesis of it.[11] But even this is only tantalizing information. We do not know, for example, who his teachers were, if indeed he had teachers in any formal sense. We do know that he was intimately familiar with Fa-tsang's works, but it is very unlikely that he was ever a student of Fa-tsang, especially in view of his later demonstrated readiness to disagree with that eminent authority.[12]

The standard hagiographies of Li T'ung-hsüan begin their story in the year 709, i.e., in roughly his 74th year, when he is said to have arrived (from where we do not really know, though we may presume it was from the capital) in the general vicinity of the city of T'ai-yüan 太原 in central Shansi. There he took up the life of an ascetic hermit and there he stayed, never altering his style of life, for his remaining 21 years. During this period he is said to have written a number of expositions of Avataṁsaka doctrine, four of which have survived.[13] By far the best known and most important of these is his 40 chüan Exposition of the Avataṁsakasūtra, the Hua-yen ching lun 華嚴經論.[14] The other three are:

a) Ta-fang-kuang fo-hua-yen ching chung chüan-chüan tai-i lüeh-hsü 大方廣佛 華嚴經中卷卷大意略敘

--a fascicle by fascicle summary of the Sūtra, in one fascicle.[15]

b) Lüeh-shih hsin hua-yen ching hsiu-hsing tz'u-ti chüeh-i lun 略釋新 華嚴經修行次第決疑論

--a brief explanation of the Sūtra in which doubts concerning the regimen of practice are resolved, in four fascicles.[16]

c) Shih hua-yen ching shih-erh yüan-sheng chieh-mi hsien-chih ch'eng-pei shih-ming lun 釋華嚴經十二緣生解 迷顯智成悲十明論

> --an explanation of the Sūtra in terms
> of ten perspectives on the doctrine of
> twelve-fold dependent origination, in
> four fascicles.[17]

It seems, however, that, like many Chinese Buddhists associated with the Avataṁsaka, Li was known best to his contemporaries not as an exigete or scholar but as a meditation adept and miracle worker (kan-t'ung-che 感通者). Indeed, the works on which we must rely for our "biographical" information about him are little more than collected tales of miracles he performed or precipitated. Although they are not very informative historically, they are often charming, and they do reflect his eminence in local traditions of popular piety.[18]

Perhaps because he was a layman, and therefore not so closely tied as a monk might have been to any particular lineage of teaching, he was free to develop his own distinctive views of the Avataṁsaka and its purport.[19] This he did with great originality and independence of spirit, even to the point, as I have mentioned, of disagreeing explicitly and by name with Fa-tsang.[20] Despite his originality, however (or, perhaps, because of it), and certainly because he had chosen a hermit's life, Li's reputation for several generations after his death remained for the most part a local one, confined largely to certain areas of Shansi.[21] There is no convincing evidence, e.g., that his thought was very well known to Ch'eng-kuan or Tsung-mi, or to any other luminaries of the late eighth, ninth, and early tenth centuries,[22] although several of his works were carefully preserved and copied by a small lineage of followers who are known

to history only in that capacity. In the mid-ninth
century, for example, a monk named Chih-ning 志寧
collated the Hua-yen ching lun together with the Sūtra
itself, thereby producing the Hua-yen ching ho lun 華
嚴經合論, the text most often used by later
students of Li's thought. Less than a century after
the collation was made the Hua-yen ching lun achieved
the signal distinction of becoming the first Buddhist
text of indisputable and acknowledged Chinese authorship to be accorded "canonical" status. This occurred
in the year 938 when Li Pien, ruler of the Kingdom of
Southern T'ang, acceded to the ardent request of
certain monks that Li's Exposition be "entered into
the Canon" 入藏. It was actually only added as a
sort of appendix to the Canon 編於藏末, but this
was to have lasting consequences. In 945 or 946, when
the monk Heng-an compiled his Continuation of the
Scriptural Catalogue of the Chen-yüan Era 續貞元錄,
he listed the Exposition as one of the texts in
the Canon he was cataloguing and made special mention
of it in his introduction.[23] It was to retain its
venerated status from then on, as can be seen in the
fact that it went on to inclusion in no fewer than
twelve of the thirty-one recension of the Canon that
we know today.[24]

In the early Sung dynasty, however, and for
reasons yet to be determined, Li was "rediscovered."
His works then came to be widely celebrated,
particularly by members of the Lin-ch'i tradition of
Sung dynasty Ch'an like Ta-hui 大慧 (d. 1163)[25] and
Te-hung 德洪 (1070-1128),[26] but also by figures
tangential to that tradition like the scholar-official
Chang Shang-ying 張商英 (1043-1121).[27] It was in

this period, too, that Li's works were first transmitted to Korea and thence to Japan. In Korea, they
came quickly to enjoy eminent status after one of
them, the Hua-yen-ching lun, proved to be a crucial
influence upon the life and thought of one of the most
important figures in the history of Korean Zen or Sŏn,
the famous Pojo Chinul 普照知訥 (1158-1210).[28]
Chinul compiled an influential synopsis of Li's
lengthy Exposition, the Hwaŏmnon chŏryo 華嚴論節
要, which was later taken to Japan.[29]

Li T'ung-hsüan's thought had, as is better
known, a similarly profound influence upon a major
figure in the history of medieval Japanese Buddhism,
i.e., Kōben 高辨 or Myōe Shōnin 明惠上人 (1173-
1232).[30] It is the connection with Kōben that is
probably more responsible than anything else for the
little attention that Li has been given in traditional
Japanese Hua-yen scholarship, the focus of that attention being a meditation on the light emanating from
the person of the Buddha. Li attached great doctrinal
significance to the Sūtra's several descriptions of
the Buddha's awesome radiance. Centuries later,
Kōben, having happened upon copies of Li's works
recently transmitted to Japan,[31] was struck by the
affinity between Li's use of the Buddha-radiance motif
as a doctrinally fertile symbol and certain forms of
visualization meditation practiced in the medieval
Japanese traditions of esoteric Buddhism.[32] He
conflated the Mikkyō 密教 techniques with Li's
symbolic interpretations, amplifying both by relating
them to his own rich inner life of dreams and visions,
and created a novel meditative and doctrinal scheme
known as the Bukkō zammai 佛光三昧, the "Sāmadhi of

the Buddha's Radiance,"[33] about which much more will be said below.

Once transmitted to Korea and Japan, however, Li's works were not forgotten in China. In fact, there was another upsurge of interest in him during the Ming dynasty, when two more synopses of his commentary on the Avataṁsaka were compiled. One of these was done by the little known monk Fang-tse 方澤 , of whose dates I am not sure.[34] The other, and surely the more interesting of the two, was by none other than Li Chih 李贄 (1527-1602), the great iconoclast of the Neo-Confucian tradition.[35] Nor was Li forgotten during the Ch'ing. His work was studied and recirculated by Tao-p'ei 道霈 (d. 1702), an influential scholar-monk of that dynasty.[36] Even today Li's works are a part of the living Buddhist tradition in East Asia. Testimony to this is found in the recent Korean publication of the Hua-yen-ching ho lun together with a vernacular commentary.[37]

The currently accepted view of Li T'ung-hsüan's place in Hua-yen history is derived from consideration of his influence upon such later figures as I have mentioned. They, especially the Korean Chinul and the Japanese Kōben, had credited Li T'ung-hsüan with the signal accomplishment of making Hua-yen Buddhism practicable. He is now known, in respect of their opinions, especially for having found amidst the profound symbolism of the Avataṁsaka and in the maze of difficult doctrine created by the earliest Hua-yen thinkers, concrete and practical guidance for the actual living of the religious life of Buddhism, i.e., for the practice of faith and meditation. It was this ability, ascribed to him by his spiritual progeny, to turn the abstract and often fantastical constructions

of Hua-yen theory and symbol to practical religious
account, to transform the stuff of scriptural myth and
metaphysics into lived salvific experience, that is
cited traditionally as the most characteristic quality
of his work and as the pith of his later influence.

Whether or not such characterizations of Li
T'ung-hsüan's work correspond to his own intentions or
to the understanding of his meanings shared by his
contemporaries and immediate followers is a question
we may never be able to answer satisfactorily. Li's
apparent idiosyncracies as a Hua-yen thinker, together
with the dearth of knowledge about his life and the
lack of early commentary on his writings, make it very
difficult to reconstruct his identity as an early
T'ang figure. The rich texture of detail and background necessary to allow our situating him in his own
time and place simply is not available to us. Moreover, the broad significance[38] his thought was to have
did not emerge in his own lifetime nor even shortly
thereafter. He did not come into his own, so to
speak, until hundreds of years after his death. These
facts--i.e., our inability to retrieve the original Li
T'ung-hsüan from the pauciloquy of history and the
emergence of his thought as a consequential force in
Buddhism only well after his own day--lead us inevi-
tably to treat not so much of Li T'ung-hsüan himself
as of his later influences, unintended and unantici-
pated though they may have been. But this is a necessity which we may well make into a virtue, for it
allows us to adhere to our purpose, stated at the
outset of this essay, to accentuate the variety of
what may be called Hua-yen and to stress its discon-
tinuities. Thus may we untether the term from any

narrow sectarian definition and from any false assumption that its history is undergirded by a "soul" (ātman) of continuous and determinate meaning, or that it is exempt from the law of "dependent origination" (pratītyasamutpāda) as that law operates in history.[39] It is upon this assumption,--viz., that Li T'ung-hsüan's thought is as much what Chinul or Koben thought it was as it is what Li himself may have had in mind--that we propose to give so much attention to those later figures. Let us begin with Chinul.

Li T'ung-hsüan as Seen by Chinul

One of the more eloquent testimonies to Li T'ung-hsüan's influence--or, to put the matter more accurately, one of the most compelling re-creations of the meaning of Li's thought--is to be found in the opening passage of Chinul's preface to his Synopsis of Li's Exposition:

> In the fall of the year 1185, as I began my retreat on Mt. Haga, my attention was fixed upon the Sŏn (Zen) theme of "the identity of one's mind with the true mind of Buddha" 禪門 即心即佛真心 , convinced that should I fail to realize this truth even kalpa-s of effort would not bring me to the bourne of sagehood. And yet I was left with doubt, the crux of which was the Hwaŏm (Hua-yen) doctrine of the "access of enlightenment" 悟入之門 . What, after all, was its point?" Therefore I sought out a certain lecturer, expert in Hwaom, and put my question to him. He replied that I should contemplate unceasingly "the

interpenetration of all phenomena." He
further cautioned me, saying, "If you contemplate only your own mind and fail to contemplate 'the interpenetration of all phenomena,' you will surely fail to gain the perfect
qualities of the fruition of Buddhahood." I
made no reply to this but thought silently to
myself, "If one uses the mind to contemplate
phenomena, then, since phenomena are obstacles, one will only fret the mind and there
will be no end to it. But, if the mind be
made clear with the purity of insight, then
entire worlds will interfuse with even a
single strand of hair, for certainly there are
no realms outside the mind."

So I returned to my mountain retreat, there
to peruse the Tripiṭaka in search of words of
the Buddha which confirmed the "Mind Lineage"
(i.e., the Zen tradition). Three years passed
before I came upon the simile of "a single
particle of dust encompassing thousands of
volumes of scripture," in the Avataṁsakasūtra's "Chapter on the Arising of Tathāgatas." Later in the same passage it is said
that "the Tathāgata's insight is also like
this--fully present in the body of each
sentient being. Of this only fools are ignorant and unaware."

Tears of joy welled up in my eyes and I
touched the text to my forehead in reverent
gratitude. Yet, I still did not fully understand how common people of these days might
acquire the first access of faith 今日凡夫最
初信入之門 . So I further consulted the

Exposition of the Hua-yen ching composed by the Elder Li. Therein, in his explanation of the first of the ten stages of faith, he says, "The Bodhisattva Crown of Enlightenment 覺首 菩薩 has three realizations. First, he realizes that his own body and mind are themselves fundamentally the dharmadhātu, immaculate and stainless. Second, he realizes that the discriminate nature of his own body and mind is itself fundamentally without distinction of subject and object 本 無能所 , being originally the Buddha of Adamantine Insight. Third, he realizes that his own mind, that marvelous insight by which he distinguishes between the genuine and the false, is itself the Bodhisattva Manjuśrī (embodiment of wisdom). In the inception of his mind of faith does he realize these three truths, and thus is he called Crown of Enlightenment." The *Exposition* says further that "the difficulties an ordinary person has in gaining access to the ten stages of faith are wholly due to his recognizing himself as an ordinary being and to his reluctance to acknowledge that his own mind is itself the Buddha of Adamantine Insight." Thereupon I put the volume aside and, with a long sigh, said, "What the World Honored One spoke with his mouth are "The Teachings." What the patriarchs transmitted in their minds is Sŏn (Zen). It cannot be that the Buddha's mouth and the patriarchs' minds contradict each other. How, then, can it be that proponents of Sŏn and advocates of "The Teachings" do not plumb the common source of truth but rather rest content in their own conventions, wasting their days in the reckless fomenting of disputes?" From that point on I have sought to amplify the mind of faith and have practiced assiduously. Many are the years I have accumulated in this effort.[40]

Chinul was a Zen monk and--like many such before and after him, indeed like many Buddhists since the inception of the religion--he was deeply troubled by apparent tensions, seeming incompatabilities, between the practicalities of his own discipline and the intellectual profundities of the more doctrinal sorts of Buddhism.[41] In his case, these tensions were heightened by institutional rivalries among the various lineages of Korean Buddhism, some of which emphasized learning whereas others were committed almost exclusively to the practice of meditation.[42] Chinul sought, in both his practice and his studies, the harmony and complimentarity between the two that he felt each demanded. He professed to have found it in Li T'ung-hsüan's explanation of the Avataṁsaka's teachings on faith. I take the crux of that explanation to be the claim that the first access of faith in the mind of the practitioner is in itself the culmination of the entire path, the very realization of final Buddhahood.

The first of the ten stages of faith, to which the passage from Li's Exposition refers, is actually the very beginning of bodhisattva practice as conceived in Hua-yen--i.e., the first of the classic 52 stages.[43] In standard Mahāyāna, i.e., in what Hua-yen has conventionally called the Mahāyāna of "the three vehicles" 三乘 as opposed to the encompassing yet higher teaching of "the one vehicle" 一乘 , the novice bodhisattva who has advanced to the first step of faith immediately after generating the aspiration to enlightenment 發菩提心 sees stretching ahead of him the daunting prospect of kalpa-s of arduous practice. Enlightenment lies so far beyond him as to suggest that the human condition, in which the newly fledged bodhisattva is still emersed and in which he is required to carry on his practice, is a dismal condition indeed, a condition from which he must strive to place himself at a very far remove.[44] The three vehicles do provide him with assistance, with expedient means said to make the transformation from ignorance to enlightenment possible. Prominent among these are the so-called "Teachings" 教. But the help they may give is not always quite obvious. "Emptiness" 空 , "dependent origination" 緣起 , "representation-only" 唯識 , "the mutual non-obstruction of all phenomena" 事事無礙 , etc. are, after all, rather difficult teachings--difficult to understand and even more difficult to apply. They may well seem more like barriers than bridges to liberation. And on what foundation--in the midst of his delusion, malice, and desire--is the still unenlightened aspirant to erect his efforts of understanding? What reason has he even to hope for success? Li's comments on "faith" (hsin 信)[45] and on the Bodhisattva Crown of Enlightenment were taken by Chinul as addressed directly to such questions and doubts as these. They were understood baldly to deny the alleged separation between the common sentient 凡夫 condition and the condition of Buddhahood. Their effect was seen to be that of shocking or stunning those aspiring to enlightenment

into a sustaining confidence in their ability actually
to accomplish their goal. The grounds for such confidence, Li suggested to Chinul, lie in the realization
that what is called "faith," even its merest incipience, is in fact not just a means to a distant end but
rather the proleptic presence of that end within the
very precincts of ignorance and suffering. "Faith" or
confidence in the possibility of enlightenment is
nothing but enlightenment itself, in an anticipatory
and causative modality. Were sentient beings themselves incapable of successful pursuit of the goal,
were that capability not resident in their very
natures, there would, on standard Buddhist premises,
be no external agency to endow them with that capability. Their situation would be irremediable. But what
is this innate capability, and where does it origi-
nate? For Li, as well as for Chinul, this capability
is enlightenment itself, in the experiential guise of
"faith."

This notion, of course, was not new with Li
T'ung-hsüan, and so was not available to Chinul only
in Li's works. However, the typical earlier Hua-yen
versions of it are couched in more abstract, more
explicitly philosophical language. Chih-yen 智儼
(602-668), the reputed "second Hua-yen patriarch," for
example, maintains that enlightenment is as much
"innate" 本有 as it is "cultivated" 修生 , as much
"innate and thereby born of cultivation" 本有修生 as
it is "born of cultivation and thereby innate" 修生
本有 .[46] He also says, "It is buddha-nature which is
the supportive cause 因 of all worldlings and nobles;
both are born from and mature upon the buddha-
nature."[47] Terms like "cause" (hetu 因) and "fruit"
(phala 果) are the more common vehicles for this

teaching in early Hua-yen, and the Hua-yen use of them is usually somewhat paradoxical, or at least athwart their common use. "Cause," i.e., the realm of practice and effort (hsing 行) leading to enlightenment, is assigned to the role of effect or fruit; fruit, the realm of attainment (ch'eng 證), is given attributes of causation and efficacy. The two are said to be "coincident" 因之與果 [48] and of "the same substance" 同體.[49] It is fruit which "constitutes the causality in cause" 在因為因 , and cause which "constitutes the fruition in fruit" 在果為果 .[50]

Now, Li T'ung-hsüan made use of such terms too. For example, in discussing the symbolism of the aura or brilliant light emanating from the person of the Tathagata, he notes that such imagery is found not only in the Avataṁsakasūtra but also in such "three vehicles" texts as The Larger Prajñāpāramitā 大品 經.[51] He maintains, however, that in the latter such imagery symbolizes the more obvious relation of "cause" producing "fruit," wherein one proceeds "by stages 漸次 from common toward saintly status 從凡 向聖, achieving the qualities of fruition 成果德 only after kalpa-s of accumulated cultivation 多劫積 修." In the Avataṁsakasūtra, he says, such imagery of radiance symbolizes rather "the achievement of cause from fruit 從果成因 ."[52]

Nevertheless, though he knew and occasionally employed the traditional termini technici, the special virtue of Li's thought for Chinul was that it tended more often to subordinate this sort of relatively abstruse discourse to a discourse more obviously addressed to concerns of practice and closer to the "vernacular" of Buddhism than to its learned tongue. Thus, in the passage from the Exposition which Chinul used, [Li makes his claim that enlightenment is already present at the outset of any striving for it, present specifically in the form of faith or confidence, a disposition available to all, even to those incapable of the feats of intellect that so much of the rest of Mahayana and of Hua-yen seem to require. Moreover, he makes this claim in a rhetorical or exegetical mode notably free of the scholastic usage most typical of "orthodox" Hua-yen.

This last point may be of special significance in explaining the peculiar attraction that Li T'ung-hsüan's thought had for Chinul, i.e., for a Zen monk who was, as many Zen monks have been, rather impatient of the emphasis on intellectual systematizing found in so much of early main-stream Hua-yen. Especially in passages in Li's writings dealing with faith and with related issues such as the possibility of achieving enlightenment "in one life" or "in the worldly body," one discerns (and assumes that Chinul also discerned) a pattern of thought that might well be identified as Li's novel and characteristic hermeneutical strategy.

In the Hua-yen literature written in China during the century or so before Li's works appeared, as in much of the rest of Buddhist scriptural exegesis of that time, one cannot help but note the predominance of an interpretive method in which a scripture is made to yield meaning by being placed under a doctrinal grid or "template" composed of elements culled from certain elaborate systems of Indian Buddhist thought. Thus the common exegetical technique of a Chih-yen or a Fa-tsang was to interpret the Avataṁsaka in terms of, say, the scholastic categories of Abhidharma, Yogācāra, and Tathāgatagarbha thought. The relatively amorphous or loosely structured scriptural

text was set in order, as it were, by the appli-
cation of preconceived theories and models--<u>dharma</u>
<u>theory</u>, causation theory, Vijñānavāda psychology,
Mādhyamika dialectic, etc. Admittedly these systems
and theories were themselves often altered as they
were made to consort with the primary text, but even
the many genuine innovations of earlier Hua-yen
exgesis were achieved by learnèd manipulation of
imported and inherited structures of doctrine which
had had their origins in other secondary texts. Li
T'ung-hsüan's work stands in sharp contrast to all of
this. He was, as we have already said, something of
an autodidact--knowledgeable in the more "orthodox"
traditions but not subservient to them--and he seems
to have been able to attend more to the text itself.
Rather than organize passages or the whole of the
<u>Sūtra</u> under rubrics taken from the various Indian
<u>śāstra</u> canons, his inclination was to find in the text
its own autonomous patterns of meaning. He saw it
with a fresh and naked eye, rather than through complex lenses provided by the various doctrinal systems
then available. As a result of this idiosyncratic
openness he was never drawn into preoccupations with
matters of doctrinal consistency and coherence. He
could instead proceed immediately to the more urgent
task of relating the text to his own situation and his
own spiritual problems. There is, consequently, a
certain simplicity and economy about his interpretations, a notable absence of extraneous matter. His
vision of the text is homogenous, not particulate, and
he was able to see in it important implications which
were, perhaps, too obvious for his more "sophisticated" predecessors and contemporaries. It may well
be this, especially, which so attracted his students

in Sung and Ming China, in Korea, and Japan. This too
may be the source of his reputed "practicality."

Let us sample a bit of his exegesis. The
following is from fascicle 22 of Li's Exposition of
the Avataṁsakasūtra, in which he treats of the opening
sections of the chapter on "The Ten Stages of the
Bodhisattva Path" (Daśabhūmika 十地品). He begins
with an explanation of the title of the chapter and is
overtly concerned to explain the use of the number
ten, there and elsewhere in the Sūtra. In particular,
he wishes to show that the Sūtra's custom of present-
ing nearly all of its topics in decades, or in higher
multiples of ten (hundreds, thousands, etc.), in no
way contradicts its consistently unitary vision. For
example, he says that although the bodhisattva may
progress through "the ten stations" (daśa vihāra 十
住), "the ten modes of action" (daśa caryā 十行),
"the ten dedications" (daśa parināmanā 十迴向),
etc., he does so without every really leaving the one
essential stage, the essence of all stages 地體,
which is "the pervasively refulgent insight of the
Tathagata" 如來普光明智 . Further to clarify this
point, he refers to another section of the Sūtra in
which ten Buddhas of Insight 十箇智佛 --The Buddha
of the Insight of Nonobstruction 無礙智佛 , The
Buddha of the Insight of Liberation 解脫智佛, etc.--
are presented. Of these he says:

> These ten buddhas all have as their single
> common foundation the one Buddha of Adamantine
> Insight. The Buddha of Adamantine Insight has
> as his foundation the pervasively refulgent
> insight of the Tathāgata. The pervasively
> refulgent insight of the Tathāgata has as its

342

foundation the insight without abode 無依住智 . Finally, the insight without abode has as its foundation the totality of sentient beings 一切衆生 .

So too with Sudhana (善財 --the protagonist of the final and longest chapter of the Sutra, the "Chapter on Entering the Dharmadhātu" 入法界品 , otherwise known independently as the Gaṇḍhavyūhasūtra). When he presents himself to Maitreya (the fifty-second of the fifty-four spiritual advisors whom Sudhana visits in his pilgrimage), Maitreya sends him back to see Mañjuśrī, who had been the very first of the fifty-four kalyāṇamitra 善知識 . The intent of this (i.e., of Maitreya's curious decision to send Sudhana back to the beginning of his long quest) is to demonstrate that, even throughout all five phases of the bodhisattva career, one never really departs from that first fruit of buddhahood which is the incipience of faith 不離初信之佛果 .

So, these "ten stages," extending from the beginning to the end of bodhisattvahood are actually but a single, unitary reality. In this sense is the chapter named "The Ten Stages." It is a chapter whose purpose is to equalize all parts of practice, to unify the many stages of advancement, and to integrate its various degrees. This, then, is a progressive cultivation in the midst of non-progression 此乃是無昇進中進修 , an advancement by degrees in the midst of an absence of all degrees 無層級中級.

In a word, the true subject of this chapter
is the one essence of all ten stages. Were it
not for the incipience of faith, the first of
the fruits of buddhahood, there could be no
completion of the ten stages. If the incipience of faith in the mind did not already
encompass the buddha-fruits of the ten or
eleven stages, then neither would there be
perfection of the mind of faith. From first
to last, they are all the one fruit of adamantine insight--the mind of faith is this fruition of buddhahood; the object of faith is
this fruition of buddhahood; the person of the
practitioner is this fruition of buddhahood.
Such is the mind of faith and thus is perfection of faith accomplishable. Neither the
cause nor the fruit of cultivation, neither
its end nor its beginning, is at all different
from adamantine insight.[53]

Also, toward the end of the long introductory section
of the Exposition, under the topic of "The Compression
and Extension of the Path from Cause to Fruit" 因果
延促者 , and after noting that other traditions and
texts of Buddhism describe the path as requiring as
many as sixteen kalpa-s or three inconceivable
kalpa-s, he observes:

The youth Sudhana accomplished Buddhahood in a
single lifetime. This illustrates that at the
very outset of the ten stations, in that one
instant, all deluded thoughts and affections
are immediately extinguished. Neither over
the three times (i.e., past, present, and

future) nor even in as little time as a moment is there anything that is "born" 無所生 . This is what the text means when it speaks of "a single lifetime." Not clinging to the notion of a "lifetime" measured in <u>kalpa</u>'s, which is but the product of the delusion of duration 存情 , one achieves a Buddhahood which is as though "unborn" 無生 because it is in truth "originally born" 本生 . This is what the text means when it speaks of "a single lifetime."[54]

In these two passages we see not only the substance of Li's overriding concerns but also typical examples of his method of putting a text into their service. He was clearly convinced that, if sentient beings were not already somehow quickened by an original or prior presence of buddhahood within themselves, then the unenlightened among them (i.e., virtually all) would not be able to mount the path <u>to</u> enlightenment; they would not have the wherewithal to transform themselves or to make of their practice a "cause" of the "fruit" of realization. Yet the practice unto enlightenment--as it was described in the <u>Avataṃsaka</u> itself, not to mention its far more elaborate descriptions in the Indian treatises earlier Hua-yen masters had used to "clarify" the <u>Sūtra</u>--was portrayed as lengthy and complex, intimidatingly so. Li seems to have shared the need, felt strongly by many Chinese Buddhists of his day, for a less remote goal of practice, a more immediately and easily available enlightenment. It would seem that he felt that satisfaction of that need did not lie, as others of his time thought it did, in subtle <u>doctrinal</u> "proofs" of the identity of ignorance and enlightenment, but in a simpler depiction of a simpler path, a path commensurable with the human condition of pervasive delusion and suffering, a path to which imperfect men and not only mythic bodhisattvas had access. Such a path he found in his fresh and doctrinally unhampered reading of the Avataṁsakasūtra. Thus he was able to see that Sudhana, a mere boy and yet also the protagonist of the culmination of the scripture, had himself achieved enlightenment in a single lifetime. He snatched this obvious and comforting fact from the welter of heroic and supernatural imagery of the text and concluded from it that such an expeditious path is available to all. He noted that at the end of his journey Sudhana was sent back to his starting point, and he drew from that a conclusion never (so far as I know) reached therefrom by earlier commentators, viz. that the beginning of the path must be somehow tantamount to its end. On this basis, he took the plethora of Buddhas, enlightenments, insights, and stages and reduced them all to the one experience of nascent faith, holding thereby that enlightenment--in its available form, in the form most relevant to the imperfections of this life and this world--is nothing other than mere faith. It is difficult to imagine, in this Chinese Buddhist context, a greater or more heartening encouragement to the aspirant than this.

The claim that it was Li T'ung-hsüan's novel hermeneutics and commentarial style, as much as or more than any substantive doctrinal innovation, which attracted Chinul's fervent attention may seem odd and dubious at first, but the manner of Chinul's appropriation of Li's writings would seem to bear it out, and in so doing would seem also to remind us of the crucial role played by method of scriptural interpretation in the construction of religious thought and practice. Apart from his <u>Synopsis</u> of the <u>Exposition</u>, Chinul wrote another work which is much concerned with Li's thought; that is the <u>Discourse</u> <u>on</u> <u>the</u> <u>Perfect</u> <u>and</u> <u>Sudden</u> <u>Attainment</u> <u>of</u> <u>Buddhahood</u> (Wŏndon sŏngbul-lon 圓頓成佛論).[55] In this work Chinul again confesses his typically Zen antipathy towards the scholasticism of conventional Hua-yen. He rails against those "doctrinalists" 敎家 and "orthodox disciples" 常徒 who allow themselves to "become mired in the marginality of words and doctrines and who are still unable to forget 'meanings,' to limn the mind, and so to realize enlightenment straightaway" 滯在言敎義理分際未能忘義了心連證菩提 .[56] Li T'ung-hsüan does not fall into such sorry company, Chinul implies, because his writings, though voluminous and profound, are "plain and simple in style" 文質 .[57] This quality, in turn, renders Li's works more suitable to the primary task of "introspective illumination" 返照 [58] of one's own mind and nature. As though to codify this distinction Chinul sets forth a <u>tripartite division of</u> approaches to liberation--the so-called <u>"three myste-</u><u>rious gates"</u> 三玄門 which he says are recognized in Zen. They are "<u>the mystery in substance</u>" 體中玄 , "<u>the mystery in word</u>" 句中玄 , and "<u>the mystery in</u> <u>mystery</u>" 玄中玄 .[59] The first is exemplified in such locutions of the standard Hua-yen principles of <u>"phe-</u><u>nomenal interpenetration"</u> 事事無礙 as, e.g., "Throughout the infinite cosmos self and other are not separated by so much as a hair's breadth, nor is there any phase of the whole length of cosmic time from its beginning to its end that is not present in this very moment." Of the truth of these and similar Hua-yen expressions Chinul has not the least doubt, but he holds them to be nonetheless insufficient and merely preliminary "because they have not abandoned the discriminate understanding that consists only in words and doctrines" 此亦是言教中解分未忘故. I think it fair to take this as a distillation of Chinul's judgement of the whole corpus of conventional Hua-yen literature. But what is there about Li T'ung-hsüan's works that places them outside this category? The answer lies, it would seem, in the definition of the second mysterious gate, "the mystery in word." This is the uncanny efficacy thought to reside in ordinary language as used for cathartic rather than constructive purposes. Language of this sort has three salient features. It is "traceless" 無跡, i.e., transformative rather than descriptive. Thus it does not function to imprint its own structure upon the world as the seemingly metaphysical usages of traditional scholastic Hua-yen were sometimes thought to do. It is also commonplace or "everyday" 平常 00 in character--i.e., more colloquial than technical, more natural than fabricated, and more consonant with the simple immediacy of quotidian experience than with the rarefaction of systematic philosophical reflection. Finally, it is purgative or cleansing in its ability to dissipate or "sweep away" 湯落 the congestion of ignorance that accumulates with clinging. Now Chinul does not explicitly place Li T'ung-hsüan's discourse under the rubric of this second mystery, but it does seem reasonable to infer such a characterization. He did say earlier in the work, while discussing the "intentionality" 旨趣 of the Exposition, that Li had meant to expose the cardinal meaning of the Hua-yen canon in such a way as to lead those of "great resolve" 大心, even in this "latter age" of the law 末世 and despite their merely "common" 凡夫 status, "to realize immediately that, upon this very plane of birth and death, the origin of the first aspiration for enlightenment is just the immovable insight of all the Buddhas" 於 生 死 地 面 上 頓 悟 諸 佛 不 動 智 以 為 初 發 心 之 源 也.[61] The references to "the latter day of the law," to the "common" rather than the "noble" condition, and to "the plane of birth and death" echo with the implications of the term "common-place" or "everyday" that is used to characterize "the mystery in word," as does the plainness of Li's prose which Chinul had also noted. It is both "traceless" and "purgative" insofar as it encourages those who understand it to "abandon once and for all the contentious mental attitude you may have developed previously in the discrimination of doctrines" 永 除 前 來 學 習 差 別 義 理 諍 論 之 心[62]. [In Chinul's estimation, therefore, its purpose was to effect a change in the reader, to release him from bondage to verbalization and conceptualization, rather than to assist him in the construction of elaborate and sophisticated systems of thought.]

These features which Chinul perceived in the form of Li's works and in their author's intentions correspond in turn to the substance of Li's vision, again as seen from Chinul's vantage point. The "traceless," "commonplace," and "purgative" qualities of the discourse fit well its central message of buddhahood's immediate availability, under the species of faith, in these very precincts of ignorance, imperfection, birth, and death. Moreover, both the form and the substance of Li's works admirably suit the needs of a Zen practitioner, i.e., of one whose

interests are perforce more practical than theoretical. Of course, Chinul's identity as a man of Zen
ought never to be forgotten, not even while considering his appropriation of Li T'ung-hsüan's Hua-yen.
According to the conceit of the "three mysterious
gates," there lies beyond even the liberating discourse of such works as Li's the still higher "mystery
within mystery." This consists of no "words" whatsoever, not even the "traceless," "commonplace," and
"purgative" words of a Li T'ung-hsüan. Rather it
consists in the characteristic metalinguistic instruments of Zen discipline, to wit, "silence," "the
staff," and "the shout."[63] The employment of these
takes one beyond even the purgation effected by discourse of Li's sort, and leads directly to experience
of the dharmadhātu itself. This, of course, is beyond
the reach of any sort of language; it is accessible
only to practice. Nevertheless, precisely in his
appreciation of this fact, Chinul found value in Li's
writings--value greater than that to be found in most
other Hua-yen literature--because they used language
in just such a way as to inspire the transcendence of
language. One might argue that other Hua-yen thinkers
had the same attitude toward language--indeed, I think
they had--but it is clear that this was often hidden
in or concealed by the cerebrations of conventional
Hua-yen usage, particularly in periods or circumstances (like Chinul's) dominated by a rhetoric of
practice. Perhaps, then, one can say that it was the
merit of Li T'ung-hsüan's thought to have preserved
the insights of Hua-yen in forms that would allow
their integration into religious contexts quite unlike
those in which Hua-yen was born. This, surely, is at

least part of what is to be learned in the study of
Chinul's encounter with "The Elder li."

Li T'ung-hsüan as Seen by Myōe Shōnin

In the year 1221, a mere eleven years after
Chinul's death, the Japanese monk Kōben (高辮 ,
otherwise known as Myōe Shōnin 明惠上人 , 1173-
1232), who was then residing at the Kōzan 高山 monastery[64] in the mountains just northwest of Kyoto,
further enlarged his already substantial corpus of
writings by completing a fascinating work entitled The
Mysterious Transmission of the Avataṁsakasūtra's
"Samādhi of the Budha's Radiance" (Kegon Bukkō zammai-
kan myōkan den 華嚴佛光三昧觀冥感傳).[65]
Nothing remotely like this short text is to be found
anywhere in Chinul's corpus. Its difference from the
works of the Korean monk can, of course, be partially
explained by reference to the differences between the
religious and cultural situations of Koryŏ Korea and
Kamakura Japan. Such an explanation would be insufficient even to its own purpose, however, and in any
case could not be extended to account for the even
more intriguing fact of the work's virtual singularity
when compared not only to Chinul's writings but to any
and all East Asian Buddhist texts. For that, one must
take special note of the overriding singularity of its
author, a figure who seems genuinely unique in the
annals of Buddhism despite the many senses in which he
can be said also to be representative of his time and
place. Yet it is an appreciation of just this singularity of text and author which may still further
expand our understanding of the range and diversity of
Li T'ung-hsüan's influence and thus of Hua-yen.

The Mysterious Transmission--actually a sort of autobiographical appendix to a longer and more theoretical treatise on the Samādhi of the Buddha's Radiance entitled Kegon Bukkō zammai-kan hihō zō 華嚴佛光三昧觀秘寶藏,[66] written in the same year takes the form of a series of questions and answers. To appreciate the first of these one must bear in mind that Kōben was a monk of the Shingon 真言 tradition and thus a practitioner of the Shingon variety of esoteric Buddhism (Mikkyō 密敎) known as Tōmitsu 東密. Among the many symbolic usages (abhiseka, mantra, mandala, etc.) observed in Tōmitsu is the performance of a Buddhist "last rite" or purification ceremony known as "Dosha kaji" 土砂加持 ,[67] i.e., the "absolution by dust," in which handsfull of dirt are sprinkled one hundred and eight times on the corpse of a deceased person to insure purgation of the consequences of bad karma, or on the body of a sick person to effect a cure. Of special relevance to the topic at hand is the fact that during the performance of this ritual a mantra is recited known as the "Mantra of the Buddha's Radiance" (Bukkō shingon 佛光真言). Unlike the Samādhi of the Buddha's Radiance, which seems to have been Kōben's invention, this mantra--Om amogha Vairocana mahāmūdra mani padmajvala pravarttaya hūm"--had long been recognized and used, and was established in the canon.[68] In light of this we can understand why the text opens with the question, "How does one know that this mantra of radiance corresponds to this samādhi?"[69] This, of course, is a crucial question for a Shingon monk and Mikkyō practitioner like Kōben. Buddhist esoterism is a rather complex array of symbols, each component of which is related to all the others according to a precise and

relatively invariable system of correspondences. Any
departure from or violation of this system (e.g.,
mismatching of colors and directions in the construction of a maṇḍala, use of the wrong mudrā at a certain
point in the performance of ritual meditation, invoca-
tion of deities in improper order in the enactment of
a ceremony, etc.) necessarily deprives the practice of
its efficacy and may even present a certain danger to
the spiritual well-being of the practitioner. In this
particular case the question was raised no doubt
because of the novelty of the Samādhi of the Buddha's
Radiance. No such samādhi was attested in the esoteric canon, and Kōben surely realized that in assert-
ing correspondence between a canonical mantra and a
samādhi of his own contrivance he was doing something
that needed explicit justification. What is especially fascinating about the Mysterious Transmission,
and what serves as a mark of what we have called
Kōben's singularity, is the form his justification
takes. Rather than weave a web of doctrinal explanation or construct some artifice of scriptural exegesis, he makes his appeal to a series of his own
visionary revelations.

Thus he tells us that in the second year of the
Jōkyū 承久 era, on the evening of the twenty-ninth
day of the seventh month (i.e., on August 28, 1220),[70]
while he was engaged in a course of meditation lasting
over a hundred days, there appeared before him a shim-
mering circle of white light in the form of a pearl
about a foot in diameter. Radiating from the left
side of this circle, up to distances of three feet,
were many beams of clear light. From the right side
arose clusters of brilliant flame. Just then he heard
the disembodied sound of the Mantra of the Buddha's

Radiance. When he emerged from this seemingly (but, as we shall see, not literally) spontaneous meditative visualization, he thought to himself that it must have had deep significance. He knew, for example, "from the formularies of other texts" 別本儀軌 that it is just such brilliant flames which were said to consume the lesser or evil realms of rebirth 有火曜光明滅 惡趣者即此義也 .[71] This seemed a pregnant fact to him, but he suggests that at first he did not know quite how to interpret it.

Having established the connection between the mantra and the samādhi by reporting their juxtaposition in a vision generated in meditation, Kōben proceeds to another question, this one of special historical interest. Noting that these "latter days" are not a time in which there are many persons inclined to practice meditation, and noting too that even those few who do practice seldom meet with success, he asks himself why one should even bother with the effort of practice. His reply--a forceful one--is that it is our responsibility to practice Buddhism assiduously, at least in appreciation of the rare privilege that is ours in having been reborn as humans and in thereby having had access to the Buddha's teachings. Moreover, he maintains that the Sāmadhi of the Buddha's Radiance is unfailing and, if practiced with abiding faith, is not difficult, not even for beginners. Here we see not only references to faith and to the possibility of efficacious practice, both reminiscent of Chinul, but also an adversion to one of the most ominous developments in the history of medieval Japanese Buddhism. We refer to the emergence of Pure Land Buddhism and to the corollary spread of belief in the arrival of mappō 末法 ,

i e., the inception of a spiritually degenerate age in which the old teachings and practices of Buddhism were widely thought to be beyond the capacity of most or all ordinary sentient beings. Kōben, well known to his contemporaries as a thoughtful but nonetheless trenchant critic of Hōnen (法然, 1133-1212), was an ardent defender of the so-called "old Buddhism."[72] The thrust of his arguments was not to deny the advent of mappō; rather it was to admit it, to deny that it deprived beings of all "self-power" (jiriki 自力), and to cite it as a reason for redoubling one's efforts at practice. To these he adds the further, though still quite traditional, argument that Buddhism is a generous tradition, abundant in "devices" (upāya, hōben 方便) precisely designed by compassionate teachers to facilitate practice, even in the most dire circumstances. Thus he emphasizes in the passage under discussion that the Samādhi of the Buddha's Radiance is especially suited to this desolate age just because it is easy to practice, provided only that practice be built upon a foundation of faith.

The next question in the text returns us to the topic of our primary concern, the influence of Li T'ung-hsüan. That question is, "From whom was this method (i.e., the Buddha Radiance Samādhi) received?" 從誰人相承得此法乎. To this reiteration of the concern with authenticity Kōben makes a reply that not only invokes the name of Li T'ung-hsüan but also echoes his spirit of self-reliance and his emphasis on practical experience. He says,

There are some who depend upon teachers (kalyāṇamitra), others who rely on volumes of scripture to ascertain that the doctrines they

have received truly derive from the patriarchs
of old. This humble monk, however, since
first he came of age, has had a deep love of
actual practice 然愚僧從盛年以來深好
實行. Thus have I shunned the vanities of
the world 更不事浮華, at times going into
the deep mountains, at other times repairing
to the ocean's shore. The pines and the
breezes have been my meditation cell; the
bright moon my hymnal lamp. Bathed in tears,
I have chanted alone, practiced alone. In
supplication to Manjuśrī I have begged for
wisdom and understanding, and in my yearning
for cultivation I have pledged myself to
Samantabhadra. Constantly mindful that this
latter age lacks true kalyānamitra, I have
relied upon the Buddhas and Bodhisattvas
mysteriously to extend their aid that the four
absorptions (dhyāna) would naturally arise,
even in these corrupt times bereft of a
teacher. I had met the dharma by virtue of
good deeds in prior lives. Now the Buddhas
have rained down their compassion and I have
abandoned the bogus dharma of fame and profit,
longing instead for the authentic path by
which to attain the true reality.

Thus did it come about that, in a spirit of
genuine humility, I was moved by the mystical
influence of the Bodhisattva Maitreya to
undertake this course of meditation. In the
summer of the third year of Jōkyū (1221), in
the sixth month, while meditating upon the
"Universal Eye" chapter of The Scripture of

<u>Perfect</u> <u>Enlightenment</u>,[73] my meditations bore auspicious fruit. My body suddenly became light and I rose into the sky, passing first beyond the realm of the Four Kings, then beyond the Trayatrimsa Heaven and the Heaven of Yama, arriving finally in the Tusita Heaven before the palace of Maitreya.[74] However, I did not immediately present myself to Maitreya, for I saw standing outside of the palace a Bodhisattva who resembled Samantabhadra. Suddenly he took a golden chalice the size of a ewer and proceeded to fill it with perfumed water. He then poured the scented water over me, bathing the whole of my body with it. With this the vision concluded.

Shortly thereafter, however, I had an auspicious dream in which there appeared before me, extending down from the sky, a bamboo scaffold. At its base was a length of rope. I grasped the rope and climbed. The scaffold had fifty-two tiers--a separate place, that is, for each of fifty-two Bodhisattvas.[75]

That same night I had another dream, one in which the Great Buddha of Tōdaiji seemed deformed, a distortion of the Buddha image. His figure was not made of bronze and gold; it was merely clay inside with an outer veneer of bronze. A repair that had been made on one side of the statue revealed clearly that it was not made of bronze. I was sick at heart to see this and desired to undertake the statue's recasting.[76]

Yet another dream befell me that night. In
this one, there appeared before me a set of
wood-blocks on which were inscribed one fascicle of the Maitreya Sūtra.[77] The blocks
were being used to print a copy of the scripture, and paper was still attached to them. I
peeled off three sheets of the printed text,
thinking that this might serve as my tutelary
scripture.

It was only shortly after these dreams had
occurred that I happened to come across a
newly imported copy of T'ung-hsüan's Exposition and in it found a passage describing the
Buddha Radiance Contemplation referred to
above. (This treatise had not been widely
available; the copy I chanced upon had just
been brought from Sung China.) When I saw
this passage, I was filled with a fervent
delight. I also read the appended biography
of the treatise's author[78] and conceived a
deep admiration for him. Thereafter, I
abandoned the meditation based on the Sūtra of
Perfect Enlightenment and took up this Samādhi
of the Buddha's Radiance.

Later in the course of that practice--on the
seventh day of the eighth month, during ves-
pers meditation--I had an experience in which
I could not be certain of whether or not I
still existed in body and mind. Then there
appeared in space the three Bodhisattvas,
Samantabhadra, Manjuśrī, and Avalokiteśvara.
Their hands held a long staff made of lapis

lazuli. With both of my hands I grasped one
end of this staff while the Bodhisattvas held
the other. They pulled me up and I clung to
the end of the staff until shortly we reached
the Tuṣita Heaven and I found myself standing
before Maitreya's palace. At that moment my
body seemed transfigured in clarity, my mind
transported in joy. There is nothing to which
I can compare that experience. Suddenly I saw
the lapis lazuli staff placed upon the jew-
elled ground. It was crested with gems and
from them gushed forth a precious water which
drenched the whole of my body. Just then my
face was transformed as though into a bright
mirror. Gradually my whole body underwent the
same transformation and little by little was
suffused with liquid crystal and grew to the
size of a great mansion. It was as though my
mind was enabled by meditation to create these
wonders by the sheer power of thought. At
that moment I heard a voice from the sky
intone, "All the Buddhas have entered you and
you have attained purity." My body then
resumed its normal shape and I found myself
beneath a seven-jewelled necklace which hung
from space. Then the transport ended.

The passages summarized and freely translated
immediately above comprise just slightly less than the
first two pages of the four page Mysterious Transmission. The remainder, however, is very much like what
we have already seen; it too consists of descriptions
of various of Kōben's meditative visions, in nearly
all of which the Samādhi of the Buddha's Radiance

figures prominently. Kōben also wrote other texts on the theme of this samādhi--the one already mentioned to which the Mysterious Transmission was originally appended, a manual-like text (Kegon ichijō jisshin ichū kaikaku shinkyō butsu-butsudō bukkō-kan hōmon, 華嚴一乘十信位中開廓心境佛佛道佛光觀法門) which gives detailed instructions on how the samādhi is actually to be performed,[79] and a fourth text (Kegon shuzen kanshō nyū-gedatsu mongi, 華嚴修禪觀照入解脫門義) which is perhaps the most systematic treatment of the topic.[80] All of these works deserve, and will surely reward, extensive study, but even our brief glimpse of but one of them-- the Mysterious Transmission--should suffice for the modest purpose of indicating the powerful impact that Li T'ung-hsüan's works had on this medieval Japanese monk.

What we have in Kōben, then, is still another "rebirth" of Li's thought. To be sure, this incarnation is startlingly different from its predecessors, including Chinul. In thirteenth century Japan the Elder Li's vision was refracted in the lense of an unusual visionary's rich interior experience, and was made both to consort with the powerful and vivid symbolism of Mikkyō and to speak to the urgent controversies of a religious revolution. But even so certain continuities do reemerge. Like Chinul, Kōben was familiar with "orthodox" Hua-yen, i.e., with the works of Chih-yen, Fa-tsang, Ch'eng-kuan, etc. After all, though ordained in the Shingon tradition, he spent years of study at Tōdaiji and thus might also be placed in the lineage of Kegon. However, Kōben too found scholasticism finally unrewarding. Thus he was drawn by his own Mikkyō heritage, but even more by his

strong personal penchant for experience rather than
doctrine, to seek what was for him a more authentic
Buddhism. Again, Li's works, found rather than
sought, spoke to that need in ways other Hua-yen texts
had not, and again the idiom in which they spoke was
the idiom of practice and experiential confirmation.
Whereas for Chinul the mode of practice was the aus-
terity of Zen and its sustenance Li's exaltation of
faith to the status of quotidian enlightenment itself,
for Kōben practice was the luxuriance of Mikkyō and it
was nourished by the rich imagery that abounded in
Li's exegesis and that so well suited the Mikkyō
monk's taste for symbolism of the "three mysteries" 三
密 of "body, speech, and mind."

The explicit Tantric notion of employing in
meditation the resident energies of body and speech,
along with those of the mind, is, of course, not to be
found in traditional Hua-yen--no more than Chinul's
Zen instruments of "silence, the staff, and the shout"
are to be found there. Certainly neither is to be
found in the writings of such as Chih-yen or Fa-tsang,
and they are absent even from the less conventional
works of Li T'ung-hsüan. Nevertheless, the freer
structure of Li's texts, their more colloquial dic-
tion, and the fact that they are more faithful to the
literary texture and imagery of the Avataṁsaksūtra
than to the conceptual architecture of systematic Hua-
yen thought, all combined to render those texts more
serviceable to Kōben than other Hua-yen texts had
been, and to lend them better to his search for
"canons" that resonated to both the plangency of his
rich inner life and the chromatics of his esoteric
tradition. Whereas the more typical expressions of
classical Hua-yen seem often to have "weighed upon"

later generations, i.e., to have threatened to impose their own strict constructions on the minds of later readers and to have been rejected therefore, Li's writings seem rather to have been susceptible to a great variety of personal interpretation. I think we may see, repeated in all of this, a pattern that was actually instrumental in the birth of classical Hua-yen itself. When Hua-yen arose in late sixth and seventh century China it was but one of several new forms of Buddhism that were based on primary scriptures (sūtra), rather than on the systematic "treatises" (śāstra) or renowned Indian thinkers that had underlain earlier lineages of Chinese Buddhism. Thus, the early Hua-yen patriarchs were not as beholden to Nāgārjuna, Asaṅga, Vasubandhu, and Haribhadra as the thinkers of the San-lun 三論 , She-lun 攝論 , Ti-lun 地論 , and Ch'eng-shih 成實 traditions had been. This, in turn, had allowed those founders of Hua-yen the freedom they needed to create a form of Buddhism more suitable to specifically Chinese religious requirements and more appropriate to the historical particularities of their time and place. This was possible because the Avataṁsakasūtra, like most scriptures, being of looser and less methodical construction, was much more susceptible to novel interpretation or creative hermeneutics than were the treatises of any Indian thinker. Sūtras, after all, were meant to appeal as much to the imagination and the emotions of devotees as to the intellects of dialecticians; their mode of expression is usually more that of dialogue, poetry, inspiration, or ecstatic vision than that of tightly reasoned argument. They are therefore more fertile ground for innovation than were the meticulously plotted but

perhaps overcultivated fields of the śāstra literature. To the irresistable dialectic force of the
writings of a Nāgārjuna, for example, a reader can do
nothing but submit, his submission being either substantive (i.e., yielding agreement) or formal (i.e.,
leading to further argument in Nāgārjuna's own terms).
By contrast, in reading a typical Mahāyāna scripture--
i.e., in contemplating visions of buddhas and bodhisattvas arrayed in scenes of mythopoeic splendor, in
savoring the wonders they perform, or in following the
subtleties of symbol and metaphor they display--one
may more easily indulge his own doctrinal creativity.
More importantly still, one may proceed more directly
to the paramount task of transforming scriptural text
into practical salvific experience. Something very
much like this is what happened in late sixth and
early seventh century China, and it produced not only
the then novel and liberating insights of Hua-yen but
also such other Chinese innovations in Buddhism as
Ch'an, T'ien-t'ai, and Pure Land. But of course
history did not stop at mid-T'ang, nor did Buddhism
halt at the borders of China. Over subsequent centuries the religious needs of the Chinese themselves
continued to change, and Korean and Japanese Buddhists
of later eras found that they too had their own
peculiar requirements.

What all of this suggests, I believe, is that
the early Hua-yen patriarchs like Chih-yen and Fa-
tsang appeared to later East Asian Buddhists like
Chinul and Kōben rather as Nāgārjuna, Vasubandhu, et
al. appeared to Chih-yen and Fa-tsang. They were
seen, that is to say, as masters worthy of respect and
study, but also as figures somewhat remote from the
urgencies of one's own practical religious life, and

their remoteness was largely a function of the impregnable systematicity of their thought, of their emphasis on a coherence and comprehensiveness of doctrine that was seen to belie or undercut doctrine's practical and experiential purpose. To be sure, there is some oversimplification in putting the matter this way. Chinul, for example, may also have had substantive disagreements with standard Hua-yen doctrine (e.g., with what appeared to him to be its exaggerated concern with the phenomenal world over and against the mind), and these may have been as important to him as his equally evident distaste for the "style" of scholastic Hua-yen discourse. Kōben's preference for Li T'ung-hsüan, on the other hand, seems not to have implied such a substantive rejection of any Hua-yen principles. Nevertheless, I think the point still stands as valid. Thus do we find Kōben speaking as much for Chinul as for himself when he posits the following contrast between Li T'ung-hsüan and the "official patriarchate" of Hua-yen:

Question: Even with a single lineage 一宗 it is not the case that all the masters are univocal in their theoretical explanations of doctrine 諸師解釋非一 . This is especially true of Hsiang-hsiang (香象 , i.e., Fa-tsang), Ch'ing-liang (清凉 , i.e. Ch'eng-kuan) and other such masters, all of whom have constructed out of this <u>Avataṁsakasūtra</u> a plethora of utterly beautiful and quite superb theoretical explantions 造數多解釋極美 盡善 . So how does it happen that now it is only in T'ung-hsüan's exigesis that we find

established this diagram (explaining the
Buddha Radiance Sam<u>ā</u>dhi)?[81]

Answer: The theoretical explanations of those
masters were more than adequate for the purpose of setting forth doctrinal principles 開
演義理諸師解釋良為可足, but the
great teacher T'ung-hsüan, seeing the welter
of exegesis (of the S<u>ū</u>tra), sighed and said,
"It is indeed a pity. One could work away at
these texts, without respite, until one were
old and gray, but it is still the practice of
contemplation (i.e., rather than study) which
discloses the true essentials. If one could
perfect the practice of sam<u>ā</u>dhi, then one
could choose just one of those theoretical
explanations on which to rely and could depend
on only a single teacher for support of one's
views, rather than produce a complex of interpretations so as to protect one's elementary
learning. Moreover, this would show care in
the joint practice of both concentration (定,
i.e., meditation proper) and dispersion (散,
i.e., differentiated worldly activities). Why
then labor to produce textual proofs one after
the other?" He expresses himself further on
this matter elsewhere, as in the following
heartfelt verse:

> Now have I met the heritage of the
>   dharma;
> It is as though I stand in the very
>   presence of the Bhagavat,
> Even though I was born well after his
>   decease.

> Having gained access to the Buddha's
> knowledge and vision,
> I revere the place where the Wheel of
> the Law was turned
> And shed passionate tears of longing.
> With simple explanation of the profound
> and subtle truth,
> Suddenly do I enter the gate of libera-
> tion.[82]

A careful student of the standard Hua-yen corpus may well wish to argue that the celebration of Li T'ung-hsüan which we see in the works of Chinul, Kōben, and others implies a misinterpretation of that corpus, that beneath the scholastic usages of Chih-yen, Fa-tsang, etc., are to be found messages of strong practical import. One may suspect, in other words, that too much attention was given to their form and not enough to their content. Perhaps. Nonetheless, such is not the view of many important figures who emerged later within the East Asian Buddhist traditions themselves, and some of them--like the two we have considered--are of such a stature as to prevent our ignoring them. The import of a passage like that quoted just above is that the practicality of a doctrinal tradition is measured as much by its hermeneutics as by its messages. This is part of what a study of the heritage of Li T'ung-hsüan can tell us about the "practical dimensions" of Hua-yen. It can do so by reminding us that the very conception of the practical dimension draws us away from consideration only of the "meaning" of doctrine towards a consideration primarily of its use. In short, we have found in even this preliminary and partial sketch of the subject that Li T'ung-hsüan's Hua-yen was held to be more _useful_ because it was seen as more accessible. Its reference to "faith" more often than to such obscure notions as "the mutual penetration of phenomena and principle" or "the ten arcane principles of dependent origination"--the pride of place it assigns to vivid imagery and pregnant symbolism over sophisticated, learned, and precisely formulated doctrine-- these may not actually have endowed Hua-yen with its measure of practical and experiential relevance, but they can, I think, be said to have preserved those aspects of the tradition and to have allowed them to be retrieved by practitioners of later generations and different religious customs. They can also be said, therefore, to have allowed the expansion of our understanding of the Hua-yen tradition beyond the limits of the conventional definitions that have been given of it. This is a task, I trust, which continuing study of Li T'ung-hsüan and his influence will advance still further.

APPENDIX

A Translation of the Earliest Surviving
Hagiography of Li T'ung-hsüan

[The following is a translation, with some (but by no
means exhaustive) annotation, of The Record of the
Life of the Elder Li,[1] a work which serves as the
fountainhead of the whole Li T'ung-hsüan hagiographical tradition.   The exact date of its composition is
not   known, but   internal evidence   suggests   the late
eighth-early ninth century, i.e., within about   a hundred years of Li's death.   Its author, Ma Chih 馬支 ,
is known to history only in this capacity; it seems he
is mentioned in no other source.   Apart from a very
brief preface   to Li's Chüeh-i lun, dated August 4,
770,[2] this work   seems   to be our earliest   account of
the legend of Li T'ung-hsüan.]

A RECORD OF THE LIFE OF THE ELDER LI,
AUTHOR OF THE EXPOSITION OF THE NEWLY TRANSLATED
MAHĀVAIPULYA - BUDDHA - AVATAṀSAKA - SŪTRA

The personal   name of the Elder Li   was T'ung-
hsüan.   No one has determined precisely where he
hailed from, and   those who have enquired at   all into
his origins say only that he was a man of the province
of Ts'ang 滄 .[3]

It was in the twenty-seventh year of   the K'ai-
yüan 開元 era--on the fifteenth day of the third
month[4]--that he came, laden with books, to the village

of Ta-hsien 大賢 in the district of T'ung-ying 同穎 , some forty li west of the seat of Yü County 盂縣 in T'ai-yüan.[5] Therein resided a certain Kao Shan-nu 高山奴 , a man known to hold the virtuous in high regard, to admire scholars, and to be unflagging in his hospitality towards both. The Elder Li went directly to Shan-nu's gate and the latter, divining Li's god-like demeanor and recognizing him as a person of extraordinary spiritual capacity, accordingly welcomed him with deep humility and invited him to "take refuge" in his retreat. Thenceforth, the Elder Li hid himself in his hermit's cell, taking as his daily food only ten dates and a single cypress-leaf cake the size of a spoon,[5] thereby to avoid all contact with those of the outside world. Without any respite, he spent all of his time engrossed in writing. In this way did he pass three years.

One day he took his leave of Shan-nu and moved five or six li further south, to an old Buddha-hall of the Ma family.[6] Next to this he built himself an earthen hut and there he dwelt in contemplation for another ten years.

At the end of that period, he once more gathered together his scriptures and writings and took to the road. He had proceeded some twenty li or more on his journey, coming to the country residence of the Han family, which is today the village of Kuan-kai 冠蓋 ,[7] when he suddenly encountered a tiger. Just there, in the middle of the road, the tiger prostrated itself docilely as though awaiting a command. The Elder spoke to it, saying, "I am about to compose a discourse explaining the Flower Garland Scripture.

You may accompany me to choose a place where I may settle down to the task." When he had finished speaking, the tiger arose and the Elder calmly petted it. He then took up his satchel of books, hung it on the tiger's back, and entrusted to the beast the task of finding the place where they should stop. At that, the tiger turned toward the Shen-fu 神福 plateau.[8] They proceeded straight in that direction for more than thirty li until they came before a grotto, whereupon the tiger sat itself down. The Elder took his satchel from the tiger's back and placed it inside the grotto. The tiger then looked about repeatedly, tucked its tail between its legs, and left.

The grotto was bright and clean throughout, and spacious. It had been naturally formed, not made by human effort. In its vicinity there had never before been any spring or stream. Yet, on the night of the Elder's arrival, there arose violent winds and lightening. They uprooted an old pine which was over three hundred ch'ih 尺 tall. The next day, where the pine's roots had been, there had magically appeared a pool many fathoms deep and over fifty paces in circumference. Its waters were as sweet as auspicious dew[9] and its hue brighter and clearer than crystal. In time, men came to call it "the Elder's Spring." Even today its waters are pure and sparkling, and have neither increased nor diminished. In years of drought it invariably responds to the prayers of the people.

On nights when the Elder was composing his Exposition, as his mind plumbed the profound principles, there would issue from his mouth a radiance

which served in place of candles or torches to illuminate the grotto.

After he had settled in these mountains, there
appeared out of nowhere two maidens of unearthly
beauty, both in the full bloom of their youth. They
were dressed in homespun clothing and wore mantles of
plain hemp to cover their heads. Nothing is said of
their names, families, or places of residence. They
regularly drew water and burnt incense for the Elder,
and they kept him supplied with paper and brushes. At
the crack of dawn they would prepare an assortment of
delicacies and place them before the Elder. After the
meals they would collect the utensils and disappear,
no one knows to where. For a period of five years
they never missed a single day. Then, when the Elder
was about to conclude his Exposition, they left
without a trace.

A careful examination of the "Old Records" of
the Avataṁsaka reveals that when Tripiṭaka Master
Buddhabhadra of the Eastern Chin was translating the
Sūtra at the Hsieh-ssu-k'ung Monastery 謝司空寺 in
Chiang-tu 江都 ,[10] there had [also] appeared two
maidens who emerged suddenly from the garden pool to
wait upon the Indian monk. Burning incense for him
and filling altar chalices with water, they were in
constant attendance upon him. With the coming of each
evening they would return to the pool. This went on
day after day, eventually becoming a regular routine.
But when the copying of the translation was completed,
these two maidens [also] vanished without a trace.
[Thus we see that] the Elder's miracle tallied with
one of old.

The Elder stood seven feet, two inches tall.
He had thick eyebrows, bright eyes, deep red lips, a
lustrous complexion, a long a full beard, and long and
well formed arms. The hair of his head was of a dark
purple color, and his body hair curled to the right.
Uncommonly handsome and truly remarkable in bearing,
he was lacking in none of the auspicious marks [of a
superior person.] He wore a birch-bark cap and clothing of coarse hemp with wide sleeves and long trou-
sers, moving about without a sash at his waist. He
was always barefoot, and did not stand on ceremony
when receiving guests.

One day, without warning, he left the mountains
to visit his old village. He arrived there just at
the time the local people were gathering for a festi-
val. Addressing them all he said, "May all of you
remain here in peace; I am about to return." They all
ceased their festivities and looked at each other in
dismay, sorry to think that the elder was to return to
Tsang Province. Wiping away their tears, they
entreated him to stay, but the Elder said, "Though we
may abide here for as many as a hundred years, there
comes a time when one must return." Thereupon, the
crowd rose up in a group to see the Elder back to his
mountain. When he reached his grotto he said again,
"Departing and abiding were ever thus; you may all
return now to your homes." Just as they turned to go
back, mountain mists arose on all sides and the sur-
roundings were indiscernible. The people walking
along the road all thought it very strange. The next
day, the senior men of the group gathered their followers together and went to the mountain to bid him
their formal farewell, but all they found was that the

Elder had already passed away while sitting   erect [in the posture of meditation].   It was the twenty-eighth day of the third month.   He had   lived to be ninety-six.   [At that time] there was a large serpent coiled up outside the grotto.   Its eyes were opened wide and its mouth gaped.   Unable, therefore, to approach, the people drew back and intoned in supplication, "We wish to collect the   earthly remains of the Elder   in order to install it in a coffin.   Would that   you, awesome spirit, would help us to accomplish that task." Thereupon the serpent withdrew into itself and disappeared.   The elders of the group shed tears as they shouldered the bier.   They chose [for the burial site] a place on the north slope of the great mountain and piled stones for a tomb, covering him to protect him from decay.   This was to become the Shih-tuo hermitage 逝多蘭若 11 of Shen-fu mountain, now known as Mount Fang 方 .

On the day the Elder passed away, and when the tomb was being constructed, clouds of smoke congealed and spread through the hills and the valleys, which quaked in response.   Two white cranes cried sorrowfully in the sky, two deer wailed to each other night after night, and the laments of the other animals filled the mountains.

The people of the village followed each other in changing to mourning clothes and supported each other in a grief as deep as if they had been bereft of Heaven itself.   Whenever they made offerings clouds gathered above the grave and this happened at every seventh day offering throughout the forty-nine days of mourning.   This was passing strange!

While he lived the Elder had made it a practice
every year toward the end of the third month to gather
together the worthy and the pious from all directions
for a maigre feast. Women were not employed in preparing the food, so highly did he value refined
sincerity in the performance of the service. Not even
the seeds of the dates or the water used in rinsing
the rice were wasted; they were to be used after the
feast so that even the dogs and the swine would be
blessed with donations. This sort of feast has been
maintained ever since, without interruption.

On the sixth day of the second month, in the
ninth year of Ta-li 大曆 (774),[12] a monk named Kuang-
ch'ao 廣超 discovered at the Shih-tuo hermitage two
treatises that had been written by the Elder. One was
the forty fascicle Exposition of the Newly Translated
Mahā-vaipulya Buddha-avataṁsaka-sūtra.[13] The other
was the single fascicle Discourse on the Ten Illumina-
tions by which Ignorance Regarding the Twelve-fold
Dependent Origination is Dispelled, Wisdom Made Manifest, and Compassion Achieved.[14] Kuang-ch'ao then
copied these and disseminated them throughout Ping-fen
拼分 .[15] Kuang-ch'ao's disciple, Tao-kuang 道光 ,
continued in his master's purpose by distributing them
throughout Yen 燕 and Ch'ao 趙 and making them known in
Huai 淮 and Ssu 泗 [16] so that later scholars in both
the North and the South would have access to them.
The establishment of the Elder's lineage was the
result of Ch'ao and Kuang's success in their task of
transmission.

The treatises of the Elder capture the whole
meaning of the Sūtra. They manifest the dharmakāya,

extend the sea of Buddha nature unto infinity, and
pervade each speck of dust in all the worlds without
ever moving. Classifying the various teachings and
tracing them all to their sources, they meld those
teachings into the Higher Vehicle. Implicit in the
Flower Store World 華藏 ,[17] they guide those who are
lost to find the Tao and those who are mired in doctrine 滯教 [18] to free themselves of their limitations. They are the very recourse to Vairocana, and
the sun and moon of Hua-yen. Had the sage not
harbored compassion for the world and had he not con-
descended to instruct the ignorant, who else would
have so methodically explained the Great Scripture and
transmitted the Great Mind? Mysterious indeed were
the actions of the Elder, and hard is it to fathom
them. Even space itself cannot match their vastness.
How vain then are our efforts to find their limits.

Recently, a monk named Yüan-chan 元覘 [19] made a
pilgrimate to Mount Fang, seeking traces of the Elder.
First he paid homage at the grave, then he visited the
grotto. In front of the grotto were three pine trees,
one of them already withered. They had all been
planted by the Elder himself. The dead one had
withered during the month just before the Elder's
passing. Even now auspicious cranes nest in the two
that remain alive.

Yüan-chan also met--in the hamlet of Chieh-
ch'ou 解愁. south of Shou-yang 壽陽 --a certain Li
Shih-yüan 李士源 , nephew of the monk Kuang-ch'ao who
had handed down the Elder's writings. Li showed Yüan-
chan a portrait of the Elder. He paid homage to it
and returned, his vow fulfilled.

There are many stories of this kind. I have chosen only the "fruits." With the "leaves and branches" I have not bothered.

Collected and Compiled by
the Cloud Dwelling
Wanderer, Ma-chih.

NOTES

1. In the early decades of the century, Japanese scholars, following an old and largely sectarian tradition, were wont to take a "patriarchal succession" approach to the history of Buddhist traditions. A classic example of this sort of treatment of Hua-yen is Yusuki Ryōei's Kegon taikei, originally published in 1915 and reprinted many times since. More familiar to western readers, as an example of this approach taken to the general history of East Asian Buddhism, is Takakusu Junjirō's Essentials of Buddhist Philosophy, first published in 1947.

2. The earliest known use of this term seems to have been Ch'eng-kuan's, in his Hua-yen-ching-shu (T1735:35.529b6).

3. There is available on these four monks a considerable amount of primary and secondary information. For a convenient summary of it, see Takamine Ryōshū, Kegon shisōshi (Kyoto: Hyakkaen, 1963), pp. 331-42.

4. This contemporary of Lin-chi (d. 867) was a third generation descendant of Ch'ing-yüan Hsing-ssu (d. 740). The standard account of his life is to be found in the Sung Kao-seng chuan, 22.

5. Pen-chi was Liang-chieh's disciple and heir. A standard biography of him may be found in the Ching-te ch'uan-teng lu, 17.

6. A detailed but highly idiosyncratic discussion of "five rank" theory is to be found in Alfonso Verdu, Dialectical Aspects in Buddhist Thought (Univ. of Kansas: Center for East Asian Studies, 1974). The Japanese literature on the subject is too vast to inventory, but a good introduction to it may be found in the Tōzan-roku vol. (#12) of the Zen no goroku series.

7. Li is mentioned only briefly in most of the standard surveys of Hua-yen. One of the most extensive treatments of his thought is probably that of

Araki Kengo, in his Bukkyō to Jukyō (Kyoto: Heirakuji, 1963), pp. 170-93. Another important work is Takamine Ryōshū's study of Li's relationship to Zen. This appeared originally in his Kegon to Zen to no tsuro (Nara: Nanto Bukkyō, 1956), pp. 98-142. More recently, Kimura Kiyotaka has published several fine articles on various aspects of Li's thought. Of these, the most pertinent to the issues covered in this essay (and one to which I am much indebted) is "Ritsugen no zentei-ron," in Sekiguchi Shindai, Bukkyō jissen-shudō no genri (Tokyo: Sankibō, 1977), pp. 253-68. Li is also attracting attention currently among some young Japanese scholars, one of whom--Inaoka Chiken--deserves special notice. His study of Li's biography--"Ritsugen no denki ni tsuite," Bukkyō-gaku seminā, 34 (Oct., 1981): 24-39--is the most thorough treatment of the topic to date.

8. This seems the most reliable date--whatever reliability may mean in the case of so legendary a figure--but other sources give as variant dates 661-757, 654-750, 652-747, and 646-740. For the details of these variations, see the Inaoka article mentioned in note #7.

9. See, for example, fascicle 11 of the Exposition in which Li employs the I-ching in order to explain an aspect of the Sūtra's pantheon and cosmology (T1739:36.789b). Towards the very end of the Exposition he actually argues for a connection between Confucius and one of the kalyānamitra of Sudhana! (See T1739:35.1002c.) These are only two of many instances of Li's referring to the Confucian canon in his Buddhist writings.

10. This Khotanese monk, who had been invited to China by Empress Wu in 695 specifically for the purpose of translating the Avataṃsaka, completed his task late in the year 699. A concise statement of the differences between his 80 fascicle version and Buddhabhadra's earlier 60 fascicle translation can be found in Kametani Seika, Kegon seiten kenkyū (Tokyo: Hobunkan, 1926), pp. 18-25 & 48-9. It follows from these dates that Li T'ung-hsüan's Exposition, having been completed before 730, was the earliest commentary on the new translation of the Sūtra.

11. The commentary that he was apparently most familiar with was Fa-tsang's Shen-hsüan chi (T1733: 35). However, since Li seems to have been purpose-fully intent on not writing a "scholars' commentary,"

we ought not to be surprised by the relative paucity of his explicit references to earlier exigesis.

12. Among the major issues on which Li disagreed with Fa-tsang, perhaps the most famous is the question of which part of the Hua-yen scripture was its essential part. Fa-tsang had held that that honor belonged to the "Chapter on the Arising of the Tathāgata," a choice that reflected his commitment to Tathāgata-garbha thought. Li, in contrast, assigned that chapter to the category reserved for those which served only the purpose of self-propagation. For Li, the pith of the Sūtra was its final chapter, "On Entering the Dharmadhātu," otherwise known as the Gandavyūha. Like much else that Li had to say about the Hua-yen Scripture, this choice seems to reflect his greater sensitivity to the text itself as opposed to schemes of doctrine that can be applied to the text. Another famous issue of dispute was the question of how many "assemblies" comprised the Sūtra. Fa-tsang maintained there were eight or nine (depending upon which translation was in question). Li argued that there were ten. In this case, however, it is Li's argument that has less foundation in the text; it was motivated more by his fascination with the symbolic potential of the number "10," the Hua-yen code for infinity. See T1739:35.744b & 770c-71b.

13. A variety of later catalogues, e.g., Uichon's Sinp'yon chejong kyōjang ch'ongnok, and several still later Japanese compilations based thereon, attribute a number of other works to Li, but none of those works survive and the attributions are questionable to say the least. See, for example, T2184:55.1167a.

14. T1739:35.721a-1008b.

15. T1740:36.1008c-1011b.

16. T1741:36.1011c-1049c. This text, more popularly known as simply the Hua-yen-ching chüeh-i lun, is a sort of summary of the Exposition. In fact, several of the later figures who claim to have been influenced by the Exposition actually cite this work more frequently than that much longer work.

17. T1888:45.767c-773c. This brief text is the only of Li's works for which something like commentary or traditional annotation exists. I refer to a manuscript of notes on the Shih-ming lun entitled Kegon jūmyō ron kutetsu, compiled in 1760 by the 20 year old

student monk Shinshō.   It is   kept in   the Library of
Ryūkoku University in   Kyoto, where   I   was fortunate
enough to secure a copy.

18.   The traditional view of Hua-yen as   an exclusively cerebral and theoretical form of   Buddhism has
led   scholars   until   very recently   to   overlook   the
interesting fact that throughout its history   it has
had very strong associations with magic   and miracle-
working.   The purported founder of the tradition, Tu-
shun, was best known to his contemporaries as   a thau-
maturge; the scripture on which it is based abounds in
imagery of   magic and of the bodhisattva   as magician;
some of   its most   popular literature (e.g.,   the Hua-
yen-ching kan-ying chuan, T2074:51) is   miracle literature; and   its holy   places (e.g., Wu-t'ai   shan) are
regions of some of China's most venerable miracle-tale
traditions.   Li T'ung-hsüan, for all of the profundity
of his thought, fits well into this picture.

19.   I cannot at this stage of my researches document my   suspicion, but I will broach   it nonetheless:
The   teacher-disciple   relationship   in   East Asian
Buddhism--particularly   as   cultivated   within   the
saṅgha--seems often to have functioned as   an institutional   restraint upon   doctrinal and   other   kinds of
religious creativity.   If this be true, then there is
further particular reason to give special attention to
the thought   of laymen   in the traditions   of Chinese,
Japanese,   and   Korean Buddhism.   However closely
related they may   have been to the clergy,   the social
contexts   of their   thought and   practice   were   quite
different   and often   freer.   It   is   no accident,   I
think, that laymen of the later   tradition--like Chang
Shang-ying and   Li Chih--were   to have so   important a
role in   fostering the study of their   predecessor, Li
T'ung-hsüan.   Morever, it may well be that East Asian
Buddhism presents many more examples of   the influence
of laymen upon the direction of Buddhist   history than
do the   Buddhisms of, say,   India, Srī Lanka, Southeast
Asia, or Tibet.

20.   See, for example, T1739:759a, where Li refers
to   Fa-tsang, somewhat formally, as "Dharma   Master Fa
of the T'ang Dynasty."

21.   The hagiography of Li   translated   in   the
appendix to this   article (q.v.) tells us that   in the
year 774 a monk named Kuang-ch'ao discovered   the Hua-
yen-ching lun and the Shih-ming lun in   the monastery
that had been   built on   the site   of   Li's hermitage,

i.e., in the mountain suburbs of T'ai-yüan in central Shansi. He then undertook to circulate them, we are further told, throughout the region of "Ping-fen" (around modern Fen-yang, still in Shansi). His disciple, Tao-k'uang, took them still further afield--into "Yen and Chao" (i.e., Eastern Shansi and Hopei) and "Huai and Ssu" (i.e., Anhui and Northern Kiangsu). That same work also notes that Shou-yang, another region of Shansi not far from T'ai-yüan, had by around 800 become a kind of center of the "cult" of Li T'ung-hsüan. The entry on Li in the Sung kao-seng chuan indicates that sometime before 988 (the year when Tsan-ning completed that collection) Li's corpus was known in the Liao-ning region of Hopei, for it recounts the unsuccessful attempt by a monk of that region to burn Li's Exposition along with a number of other texts believed to be spurious. Chih-ning, the monk who sometime between 847 and 860 collated Li's Exposition with the Hua-yen Sūtra itself, was a resident of Fukien. That he had access to Li's work indicates its transmission still further south by that time, and this is information corroborated by the account already noted of the incorporation of Li's works into the canon in 938, during the Southern T'ang. Thus it would seem that during the two centuries following Li's death his works were still somewhat less than widely known. They were preserved in his own region of Shansi and were gradually transmitted from there to as far south as the general region of Fukien. Only one piece of evidence suggests a broader distribution. That is a brief mention of Li's approach to the Hua-yen Sūtra found in a ninth century Japanese work--the Kegon-shu ichijō kaishin ron by one Fujaku who died in 851 (see T2326:72.1a-14c). Nevertheless, it seems that this early Japanese acquaintance with Li's works was short-lived, because they had to be rediscovered by Kōben nearly four hundred years later. Likewise, in China, despite the modest dissemination sketched above, it was not until the early Sung and the sponsorship of people like Chang Shang-ying, Te-hung, and Ta-hui that Li's corpus became truly famous and influential. It was at this time, one should also mention, that Ŭichon (1059-1101) brought that corpus to Korea for the first time, thereby making it available less than a hundred years later to Chinul.

22. I have come across no references to Li on the part of Tsung-mi, and only one on Ch'eng-kuan's part. The latter is to be found in the Hua-yen-ching shu yen-i (T1736:36.367c). This, together with certain

perceived similarities between the thought of the two men, has led some to suggest that Li's thought had an important influence upon Ch'eng-kuan's. The evidence for this, however, is rather slim.

23. See T2158:55.1048a-b, 1049b.

24. See Ts'ai Yun-chen, ed. Shih-san-i-chung tsang-ching-mu-lu tui-chao pian-chieh ch'u-kao (Taipei: Hsiu-ting Chung-hua Ta-tsang-ching hui, 1960), p. 64.

25. Ta-hui's familiarity with Li's works, which he seems to have owed to Chang Shang-ying, is briefly discussed by Miriam Levering in her 1978 Harvard dissertation, Ch'an Enlightenment for Laymen: Ta-hui and the New Religious Culture of the Sung.

26. This monk, an important figure in the history of both Sung Ch'an and Sung literary theory, has been very little studied. His full name was Chüeh-fan Hui-hung and his sobriquet Shih-men. He was the heir of Pao-feng K'o-wen, in the Huang-lung branch of the Lin-chi lineage. He was also a major influence upon Chang Shang-ying and is best known in Ch'an history as the advocate of "lettered Ch'an" (wen-tzu Ch'an), an amalgam of Ch'an practice with scriptural study. His place in the history of Chinese literary criticism is secured by his authorship of two works in that vein--the Leng-chai yeh-hua and the T'ien-ch'u chin-luan. His most famous collection of Ch'an writings is the Shih-men wen-tzu-ch'an, a work not found in any of the standard Tripitaka collections but included in the Ssu-pu Ts'ung-k'an. The Taishō edition of Li's Shih-ming lun includes a preface by Te-hung.

27. Chang, whose cognomen was T'ien-chüeh and whose sobriquet was Wu-chin chü-shih (Elder of the Infinite), was a many faceted figure. A protegé of Wang An-shih who was later to serve as Grand Councilor of the Sung (6.1110-9.1111), he was a prolific author of secular, Taoist, and Buddhist texts, the most famous of the latter being surely his Hu-fa-lun (Essay in Defense of the Dharma), in which he defended Buddhism from the criticisms then being levelled against it by the most famous representatives of the nascent Neo-Confucian tradition. He was also a disciple-associate of several important Ch'an figures of his day, including both Te-hung and Yüan-wu Fo-kuo (1070-1135), and appears as an interlocutor in the recorded sayings of both. Later he would be patron to

Ta-hui. His connection with the Li T'ung-hsüan corpus seems to date from the mid-1080's when he was posted as a minister to the Shansi region. In 1088, when returning from a pilgrimage to Wu-t'ai shan (on the basis of which he would write his Hsu Ch'ing-liang chuan or Continued Record of Wu-t'ai, T2100:51.1127a-1135a), he stopped in the area of T'ai-yüan, visited Shen-fu shan, and came upon Li's writings. He proceeded thereafter to sponsor the circulation of those works and seems to have been especially responsible for their growing popularity in Ch'an circles. Most standard editions of Li's Chüeh-i lun include Chang's postface to the work, and he is the author of a 1088 stele inscription commemorating Li which is preserved in the Shan-yu shih-k'o ts'ung-pien, ch. 17. I am now working on a monograph about Chang Shang-ying which I hope will appear before long.

28.   See Robert E. Buswell's forthcoming The Korean Approach to Zen: The Collected Works of Chinul (Honolulu: Univ. Press of Hawaii, 1983), which will be the first study of Chinul, and the first translation of his major writings, to be published in a western language. The Hwaŏmnon chŏryo itself was long unknown to scholars, but an early block-print of it was preserved in the Kanazawa Bunko and has recently attracted scholarly attention. In 1972 Dr. Kim Ji-kyon published a photographic reprint of it, with his own introduction, in Seoul. In 1975 the staff of the Kanazawa Bunko published a critical edition in their Kanazawa Bunko shiryo zenshū: Butten, Volume II, Kegon-hen, a work which seems, unfortunately, not to be widely available.

30.   The literature about Kōben is far too extensive to list in its entirety, but a good general introduction to the life and thought of Kōben is to be found in Okuda Isao, Myōe: henreki to yume (Tokyo: Tokyo Univ. Press, 1978). Special note should be taken, however, of an article by Kamata Shigeo which deals specifically with Koben's use of Li's writings, i.e., "Bukkō-zammai-kan no jissen hōhō," in Sekiguchi Shindai, ed., Bukkyō jissen shudō no genri (Tokyo: Sankibo, 1977), pp. 239-52. Kōben studies are particularly rich and well-developed in part because so much of Kōben's own corpus, and so many early materials about him, have survived in the care of the library at Kōzanji. The Kōzanji collection is currently being catalogued with consummate skill by a team of Japanese experts, the results of whose works comprise the Kōzan-ji shiryō sōshū, a collection in

more than ten volumes now being published by Tokyo Univ. Press.

31. Copies of Sung printed editions of Li's writings (including, no doubt, some of the very ones Myōe himself read) survive today in the Kōzanji collection. For a complete list of them, consult the series mentioned in note 30.

32. This is not surprising when one considers that in the 12th cent. Tōdaiji, where Kōben studied his Kegon, was also a center of Mikkyō practice. For a useful overview of that monastery's history in this period, see Hiraoka Jōkai, Tōdaiji (Tokyo: Kyoiku kai, 1977), pp. 121-49.

33. It is this hybrid practice that scholars usually have most in mind when they speak of Koben as the founder of the "Gonmitsu" tradition (i.e., the combination of Kegon and Mikkyō).

34. Hua-yen-ching-ho-lun tsuan-yao, 3 ch., ZZI: 88/4.

35. Hua-yen-ching-ho-lun chien-yao, ZZI:7/3.

36. In 1668, Tao-p'ei published the Hua-yen-ching-shu-lun tsuan-yao, an edition of the Sūtra collated with excerpts from Li's Exposition and Ch'eng-kuan's commentary, the Hua-yen-ching shu (T1735:35). A 1944 edition of this work was reprinted in the 1970's in Taiwan by the Tripitaka Society.

37. This magnificent work by Kim T'anhŏ is in 13 cases. It was published in Seoul in 1975 by the Hua-yen Study Society, and only 300 copies were printed. One copy may be found in the East Asian Library of The University of California at Berkeley.

38. One might well employ here the distinction that E. D. Hirsch has made between the "meaning" of a text and its "significance." The former consists in good measure of the author's intention, whereas the latter resides more in the minds of his readers. Such a distinction is, regrettably, not very fashionable these days among literary critics and theorists--so much the worse for the prospects of truly critical literary analysis. See E. D. Hirsch, The Aims of Interpretation (Chicago: The Univ. of Chicago Press, 1976).

39. I have often thought that there is implicit in Buddhism a theory of history not entirely unlike the view of history found in the writings of Michel Foucault. As the Buddhist doctrines of no-self and emptiness deny the existence of enduring personal and non-personal entities, so Foucault has argued that history too is devoid of such transpersonal entities as the Zeitgeist or the teleological "tradition," but consists solely in a succession of aggregates made up of such dharma-like qualities as "discourse," "power," etc. That, however, is the subject of a quite different essay.

40. Kim Ji-kyon, ed. Hwaŏmnon chŏryo, 1-2.

41. For a discussion of this tension see R. M. Gimello, "Mysticism and Meditation" in Steven T. Katz, ed., Mysticism and Philosophical Analysis (New York: Oxford Univ. Press, 1978), pp. 170-99.

42. For a useful survey of this period in Korean Buddhism see Eda Toshio, Chōsen Bykkyō-shi no kenkyū (Tokyo: Kokusho Kankyokai, 1977), pp. 228-38.

43. The ten faiths, the ten abodes, the ten practices, the ten stages, virtual enlightenment, and marvelous enlightenment.

44. A similar perception of the human condition led certain contemporaries of Li T'ung-hsüan in quite different directions, e.g., towards the foundation of what would become the Pure Land tradition.

45. I have translated this term as "faith" in respect of conventional scholarly usage, but a more faithful rendition might be "confidence."

46. Hua-yen-ching sou-hsüan-ch, T1732:25.62c-63c.

47. Hua-yen wu-shih-yao-wen-ta, T1869:45.532b.

48. Hua-yen I-sheng shih-hsüan-men, T1868:45.514a.

49. T1868:45.515a-b.

50. Hua-yen k'ung-mu-chang, T1870:45.586b.

51. This would have been the Pañcaviṃśati, in either Kumārajiva's translation (T223) or

Hsüan-tsang's (T220). I cannot identify which passage
Li may have had in mind, but Mahāyāna scriptures
generally abound in such imagery of light radiating
from the person of the Tathāgata.

52. Hua-yen-ching lun, T1739:36.738a.

53. T1739:36.870a4-15.

54. T1739:36.76b13-16.

55. This work is not included in the Taisho or
any of the other standard editions of the canon. I
have used the edition included in the Pojo pŏbŏ
(Dharma Discourses of Chinul), a 1963 Seoul publication edited by Kim T'anhŏ which includes the editor's
Korean translation and commentary. Being unable to
read Korean, I could make use only of the original
Chinese text. Kim's edition of Chinul's collected
works was itself based on the 1937 edition by Pang
Hanam, the Koryoguk Pojo sonsa ŏrok, published in
Kangwondo. The Wŏndon sŏngbul-lon is found on pp.
91a-120b of Kim's collection. It may also be found in
vol. 6 of The Collected Works of Eminent Korean Monks
(Seoul, 1974). As mentioned above, this and other
works by Chinul have recently been translated by
Robert Buswell in his forthcoming work. I had the
advantage of seeing a draft of his translation of this
text, and it proved very useful in solving some of the
problems I had encountered earlier when I had first
read the work myself. The translations which follow,
however, are my own.

56. Kim, ed., Pojo pŏbŏ, 91a, 101a, & 106a.

57. Kim, ed., Pojo pŏbŏ, 92a.

58. Kim, ed., Pojo pŏbŏ, 104a, et passim. This
term is used so frequently in the work as to suggest
that it is one of its cardinal themes. In fact it
labels a notion broadly characteristic of Zen generally, referring to the discovery of latent buddhahood
within oneself rather than in the outside world.

59. Kim, ed., Pojo pŏbŏ, 107a. Chinul drew these
"three mysteries" from the Records of Lin-chi. See
Chen-chou Lin-chi Hui-chao ch'an-shih yü-lu, T1985:
47.497b.

60. This is another term much used by Lin-chi and
other Ch'an masters of "the Golden Age."

61. Kim, ed., *Pojo pŏbŏ*, 92b.

62. Kim, ed., *Pojo pŏbŏ*, 92a.

63. Kim, ed., *Pojo pŏbŏ*, 107a.

64. Named by Kōben after a passage in Fa-tsang's *Hua-yen wu-chiao chang* about the light of the newly risen sun falling first on the "highest mountains," (T1866:45.483c), this monastery was established by Kōben in 1206 on Toganoo Mountain, part of which had been donated to Kōben by Retired Emperor Gō-Toba. It now houses not only the extremely valuable library mentioned above but also several of Japan's national art treasures, including the famous scroll-painting of Kōben meditating while seated in a tree.

65. Found in *Nihon daizōkyō* (hereafter: "NDZ"), enlarged and revised edition (Tokyo: Suzuki Research Foundation, 1976), vol. 74, pp. 107-111.

66. NDZ, 74, 81-105.

67. See the Kamata article mentioned in note #30.

68. Properly called the "K'uang-ming chen-yen," its *locus classicus* is fascicle 28 of the *Amoghapaśakalparāja*, T1092:20, but it was probably best known in Mikkyō through its exposition in Amoghavajra's trans. of the *Amoghapaśahṛdaya*, T1002:19.

69. NDZ, 74, 107a.

70. The most detailed treatment of this phase of Kōben's life and of the process by which he created the *Bukkō zammai* is Koizumi Haruaki, "Myōe shūhen," *Nantō Bukkyō* 42 (Dec. 1979), 67-87 and 45 (Dec., 1980), 69-100.

71. NDZ, 74, 107a.

72. Two of Kōben's works are devoted in large measure to a refutation of Hōnen. They are the *Zaijarin* and the *Shogonki*, a critical and annotated edition of the former of which is to be found in Kamata Shigeo, *Kamakura kyū-Bukkyō*, Nihon shisō taikei 15 (Tokyo: Iwanami Shoten, 1971), pp. 43-105.

73. A Chinese apochryphus given much attention by Tsung-mi and thus, in a sense, adopted into the Hua-yen and Zen traditions, T842:18.

74. For a discussion of the significance and symbolism of this magic edifice, see Luís O. Gómez, Selected Verses from the Gaṇḍavyūha (Dissertation, Yale Univ., 1967), pp.lxxvi-xcii.

75. For an outline of the final chapter of the Hua-yen Sūtra, including a brief account of Sudhana's encounter with his various kalyāṇamitra, see Jan Fontein, The Pilgrimage of Sudhana (The Hague: Mouton, 1967), pp. 5-14.

76. My translation of this passage is tentative.

77. I have not determined exactly which Sūtra this is; there are several which include the name of Maitreya in their titles.

78. This is the work translated in the appendix to this article.

79. NDZ, 74, 33-39.

80. T2331:72.74a-87c.

81. NDZ, 74, 68b.

82. NDZ, 74, 68b-69a.

NOTES TO THE APPENDIX

1. Full title, literally translated: "The Trace of the Deeds of the Elder Li, Author of the Exposition of the New Translation of the Mahā-Vaipulya Buddha-Avataṁsaka Sūtra." This work appears in all of the standard editions of the Hua-yen-ching ho lun, but is also preserved separately in the Ch'uan-T'ang-wen, fascicle 816. I have worked from the Zoku-zōkyō edition, specifically from the Taiwan reprint thereof done by Hsin-wen-feng in the 1960's. In that collection it appears in vol. 5, pp. 654a-55b. It is that version to which I will refer in what follows.

2. Hua-yen-ching chüeh-i lun hsü, T1741: 36.1011c.

3. Southeast of the modern Ts'ang-hsien in Hopei.

4. Comparison with other hagiographical sources reveals that the words "erh-shih" were mistakenly interpolated and that the date should be K'ai-yüan 7, 15th day, 3rd month--i.e., April 28, 709.

5. T'ai-yüan was the name of a fu, i.e., an "administrative" or "superior prefecture" during the T'ang. It corresponds to the modern T'ai-yüan hsien and seems most often to refer to the large city by that name (sometimes called Chin-yang) which was and still is the "seat" of the prefecture or county administration. At other times during the T'ang, the same area was known as Ping-chou. Ta-hsien and Tung-ying still appear in gazetteer maps of the region produced in Ming and Ch'ing times. Yü-hsien (not, as is sometimes misprinted, Meng-hsien) was a county of that prefecture located just to the east of the prefectural seat. According to the census of 742, Ping-chou had a population in Li's day of 126,190 households. T'ai-yüan was, among many other things, a major way-station on the pilgrimage route between Ch'ang-an and Wu-t'ai shan.

6. The Ma estates also appear in some of the early gazetteer maps. Could this be the family of our author, "Cloud-dwelling Wanderer Ma"?

7. I cannot precisely locate this village, but the gazetteer maps do note an area in the general vicinity known as "the Place of the Reclining Tiger."

8. Also known as Fang-shan ("Square Mountain").

9. An ambrosia-like liquid often found, in Chinese lore, in the presence of sages.

10. See Buddhabhadra's biography in the Kao-seng chuan, fascicle 14 (T2059:50).

11. Named after the famous Jeta Grove said to have been donated to Śākyamuni himself by Anatha-piṇḍada, one of his early lay disciples.

12. A major event in Chinese history which intervened between Li's death and Kuang-ch'ao's arrival was the An-lu-shan rebellion, which may have been partially responsible for the temporary loss of Li's writings.

13. T1739:36.

14. T1888:45.

15. See note #21 to the text of this article.

16. See note #21 to the text of this article.

17. One of the more sublime regions of the Hua-yen Sūtra's cosmology.

18. Note that this phrase was appropriated by Chinul in his Wŏndon sŏngbul-lon. See note #56 to the text of this article.

19. I can find no mention of this monk in any other text.

CONTRIBUTORS

Jeffrey L. Broughton, who took his Ph.D. at Columbia University, is an Associate Professor in the Department of Religious Studies of California State University at Long Beach.

Robert M. Gimello took his Ph.D. at Columbia University, has taught at Dartmouth College and the University of California at Santa Barbara, and is now Professor and Head of the Department of Oriental Studies of the University of Arizona.

Luis O. Gómez took his Ph.D. at Yale University, and has taught at the University of Washington and the University of Puerto Rico, and is now Professor and Head of the Department of Oriental Languages of the University of Michigan.

Peter N. Gregory, who took his Ph.D. at Harvard University, has taught at the University of California at Los Angeles and at Stanford University, and is now a Fellow of American Council of Learned Societies working at Harvard.

John R. McRae, who has just recently completed his Ph.D. at Yale University, has taught in the Department of Religious Studies of the University of California at Santa Barbara.